IT and Business

Jens Christensen

IT AND BUSINESS

A HISTORY OF SCANDINAVIAN AIRLINES SAS

AARHUS UNIVERSITETSFORLAG
2000

IT and Business
er sat med Stone Serif og trykt hos
Narayana Press, Gylling
© Jens Christensen 2000
Omslag: Kitte Fennestad
Printed in Denmark 2000

ISBN 87 7288 820 2

Udgivet med støtte fra Statens Humanistiske Forskningsråd og
Aarhus Universitets Forskningsfond

Aarhus Universitetsforlag
Langelandsgade 177
8200 Århus N

Fax 8942 5380
www.unipress.dk

Denne afhandling er af Det humanistiske Fakultet ved Aarhus Universitet
antaget til forsvar for den filosofiske doktorgrad

Århus, den 15. maj 2000
Bodil Due
h.a. decanus

Forsvaret finder sted den 27. oktober 2000 kl. 13 prc.
i auditorium 025, bygning 324, Aarhus Universitet

Contents

Tables

Figures

II 1950s to 1970s

III 1980s

IV 1990s

Abbreviations

AA	American Airline
ABB	Asea Brown Bovery
ACA	Automatic Crew Assignment
ACS	Accounting System
ADA	Airline Decentralized Accounting
ADS	Automatic Debiting of Agents
AEA	Association of European Airlines
AF	Air France
APC	Automatic Pairing System
APS	Accounts Payable System
ARN	Arlanda
AROS	Aircraft Rotations System
ARP	Airline Resource Plan (Business Plan)
ATB	Automatic Ticketing and Boarding
ATT	American Telephone & Telegraph
AWB	Airway Bill
AY	Finnair
AZ	Alitalia
BA	British Airways
BABS	British Airways Booking System
BAS	Baggage Administration System
BBC	Björn Boldt-Christmas
BCDC	Business Cooperative Data Collector
BEA	British European Airways
BEACON	British European Airways Computing Network
BFU	Information Systems Business Follow-up
BIC	Business Intelligence Concept
BM	Business Manager
BOAC	British Overseas Airways Corporation
BOADICEA	British Overseas Airways Digital Information Computers for Electronic Automation
BOWAC	Bill of Work Aircraft
BPR	Business Process Reengineering
BSD	Business Systems Division
CAB	Civil Aeronautics Board
CAD	Computer Aided Design

CAIMEX	Cargo Import Export
CAIS	Crew Allocation Information System
CARBOOK	Cargo Booking
CAREX	Cargo Export
CARIN	Cargo Information System
CARINA	Cargo Information Application
CAROLINE	Cargo Online
CAS	Cargo Accounting System
CASAS	Cargo Sales Statistics
CASE	Computer Aided Software Engineering
CATS	Catering System
CCS	Centralized Consolidation System
CC	Component Control
CEO	Chief Executive Officer
CFC	Corporate Finance and Control
CICS	Customer Information Control System
CISC	Complex Instruction Set Computing
COBOL	Common Business Oriented Language
COCA	Common Calculation System
COMACS	Commercial Accounting System
COMET	Common Methods and Tools
CPH	Copenhagen
CPU	Central Processor Unit
CRAS	Cargo Revenue Accounting System
CRC	Carmen Rule Compiler
CRIS	Cargo Revenue Information System
CRT	Cathode Ray Tube
CRU70	Crew Planning System
CRU80	Crew Planning System
CRU-S	Crew Statistics System
C/S	Client/Server
CSC	Computer Systems Corporation
CTF	City Timetable and Fares
CUTE	Common User Terminal Interface
DAP	Decentralized Accounting Processing
DASCO	Data System Computer
DB	Database
DBMS	Database Management System
DCP	Data Communications Processing
DDD	Data and Distribution Division
DDL	Det Danske Luftfartselskab (Danish Airline)

DFI   Decision Focus Incorporated
DIT   Division IT Board
DMS   Data Management System
DNB   Det nye besætningssystem (New Crew System)
DNL   Det Norske Luftfartselskab (Norwegian Airline)
DOS   Disk Operating System
DRAPRO   Data Registration and Processing in Remote Organizations
DSC   Data Systems Committee

EDI   Electronic Data Interchange
EDISS   Electronic Data Interactive Share System
EDP   Electronic Data Processing
EDS   Electronic Distribution Services
EEC   European Economic Community
EI   Air Lingus
ELOP   Electronic Long Range Data Processing Plan
ERP   Enterprise Resource Planning
EU   European Union

FATIS   Fornebu Airport Telecommunication Information System
FBU   Fornebu
FDI   Foreign Direct Investment
FFU   Failure Follow-up
FLIST   Flight Statistics System
FM   Facility Management
FORTRAN   Formula Translation

GCA   Graphic Crew Assignment
GDP   Gross Domestic Product
GE   General Electric
GL   Generation Language
GLM   General Ledger Millennium
GM   General Motors
GPC   Graphic Pairing Construction

HP   Hewlett Packert
HR   Human Resources

IATA   International Air Transport Association
IBM   International Business Machines
ICAO   International Civil Aviation Organization

ICL	International Computers Limited
IDC	International Data Corporation
IDIS	Inter-airline Debit Information System
IFIP	The International Federation for Information Processing
IM	Information Management
IMPALA	Information Management Passenger Line Accounting
IMS	Information Management System
INV	Investment System
IP	Internet Protocol
IRIS	International Route Information System
IRM	Information Resource Management
IRMA	Information Resources Management Association
ISP	Information Systems Policies
ISPG	Information Systems Planning Group
ISS	Information Systems Strategies
IT	Information Technology
ITM	Information Technology and Management
IWS	Intelligent Workstation
KPMG	Klynveld, Peat, Marwick, Goerdeler
KSSU	KLM, SAS, Swissair, UTA
LAN	Local Area Network
LEVEL	Departure level control system
LH	Lufthansa
LIPS	Linta Production System
LKS	Line calculating system
LOCS	Load Control System
LRS	Line Route System
LUCAS	Local Users Cargo System
MACS	Mail Revenue Accounting System
MAD	Marketing Automation Division
MASAS	Mail Statistics System
MATS	Material Supply and Inventory Control System
MCC	Movement Control Center
MESCO	Message Computer
MIS	Management Information Systems
MNC	Multinational Corporation
MOCO	Modification Control
MOPS	Maintenance and Overhaul Planning System

MRS	Maintenance Requirements System
MS	Microsoft
MVS	Multiple Virtual Storage
NADAC	North American Division Accounting System
NCP	New Crew Planning
OBS	Online Budgeting System
OD	Operation Division
OECD	Organization of Economic Cooperation and Development
OPDOC	Operations Documentation
OPS	Operations Control System
OPUS	Operations Control System
ORD	Origin Destination Movement Management System
ORS	Online Registration System
OS	Operating System
OSI	Open Systems Interconnectivity
OSL	Oslo
PA	Personnel Administration System
PADOCS	Passenger Document System
PAH	Palco Aircraft Handling
PALCO	Passenger check-in and Load Control System
PARS	Programmed Airline Reservations System
PAS	Passenger Accounting System
PASAS	Passenger Sales Statistics System
PC	Personnel Computer
PCI	Passenger Check-In System
PENG	Planning of liquidity
PERS	Personnel Registration & Planning System
PERS/PINS	Personnel and Personnel Insurance System
PNR	Passenger Name Record
PORS	Planning and Resource Disposing System
PUSS	Purchase Statistics System
QUALISAS	Quality SAS System
R/2, R/3	Real-time-processing
R & D	Research and Development
RECS	Revenue Control System
REFLEKS	Resultatorientering og Flexibilitet (result and flexibility)
RELS	Reliability System

RES	Reservation System
RESAID	Reservation Inventory Documentation
RESCO	Reservation Computer
RISC	Reduced Instruction Set Computing
ROCO	Rotables Control System
RODOS	Route Documentation System
ROW	Rest of the World
SA	Swissair
SAA	Systems Application Architecture
SAGE	Semi Automatic Ground Environment
SAP	Systems, Applications, and Products in Data Processing
SAS	Scandinavian Airlines System
SASCO	SAS Computer
SASMO	SAS Data Models
SCOL	Schedules Control System
SCOT	Social Construction of Technology
SD	SAS Data
SDD	SAS Data Denmark
SDG	SAS Data Group
SDN	SAS Data Norway
SDS	SAS Data Sweden
SEK	Swedish 'Kroner'
SFA	Sales Force Automation
SITA	Societé International de Télécommunications Aeronautique
SIW	Systems Information Warehouse
SK	SAS
SMART	Scandinavian Multi-Access Reservations for Travel Agents
SME	Small and Medium-sized Entreprise
SNA	Systems Network Architecture
SOB	Sales on Board System
SOBOB	Sales on Board System
SQL	Structured Query Language
SPAS	Cargo Sales follow-up system
SPI	Statistical Passenger Information System
SRI	Stanford Research Institute
STREPS	Station Resource Planning System
TACS	Ticket Accounting System
TARGET	Follow-up on routes
TCP	Transmission Control Protocol
TD	Technical Division

TDB	Timetable Database
TEDOC	Technical Documentation
TICS	Ticketing Computer System
TNC	Transnational corporation
TO	Technical Order System
TOPRO	Traffic Operations Procedure System
TOPST	Traffic and Operations Statistics
TP	Traffic Projection
TPTS	Timetable Planning Traffic System
TQM	Total Quality Management
TRAF	Traffic Planning System
TRAPS	Traffic Planning System
TRAST	Traffic Revenue Statistics System
TSD	Traffic Services Division
TSST	Traffic Statistics System
TTP	Traffic Timetable Program
U	Univac
UA	United Airlines
UN	United Nations
V	Virksomhed (corporation)
VAS	Value Added Services
VIA	Vertical Industry Applications
VM	Virtual Machine
VTAM	Virtual Telecommunications Access Method
WAN	Wide Area Network
WWW	World Wide Web

Preface

The arrival of Jan Carlzon as the new SAS CEO in 1980 was the beginning of a business revolution. A process started that would involve all Scandinavia, not only in business but in politics as well. In a conspicuous and charismatic way, Carlzon challenged well-established structures and mentalities, labeling such sentences as: "Our most important asset is a satisfied customer". "Tear down the pyramids of bureaucracy". "It is the companies and not the State that create welfare". "We are all managers in our jobs". This was a challenge to a deeply rooted social fabric and thinking that went far beyond the borders of corporate SAS. Barriers to overcome were tremendous. Yet, a different approach had been set to work that caught my attention, too. Maybe we were about to move from one era to another.

In retrospect, it took more than a decade until change stepped up from slow to fast speed. What used to be a hesitant practice turned into a true transformation. Meanwhile, information technology revolutionized to present a tool of immense potentials. Even politics transformed to unleash expanding business and technology. The visions of the eighties were about to materialize.

Then in 1994 when Jan Stenberg took over after Carlzon's long presidency and determinedly attacked left-over legacy structures of the organization, I decided to investigate the outcome of the SAS case and to see, in what way the history of the company applied to general developments of the postwar world. In particular, I was preoccupied with the ubiquitous information technology without which there would be no business at all.

A number of leading SAS people have made available to me their profound knowledge of the various parts of corporate SAS. Without this it would not have been possible to make the written sources speak of all the changing activities that add up to form a whole business of the size of SAS. I thank you and others for their support.

1 · SOURCES AND THEORIES

Introduction

Scandinavian Airlines[1] (SAS) was started in the early post-war years and expanded enormously during the second half of the twentieth century. The company joined the club of leading international airlines from the very beginning and never lost that position over the years. By and large, the growth of SAS and the airlines industry followed the general trends of economic development in the industrialized world. Airlines grew to meet the increasing national and international demands of trade and transport. The remarkable post-war development of aircraft technology and airlines also influenced the economy, moving people and goods in large numbers around the world in hours. As air transport and business in general increased in speed and volume, so did the information transactions that handled these activities. Soon, management realized that capabilities for information processing formed a crucial barrier as well as offering a potential for the economic growth of airlines.

Computer technology, along with electronic communications, presented the new tools needed to carry out the ever-growing expansion of airlines and air transport. Early in the history of modern airlines, computers and electronic communications were introduced to handle the enormous amount of information that had to be transactioned at high speed throughout the day and that often needed to be communicated worldwide. Later, when digitalization integrated computers and communications into a so-called information technology (IT), airlines saw even more radical changes.

Airlines were not alone in struggling with the limits of traditional tools of information processing. Soon after World War II, all large industrial corporations, including large government agencies, increasingly felt the need for new technology that would permit them to reap the fruits of further economic growth and industrialization. Computers became the technological solution to these ambitions. From the 1950s, computers, computer applications, and telecommunications spread throughout the large organizations of the world, to be followed by small businesses, much later. Ultimately these technologies were integrated into one information technology. At the turn of the twentieth century, IT is no longer just an important tool of business; it has become the basic infrastructure of a globalized economy. Thus, developments in IT are

---

1   Formerly, Scandinavian Airlines Systems.

part of a radically changing post-war world that includes political economy. Nations and national governments continued to form the framework of economic and social activities but by the end of the twentieth century, radical changes in business and technology challenged this legacy of history, including mainstream social science theory.

New kinds of qualifications and a different organization were required to develop, operate and manage computers, applications, and communications. In addition to the department that handled traditional functions such as production, distribution, marketing, accounting, and personnel, a new IT business department was created to include computer professionals. For three decades, the IT department handled a growing number of computer applications and worked alongside the other functions of large corporations. However, from the late 1980s and early 1990s much changed in this traditional structure of business and organization.

The growing demand for IT spawned an industry of vendors that also did much to make firms adopt the new computer technology. It was a mutual process, fuelled by the interaction of users and producers of IT. The IT industry grew rather gradually for some decades, but since the late 1980s a digital revolution made capacity and applicability explode. A huge and dramatically expanding industry developed to offer IT solutions to any kind of business activity. As a consequence, the IT industry was turned into *the* growth sector of the world economy on the one hand, and *the* enabler of a general business expansion and globalization on the other.

IT is more than a set of machines and procedures. It processes and gives access to the fundamental resource of all business activities, namely information or knowledge. Computer applications are the meeting place of IT and business. Since the 1960s, their relationship has become increasingly close. Business remains the driving force, however, whereas IT is the needed enabler for growth and change.

From the late 1950s, computer applications became an increasingly integrated part of corporate SAS. IT in general, came to mean life or death to the company. On the one hand, IT forms a technology of its own. It is a particular complex of applied tools in the organization and vendor industries in the marketplace. On the other hand, IT runs a firm's information and is, thus, the lifeblood of the business. In the context of an airline, information processing means recording and managing all airplane activities, personnel, and customers, including relations with authorities, other airlines, and international airline organizations.

If you want to dig into the heart of a modern business firm such as SAS you have to deal with the relationship of IT with the organization, and its role in striving to build and improve the company's ability to stay in business within the airlines industry. This is my first and primary reason for the approach taken here. Secondly, I want to see IT from the perspective of business applications, rather than that of techniques. Thirdly, IT is deeply rooted in the environment of business and business organizations and must, therefore, be understood in relation to its historical background. Fourthly, SAS is embedded in the overall post-war environment of IT and business. In all four respects, I have structured this account into three different historical periods: (a) the pre-1980 post-war years, (b) the 1980s, and (c) the 1990s. To conclude, this is intended to be a business history of SAS that focuses on the significance of IT within that firm, and on the background of general business and technology developments.

Sources

SAS

Writings on SAS History

Three books have been written on the history of SAS. These celebrated its twenty-fifth, fortieth, and fiftieth anniversaries respectively.[2] The twenty-fifth anniversary book is of particular interest, because it presents the history of the founding decades of the 1950s and 1960s based on sources that in some cases no longer exist. Unfortunately, the author focuses on the political history of SAS, and only includes the history of the organization to some degree. Some factual information is presented here and in the other two books, however, that may not be found elsewhere. To my knowledge, no research has ever been published on the history of SAS.

Documents

Except for most of the records of the board of directors, all relevant internal files have been available for this study of SAS. Many older documents of the pre-1980 years were scrapped, unfortunately, when SAS moved into new headquarters in Stockholm in 1986.[3]

Since the late 1960s, SAS Management has produced internal, annual business reports on corporate and divisional levels that include updated future three-year plans. These company reports and plans were relatively small in size before 1980 and are only preserved to some degree. That applies to long-term plans for aircraft investments, too. Since the strategic reorientation of SAS in 1980/1981, these current business papers were upgraded to present a wider and deeper analysis of plans, achievements, and problems on corporate and divisional levels, including the IT field. Thus the business and IT developments of SAS during the 1980s and early 1990s are well covered. For the IT field in particular, the changing character and plans of IT users and producers at SAS are fairly well recorded during these years of transition and transformation. That includes statistics of IT costs, personnel, and capacity.[4]

---

2   Buraas, A. (1972), *Fly over fly. Historien om SAS* (a history of SAS) (Oslo: Gyldendal). Berthelsen, S. (Red.)(1985), *Et liv i luften* (a life in the air)(Copenhagen:Bogan). SAS (1996), *The First Fifty Years* (Stockholm: SAS).
3   Interview: *Torsten Bergner.*
4   Although, several sources often have to be combined.

Besides these general corporate and divisional sources, a continuous line of files on IT matters from the early 1960s to mid 1990s have been available and left intact, it seems.[5] Documents still in use in the late 1990s have only been available in a few cases. Files on SAS IT developments include correspondence, minutes of meetings, memos, and plans on corporate and divisional levels as well as developments of the IT department.

While strategic developments of SAS business and IT may be seen through internal documents, IT applications must be complemented by other sources to understand the changing contents of these business tools. One group of sources is systems descriptions of computer applications. Neither SAS Data nor SAS kept any central archive of these handbooks. They followed the person in charge of the system and often vanished.[6] Systems descriptions of past and present applications have been available in some cases.[7] These handbooks include a short history of the making and changes of each major system. As most basic SAS systems originated in the 1960s and 1970s and core functions did not change that much over the years, they make up a useful source to SAS IT applications.

Other Contemporary Sources

Since 1946/47 SAS has issued an annual report. This report contains information on the changing conditions of the SAS business and organization over the years, including statistics, and to some degree, the airlines industry in general. This source adds useful knowledge, particularly for early SAS history. The International Air Transport Association (IATA) and the International Civil Aviation Organization (ICAO) of the United Nations (UN) present annual statis-

---

5   This may found in the so-called SAS "Data Management" files, including planning material of SAS Data. In general, "SAS Data" stands for SAS' IT organization throughout the years, although it was renamed Scandinavian Airlines Data in 1990. "Data Management" stands for all IT-files in SAS' archives, including systems descriptions.

6   Some survived, however, particularly those of the MOPS (Maintenance and Overhaul Planning System) system. All MOPS planning material and handbooks are available from its origins in the 1960s and all through its long history of development during the 1970s and 1980s, until new developments and plans stopped around 1990. This material shows that it is possible to follow the main steps of planning and re-planning, including descriptions of system functions and information flows. However, much information is not written down and exists only as tacit knowledge in the mind of those involved, or may be found in correspondence and memos on division level.

7   Mainly, Cargo, Maintenance, Accounting, and Personnel. For the sake of details, however, it would have been useful if all systems descriptions had been available. This material is listed under SAS Archives in the list of Sources.

tics and reports of the international airlines that also include useful information on SAS.[8] During the latter part of the pre-1980 years, the SAS Yearbook provided information on all the various functions that together helped SAS run and expand.[9] This useful source on the SAS organization was closed down in 1981 when competition began to replace the more open attitudes of monopoly times.

Since 1970, an in-house organ has reported on the activities of the IT department.[10] Much useful information on new applications and matters of computer operations and organization may be found in this internal communications link between IT management and computer professionals, including discussions on vital changes in the IT organization within SAS.

Interviews

A number of interviews were carried out to cover the history of IT and its business relations.[11] They included general perspectives of IT and business in the company, fundamental functional business applications, the management of the IT department and division, and developments in computers, systems, and communications.

IT applications, or information systems, make up the core field of IT and the interrelationship of business and IT. A number of persons were interviewed to reconstruct this vital history of SAS. To do so properly, the parallel character of systems and functions of the SAS organization must be considered.

By the late 1990s, SAS deployed about 440 information systems to run the business.[12] These several hundred applications were organized around a few large central systems based on the main functions of the company, such as traffic, reservations, cargo, check-in, crew, maintenance, accounting, and personnel. The divisions and basic functions of the SAS business managed and operated these fundamental activities, while SAS Data and its computer professionals handled the corresponding information systems. One might say

---

8 Particularly, IATA, *World Air Transport Statistics* (Geneva: IATA), that covers annually the individual airlines, too.

9 SAS, *Yearbooks 1967 to 1980*.

10 *Data Services News*, 1970-1979. *Data Services Bulletin*, 1980-1981. *Data News*, 1981-1985. *Data Ventilen*, 1986-1987. *UPTIME*, 1988-1995 (Sweden/Norway). *Profil*, 1989-1995 (Denmark). *Linje 1*, 1995-1998.

11 Most of these interviews were carried out in 1995, the remainder part in 1997, and one in 1998 (see the list of Sources). When needed, interviews were in some cases clarified and updated with the persons interviewed.

12 SAS Data, *Organization Papers*, 1997.

that each central business function was matched by a similar IT function; and this had been the case for decades.

To catch the business perspective as well as the IT approach, interviews of functional managers of business and corresponding IT systems were carried out for all major fields of the organization, including present managers and whenever possible, previous managers. In some cases, key persons were also interviewed to provide a more complete understanding of the character and history of systems and functions.

Many of the persons interviewed had a long history with SAS, including those in charge of the first reservations systems of the 1950s and the 1960s. By and large, the interviews covered the whole history of all vital information systems of SAS. However, few of those involved in the business functions of the early systems could be interviewed. For one thing, they were not around any more and moreover, the IT department of those days came to monopolize IT developments. Not all pioneering computer professionals and managers were available, but actually in some cases they were. It was only possible to take this double perspective of business and IT on the information systems from the 1970s, also because IT developments previously used to be the monopoly of computer professionals.

None of these interviews disagreed in matters of fact or the functions of the information systems, past or present. Differences of opinion may be seen, however, when it comes to motives and causes of failure, postponement, and change of systems throughout the years. Such differences may be clarified when they are matched with other sources.

Interviews with managers of business functions and corresponding IT applications were undertaken not only to reconstruct the chronology of SAS information systems. They were also needed because information systems are meant to support business functions. Furthermore, the nature of these IT applications and their developments could not be fully understood unless the business history of these functions and their position as part of a corporate and wider environmental context had also been established. Business aims were deeply embedded in IT applications from the very beginning. Behind systems functions and information flows, there is a world of business that must be brought to light to discover the essence of these systems. IT applications are tools to run the business.

Except in minor cases, interviews never made up the sole source of this history, however. Documents, handbooks, and company plans ensure a firm chronology, including how and why things developed and changed. Contemporary written sources add to this picture. For matters of recent developments, however, only such sources as in-house organs and annual reports complement the information from the interviews.

Previous and present managers of the IT department and division at top and middle levels were interviewed to cover its history in general as well as its main functions of computer operations, communications, and systems developments. The same method of analysis was employed here as for information systems. By way of matching interviews, records, and other contemporary sources, a general and functional history of SAS was reconstructed. Here too sources were less plentiful for the early and recent years of developments. However, the outline of the history is always clear.

Finally, it must be noted that a detailed reconstruction of the decision-making process is not intended. What matters here is a history of IT and business structures and functions in their proper context.

Environment

Thorough studies on computer history are rare, and when it comes to the analysis of computer applications and their integral development in a particular industry or firm, such research is practically nonexistent. Much research is done on the older history of information processing and its industry, and through the years, social scientists have covered the field of IT management in user organizations, and have developed tools and methods for best practices.[13]

The rapidly expanding industries of present IT business applications are being continuously analyzed by consultancies, mainly American ones, such as International Data Corporation (IDC).[14] Such consultancies constitute an important source of the radical changes of the 1990s. In recent years, they have also included other functions and business departments, such as accounting, personnel and production. This new trend is a consequence of the growing enterprise-wide integration of functions and computer applications as well as the outsourcing and commercialization of an increasing number of former bureaucratic functions.

Few studies cover post-war business developments.[15] Until recent transformations, little was done to dig into the process of increasing world industrialization and the challenges of modern business. Most studies were undertaken in response to the quest for economic growth and business reform by

---

13 Cortada, J. W. (1996), *Information Technology as Business History* (Westport, Conn.: Greenwood Press), pp. 159-187, and passim. See also below, the chapter on theories: *Information Technology*.
14 See below, the chapter on the 1990s: *Environment*.
15 Maddison, A. (1995), *Monitoring the World Economy* (Paris: OECD), is one good exception, in addition to his previous studies.

the Organization of Economic Cooperation and Development (OECD) and other international organizations,[16] and they include a general analysis of IT developments, showing the growing significance of IT to globalization and innovation.[17] Published research on Transnational Corporations is expanding heavily, reflecting the ongoing strong movement from international trade to international production.[18]

There is a considerable volume of literature on the early history of airlines, including the International Air Transport Association (IATA).[19] Developments of the past two decades are primarily covered by international organizations, such as OECD and the European Union (EU).[20] During the years, IATA, the International Civil Aviation Organization (ICAO), the Association of European Airlines (AEA), and aircraft companies, such as Boeing, have produced valuable statistics of air transport developments.[21]

Computer applications and their development in the airline industry have been covered in two pieces of research.[22] One deals with the SABRE reservations and distributions system from its origins until the 1980s. The other analysis covers data processing within British Airways from the 1950s until the early 1990s.

---

16 OECD (1992), *Technology and Economy* (Paris: OECD), is a good example.
17 OECD (1997), *Information Technology Outlook* (Paris: OECD), and previous publications.
18 UN, *World Investment Reports* (New York: UN), annual since mid 1980s.
19 Sterling, C. H. (1996), *Commercial Air Transport Books* (McLean Virginia: Paladwr Press), is a general bibliography of this literature. Few business studies have been made on the history of airlines, primarily on the pre-1980 period.
20 For example, OECD (1993), *International Air Transport* (Paris: OECD), and publications of previous and later origin. Mainly, they deal with challenges of deregulation, open competition, and increasing air traffic. Recently, an interesting piece of historical study was published on some leading European airlines: Dienel, H.-L., and P. Lynth, P. (Ed.)(1998), *Flying the Flag. European Commercial Air Transport since 1945* (London: MacMillan Press). From a comparative perspective, it brings a more detailed analysis of such airlines as Air France, Lufthansa, British Airways, KLM, Alitalia, and LOT, including an outline of the American experience. Developments of the airlines' organizations and the radical changes of the 1990s are dealt with only slightly, however.
21 Such as, IATA, *World Air Transport Statistics*.
22 McKenney, J. L. (1995), *Waves of Change. Business Evolution through Information Technology* (Boston, Mass.: Harvard Business School Press), pp. 97-140. Harris, B. (1993), *BABS, BEACON, and BOADICEA. A History of Computing at British Airways and its Predecessor Airlines* (Hounslow, UK: Speedwing Press). The latter book is, to my knowledge, the only coverage of airline computing. A writer who has seen it at first hand uncovers valuable information. Unfortunately, however, computer applications are not of prime interest to the author.

Method

The difficult task of reconstructing the IT and business history of SAS had to build on a number of sources. Documents were complemented by interviews of SAS and SAS Data top management to outline the development of strategy. In addition to documents, developments of IT applications and their respective business functions were reconstructed by way of numerous interviews of functional business and functional IT managers. Contemporary written sources of various kinds added to this picture. As a complementary method, business and technology perspectives were always held up against each other.

When analyzing a business firm it is not always apparent in internal sources why and how technology and business changed over the course of time. Often this is tacit knowledge. What everybody knows, or thinks they know, does not have to be written down. Furthermore, reasons of business secrecy, disagreement by management, or clash of interest between employees and management might put fundamental business information in a category that is close to taboo. To open this "black box" and present a proper interpretation of the content and reasons for changing IT and business relations over the years, you have to link the history of SAS to environmental developments of business and IT, in the airlines industry and in general. This is even more relevant as the structure and development of SAS are deeply rooted in this environment.

Understanding the ways and causes of business and technology developments is no simple task. Theories help in making sense of these matters.

Theories

Business Environment

Business is shaped and transformed by and within industrial capitalism. Industrial capitalism is the dynamic economic system that took hold of Western societies during the nineteenth century and continued during the twentieth century to dig deeper into more and more fields of human life. To day it is everywhere.[23] Instead of a subsistence economy, goods are produced to

---

23 The approach, that industrial capitalism is a dynamic system expanding by continuous industrialization including a few profound restructuring processes, is inspired by a number of sources. This view was first presented by Marx in his studies of the capitalist system, K. Marx (1962-1966/1867-1894), *Das Kapital,* I-III (Berlin: Dietz Verlag), and later adopted by the economist: Schumpeter, J. A. (1961/1934), *The Theory of Economic Development: An Inquiry into Profits, Capital, Credit, Interest, and the Business Cycle* (Cambridge, Mass.: Harvard Univ. Press), and Schumpeter (1939), *Business Cycles: A Theoretical, Historical and Statistical Analysis of the Capitalist Process,* I-II (New York). Marx inspired a profound restructuring approach, such as that of industrial revolutions, while Schumpeter gave inspiration to theories of long waves and business reform each the length of half a century, based on changes in technology. A modern application of this approach may be found in: Freeman, C., and Perez, C. (1988), "Structural Crises of Adjustment", in Dosi, G., et al (Ed.), *Technical Change and Economic Theory* (London: Pinter Publishers). A third and still lower level of abstraction is that of economic growth, such as: Rostow, W. W. (1960), *The Stages of Economic Growth: A Non-Communist Manifesto* (Cambridge, UK: Cambridge Univ. Press) and Kuznets, S. (1971), *Economic Growth of Nations:Total Output and Production Structure* (Cambridge, Mass.: The Belknap Press of Harvard Univ. Press). Economic outlooks of current business cycles might be considered a fourth level of approach. All four levels of economic development are deployed here.

In business history, the studies of Chandler, A. D. Jr. (1962), *Strategy and Structure: Chapters in the History of the Industrial Enterprise* (Cambridge, Mass.: The M. I. T. Press), Chandler (1977), *The Visible Hand. The Managerial Revolution in American Business* (Cambridge, Mass.: The Belknap Press of Harvard University Press), and Chandler (1990), *Scale and Scope. The Dynamics of Industrial Capitalism* (Cambridge, Mass.: The Belknap Press of Harvard University Press), have paved the way for our understanding of the importance and ways of the modern industrial firm in creating the dynamics of industrial societies. According to Chandler, environmental changes in society and business were reflected in long-term goals of large firms, strategy that determined the organization and structure of the enterprise. So, structure followed strategy that responded to and influenced society, too. As we shall see, Chandler's intellectual achievement might be so modified that although structure followed strategy, new structures did not easily follow fundamental

create a profit by selling in an unknown market. Being gradually forced to make a livelihood by managing their own business or more often being wage earners, the existence of people came to be dependent on a market economy. This was a self-perpetuating process of industrialization that created new and so-called industrial societies. Nations and national governments helped to shape open markets for an economy ruled by considerations of profit and competition and by a class of interests between private ownership and wage earners. In various degrees, it spread across countries and formed a kind of international division of labor, regulated and protected by governments.

The development of capitalism and industrialization has not been a smooth process. On the contrary, it has been marked by a lack of equilibrium

---

changes of strategy, because organizational designs were and are much more deeply rooted in fields of social interest and technology than in concepts of strategy.

Porter, M. E. (1990), *The Competitive Advantage of Nations* (London: The MacMillan Press) has guided us into the transforming nature of current business. This applies to a general approach and to a number of vital concepts. The big United Nations project on transnational corporations and foreign direct investment during the 1990s has followed the paths of business globalization and reform in its annual World Investment Report and the multi volume publication, Dunning, J. H. (Ed.)(1993-1994), *United Nations Library on Transnational Corporations*, I-XX (London: Routledge). Piore, M. J., and Sabel, C. F. (1984), *The Second Industrial Divide. Possibilities for Prosperity* (New York: Basic Books) introduced the idea of emerging fundamental changes in industrialization. Hammer, M., and Champy, J. (1993), *Reengineering the Corporation: A Manifest for Business Revolution* (New York: Harper Business), and OECD, *Technology and Economy*, focused on the break through of the present business revolution, dealing with the replacement of Fordist organizations with the dynamic combination of transformed firms and revolutionary IT.

Other studies have contributed to our understanding of industrial capitalism's general history, such as Maddison, A, (1991), *Dynamic Forces in Capitalist Development* (Oxford: Oxford University Press); Maddison, *Monitoring the World Economy*. Rosenberg, N., & Birdzell, L. (1986), *How the West Grew Rich: The Economic Transformation of the Industrial World* (London: Tauris); Landes, D. S. (1998), *The Wealth and Poverty of Nations. Why Some Are So Rich and Some Are So Poor* (London: Little, Brown and Company). The dynamic approach tying all this together is that of competitive advantage, as pointed out by Porter.

In general, business history is seen from the perspective of predominant industrial models that come close to the idea of business paradigms. The paradigm concept, introduced by Kuhn, T. S. (1964), *The Structure of Scientific Revolutions* (Chicago: The University of Chicago Press), became a generalized concept for fundamental restructuring of other fields then science. Over long periods of time, a certain way of organizing and creating competitive advantage has dominated business life. Of particular importance was the breakthrough and diffusion of the multi-unit and bureaucratic corporation from the late nineteenth century to the late twentieth century. During the 1990s, this first widespread business model was violently attacked and replaced by a different industrial model of global, networked, core business firms. These two models correspond to radical changes in the business environment.

on all levels. Nevertheless, competition and the market economy make businesses strive towards best practices and an industrial system of equilibrium. In this way, a certain general system tends to dominate industrial business for a long time. When the potentials for one way of doing things are exhausted, a deep crisis hits the system and its firms, followed by a radical restructuring and transformation of industrial capitalism to regain profitability. Such profound processes of change show that capitalism has a strong capacity to survive and adapt. Capitalism does not lie down to die: it is a system of winners that will accept no failures in the long run.

In industrial capitalism, the firm is the core unit and the focus of analysis. Information technology is always used within the context of the firm.

Theories of the Firm

Neo-Classical and Transaction Cost Theories

Neo-classical economic thinking dominated the social sciences during most of the twentieth century. And being of no particular interest to neo-classical economic theory, until recently social scientists paid little attention to the firm.

According to classical theory (i.e., economic theory until the late nineteenth century), the economy grew by way of firms' increasing specialization of labor and size of the market. However, neo-classical economic theory moved the focus of interest from the production process to exchanges in the market. Since then, economic development and the working of the market economy were considered to be one and the same. The market economy was a self-regulating system, ruled by the equilibrium of supply and demand. The system worked perfectly as a mechanical machine, if only human beings did not interfere and just acted according to the rules of the game. Economic man followed his individual economic interests on the basis of private ownership. Fully informed by prices, man acted rationally, choosing the road that would maximize his profit.

Why did firms exist in such a world, at all? Neo-classical theory viewed the firm as a legal entity with a production set.[24] Private ownership called for

---

24 Chandler, A. D., Jr. (1992): "Organizational Capabilities and the Economic History of Industrial Enterprise", in *Journal of Economic Perspectives*, vol 6, no. 3, p. 85. Dosi, G., and Malerba, F. (Eds.), *Organization and Strategy in the Evolution of the Enterprise* (London: MacMillan Press), pp. 2-14. Nelson, R. R., and Winter, S. G. (1982), *An Evolutionary Theory of Economic Change* (Cambridge, Mass.: The Belknap Press of Harvard University Press), is one long demonstration of the character and deficiencies of the neo-classical theory of the firm.

legal entities and the firm was just a framework of one or more production units as any other actor in the market. In case of several production units, the firm was just considered the sum of these units, not allowing for any synergy effect. Neither did micro-economy take any particular interest in technology as a dynamic factor. As a consequence, neo-classical theory hardly developed any micro-economic theory, because it all worked according to the rules of the macro-economy.

The domination of neo-classical theory in the social sciences did not leave much room for sociology or organization theory of the firm. The firm was looked upon as a structure to carry out profit maximization. The organization worked like a machine and economic man was rational man, too. Very little attention was paid to the internal organization of firms and to all those features of economic coordination that did not correspond to pure market interactions.

Whether academics took notice or not of firms, large corporations and agencies of the twentieth century built hierarchical control systems of their operating processes based on specialization and routinization of activities.[25] These "closed" systems of organization increased productivity and reduced uncertainty but depended on stable environments for successful management. Why managers might consider internalization of activities more profitable than leaving them to the market did not bother neo-classical theorists.

Until the crisis of the 1970s, little was added to this rational complex of thinking. The breakthrough of the crisis, its prolongation, and the inability to explain and remedy it began to create doubts as to whether man was so perfectly informed and rational after all. Gradually, bounded rationally substituted for the axiom of total rational man in the social sciences. Rationality was conditional because it was a social activity. This so-called principal-agent theory accepted the neo-classical firm as a production set, but gave it managers and was more specific about its assets.[26] Managers were needed to cope with imperfect information of outsiders (suppliers, etc.) and insiders (employees, etc.). The agency literature saw the firm as a nexus of contractual relation-

---

25 Chandler, "Organizational Capabilities and the Economic History of Industrial Enterprise", pp. 80-99, discusses the historical relationship of organizational capabilities and theories of the firm. See, also Applegate, L. M. (1994)"Managing in an Information Age", in Baskerville, R., et al (Ed.), *Transforming Organizations with Information Technology: Proceedings of the IFIP WG8.2 Conference on Information Technology and the New Emergent Forms of Organizations, Ann Arbor, Michigan, USA, 11-13 August, 1994* (Amsterdam: North Holland), pp. 22-31.
26 Chandler, "Organizational Capabilities and the Economic History of Industrial Enterprise", p. 85. Dosi and Malerba, *Organization and Strategy in the Evolution of the Enterprise,* pp. 2-14.

ships. In this view, the firm was only a collective name for a set of contracts, hence there was no black box to open, except to unveil the underlying contracts linking individual agents.

Transaction cost theory moved one step further to update neo-classical theory.[27] Like agency theory, transaction cost theory focused on information asymmetry and the resulting information costs. While agency theory concentrated on the information concerning relations between principals and agents, transaction cost theory focused on the problems of imperfect information involved in transactions. The firm was organized to economize the costs of production and transactions. Bounded rationality and even specific assets of the firm determined whether transaction costs were internalized within the firm or left to be carried out in the external market.

Still, to Oliver E. Williamson, the leading figure of this approach, the transaction and not the firm was considered the basic unit of analysis. Furthermore, its static flavor made no link to the dynamics inside the organizational black box. Recently, Williamson introduced the term "governance" to allow more room for firm assets in his theory, but a change of focus from transactions to the firm did not take place.[28] Increasing business interest in core competence and outsourcing of non-core activities has given transaction cost theory a true revival, because transaction costs reductions are given high priority. Still, it is not a theory that includes the proliferating dynamic importance of firms and management.

So to all classical economic and sociological thinkers and their revisionists, the firm and its organization was an abnormality. An opposite approach exists, however, which considers the firm *the* dynamic unit without which there would be no modern industrial economies.

Evolutionary and Contingency Theories

Since the 1980s, evolutionary economic theory of the firm challenged neo-classical and transaction cost theories as a strong candidate for a new paradigm. Nelson and Winter, the main proponents of evolutionary theory, saw

---

27 Chandler, "Organizational Capabilities and the Economic History of Industrial Enterprise", pp. 85-86. Dosi and Malerba, *Organization and Strategy in the Evolution of the Enterprise*, pp. 2-14. Transaction costs theory has spawned much literature since Williamson published his central book: Williamson, O. E. (1975), *Markets and Hierarchies: Analysis and Antitrust implication. A Study in the Economics of Internal Organization* (New York: Free Press) and follower, Williamson (1985), *The Economic Institutions of Capitalism: Firms, Market, Relational Contracting* (New York: Free Press).

28 Williamson, O. E. (1996) *The Mechanisms of Governance* (New York: Oxford University Press).

the firm and not the transaction as the main unit of analysis.[29] Moreover, the firm was viewed from a production rather than an exchange perspective. Production factors of the firm were not static ones that might be substituted for by factors in the market or just left to the market when considered profitable. Production and firm activities were developed to be a unique competence, the core of a firm's competitiveness that did not copy easily. Thus, the firm was more than the sum of its parts or production units. Corporate organizations might be considered behavioral entities each characterized by a specific competence. This competence was largely embodied in routines, and evolved over time as the outcome of internal learning and response to external changes. Firms were social units of problem-solving procedures and abilities.

Evolutionary economic thinking emerged to meet the growing problems of adaptability to changing economic environments. In the field of organization theory, a contingency approach took over to match the economic theory of change and bounded rationality.[30] The black box and closed system approach of the firm gradually gave in to open system considerations and organization theory began to look for methods to improve environmental adaptability. One central aspect of organization theory of the 1980s was a rising preoccupation with strategic management.[31] Western corporations worked desperately to regain their lost competitiveness, and this search for new ways of doing business made strategic management of primary interest to management as to social scientists.

In the evolutionary approach to the firm, there is often an intrinsic tension between learning and adaptation.[32] Firms may often face the choice between radical innovation and gradual modification of existing knowledge, seeking to adapt to changing environments.

The dilemma springs from the different nature of learning and adaptation. Learning, that is the cumulative development of skills and knowledge, becomes institutionalized in the form of routines. Adaptation refers to the responses to a firm's environment. Situations of *competency traps* may occur if

---

29 Nelson and Winter, *An Evolutionary Theory of Economic Change*. Chandler, "Organizational Capabilities and the Economic History of Industrial Enterprise", p. 85. Dosi and Malerba, *Organization Strategy in the Evolution of the Enterprise*, pp. 2-14.

30 Mintzberg may be considered the leading proponent of this approach, see Mintzberg, H. (1979), *The Structuring of Organizations: A Synthesis of the Research* (Englewood Cliffs, New Jersey: Prentice-Hall), Mintzberg, H. (1983), *Structure in Fives: Designing Effective Organizations* (Englewood Cliffs, New Jersey: Prentice-Hall), Mintzberg, H., & Quinn, J. B. (1988), *The Strategy Process: Concepts, Contexts, Cases* (Englewood Cliffs, New Jersey: Prentice-Hall).

31 See, for example, Mintzberg & Quinn, *The Strategy Process*.

32 Dosi and Malerba, *Organization Strategy in the Evolution of the Enterprise*, elaborates on this topic.

organizations reflect past performance rather than focus on innovations in order to adapt. In changing environments, organizational learning may cause organizational inertia and lock-in, making firms unable to survive unless they are capable of a fundamental reorientation. In particular, this is the case when what used to be incremental changes turns into paradigmatic reform.

This theme also applies to the nature of technological change. Technology, forming the base of competitive advantage in periods of gradual technical change, may lock in firms' activities and cause inertia in times of radical technological change. In this situation, core capabilities of firms become core rigidities. So radical business and technology reform is the true test of a firm's organizational ability to adapt and innovate, to see if competence is more than routinized knowledge. The competence-based view of the firm implies that history counts and lock-ins into particular trajectories ought to be expected.

Since the 1980s, many business writings have drawn on the combined approaches of evolution and contingency. Furthermore, when radical changes of business and technology took place from about 1990, a converging model of the firm emerged.[33] Firms came to be considered collections of resources, some of which were transferable, while others were firm specific. A new international division of labor, including globalization, a focus on core business, outsourcing, and reorganization created much interest in transaction cost theory, on the one hand. On the other hand, these recent upheavals of modern business demonstrated the dynamic capabilities of the firm. So, the firm came to be considered a unit of three strongly related features: its strategy, its structure, and its core capabilities.

Models of Organization

In this way, theories increasingly adapted to the changing demands of business. Recently, social science has begun to integrate history into its approach. Changes of business and organization are of such a profound nature that it

---

33 This emerging process may be found in Williamson, O. E., and Winter, G. (Ed.)(1991), *The Nature of the Firm: Origins, Evolution, and Development* (New York: Oxford University Press). Montgomery, C. A. (Ed)(1995), *Resource-Based and Evolutionary Theories of the Firm:Towards a Synthesis* (Boston, Mass.: Kluwer Academic Publishes). Dosi and Malerba, *Organization Strategy in the Evolution of the Enterprise.* See also, Langlois, R. L., and Foss, N. J. (1997), *Capabilities and Governance: the Rebirth of Production in the Theory of Economic Organization* (Copenhagen: Danish Research Unit for Industrial Dynamics), illustrating that the long journey of social science theories of the firm paying no attention to its true dynamic dimension may have finally come to an end. Through the years, the Harvard Business Review has presented all leading contributions in organization theory.

calls for broader reflections. A. D. Chandler's fundamental studies of the origin and establishment of American corporations paved the way for a hesitant rapprochement.[34] The American economist M. E. Porter integrated Chandler's insight in his coverage of current international business.[35] During the 1990s, a structural and historical approach emerged in the social sciences alongside traditional methods of generalization and quantification. A historical perspective of changing paradigms of business models and organizations appeared.[36]

Since the start of industrialization, at least three models of organization may be found.[37] While craft and entrepreneurial structures dominated the early industrial era of the nineteenth century, the mass-producing industrial era of the twentieth century organized its activities based first on functional, and later, on divisional hierarchies.[38] Since the 1960s, increasing environmental changes pressed management and theorists to develop various modifications and additions to a domineering hierarchy. In this way, the old paradigm of bureaucracy was increasingly challenged. But it took until the early 1990s when a new paradigm of business and organization emerged.

So, two management paradigms of large firms may be seen in the second half of the twentieth century.[39] One was the hierarchical multi-unit enterprise that dominated business throughout most of the century. The second was the

---

34 Chandler, *The Visible Hand*, and Chandler, *Scale and Scope*.

35 Porter, M. E. (1980), *Competitive Strategy: Techniques for Analyzing Industries and Competitors* (New York: Free Press). Porter, M. E. (1985), *Competitive Advantage: Creating and Sustaining Superior Performance* (New York: Free Press). Porter, *The Competitive Advantage of Nations*.

36 This is shown in Dosi and Malerba, *Organization and Strategy in the Evolution of the Enterprise*. Chandler, A. D., Jr., Hagström, P., and Sölvell, Ö. (Eds.)(1998), *The Dynamic Firm. The Role of Technology, Strategy, Organization, and Regions* (New York: Oxford University Press). Dosi, G., Teece, D. J., Chytry, J. (Ed.)(1998), *Technology, Organization, and Competitiveness: Perspectives on Industrial and Corporate Change* (Oxford: Oxford University Press).

37 Applegate, "Managing in an Information Age", pp. 22-31. See also, Dosi, G., Giannetti, R., and Toninelli, P. A. (Eds.)(1992), *Technology and Enterprise in a Historical Perspective* (Oxford: Oxford University Press).

38 This is the topic of all Chandler's studies. Already, in his first major study, *Strategy and Structure*, Chandler established the theoretical and historical link between strategy, long-term policies of a firm, and structure, i.e., the way the firm organized to carry out its strategy. While mainly focusing on management considerations, Chandler did not dig much into the nature of structural practice, namely the problems of making an organization work according to a strategy. Hundreds or even thousands of people in large corporations and current technologies are always deeply embedded in broader structures of knowledge, capabilities, culture and power that do not easily change. This was most clearly seen when these multi-unit organizations launched their recent transformation projects.

39 OECD, *Technology and Economy*, pp. 89-106.

flexible networked core business model of the 1990s. The hierarchical model, sometimes called Fordism, laid a premium on scale and internal integration of the value chain, mechanization, high specialization, and strong management control, and depended on stable and growing markets. The flexible networked model adopted networking, sub-contracting, and "just-in-time" delivery, thereby reversing the trend of ever-greater internal integration. While focusing on core business, work and hierarchy was reorganized to downsized levels of high adaptability to market changes. Innovative capability, global reach, and low transactions costs replaced the machine-line stability of hierarchy. Business globalization and information technology revolutions were fundamental preconditions and attributes of organizational reform.

In between these two paradigms, incremental additions to the hierarchical model were being developed during the 1960s, 1970s and 1980s.[40]

In the late 1990s, new dimensions were added to the networked model of organization as the Internet moved in to be an electronic infrastructure for business relations.[41] A virtual model of the networked organization appeared that might create flexible forms of organization of an unseen nature.

Competitive Advantage

Unhampered by mainstream theories of economy, the American economist M. E. Porter focused on the creation of competitive advantage, the core field of business, and the changing realities of the business environment. Since 1980, Porter developed a number of fundamental concepts; particularly concerning the ways firms create and sustain competitive advantage. In his paramount 1990 study, he combined the competitive advantage approach with numerous studies of how leading firms in a variety of countries created, sustained or eventually lost a position of international competitiveness. On this basis, he developed a general understanding of the dynamic and innovative nature of the current business world that firms had to live up to if they wanted to stay in business.

Because his concepts have become highly influential tools in creating a proper knowledge of our transforming business world and produced much inspiration for this piece of research, Porter's approach will be presented at some length.

"The basic unit of analysis for understanding competition is the industry.

---

40 Applegate: "Managing in an Information Age", pp. 22-31.
41 OECD (1998), *The Economic and Social Impacts of Electronic Commerce* (Paris: OECD), Chap. 5. See, also Igbaria, M., and Tan, M. (Eds.)(1998), *The Virtual Workplace* (Hersey, USA: Idea Group Publishing).

An industry (whether product or service) is a group of competitors producing products or services that compete directly with each other."[42] "The industry is the arena in which competitive advantage is won or lost. Firms, through competitive strategy, seek to define and establish an approach to competing in their industry that is both profitable and sustainable." "Competitive strategy must grow out of a sophisticated understanding of the structure of the industry and how it is changing. In any industry, ... the nature of the competition is embodied in five competitive forces: (1) the threat of new entrants, (2) the threat of substitute products or services, (3) the bargaining power of suppliers, (4) the bargaining power of buyers, and (5) the rivalry among the existing competitors."

"In addition to responding to and influencing industry structure, firms must choose a position within the industry. Positioning embodies the firm's overall approach to competing."[43] There are two basic types of competitive advantage: lower cost and unique differentiation.

"Competitive advantage grows out of the way firms organize and perform discrete activities ... Firms create value for their buyers through performing these activities. The ultimate value a firm creates is measured by the amount buyers are willing to pay for its product or service. A firm is profitable if this value exceeds the collective cost of performing all the required activities. To gain competitive advantage over its rivals, a firm must either provide comparable buyer value but perform activities more efficiently than its competitors (lower cost), or perform activities in a unique way that creates greater buyer value and commands a premium price (differentiation)."

"The activities performed in competing in a particular industry can be grouped into categories ... in what I call the value chain. All the activities in the value chain contribute to buyer value. Activities can be divided broadly into those involved in the ongoing production, marketing, delivery, and servicing of the product (primary activities) and those providing purchased inputs, technology, human resources, or overall infrastructure functions to support the other activities (support activities). Every activity employs purchased inputs, human resources, some combination of technologies, and draws on firm infrastructure such as general management and finance ... Strategy guides the way a firm performs individual activities and organizes its entire value chain. Activities vary in their importance to competitive advantage in different industries ... Firms gain competitive advantage from conceiving of new ways to conduct activities, employing new procedures, new technologies, or different inputs."

---

42 Porter, *The Competitive Advantage of Nations*, pp. 33-35.
43 Ibid., pp. 40-41.

"A company's value chain for competing in a particular industry is embedded in a larger stream of activities that I term the value system."[44] The value system includes suppliers, distributors and buyers. "Competitive advantage is increasingly a function of how well a company can manage this entire system. Linkages not only connect activities inside a company but also create interdependencies between a firm and its suppliers and channels. A company can create competitive advantage by better optimizing or coordinating these links to the outside."

"Firms create competitive advantage by perceiving or discovering new and better ways to compete in an industry and bringing them to market, which is ultimately an act of innovation. Innovation here is defined broadly, to include both improvements in technology and better methods or ways of doing things", be they incremental or radical.[45]

The most typical causes of innovations that shift competitive advantage are the following: "1. New technologies. Technological change can create new possibilities for the design of a product, the way it is marketed, produced, or delivered, and the ancillary services provided" ... "2. New or shifting buyer needs" ... "3. The emergence of a new industry segment" ... "4. Shifting input costs or availability" ... "5. Changes in government regulations."

These innovative factors result in competitive advantage for those companies that "can perceive their significance early and move aggressively to exploit them. In a remarkable number of industries, early movers sustained position for decades ... Early movers gain advantages such as being first to reap economies of scale, reducing costs through cumulative learning, establishing brand names and customer relationships without direct competition, getting their pick of distribution channels, and obtaining the best locations for facilities or the best sources of raw materials or other inputs. Moving early can allow a firm to translate an innovation into advantages of other sorts that may well be more sustainable. The innovation itself may be copied but the other competitive advantages often remain" ... "Every significant structural change in an industry creates opportunities for new early movers" ... but "early movers will not succeed unless they correctly forecast industry changes."

"The sustainability of competitive advantage depends on three conditions. The first is the particular source of the advantage. There is a hierarchy of sources of competitive advantage in terms of sustainability. Lower-order advantages, such as labor costs or cheap raw materials, are relatively easy to imitate ... Higher-order advantages, such as proprietary process technology,

---

44 Ibid., pp. 43.
45 Ibid., pp. 45-48.

product differentiation based on unique products or services, brand reputation based on cumulative marketing efforts, and customer relationships protected by high customer costs of switching vendors, are more durable."[46]

"Second, higher-order advantages usually depend on a history of sustained and cumulative investment in physical facilities and specialized and often risky learning, research and development, or marketing ... that gives the advantages a dynamic character."

"The third, and most important, reason competitive advantage is sustained is constant improvement and upgrading. Virtually any advantage can be replicated sooner or later if a leader rests on its laurels." In the long run, "sustaining advantage demands that its sources be expanded and upgraded, by moving up the hierarchy to more sustainable types ... Sustainable advantage requires change. It demands that a company exploits, rather than ignores, industry trends. It also demands that a company invest to close off the avenues along which competitors could attack ... To sustain its position, a firm may have to destroy old advantage to create new, higher-order ones."

Change, however, "is extraordinarily painful and difficult for any successful organization. Complacency is much more natural. The past strategy becomes ingrained in organizational routines ... Reconfiguring the value chain is difficult and costly. In large firms, sheer scale also makes altering the strategy difficult ... Companies that manage to overcome inertia and the barriers to changing and upgrading advantage are most often those that have been stimulated by competitive pressure, buyer demands, or technical threats. Few companies make significant improvements and strategy changes voluntarily; most are forced to. The pressure to change is more often environmental than internal."

These basic principles of competitive strategy apply whether a firm is competing domestically or internationally. Increasingly, firms compete globally because industries globalize. In global industries, firms have to compete internationally in order to achieve or sustain competitive advantage. "A global strategy is one in which a firm sells its product in many nations and employs an integrated worldwide approach to doing so."[47] "The strategic choices unique to global strategy can be summarized in two essential dimensions " 1. "Configuration: Where, and in how many nations, each activity in the value chain is performed." 2. "Coordination: How dispersed activities, or activities performed in several different nations, are coordinated." "Industries globalize because shifts in technology, buyer needs, government policy, or country infrastructure create major differences in competitive position among

---

46 Ibid., pp. 49-52.
47 Ibid., pp. 54-55.

firms from different nations or make the advantages of a global strategy more significant."[48]

"Strategic alliances ... are a prominent tool in carrying out global strategies. These are long-term agreements between firms that go beyond normal market transactions but fall short of merger."[49] Strategic alliances include joint ventures, licenses, long-term supply agreements, and other kinds of interfirm relationships. Companies enter into alliances to gain a number of benefits", such as economies of scale, learning, access to markets, risk spreading, and to shape the nature of competition in an industry. Alliances can offset competitive disadvantages, while preserving independence. "However, alliances carry substantial costs in strategic and organizational terms, and they frequently fail or evolve into a merger."

What the paramount study of Porter learned was that economies of the late twentieth century were turning into a permanent state of innovation and globalization, where demand-driven economies replaced more supply driven economies of the past. To be competitive, companies had to compete globally. Sustained competitive advantage grew out of a new approach and practice based on the following principles: 1. Competitive advantage grows out of improvement, innovation, and change. 2. Competitive advantage involves the entire value system. 3. Competitive advantage is sustained only through relentless improvement. 4. Sustaining advantage demands that its sources be upgraded. 5. Sustaining advantage requires a global approach to strategy.[50]

Services

Airlines form a service industry. But what is service? Porter has presented a conceptual framework of understanding service industries that replaces the hitherto poor aggregate thinking.[51] If for example maintenance, transport,

---

48 Ibid., p. 63.
49 Ibid., pp. 65-66.
50 Ibid., pp. 578-583.
51 Ibid., p. 241. The significance of the traditional division of industries into tangible and intangible sectors of manufacturing and services is more formal then real when it comes to business. It is true that services cannot be stored in the same way as manufactured products, but still they are products to be produced and sold under competitive conditions just like any other product. Governmental regulations, slow developments of service industries, and traditional methods of production in manufacturing in the past worked to blur this state of affairs. The various perspectives of the service industry were dealt with in numerous OECD reports and elsewhere, particularly in the 1980s when services continued to grow more then manufacturing. They failed to see the link between manufacturing and services and that the state of affairs was historical rather than conceptual, however.

cleaning, training, etc. are performed in-house by a manufacturing firm, the employees and revenues involved are counted as manufacturing employees and income in the national accounts and are not considered part of a service industry. If individual companies provide the same activities, however, employees and revenues account for service industry. According to this approach we are moving rapidly into service societies because non-production industries occupy an increasing majority of the working population. Pure statistical measures produce no knowledge of competitive conditions and wider economic relations of service activities, however.

"The term 'services' encompasses a wide range of industries that perform various functions for buyers, but do not involve the sale of a tangible product. Services can be broadly divided into those provided to individuals and households, and those provided to businesses and institutions. Given the enormous breadth and variety of service industries, there is no generally accepted taxonomy of services.

To understand the role of services in the economy as well as the reasons for such ambiguities, the role of services in both firms and households must be understood. The tool for doing so is the value chain. Buyers who are firms or institutions (hospitals, schools, etc.) have value chains, just as do the firms that sell to them. Households also have value chains, because they perform discrete activities on a more or less regular basis.

Services provided to both firms and households are growing rapidly. There are three basic drivers of this growth: a growing underlying need for service functions, many of which are increasingly sophisticated; de-integration of service activities formerly performed in-house to specialized outside service vendors; and the privatization of public services, which is sometimes a result of the other two drivers."[52]

"Under intense competition themselves, many firms find it harder and harder to justify inefficient or ineffective in-house service departments ... The net result of all these developments is a large and rapidly growing services sector in most nations, a proliferation of new types of services, and the emergence of a new breed of larger, more sophisticated service companies. Modern technology and modern management techniques are now penetrating services, at an arguably faster rate than they penetrated manufacturing some time ago."[53] Information technology has been a vital tool in revolutionizing the value chains of service and manufacture.

All this illustrates that there is a close connection between service and manufacturing industries and that many service industries have been created

---

52 Ibid., p. 241
53 Ibid., pp. 246-247.

through the de-integration of service activities by manufacturing and service firms. Whether tangible manufacturing or intangible service production, all activities fall within the integrated value chains of business. History decides if services are done in-house, by the State, or they are left to the market.

Information Technology

Technology

The study of applied technology in firms is of recent origin. More then anything else, computers, and in particular, information technology developments have created this interest.

In neo-classical theory, technology was a largely unexplained residual.[54] Profit maximized in a system of moving equilibrium where new technologies were mysteriously turned into economic growth. In real life, however, technical advance resulted from profit-oriented investments by firms and profits from successful innovations were based on the creation of disequilibrium, destructing so to speak the profitability of old technology.

Increasing industrialization and technological development since the 1950s called for a different approach to explain how technology and change in firms interlinked. The Schumpeterian model of competition and innovation of the Inter-War period became a good candidate for a dynamic perspective of the firm when combined with evolutionary theory.[55] Schumpeter spoke of technology and innovation in the same breadth. Innovation came through new products, new methods of production, new markets, new sources of input, and new ways of organization. In large firms, new products were typically developed in an R & D department, leaving various departments to take care of the other dimensions of technology innovation.

The large bureaucratic organization of the twentieth century was organized around standardized, functional activities and not on an innovative basis, however. The firm was not a change organization. Most change originated in the separate department of R & D, but management might initiate organizational innovations, such as the introduction of divisions or new methods in production and distribution to overcome problems of profitability and competition. Firms and economies changed and grew, but such changes were not conceptualized within a neo-classical theory of the firm. But since the 1950s and

---

54 Nelson and Winter, *An Evolutionary Theory of Economic Change*, pp. 197-204.
55 Ibid., pp. 275-281.

1960s, technology moved in as *the* change factor in social science theories.[56]

To make technology an integrated part of firm theory took until the 1980s, however, when corporate management made computers and information technology an important tool for regaining a competitive edge. Evolutionary theory prepared the way for a proper understanding of the importance of technology to the firm.[57] Firms or rather management searched and selected new technologies in their business environment pressed by competition and profitability considerations, on the one hand. On the other hand, these new technologies were turned into an improved business performance in an interactive learning process with existing routines, skills, and structures. How or whether organizations reaped the benefits of new technologies only gradually became part of an evolutionary theory of the firm.[58]

Eventually, management and theorists at micro- and macro-level realized the importance of removing internal and external barriers to change, as pressure for profound innovation increased.[59] At the same time, it was understood that to create a permanently innovative organization you could not restrict change to individual departments for R & D and information technology. The radical transformation of organizations, technology and business environments of the 1990s produced this multi-dimensional and integrated view of technology and innovation.[60] The firm was a dynamic unit and technology covered all dimensions of the value-creating process of the company, including relations and infrastructures of the wider value system complex. Technology was not just defined as technique with some vague social additions.[61] Technology in a firm context equalized the methods deployed in producing the activities of the value chain.

---

56 Rosenberg, N. (1982), *Inside the Black Box: Technology and Economics* (Cambridge: Cambridge University Press), pp. 3-34. See also: Freeman, C. (1982), *The Economics of Industrial Innovation*, 2nd Ed. (London: Pinter). The organization theory perspective may be seen in Mintzberg, *The Structuring of Organizations*.

57 Nelson and Winter, *An Evolutionary Theory of Economic Change*, pp. 72-136, 246-281.

58 Dosi, *Technical Change and Economic Theory*, pp. 1-8, 124-147, and passim. This was the first general attempt to cover the problem of technological change.

59 OECD, *Technology and Economy*, is dedicated to the study of unleashing dynamic economic forces by firm reorganization and IT developments. On a macro-level, this is studied in OECD (1996), *Globalization of Industries* (Paris: OECD).

60 Chandler, Hagström, and Sölvell, *The Dynamic Firm*, pp. 1-12, and passim. The conceptual transformation of technology and firm of the past decade is seen in this volume. See also, Dosi, Teece, Syntry, *Technology, Organization and Competitiveness*.

61 This is basicly the case with the socalled "SCOT" (social construction of technology) method. Technology is considered an artifact related to some social group of society, e.g., women, young men, etc. (see, Bijker, W. E., and Law, J. (Eds.)(1992), *Shaping Technology, Building Society* (Cambridge, Mass.: The MIT Press). Furthermore, the SCOT method is applied to the analysis of technological systems, e.g., the electrical system (see for example, Hughes, T. P. (1983), *Networks of Power.*

IT

IT and Organization

Since its start in the 1960s, a separate department handled and managed the increasing computerized sectors of large firms in pretty much the same way as the other and well-established departments of manufacturing, accounting, sales, and so forth. As a new and rapidly changing technology, computers, or IT as we call it, spawned an escalating amount of literature on almost any aspect, including engineering and operation, systems development, and information management.[62] Theories and methods lagged behind, however, seeking to keep step with technology developments. Furthermore, as noted, it took some time before social science and history began to integrate IT into a new conceptual framework of the firm.

Since the late 1970s, the organizational development of IT and business interrelations were most often conceived of in terms of various stages of growth.[63] The most widely known and utilized was the Nolan four-stage model of 1974. It was later developed into the six-stage model (1979), which is most commonly employed.[64] Many other academics elaborated on that model and developed variations of their own. The stages of growth in Nolan's model went from initiation at one end to maturity at the other. Like other models, Nolan's was based on the idea that organizations pass through a number of identifiable growth phases in utilizing and managing IT. These stages of growth were employed to identify the organization's level of maturity in IT and business relations, with a view to identifying key issues associated with further IT development.

Electrification in Western Society, (Baltimore: The John Hopkins University Press). Although SCOT deals with the social shaping of technology and has produced much useful knowledge, it never leads to a true understanding of the way technology is changing within its primary context of the firm and industrial economy. Wit, D. de (1994), *The Shaping of Automation. A Historical Analysis of the Interaction between Technology and Organization, 1950-1985* (Hilversum, the Netherlands: Verloren), is another example of the applied SCOT method.

62 Cortada has produced a useful overview of the state of IT literature in the following publications: Cortada, J. W. (1996), *A Bibliographic Guide to the History of Computer Applications, 1950-1990* (Westport, Conn.: Greenwood Press). Cortada, J. W. (1990), *A Bibliographic Guide to the History of Computing, Computers and the Information Processing Industry* (New York: Greenwood Press). Cortada, J. W. (1996), *Second Bibliographic Guide to the History of Computing, Computers, and the Information Processing Industry* (Westport, Conn: Greenwood Press).

63 Galliers, R. D., Leidner, D. E., and Baker, B. S. H. (Ed)(1994), *Strategic Information Management* (Oxford, UK: Butterworth-Heinemann), pp. 31-60.

64 Nolan, R. (1979), "Managing the Crisis in Data Processing", in *Harvard Business Review*, March–April, pp. 115-126.

Nolan postulated that growth phases developed according to the changing IT cost share of total business revenue, following an S-curve over time. More importantly, he claimed that this curve represented an organizational learning path of IT use within the organization. The organization's stage of maturity with respect to IT use may be shown on the basis of four major growth processes. First, is the scope of application portfolio throughout the organization (covering an increasing number of activities and moving from operation to management levels). Second, is the focus of the IT organization (moving from a "closed" centralized department in the early stages to information management in maturity). Third, is the focus of the IT planning and control activity (moving from internal focus in the first stages to an external focus in the later stages). Fourth, is the level of user awareness (moving from a reactive position to centralized IT initiatives in the first stages to partnership in maturity).

Nolan put forth his model at an early stage of IT developments when database technology and data management was hot news. It lacked a strong organizational and management focus and provided little help for the IT manager in creating a successful department, but the idea of stages of growth caught on. What academics and consultants did since then was to update the original Nolan model and to turn it into a method for IT planning. Earl's model of the 1980s, for example, argued that organizations would pass through a number of different learning curves as new kinds of IT moved into the organization, including PC's, office automation and telecommunications, and as the focus shifted towards strategic information.[65]

By the early 1980s, large corporate IT departments were well established throughout the industrialized world, alongside other functional departments.[66] Computer professionals produced information systems and operated big centralized systems in a world largely separated from the other business functions that used IT. While IT was introduced to automate and speed up an increasing number of activities, including producing reports for planning and control, it did so on the basis of existing organization structures. Emerging and growing needs for business change started a process, however, that would eventually transform the traditional perspective of IT and business relations.

---

65 Earl, M. (1989), *Management Strategies for Information Technology* (London: Prentice Hall), pp. 27-32.
66 Cortada, *Information Technology as Business History*, pp. 221-246. The widely used textbooks of Davis, G. B. (1974), *Management Information Systems: Conceptual Foundations, Structure, and Development* (New York: McGraw-Hill), and Davis, G. B., and Olson, H. B. (1985), *Management Information Systems: Conceptual Foundations, Structure, and Development*, 2nd Ed., (New York: McGraw-Hill), present a good view of the state of art by the early 1970s and early 1980s.

From about 1980, American human-relations management merged with European socio-technical and democratic trends into a user-oriented approach to systems development.[67] It was based on the idea of the organization as an open system, leaving much room for social factors to determine computer systems. This approach took two directions. Particularly in Scandinavia, some focused explicitly on the relationship of user organization employees with systems developers. Inspired by a labor process approach, this group of academics strove to go against management endeavors to use IT for purposes of labor de-skilling and removal. However, in so doing they omitted true business considerations. Others looked for ways of increasing business benefits. The former "democratic" approach reached its peak in the early and mid-1980s, but lost ground as a management or firm view took over in organizations.

Since the mid-1980s, the engineering and bureaucratic way of organizing IT resources, separated from business and dominated by computer professionals, was being challenged by a business or organizational perspective.[68] Investing heavily in automation and integration, corporations gradually adopted a general management view of IT, seeking to raise productivity and regain competitiveness. The IT management literature was most attentive to these changes.

Based on concepts imported from diverse areas of business studies, a restructuring of the IT management field took place. What used to be a rather technical subject connected with the development and management of computer-based systems became transformed into an interdisciplinary area of study.[69] The use of IT for strategic purposes to support or shape the competitive strategy and strength of the enterprise moved to the top of the agenda. A process started to match IT with internal functions and authority levels of the firm as well as competitive perspectives of external markets and competitors. In aligning IT with organizational strategies and goals, Michael E. Porter's

---

67 Most of Friedman, A., with Cornford, D. S. (1989), *Computer Systems Development: History, Organization, and Implementation* (Chichester: John Wiley), is dedicated to the study of user relations in the 1980s, paying little attention to the management and business approach, see pp. 169-305.

68 Galliers, Leidner, Baker, *Strategic Information Management*, pp. 1-24.

69 First by mid 1980s, some social scientists and corporations began to consider IT a tool to improve competitiveness through the existing ways of organizing business activities, making technology so to speak the driving force, see: McFarlan. M. W. (1984), "Information Technology Changes the Way You Compete", in *Harvard Business Review*, May-June, pp. 98-103. Porter, M. E. and Miller, V. E. (1985), "How Information Gives You Competitive Advantage", *Harvard Business Review*, July-Aug., pp. 149-160. Synnott, W. R. (1987), *The Information Weapon: Winning Customers and Markets with Technology* (New York: Wiley). Then by late 1980s, the focus moved to the strategic level, still under the existing framework of organizations. This is clearly seen by such widespread publications as Wiseman, C. (1988) *Strategic Information Systems* (Homewood, Ill.: Irwin). Earl, *Management Strategies for*

works on competitive strategy and competitive advantage eventually became widely used. He determined competitive forces, generic strategies, and the sources of competitive advantage, which were seen as stemming from the way firms organized and performed their discrete activities in the so-called value chain. Consideration of critical success factors was a different method for defining the strategic information needs of an organization. New technologies, such as networking, PCs, relational databases, and 4GL for increased productivity of systems development, added to this change of perspective. Endeavors and needs to reform corporations and business in general created the pressure for such change of perspective.

Nevertheless, barriers to change still existed because of the unfamiliarity of general and functional management with the potentials of IT, and IT managers and professionals' superficial understanding of business requirements.[70] It took the profound business reform and escalating IT developments from the early 1990s to create an environment for transformation.[71] That speeded up the process of actual change and the learning processes of IT and business managers and employees. The business side became familiar with the character and potential of IT, just as the IT side re-qualified in theories and methods of economy and organization.

Rarely did academics and consultants undertake any fundamental research in the changing IT and business environment. They tried to adapt methods for IT and business alignment to what they observed, often based on small case studies.[72] Furthermore, the stages-of-growth approach did not real-

---

Information Technology. McNurlin, B. C., and Sprague, R. H., Jr.(1989), *Information Systems Management in Practice*, 2nd Ed. (Englewood Cliffs, New Jersey: Prentice-Hall). The strategic business approach of these books is much different from the technology management perspective of publications of the early 1980s.

70 This problem of transformation is the subject of: Applegate: "Managing in an Information Age", and Allen, T. J., & Morton, S. S. (Ed)(1994), *Information Technology and the Corporation of the 1990s. Research Studies* (New York: Oxford University Press). Galliers, R. D., and Baets, W. R. J. (1998), *Information Technology and Organizational Transformation: Information for the 21ˢᵗ Century Organization* (Chichester: Wiley).

71 The Oticon case is an example of that reform: Bjørn-Andersen, N., and Turner, J. A., "Creating the Twenty-First Century Organization: The Metamorphosis of Oticon", in Baskerville, *Transforming Organizations with Information Technology*, pp. 379-394.

72 This is reflected in textbooks of the 1990s, such as Applegate, L. M., McFarlan, F. W., McKenney, J. L. (1992 and 1996), *Corporate Information Systems Management*, 3rd and 4th Ed. (Chicago: Irwin). Sprague, R. H., Jr., and McNurlin, B. C. (1993), *Information Systems Management in Practice*, 3rd Ed. (Englewood Cliffs, New Jersey: Prentice-Hall). Earl, M. (1996), *Information Management: the Organizational Dimension* (Oxford: Oxford University Press). Willcocks, L., Feeny, D., Islei, G. (1997), *Managing IT as a Strategic Resource* (London: McGraw-Hill).

ly differentiate between changes of more or less profound importance. Finally, dominated as they were by optimistic and "hyped" views on technology, they did not investigate the problems of changing business and IT legacy systems. Increasingly, since about 1990, IT and business relations took on organizational perspectives. As business environment and organizations changed radically, IT considerations did, too. Furthermore, information technology developments created business potentials of quite new and revolutionary dimensions. While most academics and consultants stuck to a stages-of-growth approach, changes seemed so radical that they called for new paradigm-like understandings.

Strategic alignment of IT and business were faced by new challenges.[73] First, markets liberalized. Second, a reorganization of firms took place, by way of so-called business process reengineering (BPR) creating an entrepreneurial market-oriented organization of continuous innovation and adaptation to change. Third, firms and industries globalized. Fourth, business focused on core competence and began to outsource non-strategic functions, creating a basis for an increasing number of industries. Fifth, IT moved from in-house to market sourcing. Sixth, escalating digitalization turned IT into a ubiquitous technology. Seventh, IT became an enterprise- and industry-wide tool for internal and external integration of increasing aspects of value creation. Eighth, new technologies had to be assimilated into the organization and integrated with legacy systems, moving through stages of learning. Ninth, proprietary standards were replaced by open standards and the IT infrastructure of one organization became part of a global electronic infrastructure. Tenth, an information age of non-hierarchical networked organizations and societies emerged, fueled recently by the advent and breakthrough of the commercial Internet. Eleventh, IT management had to adapt flexibly to all this transformation.

All these new trends and challenges of the 1990s radically changed the premises of IT management. No longer had the various functions to be organized and executed within a bureaucratic framework. General management could choose as it pleased to outsource or keep these activities internal to the

---

73 This changing nature of IT and business relations are reflected in such publications as: Davenport, T. H. (1993), *Process Innovation. Reengineering Work through Information Technology* (Boston, Mass.: Harvard Business School Press). Coleman, K. G., et al (Ed)(1996), *Reengineering MIS. Aligning Information Technology and Business Operations* (Harrisburg, USA: Idea Group Publishing). Deans, P. C., and Karwan, K. R. (Ed.)(1994), *Global Information Systems and Technology. Focus on the Organization and its Functional Areas* (Harrisburg, USA: Idea Group Publishing). Furthermore, it is seen in numerous articles in the Harvard Business Review, Sloan Management Review and IT reviews such as MIS Quarterly and Information Management, including conference proceedings of IRMA and IFIP.

organization. IT became a business as any other business, while the IT and business alignment process of organization and learning moved to still higher levels of integration and impact, in theory and practice.

IT Eras

The IT management approach and literature never focused specifically on the history of IT and business relations. It did so indirectly, however, adapting to the changing character and challengers of IT. Frequently, a short notice on historical eras slipped into the textbooks. A widespread version pointed out three such eras.[74] First, the data processing era, 1960-1980, focused on automating manual transaction processing systems using centralized mainframes. Second, the microcomputer era, 1980-1990/95, allowed non-computer professionals to use computers to access, analyze, and present data. Both of these eras had an internal focus. Third, the emerging network era, 1990/95-, overlapping with the micro era, is a consequence of the fusion of computer and telecommunications technology.

Some texts listed four eras, stressing more technological fields of developments.[75] During era I, transaction processing of back office functions on mainframes dominated the 1950s, 1960s and early 1970s. In era II, from the early 1970s to the mid 1980s, databases, systematic systems development, decision support for management, and end-user terminal communication moved computers into still wider fields of operation and functional management. Era III of the mid and late 1980s stressed the strategic potentials of IT in creating a competitive advantage. In era IV, from about 1990, integrated computers and telecommunications, as well as the integrated architecture of a ubiquitous technology, made IT a general strategic tool of organizational reform and competitive advantage, integrating all previous eras. Unlike the earlier eras, in era IV, IT was seen from a business and not a technological perspective.

---

74 Nolan, R. and Croson, D.C. (1995), *Creative Destruction. A Six Stage Process for Transforming the Organization* (Boston; Mass.: Harvard Business Press), p. 6.
75 Applegate, "Managing in an Information Age", p. 37. See also, Applegate, McFarlan, McKenney, *Corporate Information Systems Management*, 1996, pp. 10-12, 353-364. The era concept tends to focus on technical development of computers and networks rather then applications, however. From a systems development point of view, Friedman, *Computer Systems Development*, presented the following eras up to the late 1980s (pp. 321-352): 1. A hardware constraint period until the mid 1960s. 2. A software constraint period from the mid 1960s to the early 1980s. 3. A user-relations constraint period during the 1980s. 4. A future radical change of computer applications, dealing not only with internal but also external relations of the organization. While it is an interesting study on the history of systems development literature up to the late 1980s, Friedman does not relate it to business developments.

In a few cases, the era approach has been based on studies from a more profound information perspective. Three phases might be found.[76] First was the classical period of industrial corporations from the late nineteenth century to about 1960. Information technology was mechanical and rather simple, but the bureaucratic organization had developed fundamental pre-processing structures for information processing and management that the arrival of IT did not change fundamentally. That included such basic business functions as production, marketing and sales, finance and accounting, procurement and inventory, research and development, and clerical and secretarial activities.

Second was the period from approximately 1960 to approximately 1990, when IT was introduced and spread throughout all basic corporate functions and departments. Automation of operation and reporting enabled productivity rises and improved management capabilities. The advent and spread of the computer allowed for increasing business activity and economic growth of an industrialized world. Inflexible organizations with lingering bureaucracies, mass production and mass marketing, and stand alone information systems, created strong barriers to radical change and expansion, however.

In the third phase, since about 1990, political, organizational and technological barriers were gradually being removed and replaced by revolutionary change and the growth of open, integrated, and networked economies and organizations. IT became a ubiquitous technology and infrastructure.

In his historical outline of IT business applications, Cortada utilized the following historical periods.[77] 1. The introduction of computers, 1945-1952: business meets the computer. 2. Initial implementation of computers, 1952-1965: computers come to commerce. 3. The era of major adoption in business, 1965-1981: computers become part of the corporate scene. 4. Extensive imple-

---

76 Jönscher, C. (1994) "An Economic Study of the Information Technology Revolution", in T. J. Allan & M. S. S. Morton (Ed.), *Information Technology and the Corporation of the 1990s*, pp. 5-42. The information approach from a structural historic perspective was developed by Beniger, J. R. (1986), *The Control Revolution. Technological and Economic Origins of the Information Society* (Camdbrige, Mass.: Harvard University Press). He demonstrates that the foundation of information societies was created during the second industrial revolution of the late nineteenth and early to mid twentieth centuries, based on the large bureaucracies and pre-processing corporations that dominated these societies. Since the 1950s, computers just took over information processing of existing routines.

77 Cortada, *Information Technology and Business History*, pp. 159-187. To my knowledge, this is the only general historical study of IT and business developments. Cortada focuses primarily on the US. While his observations on the post-1981 era are few, the period pre-1981 is covered more thoroughly. Generally speaking, he subscribes to an approach of continuous development and stresses how surprisingly little research exists on the business application of computers.

mentation to all corners of business, 1981-1995: the microcomputer era. Although the author presents much relevant information on the first three eras, the post-1981 period is not well covered.

A Theory of Information Management

On a purely theoretical basis, an attempt has been made to construct a theory linking information and business management.[78] The extended firm concept is taken to be the basis of the information requirements of management to run his business efficiently. By way of a cycle analogy, a model for theoretical thinking around economic, organizational, and informational business relations is developed. Many kinds of cycle interdependence are created between natural processes of materials, energy, and people on the one hand, and economics, organization engineering, and management on the other.[79] This complex of interdependence works in a common social sphere of human interaction by way of information interchange, information meaning something intentional. It is the task for what he calls "the science of informations" to understand this interchange of information and for management to match information from these interrelated cycles with the business system so that the firm performs effectively. Without IT and information management systems, management would be unable to compete.

Many theoretical themes and discussions are raised in this treatise. In the end however, it is hard to judge the analytical importance of such a theoretical and normative approach when real world affairs are left out, or just taken for granted. The meaning of information is also obscure. It is never confronted with business realities and seems to be connected with matters of interchange or transactions rather than production. IT and information interact ubiquitously with business, but how and why?

---

78 Pedersen, M. K. (1996), *A Theory of Informations* (Roskilde, Denmark: Samfundslitteratur & Roskilde Universitetsforlag).
79 Ibid., pp. 279-318.

Approach

In this context, IT is considered a tool for processing business information. Business information constitutes the fuel for the value-creating activities of firms. The organization of the firm structures the way information is produced and moves, while IT facilitates speed and new capabilities. General business developments, followed by industry level business, make up the framework and generator of IT. In this way, IT is structured by business and the organization, which also works to perpetuate existing forms and functions. On the other hand, IT is an enabler of business development and industrialization.

Over the years, as IT spreads into every corner of organizations it turns into a precondition for the existence and expansion of large firms. The transformation of business and the networking and electronic infrastructure revolution of the 1990s move the interaction and dynamics of business and IT up to a much higher and escalating level. While business remains the driver of development, IT has become the key to change and expansion to such a degree that business has to align along the potentials of technology, too.

According to the contextual nature of IT and the business relationship, the history of the past four to five decades is divided into two paradigm-like eras, including the transition period of the 1980s.

II · 1950s–1970s
EXPANSION AND CRISIS

Environment

Economic Development

The two decades from the 1950s to the early 1970s were years of unparalleled prosperity. Economic growth and international trade grew faster than in any other period, accelerating particularly in Europe and Asia.[80]

Western economies worked within a stable international order, reinforced by a common communist enemy. The US played its leadership role, providing capital for Europe and Japan to recover from the Second World War, fostering procedures for cooperation and liberal trading policies, and being the basis of international monetary stability. Western colonies were transformed into states, and financial aid and trade stimulated world economy.

Domestic policies were devoted to promoting high levels of demand and employment in advanced countries. Growth was faster than before, inflation was low, business cycles virtually disappeared, and investments and expectations rose to unprecedented levels.

The potential for growth was very large. Throughout Europe and Asia there was substantial scope for recovery from the years of depression and war. And even more importantly, the American lead country continued to accelerate technical progress and diffuse new technologies by heavy investments or by technology transfer to Western Europe, Japan, and other Western offshoots. By copying the consumption patterns, technology, and organizational methods of the USA, these follower countries were almost able to catch up to and reach American levels of productivity and welfare. An important condition for this successful catch-up was the fact that Western Europe and Japan had a human capital with high levels of skill, education, and science. More than anything else, perhaps, this was crucial to the fast catch-up. Everywhere there was much room, need and will for recovery, especially in Europe and Asia. And everybody imitated the technology and business of the USA.

By the early 1970s, other advanced economies of the world had almost caught-up with the USA. Enormous production capacities were developed, and the dynamic markets of automobiles and other consumer durables showed clear signs of saturation. Then a recession led Western economies to waver. Inflation and unemployment rose, economic growth and profits fell,

---

80 Maddison, *Monitoring the World Economy*, pp. 73-78.

and technical progress slowed down. Inflation was worsened by the two oil shocks of 1973 and 1979-1980. Economies were destabilized by these price increases, terms-of-trade losses and balance of payments problems, including the collapse of the post-war fixed exchange rate system. Traditional economic policies failed and corporations were unable to adjust and create new potentials of growth. In Asia, however, the golden age continued, as Japan and NICs (newly industrialized countries) kept on expanding. Furthermore, Japanese corporations started a proper invasion of Western markets by way of a very competitive production of automobiles and electronics.

The Western industrial world entered a time of troubles. One economic disruption succeeded another. As the conviction spread that events could not be explained – much less reversed – by the theories and policies of the preceding epoch, the economic disruptions merged in the public mind into a general crisis of the industrial system. How could the institutions that had generated stability and prosperity suddenly cause inflation, unemployment, stagnation, and social unrest?

Since about 1970, Fordism, the dominant Western business model, encountered growing difficulties as a consequence of declining economic growth and productivity.[81] Three broad sets of factors account for this slowdown.

The first was the technological exhaustion of the main clusters of innovation in large mechanical and electrical engineering and automotive industries.

The second factor concerns the breakdown of worker acceptance of the Fordist approach to the organization of production when labor started to rebel against the monotonous character of assembly-line tasks from the mid 1960s onwards in Europe and the USA.

A third major weakness of Fordism became apparent after the recessions of 1974-75 and 1979-82, followed by uncertain macro-economic conditions in the 1980s. Fordist scale economies of undifferentiated mass production lacked flexibility towards changes in consumer demand. This rigidity characterized the whole approach of Fordism, being based on supplier domination over consumers.

These factors might not have sufficed to challenge the Fordist paradigm of industrial management and work organization deeply or rapidly, had Japanese corporations not strongly entered Western markets, in particular the USA domestic market. Many major American and European firms that used to

---

81 See below, *Organization*.

dominate their domestic markets acted with conservative reactions to this set-
back. In steel, consumer electronics, and automobiles, but also in food processing and many other industries, firms reacted to declines in growth and
profits as if they were of a purely cyclical nature.

Until the late 1970s, management and politicians stuck to the old system
and old policies. Then, a new policy was introduced in the USA, followed by
other industrial countries.[82] Gradually, governments eliminated restrictions to
market entry and pricing, restoring the pressure of the market on wages and
prices. Next, Western corporations began to realize the need for fundamental
organizational reform.

Organization

By the time SAS was formed in the early post-war decades, the hierarchical
multi-unit enterprise was the dominant business institution in most sectors of
Western economy. This was, therefore, the natural pattern of organization to
follow. This type of corporation originated in the second industrial revolution
around 1900, when enterprises in capital-intensive industries moved in to be
the dynamic force of industrialization.[83] These firms grew in similar ways.

All exploited the cost advantages of scale and scope by investing in large
production facilities. These potential cost advantages could not be fully realized unless a constant flow of inputs from suppliers, flow of materials through
the plant, and flow of outputs to intermediaries and final users was maintained and coordinated to assure effective capacity utilization.

Such coordination could not happen automatically. It demanded the constant attention of a managerial team or hierarchy. The entrepreneurs organizing these enterprises created national and then international marketing and
distributing organizations. They then had to recruit teams of lower and middle managers to coordinate the flow of products through the processes of production and distribution, and teams of top managers to monitor current operations and to plan and allocate resources for future ones. The firms who
made these investments in manufacturing, marketing, and management essential to exploit fully the economies of scale and scope quickly dominated

---

82 Piore and Sabel, *The Second Industrial Divide*, pp. 165-193.
83 Chandler, *The Visible Hand*, and Chandler, *Scale and Scope*, laid the ground for our
    understanding of the dynamic nature and importance of the modern corporation.
    In "Organizational Capabilities and the Economic History of Industrial Enter-
    prise", pp. 79-99, Chandler relates his conclusions explicitly to the development
    of the firm.

their industries, and even the national economies in which they operated. Most continued to do so for decades.

These organizational capabilities were created during the knowledge-acquiring processes involved in: organizing production, scaling up production processes, commercializing a new product, moving into new markets, adapting to customers' needs, working with suppliers, and learning the ways of recruiting and training workers and managers. Even more important were those routines acquired to coordinate these several functional activities, including strategic responses to competitor moves.

This dominant model of business is sometimes called "Fordism", because its core technology was based on mass production, striving to adapt the environment to the capabilities of the organization.[84]

Modern enterprise, by bringing many units under its control, began to operate in different locations, often carrying on different types of economic activities and handling different lines of goods and services. In this way, more and more functions were added to the bureaucracy. Some also expanded by diversifying into related industries and products, to keep their leading position in the market and such companies consequently adopted a multidivisional structure. Top management governed and integrated all these units into one firm, under the supervision of a board of directors. The activities of these units and the transactions between them thus became internal, instead of being carried out by other companies in the marketplace. Each unit had its own administrative office, its own managers and staff, its own set of books and accounts, and its own resources of facilities and personnel to carry out a specific function in a specific geographical area. Each unit could theoretically operate as an independent business enterprise.

All these structuring procedures were developed by management to ensure control of activities. This bureaucracy produced a continuous flow of information from top management to operators at the bottom and back again by way of an endless flow of reports and communications.[85] This increased control structure brought reliability and hence predictability of processes and flows, which in turn meant economic returns on the application of information processing technology. Furthermore, information processing and flows needed themselves to be controlled by increasing levels of bureaucracy and pre-processing procedures, finally placed under computer control.

The activities of the organization were broken down into distinct units of

---

84 OECD, *Technology and Economy*, pp. 92-94.
85 Beniger, *The Control Revolution*, pp. 291-436. You might say that Beniger's studies added an information processing perspective to Chandler's fundamental research.

specialization, each responsible for one major task associated with making and marketing a product.[86] These units were subdivided into smaller and smaller units until the job of each individual in the organization was specified in detail. Founded on the concepts of simplification, routinization, and control, the bureaucratic hierarchy minimized uncertainty to operate smoothly. Hierarchical chains of authority linked the various levels of the organization, and personnel behavior was codified in detailed policies, procedures, and job descriptions that facilitated tight control through direct supervision. Two central concepts developed to control work processes. One, a job was a precisely defined aggregate of well-specified tasks. Two, seniority, that is, the length of service, was a criterion in the allocation and progression of jobs. Workers' income, employment security, and degree of autonomy all depended on the definition of their jobs and on seniority. Management control was limited by these fundamental principles of labor.

Labor organized according to the division of labor in corporations and between corporations. Highly specialized labor unions or industrial unions, along the lines of corporate organization, appeared in all industrial societies. In smaller countries, particularly in Scandinavia, organized labor played a strong role during the twentieth century.

This process of industrialization developed within a national framework supported increasingly by national government and state apparatus to enable continued growth and stability.

Finally, an international division of labor emerged and worked as a vital dynamic force of industrial development, particularly in smaller countries such as the Scandinavian ones.

In spite of some adaptability, the classical organization or the bureaucratic hierarchy tended to work as a machine.[87] It worked to ensure, so to speak, that it was "sealed off" from influence of the uncertainties of the environment. As the industrial environment became increasingly volatile from the 1960s, corporations began to look for ways to create more flexibility. Matrix organizations, project groups, and other efforts to reform organizations were introduced, but the hierarchy always remained in charge while entrepreneurial gains were hard to obtain.

---

86 Piore and Sabel, *The Second Industrial Divide*, pp. 19-35, and passim.
87 Applegate, "Managing an Information Age", pp. 22-35.

Scandinavia

Scandinavia is situated on the periphery of Europe, and compared with European centers its population density is low.[88] The large distances, except in Denmark, are favorable to air transportation. The three nations of post-war SAS, Norway, Sweden, and Denmark, experienced the world's fastest growing industrialization and growth in welfare. These small national economies depended heavily on international trade and transportation and with the expanding economy, the need to link Scandinavia to the rest of the industrialized world grew in time. That paved the way for an early international network of airline routes.

Another important side of Scandinavian development was the breakthrough in a large government sector. The state intervened to handle a number of welfare activities that tended to raise and equalize the level of living conditions. Furthermore, all through the twentieth century, class-relations in Scandinavia were based on organized cooperation through collective agreements. These agreements laid down which organized group of workers should do what kind of job at what time and for what payment. As a result, Scandinavians came to live with a heavy burden of taxes and high wages compared with the rest of the industrialized world.

The resulting pressure on companies created strong motives for automation, including the introduction of computer technology. Finally, management of companies lived in a world that was much regulated and left little room for action. This Scandinavian model of society seemed to suit the bureaucratic organization of SAS that emerged, including a highly developed division of labor, cemented by unions, collective agreements, and management culture. Conversely, this structure created a strong barrier when SAS later wanted to transform its strategy in response to a changing environment.

---

88 Thomsen, R. (Ed.)(1975-76), *Hovedlinier i Nordens Historie*, 3-4 (Copenhagen: Gyldendal) (an outline of Nordic history).

The Aircraft Industry

Since the Second World War, the two American aircraft manufacturers Boeing and McDonnell-Douglas have dominated world air transport technology.[89] The French aircraft industry gained a niche in the early European market, followed by the combined and more successful French-British-German efforts of Airbus since the 1970s.

Aircraft technology developed at the speed of lightening during these three decades. Every decade saw one or two new generations of aircraft technology appear in the market. The arrival of the jet plane in the late 1950s marked a revolution in air transport. All leading airlines of the world purchased these new airplanes and during the early 1960s, jet planes replaced hundreds of propellers.

In the late 1960s, a second generation of jet planes was introduced. To some degree, they used the new technology of integrated circuits instead of electro-mechanical devices. The technology of these second-generation jet planes reached its climax when wide-body planes arrived during the 1970s. A simultaneous crisis ended the expanding line of aircraft technology. The airplane market slumped, and aircraft manufacturers had to come up with something new and more flexibly adjusted to new kinds of market demands.

The Airlines Industry

Air transport is a business that grows according to trends of macro-economic growth, but only faster.[90] The rate of air traffic growth has been the double of world GDP since the early 1950s when economic expansion began. Except for its setbacks when moving from propellers to jet planes in the early 1960s, the airline industry expanded until the oil crises of the 1970s reduced growth.[91]

---

89 Selling, R. (1992), *Legend and Legacy: The Story of Boeing and its People* (Seattle: Boeing). WWW: Boeing homepage (includes the McDonnell Douglas history). Ceruzzi, P. E. (1989), *Beyond the Limits: Flight Enters the Computer Age* (Cambridge, Mass.: MIT Press). A detailed description of changing McDonnell Douglas models may be found in SAS, *Yearbooks*, 1967-1980.

90 OECD (1993), *International Air Transport* (Paris: OECD), pp. 21-73.

91 The CEO of SAS and chairman of IATA, K. Hagrup, published an interesting book on the postwar developments of the airlines industry and the problems caused by the 1970s crisis: Hagrup, K. (1975), *LUFTFARTEN og fremtiden* (aviation and the future) (Copenhagen: Chr Erichsens Forlag). It also demonstrates that his solutions stuck to the mass-producing perspective of Fordism.

The economic importance of air transport is why the sector has been treated as a strategic issue by national governments. Except for the large American industry and market, each nation had one monopoly airline, and governments claimed sovereignty of national airspace. To allow international air transport, a system of bilateral and multilateral agreements developed. Practical cooperation on fares, documents, interline accounting, and so on, was taken care of by the International Air Transport Association (IATA), and by United Nation's (UN) International Civil Aviation Organization (ICAO) for technical matters. As a result, air transport was a regulated industry.[92]

Passenger and freight traffic grew rapidly from the early 1950s, first in the USA, then followed by Western Europe during the 1960s and early 1970s until the slowdown, caused by shocking increases in oil prices, occurred. During the 1960s and 1970s, expanding air tourism contributed increasingly to growth of air traffic.

During the 1950s, the number of airlines expanded greatly when all industrial nations started or reconstructed a national airline. Newly industrialized countries of Latin America and Asia followed suit. During the 1960s, the new de-colonized states of Africa established airline companies, too. Around 1970, the transport capacity of the world's airlines was enormous and although traffic grew, problems of over capacity began to loom on the horizon. As production capacity kept on growing during the 1970s and economic stagnation and crisis brought newly blooming capitalism to an end, the airlines also ended up in a deep crisis in the late 1970s.

A smaller group of large American, followed by Western European, and later on East Asian, airlines dominated world air transportation from its very beginning. The American flight market developed earlier and expanded more than the rest of the industrialized world, because of the head start of the American economy after the Second World War. Airlines such as American, United, and PanAm led the American airlines industry. After 1978, deregulation of the American airlines industry led to some replacement and consolidation among the leading companies.

In Western Europe, every country had its national airline.[93] As a result of industrial recovery and expansion, the leading industrial nations also came to dominate the European airlines industry. British Airways, Lufthansa, and Air

---

92 On the particular important role of IATA, see: Brancker, J. W. S. (1977), *IATA and What It Does* (Leiden: Sitjhoff).
93 For West European airlines in particular, see also: Dienel and Lynth, *Flying the Flag*, pp. 18-194.

France led the pack, followed by the medium-sized companies SAS, KLM, Swissair, and Alitalia. In East Asia, All Nippon Airlines, Japan Airlines, Qantas Airways of Australia, Singapore Airlines, and Thai Airways were among the leading airlines of the region. They lagged behind Western airlines until the 1980s. In Latin America Varig of Brazil became one of the leading airlines. Except for South African Airways, no African airline developed to become a leading airline of the region. Outside the capitalist world, Aeroflot of the Soviet Union grew to become the largest airline of all at the end of the 1970s. Airlines of the communist world kept outside the regulated air systems of the capitalist world, except for necessary cooperation for technical reasons.

As a rule, the various airlines served their home markets in domestic and international flights. All leading airlines of the capitalist world were part of the international regulated air transport system of IATA, until the late 1970s. Consequently, no direct competition was strong enough to break the system of monopolized markets. Only since the 1980s, the monopoly has been increasingly attacked.

All leading airlines went through the same lines of development. A large, bureaucratic, Fordist organization, based on a combination of functional departments and highly specialized jobs ruled by hierarchically structured management, came to dominate these airlines from the 1950s onwards.

Sophisticated aircraft technology, that allowed airlines to fly an increasingly large number of passengers and amount of freight, at greater speed and frequency, at a relatively declining price, became the most important economic tool of development. In addition, a combination of pre-processed structuring of work and information flow and computer technology was introduced to reduce costs and improve productivity of labor even more. Computer technology enabled airlines to handle the rapidly growing number of transactions, too, without which they would hardly have been able to grow into such large corporations.

World Statistics of Passenger Scheduled Services[94]

	1970	1975	1980
Total passengers, mill.	312	436	645
Shared international passengers,%	23.7	24.2	25.0
Share USA,%	52.4	47.2	45.6
Share Europe,%	21.9	21.7	20.0
Share Asia,%	11.1	13.8	16.5
-Japan,%	5.2	6.3	7.0
Share, ROW,%	14.6	17.3	17.9

Source: UN, *Statistical Yearbooks,* 1970, 1975, 1980.

Passenger Statistics of International Airlines[95]

	1970	1975	1980
Air Canada	7.3	10.4	13.0
American Airlines	19.2	20.8	25.7
Delta Airlines	16.2	26.8	-
Eastern Airlines	22.3	27.6	39.5
Pan American	10.1	7.4	-
Trans World Airlines	13.9	15.9	20.6
United Airlines	28.1	29.3	32.8
Varig	1.4	3.0	4.4
Air France	6.1	8.0	10.9
Alitalia	5.6	5.8	7.3
British Airways	10.4	12.4	16.1
Iberia	5.6	9.8	13.8
KLM	2.4	3.1	3.8
Lufthansa	6.5	9.4	13.0
SAS	5.1	6.7	8.3
Swissair	3.4	4.7	6.0
Japan Airlines	6.1	8.9	13.3
Qantas Airways	0.7	1.4	2.0

Source: IATA, *World Air Transport Statistics,* 1970, 1975, 1980.

---

94 World figures are exclusive of Sovjet and China. Sovjet Aeroflot was the world's largest airline, reaching 73 million passengers in 1970, 98 million in 1975 and 104 million in 1980 (UN, *Statistical Yearbooks*).

95 In millions of passengers.

The IT Industry

From the 1950s to the 1970s, the computer industry was primarily a hardware industry. The major portion of revenues came from hardware, with software gradually increasing its share, from approximately 1/4 in the 1950s to 1/2 by the early 1980s.[96] Hardware revenues did not grow just because the number of computers sold increased, but also as sales of peripheral equipment rose. The real breakthrough in computer sales came from the mid-1960s to the early 1970s, then slowed down during the recession, and continued a steady expansion during the 1970s into the early 1980s.

Computer technology developed rapidly, as computers moved from first generation core technology (vacuum tubes) of the 1950s, to second generation computers (transistors) around 1960, and third generation computers (integrated circuits, including microprocessors) from the mid 1960s. The third generation computers inaugurated the modern computer and the modern computer industry.

American corporations dominated the industry worldwide, led by IBM, and followed by such American vendors as Remington Rand (including Univac) and Burroughs. Since the mid-1960s, computers have turned into a multi-billion dollar industry.

Mainframes, used in large corporations and government agencies, completely dominated computers and computer systems during these decades. From the 1960s, and particularly since the 1970s, terminals rose in number as networking spread in organizations, by way of telephone systems linked to computers. The use of magnetic storage media for input/output equipment also expanded since the 1960s, while the value of punch card equipment declined. Online information storage on disks replaced magnetic tape storage during the 1970s as online applications rose and batch applications declined.

The cost per transaction executed on digital computers declined steadily over the entire period, and processing speed grew by a factor of over 1,000. Computer memories also saw a dramatic change. Between the mid-1950s and the late-1970s, the price of disk storage declined by a factor of 100.

At first, batch processing dominated computing, with for example weekly reports mailed to customers. In the 1960s, telecommunications made it

---

96 Cortada, *Information Technology and Business History*, pp. 51-81. Christensen, J. (1993), "Historical Trends in Computer and Information Technology", in P. B. Andersen, B. Holmqvist, & J. J: Jensen (Ed.), *The Computer as Medium* (Cambridge: Cambridge University Press), pp. 422-439. Unlike the post-1980 age, this first era is well-covered in the research literature, except, unfortunately, for business applications and vendor histories.

possible to transmit information to a customer over a telephone line to a specialized terminal or printer, and this was the way information was delivered up to the 1990s. During the 1970s, one could access a service bureau computer via a terminal, and services expenditures increased during that decade.

A software industry began to emerge in the second half of the 1970s, but on a very limited basis, when IBM decided to un-bundle application software in 1969. Hardware vendors, such as IBM and Remington Rand/Univac, kept on bundling hardware, operating systems and other basic utilities, including the new database management systems of the 1970s. As a rule, software was thought of as ancillary to hardware. The large vendors in the computer industry did not focus on the software market until the mid-1980s.

While users typically did not build their own computers, they normally developed all their application programs. By the late 1970s and early 1980s, perhaps 85% of all expenditure on software went to the salaries of employees who wrote these programs, including programmers and systems analysts. Another 5% went to cover the costs of program development by software manufacturing firms. The remaining 10% was used to rent or buy software packages or services. It is interesting to note that by the early 1990s, just before the start of the client/server revolution, mainframe applications still accounted for about 90% of all software expenditures, according to a rough estimate.[97]

Since the breakthrough of the IBM 360-family of the mid-1960s, and other third generation computers, including their operating systems, the use of programming languages, such as Fortran and Cobol proliferated, although not totally replacing assembler language. The microprocessor of the early 1970s paved the way for smaller computers, so-called mini- and microcomputers of the late 1970s, and software packages began to appear in the marketplace.

As the number of mainframe computers installed increased, so did the demand for programmers and systems analysts to develop and write more applications. By the early 1970s, the entire industry was experiencing a shortage of qualified programmers. By then, the effective use of information processing could mean life or death for many organizations. Furthermore, the growing size and complexity of applications caused delays, excessive budgets and problems of information management. Accordingly, a kind of software crisis arose.

Consequently, pressure increased to develop software faster, better, and with decreasing amounts of technical expertise. The computer industry developed many techniques for the design and creation of software applications, such as structured and moduled programming to reduce complexity, project

---

97 See below: the 1990s, *IT Industry and Applications*.

management for overall control of systems development, and database management systems to improve the usability of data that used to be organized in simple files.

IT Management

The use of computers in business required an army of specialists, who, in turn, called for a smaller army of managers and executives to run IT departments. These departments and divisions had to function within the broader context of the companies of which they were a part. When executives wanted to exploit computers, their tool was the IT department.[98]

Taking a historical perspective of the evolution of IT departments, you might observe three phenomena. First, these units changed very slowly over time, and their structure, job titles, and approaches to work evolved more slowly than the technology they used. Second, IT departments developed their own culture and professional associations, just as other business people did in their fields. Third, they took on a life of their own, constantly trying to expand and justify their value to the companies or government agencies of which they were a part. Similar observations may be made in departments of accounting, manufacturing, distribution, or marketing and sales. In short, IT departments were always an integral part of mainstream business. If anything changed over time it was that they became an even more important part of their companies.

One of the greatest challenges facing executives was how to use computer technology. The first computer applications simply sought to automate highly repetitive functions and to overcome information bottlenecks, without changing the existing organization. By the late 1970s, a new concept of thinking and practice had appeared. In the 1960s and 1970s, as the number of applications using computers grew, it became increasingly obvious that companies had become highly dependent on computers. An increasing number of decisions could not be made without facts that were stored in computers and it was generally thought that decision-making required more facts than in the past. Thus, information became of major concern to management.

One reason for this growing concern with information was that budgets for data processing grew to a share of two or three percent, on average, of total costs in large corporations. Roughly two thirds of this budget was allocated

---

98 Cortada, *Information Technology as Business History*, pp. 224-241. Friedman, *Computer Systems Development*, pp. 69-167.

to salaries. As the investments and value of IT grew, so requirements for IT management rose.

Computers were first installed in commercial settings during the 1950s. It had already become evident to many companies that the huge cost of acquiring and caring of computers called for centralized operations. Since accounting was the first function to use computers, it was natural for this department to take general responsibility for their use. However, during the 1960s, as computers became increasingly important to the operations of the enterprise, the role of IT management changed. IT managers rose in status, from third to second level management and even to the first level of senior executives. The elevation of the IT manager continued to the point when, in the late 1970s, such managers frequently had become senior vice presidents of major corporations, a position many continued to attain in the 1990s.

Despite the enormous investments made in computers, relations between the IT department and the rest of the company were anything but smooth. The IT department was often blamed for not serving the other departments well, running data processing as they pleased, and furthermore, for not getting much value out of large investments. IT managers seemed under constant siege in the 1970s and particularly so in the 1980s.

Computer professionals divided into different groups. Systems analysts designed software applications. Their jobs grew out of the pre-computer era "methods department". The other large group was comprised of programmers. No population grew as quickly or became as visible as this one. Essentially, programmers played the same role for four decades. They took the work of the analysts and wrote software programs to instruct computers in what to do. Computer operators formed the third group. These were the people who actually ran the machines. Like the other occupations, their functions have remained essentially the same. Keypunch operators (later responsible for data entry into terminals), formed a fourth group, which collected and typed data into machines. While the other three groups consisted almost exclusively of men, the majority of the fourth group was women and they were at the bottom of the hierarchy. These data entry clerks disappeared when end-user computing took over during the 1980s. A fifth group of technicians working in the department of communications eventually also joined the IT department.

For all these populations, recruiting and training became a major focus area early on, as the requirements for qualified personnel always seemed to lag behind availability. In the 1950s and 1960s, most recruitment occurred from within organizations, later it focused on a national labor pool, including computer science graduates.

IT Applications

As a consequence of increased industrialization and expanding government activities, IT applications were widely introduced from the late 1950s and early 1960s.[99] Most applications carried out administrative routines, such as accounting and salaries. Information bottlenecks and most importantly, the pressure for improved productivity, typically justified the use of computers. From the mid-1960s to 1980, all large Western corporations and government agencies introduced and developed computer applications for all their main business and administrative functions.

The main reason for doing so was probably that computers became more reliable, bigger, faster, easier to use, and therefore able to handle larger amounts of data. The two biggest technological changes involved the widespread acceptance of disk drives in which to store direct access information, and the implementation of online systems. Thus, while batch processing continued to expand all through the 1960s and 1970s, online processing grew from almost zero in commercial environments to becoming the preferred choice by the end of the 1970s. In other words, as the 1960s and 1970s progressed, more applications were being developed that were online rather than batch, and terminals were installed in large numbers. So were disk drives as they became less expensive and more reliable.

Like the organizations they served, the systems worked separately and were rarely integrated. The labor process of business and government agencies and the way it was organized did not change radically. Rather, manually and mechanically processed systems were converted into computer applications, and the new technology was more or less absorbed by the existing bureaucracies. The IT department was just another unit added to the other departments of the corporation or the agency.

What IT applications were implemented? First, accounting and manufacturing applications were implemented more widely in companies and across organizations. Batch systems were enhanced with online applications, including use of terminals and in the second half of the 1970s, distributed processing, mostly for data collection and data presentation.

---

99 Cortada, *Information Technology as Business History*, pp. 162-176. This is primarily an American story, followed somewhat belatedly by Western Europe and Japan, it seems. No comprehensive study has been found on the history of IT applications in any company. The British Airways study is the best one available, although it does not really focus on information systems (see below). Thus far, we shall have to make do with this general picture.

Second, the spread of terminals and database management systems during the second half of the 1970s paved the way for the beginning of word processing and decision-making support systems. Both did not really spread until the 1980s, however.

American industries and government agencies led the adoption of computer applications, followed somewhat belatedly by their West European counterparts and Japan, although these countries caught-up in time. Some industries were extensive users of computers by the late 1970s. All major companies in the service industry and in manufacturing and utilities used computers, not only for normal accounting applications but also for some manufacturing and logistical operations.

The conclusion is that IT applications were initially developed in the 1960s and then diffused until they were in relatively wide use by the end of the 1970s. By 1980, large corporations and government agencies dominated the field of IT applications, whereas medium-sized companies only used computers to a limited degree, mainly for accounting functions. Small companies were yet to introduce IT. IT was primarily used for operative purposes, including some planning on the tactical level. Strategic management lay outside the realm of computing.

Airlines IT

From the late 1950s to the 1990s, two vendors completely dominated the airline information technology, namely Unisys (originally Univac, later Sperry) and IBM. Until the early 1980s, they divided the airlines of the world almost equally between them, until IBM became more dominant. But Unisys still held strong positions. The core reservation systems on third generation computers, including passenger name recording (PNR), were mostly IBM-based in North America (except in the case of Air Canada), and Unisys-based in Western Europe (except for Alitalia and later, British Airways).[100]

IBM and Unisys were primarily vendors of hardware and operating systems. They took part in systems development of all major reservation systems and a number of cargo systems. Both launched standard systems of these two vital functions of any airline, based on a pioneering airline system. As a rule, however, functional applications of all leading airlines of the world were made in-house by internal IT departments. IBM and Unisys (called Univac at the time) were both main vendors for SAS.[101]

---

100 See list: *Airlines with PNR-Reservations Systems 1970.*
101 See below the chapter on: *Airlines IT,* in the 1980s, including the figure: *Airlines IT Cost Share of Total 1983.*

Airlines with PNR-Reservation Systems 1970

List of PNR-airlines

Airline	System	Computer	Cutover
Air Canada	EXEC 8	U1108	MAY 70
Air France	EXEC 8	U1108	JUN 69
BEA	CONTORTS	U 494	JAN 67
CDC[x)]	STARS-SOLAR	U 494	Spring71
Iberia	STARS	U 494	MAY 70
Lufthansa	STARS	U 494	DEC 71
Northwest	OMEGA-TCS	U 494	JAN 70
Trans Australian	OMEGA-TCS	U 494	MAY 72

[x)] Shared system for: Southern
Shawnee
Wright
Altair
Varig
SAS, NAD

Airline	System	Computer	Cutover
Aer Lingus	I-PARS	I360/50	DEC 69
Alitalia	I-PARS	I360/65	APR 68
Allegheny	PARS	I360/65	OCT 70
American Airlines	SABRE	I7090	JAN 69
BOAC	I-PARS	I360/65	OCT 68
Braniff	PARS	I360/65	MAR 69
Continental	PARS	I360/65	MAY 68
Delta	PARS	I360/65	OCT 68
Eastern	PARS	I360/65	JUL 68
Frontier	PARS	I360/65	SEP 68
JAL	I-PARS	I360/65	NOV 70
KLM	I-PARS	I360/65	JUL 70
MCS[x)]	PARS	I360/65	70/71
Mohawk	PARS	I360/50	Spring69
National	PARS	I360/65	OCT 70
North Central	PARS	I360/65	JUN 70
Northeast	PARS	I360/65	MAY 69
Pan American	PANAMAC	I7080	JAN 69
Qantas	I-PARS	I360/65	JAN 72
South African	I-PARS	I360/50	NOV 70
Swissair	I-PARS	I360/65	APR 69
TWA	PARS	I360/75	NOV 71
United	PARS	I360/65	APR 71
Western	PARS	I360/65	Spring69

[x)] Shared system (owned by Contental) for Ozark
Piedmont
Air West

I = IBM   U = UNIVAC

Source: SAS, Data Management, Sept. 1971.

SABRE

Reservations systems have always been central to airline operations, and SABRE, the reservations system of American Airlines (AA), led the way in IT development of airlines.[102] Since the late 1940s, a growing number of passengers and a need to increase productivity and revenue made AA look for an electronic reservations system instead of the existing manual one. Reservation information processes involved three steps: availability, inventory, and passenger names. Seat availability and inventory control were tackled first, starting with seat availability.

In the late 1940s, AA introduced the first electromechanical system for seat availability control in its Boston reservations office. However, to improve operation of reservations, inventory control had to be automated. In the early 1950s, the first computer system for storing and online updating of reservations in inventory was introduced. An "agent set", a kind of terminal that used a destination plate to link it with AA's telephone network, was designed to ensure quick communication between the agent and the central system.

During the 1950s, the availability and inventory system spread throughout AA's sales offices and agents, although both systems suffered from many problems of inaccuracy and slowness. AA even tried to automate the third step – passenger names – but failed to do so. The two systems that had been implemented never produced the intended productivity increase as they only affected a subset of the total reservations process. Furthermore, computer technology was still at a rudimentary stage, and particularly online processing was quite new (except for the military project of Semi Automatic Ground Environment, SAGE). Accordingly, making radical changes to the reservations system would imply a totally integrated computer system, based on more sophisticated technology.

From the mid-1950s, AA planned for a transition to jet planes. Increased seating capacity and speed of planes added considerably to the importance of seat inventory control since jets traveled faster than the existing reservations system could transmit messages and adjust inventories. Consequently, AA management began preliminary studies for a total IT system with IBM. In 1959, AA and IBM agreed on a project to develop an IT reservations system that was to be called SABRE.

SABRE was intended to integrate seat availability, inventory, and passenger name information, and required rapid and direct access to large databases by way of disk files. Based on second-generation computer technology, SABRE

---

102 McKenney, *Waves of Change*, pp. 97-140.

was developed during the period from 1960 to 1964, and from 1964, replaced the old system. Response time was much faster than in its predecessor and most important, online booking information was immediately available throughout AA's network and offices. The benefits were quickly seen in improved customer service and a growing load factor and revenue.

Initially a technical solution to a transaction-processing crisis, SABRE's database gave AA accurate and timely information for strategic planning and analysis, never seen before, of such areas as crew scheduling, food services, and fuel. Furthermore, more and more functions of AA were computerized around SABRE. The basic structure of AA and its corporate strategy did not change, however. Primarily, SABRE caused a radical jump in productivity and service. Furthermore, SABRE set a new standard for efficiency of airlines operations that pressed the whole airline industry to follow suit.

The success of SABRE, and minor projects for Delta and Pan American, encouraged IBM to create a standardized airline reservations system, called PARS. Eastern Airlines chose to expand IBM's PARS to meet its own needs rather than build a system from scratch. In 1968, with this PARS II, Eastern Airlines set a new technological standard for large-scale reservations systems, eroding the dominance of AA's SABRE. Trans World Airlines and United Airlines failed to develop an even more sophisticated reservations system from scratch in 1969-70, underestimating the complexity of their requirements and overestimating the capability of the available technology. In 1971, they both bought Eastern's software PARS II, implementing it in 1971.

Since its start in 1964, SABRE had struggled with problems of peak capacity, adding IBM 360s and more disk files to increase transaction capacity. When this did not suffice, AA turned to the Eastern Airlines system and during the period from 1970 to 1972, the SABRE software was gradually converted to PARS II. The management of AA found that plans for an integrated management system based on SABRE exceeded the technology and organization of the day. By 1972, nine out the ten U. S. trunk airlines had adopted the PARS II standard. PARS II had more service functionality then SABRE, including computerized ticketing and hotel and rental car reservations.

The 1970s saw a third transformation of airline reservations systems. In 1976, the two leading reservations systems, SABRE of AA and APOLLO of United Airlines (UA), made their systems available to travel agents and commercial accounts. AA and UA started to put their newly installed terminals into agents' offices, increasing sales significantly. Automating connections between agents and airlines was such a success that AA intensified its efforts, recognizing the importance of gaining a loyal distribution channel.

Within a few years of the late 1970s, SABRE was transformed from a passenger service system to a sales distribution system, receiving messages from thousands of travel agents throughout the country. Spreading rapidly into most agencies, the other airlines were compelled to enter into co-host agreements with APOLLO and SABRE. In 1983, SABRE accounted for 43% of the revenues booked through the systems by travel agents and APOLLO for 27%.

Deregulation of the American airlines in 1978 reinforced the trend to transfer the reservations function from the airlines' own offices to travel agencies. Price competition caused the carriers to multiply the variety of fares and frequency with which they were adjusted, and as passenger inquiries changed from simple seat availability to comparative price shopping, interaction between travel agents and the carriers' schedules and fares became indispensable.

In this competitive environment only the reservations systems of the largest carries could participate. APOLLO, and more particularly SABRE, had created an industry wide distribution system covering all of the USA. SABRE became a "cash cow" for AA putting the airline in front of the screen of travel agencies and receiving revenue from every booking made by airlines subscribing to SABRE.

British Airways

British Airways was not formed until BEA (British European Airways) and BOAC (British Overseas Airways Corporation) merged into one airline in 1972.[103] Until then, BEA and BOAC were two independent companies.

During the 1940s and 1950s, punched card accounting machines dominated the office technology of BEA and BOAC (as was true for any large organization of the time) and early computing was much influenced by punched card thinking. The first computer applications of the late 1950s (BOAC) and the early 1960s (BEA) did passenger revenue accounting, payroll, load factor statistics, inventory control of technical spares, and similar jobs, and were developed on British made computers and IBM 650. There were many technical problems with these first generation computers with vacuum tubes.

The second-generation computers of the early 1960s, such as the IBM 1400 and the British ICL 1904E, had much improved capacity and speed. All these systems were batch oriented and did not break radically with the punched card technology. Furthermore, BEA and BOAC relied on their own telegraph and telephone network in cooperation with the interline company SITA (Société International de Télécommunications Aeronautique). From the early 1960s, a computer center was based in BEA and BOAC.

---

103 Harris, *BABS, BEACON, and BOADICEA*, pp. 7-284.

What really changed the line of computing was the coming of an online reservations system, just like in the USA. Although BEA and BOAC had introduced jet planes and passenger traffic had increased enormously since 1960, computerized reservations systems came late. Huge and growing numbers of clerks handled the combined manual and punched card systems of the two airlines. Until the mid-1960s, computing did not surpass the field of finance and traffic statistics, apart from experiments within operations research.

Instead of developing a reservations system from scratch, BEA, and later BOAC, looked to the systems already introduced in the USA. In 1962, an invitation to tender was sent to a few potential suppliers, primarily IBM and Univac. IBM was the leading manufacturer of online airlines system, but Univac turned out to be more appropriate for the needs of BEA than IBM.

The first BEA reservations system, the British European Airways Computing Network (BEACON), was developed between 1965 and 1967. The code of Eastern Airlines' system was adjusted to the needs of BEA, based on Univac 494 machines and electromechanical rather than computer terminals. At the same time, automatic processing of reservations telegraph messages was introduced. Just like its American models, BEACON covered the three primary processes of reservation: seat availability, inventory control, and passenger name recording.

During the late 1960s and early 1970s, a study group developed the concept for computerization of all major functions of BEA.

BOAC had less immediate passenger volume pressure then BEA, so BOAC did not come up with a company-wide computer strategy, including plans for a full reservations system, until 1965. Tenders were invited and in 1965, BOAC and IBM agreed on a project based on the IBM 360 and its standard system PARS. Transfer to the new system, called BOADICEA, which stood for British Overseas Airways Digital Information Computers for Electronic Automation, took place in 1968. To run the reservations systems, BOAC formed a central computer and telecommunications organization, as did BEA shortly afterwards

Unlike BEACON, and also unlike SASCO, the SAS Computer System, BOADICEA was based on computer terminals. Just like SASCO, it had an online computer as well as a fall back computer, including a standby computer for pre-processing the real-time system. BOADICEA did the three main processes of reservations, ticketing, and electronic messaging between reservations offices and airports. It included a number of additional facilities, such as special meals; group bookings, seat protection for "very important persons"; bookings for hotels, tours, and cars; provision of flight and station information; departure processing links; handling schedule changes and passenger reallocations; and dynamic application of overbooking profiles. BOADICEA had a more modular design than BEACON and could, therefore, be easily expanded. It placed more emphasis on the integration of communications across a worldwide network.

BOADICEA revolutionized computerization of BOAC, even more than BEACON did BEA, and continued to be the basis of its reservation system until the 1990s.

Passenger reservations systems were the vital first step in a process to automate key business activities. During the late 1960s and the early 1970s, several online systems added to the reservations systems of both airlines, including check-in and load control, operations control, timetables, crew scheduling, some maintenance functions, finance, a joint airlines' and freight agents' system of customs entry, interline revenue accounting, tariff control and distribution. Long-term management planning of aircraft fleet, forecast of passenger traffic, marketing strategy, timetables, crew scheduling, and revenue accounting drew on a separate group that used computers for operation research. The value of these online systems increased as communications networks were extended by SITA and BOAC.

The new online airline systems developed within the IT departments of BEA and BOAC created a potential for sales to other airlines. That was quickly recognized by BOAC, which sold such systems as IPARS (to Qantas, KLM, etc.), a departure control package (to KLM, Swissair, South African Airways, etc.), and one for tariff control and distribution (to 23 airlines). By 1972, BOAC was operating what was probably one of the largest and most effective software houses in Europe. This continued under BA for the next two decades.

During the first half of the 1970s, BEA and BOAC were being merged into British Airways. A special management group was formed to handle the integration of the two sets of information systems into one. The largest project was to convert the reservations systems of BEACON and BOADICEA into one, called BABS, the British Airways Booking System. It went on from 1972 to 1976, including new facilities, such as the extension of fare classes from three to eighteen, and the capability for regular customers to book a sequence of flights for the same day of the week over an extended period of several months. When converting all other systems, facilities were added and automated in online systems of check-in/load control, revenue accounting, crew, maintenance, accounting, and salaries, including increased integration and networking. In each case, investments in hardware, software and expertise were substantial, and no compromise solutions appeared feasible, due to the radically different nature of the hardware architectures of IBM and Univac for reservations, and of British ICL for finance.

Within the two IT departments of BEA and BOAC, fundamental differences of computer philosophy had emerged. BEA used several manufacturers for competitive reasons, whereas BOAC thought using one supplier would achieve greater rationalization. These differences in approach stemmed from differences in the cultures of the two airlines. The overall problem of creating a merged computer organization and technology was not an easy task, and it was clearly accentuated by differences in culture. Furthermore, skilled staff was in short supply, and pressure was growing for online development of applications and communications.

During the latter part of the 1970s, the new computer department began to make progress, in spite of all the technical and cultural problems of the merger. A common worldwide data communications system, including the concepts of computer-to-computer communication and networking, was well established. This paved the way for the growth of online systems in applications.

Airline traffic was increasing steadily, particularly in the leisure field. Since the mid-1970s, BA had introduced several systems based on IBM Information Management System (IMS). The first database system developed by BA, which included a number of functions such as component control and stock control, was used in technical maintenance. Other departments were quick to see the advantages of online access to records and databases, including personnel and finance, which had previously only been available through batch-processed reports. The decision to place the General Ledger System (Finance) on IBM/IMS eventually signaled the end of BA's use of ICL based systems.

The philosophy was still one of large centralized installations supporting networks of "dumb" terminals, and for many applications, large volume batch processing.

Minicomputers had already appeared during the 1960s, but only spread from the late 1970s. Minis were introduced for data preparation of the increasing volumes of revenue and accounting data, replacing the punched cards and consequently, many of the women employed as punch operators. The data entry process was improved by data recorders that captured keystrokes directly to magnetic tapes instead of physically to punched cards. Electronic keying, by way of keyboard and display terminal, dominated data entry during the 1970s and into the 1980s. In remote offices, minicomputer applications were introduced from the late 1970s for processing airway bills and tickets, including data capture, pricing, and interline prorating based on the IATA system. Still, terminals as well as minicomputers were based on large central computer applications.

While the first half of the 1970s tackled the difficulties of the merger, the latter half of the decade achieved a great deal in setting up the technology platform for the new airline. Telecommunications created a truly worldwide network at a high level of performance, and mainframe computers had been rationalized, based on IBM operating system technology.

With the volume of traffic now being routinely handled by operational staff, and its computers used for tactical planning and control during the 1970s, BA developed one of the largest computing operations in Western Europe.

SAS Business

Origins 1946-1951

Between the two world wars, the Danish Airline (DDL), the Norwegian airline (DNL), and the Swedish airline (ABA), pioneered scheduled air transport to a number of European and Scandinavian cities.[104] Coordinated flights between Scandinavia and New York started in 1946 under the name "Scandinavian Airlines Systems" (SAS). The same year, SAS inaugurated a second route to South America, adding the Far East and Africa to its intercontinental routes in the early 1950s.

Whereas SAS profited from its intercontinental flights, the three national airlines made consistent losses on their European destinations. The time had come for SAS to include all international traffic. European SAS was formed in 1948. It was not a success and in 1951, SAS was restructured into a consortium, which handled all the operations of the three airlines, including domestic services. Ownership was equally divided between state and private capital. For a period of 25 years, the respective Scandinavian governments granted the concessions permitting scheduled airline services within the framework of the SAS Consortium. Assets and liabilities, expenses and revenues, losses and profits were to be shared between the three partners in a ratio of 2/7 each for Denmark and Norway and 3/7 for Sweden. The three boards of directors merged into one board, and a new management was appointed.

During its first year of operation, the SAS Consortium had 6,500 employees and flew 1/2 million passengers to 67 destinations in 56 aircraft.[105]

---

104 SAS, *Annual Reports*, 1946 to 1951. Buraas, *The Making of SAS*, passim. Buraas (1979), *The SAS Saga: A History of Scandinavian Airlines System* (Oslo: Gyldendal), passim. SAS, *The First 50 Years*, pp. 1-33.
105 SAS, *Annual Report*, 1950/1951.

SAS Statistics [106]

	1950	1960	1970	1980
SAS Group				
Revenue/bill. SEK	-	-	2.0	9.3
Personnel/000	-	-	14.6	24.1
SAS Airline				
Revenue/bill. SEK	0.2	0.7	1.5	7.3
% Traffic of Group	94	90	74	68
% Passenger of Traffic	85	85	78	81
% Cargo of Traffic	10	10	19	16
Passengers/mill.	0.5	1.8	5.1	8.4
Personnel/000	6.6	14.6	13.0	16.8
% Traffic and Sales	20	20	20	19
% Crew	13	14	18	20
% Maintenance	30	30	26	24
% Others	37	36	37	36

Sources: SAS, *Annual Reports.* IATA, *World Air Transport Statistics.* Buraas, *Fly over fly: Historien om SAS.*

---

106 Figures for SAS Airline/the Consortium include SAS subsidiaries until 1970. Revenue and personnel for 1970 are estimates. Only in 1976/77, was the SAS Group formally separated from the SAS Airline/Consortium. The annual reports cover 1950/51, 1959/60, 1969/70, and 1979/80.

   In addition to traffic, revenues include: technical maintenance, station services and ticket sales for other airlines, sales on board and in airports, income from other customers of SAS' subsidiaries, and sales of airplanes.

   Separated figures of personnel for Traffic and Sales, etc. are based on IATA, *World Air Transport Statistics for 1970 and 1980*, while the figures for 1950 and 1960 are estimates based on annual reports and Buraas, *Fly over fly. Historien om SAS* (A History of SAS), passim. "Traffic and sales" cover airport handling, reservation, sales, and marketing. It is assumed that 'Others' includes back office figures.

Regulated Air Transport

Every airline, including SAS, operated within a regulated world of air transportation. The Scandinavian governmental concessions of 1951 formed the basis upon which SAS was permitted to operate scheduled airline services within the framework of the SAS Consortium, and they did so for decades.[107]

The company was subject to the regulations of Danish, Norwegian, and Swedish commercial air transport, and to international agreements concluded by the three governments. Operations were to be performed by personnel, equipment, and a traffic organization approved by the respective authorities and in accordance with approved technical and operational regulations. The company was to sustain a maintenance organization consisting of workshops. Operational reports, statistical information, traffic programs, timetables and fares, regulations for services and for the carriage of passengers and cargo, the acquisition of new types of aircraft and engines should all be submitted to the authorities for approval. The company was obligated to a reasonable extent to maintain traffic on the routes it had been granted permission to serve, and was obligated to operate scheduled services in Scandinavia. Attached to the respective concessions were route lists with specifications of the routes, including intermediate stops the company had permission to serve in scheduled operation on domestic, inter-Scandinavian, and international flights.

International scheduled air transport was based on a system of regulation, too. According to the Chicago Convention in 1944 and the Bermuda Conference in 1946, each nation had sovereignty of its air space, and all air traffic in and out of the country was reserved for the national carrier in cooperation with the country of destination, the so-called "Third and Fourth Freedom". Traffic rights for the airlines of third party countries were subject to negotiation, the so-called "Fifth Freedom".

Technical and security matters were agreed upon or recommended within the framework of the International Civil Aviation Organization of the United Nations (ICAO). ICAO worked, in cooperation with the International Air Transport Association (IATA), on a wide field of technical matters. It dealt with the standardization of navigational aids, questions on air traffic control, ground communications, charts, and the compilation of traffic and accident statistics. It also defined standards and issued recommendations adopted by aviation authorities all over the world.

---

107 SAS, *Annual Report*, 1950/51. Buraas, *The Making of SAS*, passim. SAS, *Yearbooks*, from 1967 to 1980, cover this subject through the years.

IATA was dedicated to the coordination of the world's scheduled air services. Except for the Soviet Union and China, all leading airlines of the world
were members of IATA. Since the Second World War, IATA has built and practiced a globally regulated scheduled air service. The objectives of IATA were
numerous. It created uniform fares and rates, conditions of carriage, documentation, and so on, so that passengers and cargo could fly about anywhere
in the world on tickets or airway bills issued by just one IATA airline. Interline
revenue was exchanged centrally in the IATA clearing house in Geneva. IATA
airlines followed a comprehensive manual with rules and regulations, and
IATA compiled a worldwide table of fares.

Airlines also cooperated in technical and operational matters through
IATA, developing standards and practices and exchanging experience and information on matters of maintenance, operations, flight safety, pilot training,
aircraft noise, computer development, and so forth. Many committees and
conferences were responsible for the practical uniformity that IATA strove to
achieve in the scheduled airline industry. International passenger fares and
cargo rates were set and coordinated at regular general traffic conferences.
More than anything else, the system of a worldwide agreement on fares and
rates made IATA the symbol of a regulated airline industry.

While the concessions ensured SAS a monopoly of scheduled air traffic for
Scandinavia, the international regulations excluded most international price
and route competition. On the other hand, regulations created a worldwide
airline industry. Although this system of concessions and international uniformity worked until about 1980, and in many ways until the 1990s, in fact
it began being gradually broken down from the 1970s.

The 1950s Planes and Routes

When the Consortium started in 1951, SAS had 59 propeller planes, mostly
DC-3s and DC-4s (rebuilt gunfighters of the Second World War). During the
early fifties, a new generation of aircraft took over, the DC-6 and DC-7 for
European and intercontinental routes, respectively. The Metropolitan propeller replaced DC-3 and DC-4 on domestic routes from the mid-fifties. Of the
two leading airplane manufactures of the world, McDonnell-Douglas was for
decades the favorite supplier of SAS. Only in the nineties, did Boeing take over
that position.[108]

---

108 SAS, *Annual Reports*, 1951 to 1960. Buraas, *The SAS Saga*, passim. SAS, *The First 50
Years*, pp 26-65.

All leading airlines invested in new technology to improve capacity, speed, and comfort, and SAS had to follow suit. This was the beginning of a continuous technological race. The airlines competed by presenting the most sophisticated airline technology to the public. This race was speeded up by the arrival of jet technology in the late fifties. SAS placed the French Caravelle in European scheduled service in 1959 and the DC-8 in intercontinental traffic in 1960. The Caravelle jetliner in Europe and the new Metropolitan propeller on domestic routes indicated its intentions to develop the European and particularly the domestic markets of Scandinavia.

The outline of the SAS route network was built during the first half of the 1950s. SAS extended its traffic program to include almost all destinations of interest for the Scandinavians throughout the world. SAS benefited also from its rapid expansion and the slow recovery of many war-torn countries that were unable to start their own national airline. By the mid-fifties, SAS served about 80 cities in about 40 countries (compared with the approximately 100 cities in about 50 countries by the late 1990s). The age of pioneering had come to an end.[109]

During the second half of the 1950s, international air transport took on new dimensions of expansion. European national carriers were established and SAS no longer enjoyed generous traffic rights, even having difficulties in keeping those already given. Traffic rights were restricted to mutual agreements between two countries. Only in third world countries could traffic rights still be achieved by way of cooperative agreements, such as the long-standing cooperation between SAS and Thai International Airways.

Since the mid-1950s, SAS had expanded mainly by way of improved aircraft technology and as a consequence of international economic growth, allowing a growing number of passengers and amount of cargo to be transported by air.

The USA formed the economic center of the post-war world, and the American domestic air service exceeded that of Europe by miles. As a result, the dynamics of SAS was linked to cross-Atlantic air transport in the 1950s. Scheduled air transport in Scandinavia and especially domestic flights were rather undeveloped until the late 1950s. In Norway SAS and Braathens shared the market with Braathens serving the densely populated southern Norway whereas SAS connected north and south. SAS provided scheduled air transport between the main Swedish cities and owned half the shares of the domestic

---

109 *Betänkande avgivet av skandinavisk kommitté för Reorganisation af SAS*, 1961 (Stockholm), pp. 32-36.

airline Linjeflyg. A similar structure was established in Denmark. SAS flew the trunk routes and was the leading shareholder of a newly formed company, Danair, which took care of the other routes. Finally, the Greenland airline, Grønlandsfly, was formed in 1960, with SAS as a co-owner.

During the 1950s, SAS quadrupled its traffic and revenue. Traffic increased from almost half a million to almost two million passengers, and cargo grew at the same speed. Revenue rose from less than 0.2 million to more than 0.7 million SEK (Swedish 'kroner'). Passenger traffic covered 80% of SAS' traffic revenue.[110]

1950s The Organization

Increasing investments in new aircraft technology and growing mass transport resulted in a relative decline in air transport prices (i.e., air transport prices rose at a much slower pace than prices in general). Costs, such as wages and duties, kept on rising, however. Accordingly, SAS profited less and less from every passenger and piece of cargo. To stay profitable, SAS was forced to reduce costs to compensate for declining prices. One way to do that was to keep on investing in front-line aircraft technology and improve capacity continuously. A second road to follow was to raise the load factor by massive marketing and other efforts to encourage more people to fly. A third method was to organize the working process in a more productive way. SAS took all three roads, beginning with a focus on front-line airplane technology.

In the late 1940s, SAS had already created the framework of a multi-functional organization managed by several layers of management and operated by many specialized groups of personnel.[111] This was a classical bureaucracy of the kind that had dominated large corporations of industrial society for decades. The merged SAS of 1951 continued this line of organization.[112] The structure of multi functional units and of a specialized working force formed the basics of the SAS organization. A pyramid of layers from top management to workers regulated authority and flow of information. A highly specialized and stratified bureaucracy made the machine of the SAS organization work from its very beginning. This formed the basic foundation of a rational organization.

---

110 See in the text, SAS Statistics.
111 SAS, Annual Reports, 1951 to 1960. Betänkande avgivet av skandinavisk kommitté för Reorganisation af SAS, pp. 7-31. Buraas, The SAS Saga, passim. SAS, The First 50 Years, pp 26-65. By way of interviews, Berthelsen, Et liv i luften, covers some developments of SAS functions.
112 SAS, Dagens SAS, 28/4 1951.

Planes and routes made up the basics of SAS traffic and organization. Long-term planning, negotiations, and investments concerning planes and routes were strategic head office activities from the beginnings of SAS, involving both technical and commercial competence. Forecasts of economic growth, information about new aircraft technology, statistical travel patterns of Scandinavians, and existing and potential routes formed the strategic platform for SAS management. The timetable, developed at head office, structured the activities throughout the organization. It was the functional result of strategic traffic planning, and appeared every six months.

Long-term planning and the creation of the timetable made up two basic aspects of management on the strategic and tactical level, respectively. They were parts of the organizational tools of running the organization effectively. Such "pre-processing" structures were created to manage rationally the other activities of the company, too.

Reservations and sales, including marketing, formed the lifeline of SAS' relations with customers. During the 1950s, it became ever more difficult to handle the growing number of transactions and passengers by way of manual and mechanical systems. The coming of mass-transport jet planes threatened to turn this bottleneck into a crisis of transactions and lost revenue. From the late 1950s onwards, computer systems were developed to solve this core problem of SAS. In addition, the communication system of SAS was a vital part of reservations from the late 1940s.

Marketing worked in a rather traditional way. Flying was still some kind of an adventure and pretty costly. Until the late 1950s, Europe recovered slowly from the war setbacks, and only the American economy, developing at a much higher level of activity, was able to attract many businessmen and some officials. Nevertheless, the pleasure of air-travel was generally reserved for the wealthy.

To implement the traffic of the timetable, preplanning of crew structures had also to be developed. Crew planning had four time dimensions. One was long-term planning or master planning, which combined the timetable, rules of security, and collective agreements into a rational plan weeks before departure. The second was concerned with medium-term planning (i.e., scheduling), which provided the plans with names. Three was short-term planning that dealt with individual changes caused by illness, and so on. The fourth involved plans enforced by the Operational Control Center that took over placement, so-called "disposal", of crew in action. The Operation Control Center in Copenhagen handled ongoing and future traffic although crew planning was also a head office function in Stockholm.

Maintenance of airlines expanded during the 1950s and created problems of efficiency. It was not until the following decade, however, that a modern technical organization, based on a new philosophy, was developed to suit the growing traffic. Technical maintenance was organized nationally in different workshops in the three countries. In the late 1950s, SAS agreed on technical cooperation with Swissair to cut costs in maintaining the new jet planes.

Accounting, using a traditional system of bookkeeping, was dealt with at all three national offices and aggregated at head office. Traffic statistics were kept in the same way. Results, which included monthly reports, came out once a year.

These and other functions, such as ground activities at airports and office work, were from the very start based on collective agreements between SAS management and national unions in each of the three countries. The collective agreements laid out the organizational outline of the working process of the airline, covering such areas as working hours, wages, the kind of work done by each specialized group, rules of insurance, and pensions. In this way, organized labor put many restrictions on management, while employees enjoyed relative security in working conditions.

Finally, SAS was marked by the fact that it was a consortium covering three countries. In the 1950s, most operational and tactical activities were managed at national level by three geographical organizations, such as sales, accounting, and maintenance. Similar geographical units were established for the rest of the world. Consequently, head office and strategic management was rather weak, and the SAS of the 1950s, to a high degree, was built around the three national offices. Head office took care of overall traffic planning and investments and some centralized rules of procedure, such as reservations, tickets, and check-in and load control. In most other cases, head office just laid out guidelines according to national and international rules of agreements, rather than acting strategically as a true top management.[113]

Adapting to the regular introduction of new aircraft technology, increased productivity of the organization was primarily obtained by reducing the growth of personnel compared with the increase in traffic and revenue. This relative reduction was mainly achieved by creating pre-processing and pre-planning structures within the organization. While the number of employees more than doubled, from 6,600 to 14,600, revenue and traffic quadrupled during the 1950s. As a result, labor productivity grew. Until the arrival of the computer in the late 1950s, mechanical and automatic tools of technology in information processing played a minor role, apart from some punched card machines.

---

113 *Betänkande avgivet av skandinavisk kommitté för Reorganisation af SAS*, pp. 7-20.

The growing traffic and personnel increased pressure on the SAS organization, however. The introduction of jet planes in the late-1950s made it clear that SAS had to reform its organization to be able to handle the much-increased activities and to ensure a continuous reduction of costs. As a result, every function and department was transformed during the late 1950s and early 1960s.[114] Furthermore, the new information processing technology of computers was introduced to overcome the transaction crisis caused by expanding traffic, particularly in reservations.

The 1960s Planes and Routes

SAS, and all other leading airlines, invested heavily in jetliners around 1960 and capacity increased so much and so fast that traffic lagged behind. For instance, the supply of seats on the North Atlantic routes rose by 47% during the first half of 1961 whereas traffic only grew by 12%. As a result, all international air transport was struck by a general crisis in the early 1960s.[115]

Only in 1963, did SAS show a profit again. The gap between production and traffic was narrowed and SAS reached its usual load factor. The network of routes changed little and growth was mainly caused by larger and faster planes and by increased frequency of flights. SAS flew the DC-8 on intercontinental routes, the Caravelle on European routes, and the Metropolitan propeller on domestic routes.

The break through in jet planes occurred during the first half of the 1960s. Aircraft technology changed so swiftly, however, that SAS and all other major airlines started ordering the next generation of jet planes in the mid-1960s. From the late 1960s onwards, the DC-8-62/63 served intercontinental routes, while the DC-9-41 gradually substituted for the Caravelle in Europe, and the DC-9-21 introduced jet flight on domestic routes. The capacity of the second generation of jet planes surpassed that of the first generation, including cargo, and its technology was more sophisticated (for example, integrated circuits replaced mechanical equipment). SAS had to follow the other airlines and be able to present the best technology to Scandinavian passengers, especially on the North Atlantic routes where competition was fierce. SAS therefore invested more than ever.[116]

---

114 *Betänkande avgivet av skandinavisk kommitté för Reorganisation af SAS*, pp. 23-31.
115 SAS, *Annual Report*, 1961/62.
116 SAS, *Annual Reports*, 1960 to 1970. Burras, *The SAS Saga*, passim.

During the 1960s, production and traffic increased more than in any other decade – on average 20% annually. Revenue and the number of passengers trebled reaching 2 billion SKR and 5 million passengers in 1969/70.[117]

The traffic pattern changed somewhat during the 1960s. Competition intensified on the North Atlantic routes, the center of SAS traffic, making it still harder to achieve a profitable business. Domestic flights improved, on the other hand, as did the European routes, although charter flights put a heavy pressure on the Mediterranean routes.

Cargo presented the most remarkable growth of all fields of air service, however. Air Cargo was able to take advantage of the growing international trade in industrial products. A market was developed for perishable goods, important spare parts, and light industrial products that had to reach the market quickly. Compared with global sea and land transport, air cargo had only a small share of the market, although air cargo transported relatively valuable products. To SAS and other major airlines increasing air cargo was of growing importance, however. These were the glory days of cargo.

Gradually, SAS traffic moved from passengers to cargo. In the mid-1960s, SAS introduced freight planes and started a huge program to expand and modernize Scandinavian airport terminals, including ground equipment, and freight capacity was considerably increased by the second-generation jetliners. Three-quarters of all SAS cargo was carried on intercontinental routes, dominated by the North Atlantic area, but SAS was trying to expand European cargo traffic, too. Cargo showed such a growth rate that it was predicted that it would equal the importance of passenger traffic by the middle of the 1970s.

The comparative predominance of intercontinental routes (primarily on the North Atlantic), compared with European, Scandinavian, and domestic routes did not change during the 1960s. Only the relative growth of cargo made a difference.

The prime goal of SAS was to fly as many passengers and as much freight as possible. However, as the 1960s proceeded, declining prices on the one hand and increasing costs on the other, reduced profits and forced SAS to strive still harder to increase productivity and cut costs

---

117 See, *SAS Statistics*, in the text.

The 1960s The Organization

During the crisis of 1961-62, SAS was reorganized to meet the challenge of the jet age.[118] A thorough program of rationalization was carried out, cutting down personnel from 14,600 in 1960 to 12,700 in 1965, while traffic kept on growing rapidly. Expanding subsidiaries and affiliated companies of the SAS Group caused the number of employees to rise to 14,600 again in 1970.[119]

To some degree, management came up with a new organization structure.[120] SAS was to be more business minded, paying less attention to its three-nation foundation. Catering became a subsidiary company. The board was much reduced in number, and the board and the leading executive manager, the president, were given authority and responsibility corresponding to those of a joint-stock company.

On the one hand, head office and the regional offices were given more powerful tools of management, while on the other hand, economic responsibility was more decentralized. The basic regional structure did not alter, however. SAS was made into a company based on divisions, which were partly functional and partly regional. The new management consisted of the president, and the vice presidents of the departments of Technical and Operations, Marketing, Finance, Administration (a separate department since the late sixties), and the three Scandinavian regions (including North America until 1970). This structure existed until 1980.

Marketing developed more systematic and aggressive methods to retain the profitable load factor of an expanding production. Marketing targeted businessmen, tourists, and retired people as separate groups or segments, aiming, in particular, at increasing traffic during the dull winter months. "Wonderful Copenhagen" was the famous slogan used to attract American tourists. Modern Scandinavian design was used to improve and modernize sales offices around the world. The electronic reservation system of 1965, including check-in and load control, was of particular importance, and so was an improved communication system. Computerized systems changed the core of the SAS organization and paved the way for an imminent future of airline operations based on computers. Preparing for a comprehensive introduction of computer systems, vital parts of SAS' information flow were thoroughly analyzed, thus

---

118 *SAS Nytt*, no. 4, 15, 16, 18, 1962
119 SAS, *Annual Reports*, 1960 to 1970. SAS, *Yearbooks*, 1967 to 1970. Burras, *The SAS Saga*, passim. Berthelsen, *Et liv i luften*, passim. SAS, *The First 50 Years*, pp. 26-65. See also in the text, *SAS Statistics*.
120 *Betänkande avgivet av skandinavisk kommitté för Reorganisation af SAS*, pp. 23-43.

creating a deeper understanding of the organization and potential for improvement. As a result, computer systems contributed to improved revenue
and particularly, to a rise in productivity by cutting down on the need for personnel. Finally, other leading airlines had or were introducing computerized
reservation systems and forced SAS to do the same thing.

The tremendous aircraft technological development challenged the organization and know-how of the Technical and Operations Department. Technical
maintenance prepared for the changing jet technology through re-education
and reorganization. The second generation of jet planes introduced a gradual
change from mechanical to digital technology, postponing the final breakthrough until to the 1980s and 1990s, however. More important in the 1960s
and 1970s was the changing character of maintenance. Thus far, maintenance
had been based on the idea of making repairs whenever a technical fault
arose. To increase security and productivity, maintenance work was reorganized according to principles of prevention. Prevention demanded much
planning and processing of the flow of information to make sure that the
planes were taken down for maintenance before faults actually happened. Of
course, unforeseen problems were still to be taken care of. Furthermore, from
the late 1960s the labor process in workshops was specialized according to the
types of aircraft, rather than in working fields. The technical cooperation with
Swissair of the late 1950s was extended to include KLM for maintenance of
the new wide-body airplane, the B-747.

The Administrative Department dealt primarily with accounting, personnel, property administration, and Data Services. The accounting function developed a new common accounting plan for SAS' first computer-based accounting system, ACS of 1967. The Administrative Department only took care
of salaries and similar common issues, and started preparing for the first computer system. Training and collective bargaining were preserves of the line organizations and regions. During the 1960s, the SAS working organization
came to be based on more than 30 collective agreements covering all non-
management groups of SAS. Accordingly, the structure of collective bargaining and agreements deepened its influence on SAS.

The Technical and Operations Department was an essential part of the
highly structured way of organizing SAS. This department covered the most
import employee groups, including pilots, cabin attendants, mechanics, and
engineers. Because the main strategy of SAS stressed the importance of new
aircraft technology and increasing productivity of employees, the Technical
and Operations Department played a central role in developing the SAS organization. This department clearly showed the bureaucratic and technological thinking that dominated and made the SAS organization a machine that
worked like an airplane.

International regulations imposed by IATA strengthened, too. The 1960s were truly the high tide of a regulated airlines industry. This contributed to the machine-like structure and operations of the SAS organization.

Generally, SAS kept the multi-unit, bureaucratic structure of the 1950s. Strategic management was strengthened, however, and the management of functions deepened to increase productivity in a rapidly expanding organization, where unit costs grew and prices fell. Rational mass-production had clearly become the strategy for SAS as it was for all other leading airlines of the time.

The 1970s Planes and Routes

SAS continued to expand during the early years of the 1970s. From 1970 to 1975 the number of passengers rose from 5 to 7 million, reaching 8 1/2 million in 1980. Revenue increased from 2 to 4 billion SEK from 1970 to 1975 and to 9 billion in 1980. During the early years of the 1970s, cargo reached its peak. The rapid expansion of the 1960s stopped, and cargo never fulfilled the promise of equalizing its importance in relation to passenger traffic. While the network of routes remained largely unchanged, an increase in the frequency and number of flights made SAS a true "mass production" company. As the second generation of jets took over the SAS traffic – the DC-9-41 in Europe and the DC-9-21 on domestic routes – SAS sold its first generation of jet planes and its last propellers.[121] On intercontinental routes, the so-called wide-body planes, B-747 and DC-10, replaced the DC-8, during the 1970s. The new planes increased capacity significantly, including cargo.

Profits were low, however. The fierce competition on the main North Atlantic routes made passenger traffic almost unprofitable. Only cargo traffic had reasonable results on the Atlantic. Europe and Scandinavia did better, but low prices and high costs made SAS profitable only by way of selling old planes. The world economic crisis of 1973/74 put even greater pressure on SAS, although less than most other airlines, because SAS had already finished most of its large investment program.

In spite of the crisis, SAS, like other airlines, continued its policy of expansion during the second half of the 1970s. The IATA forecasts were still optimistic. Accordingly, SAS hastened the delivery of new wide-body planes. The company even increased its orders from two to five, and the number of cargo routes kept on growing too. Evidently, SAS management decided to meet the

---

121 SAS, *Annual Reports*, 1970 to 1980. Buraas, *The SAS Saga*, passim. Berthelsen, *Et liv i luften*, passim. SAS, *The First 50 Years*, pp. 26-65.

fierce price competition with new aircraft technology aimed at an even greater "mass production".[122] SAS invested heavily in these expensive wide-body planes. In 1975 SAS had one B-747 and one DC-10. Five years later the wide-body fleet had grown to six B-747s, including two combi-planes, five DC-10s, and four Airbuses, besides eight older DC-8s.

The purchase of wide-body planes was extremely costly, but logically it continued a strategy that had driven SAS since the 1950s. In the late 1970s, it was just exercised in its widest sense. SAS strove to reduce unit costs to meet the problems of declining transport prices and rapidly rising costs of wages, duties, and so on.

In spite of all its efforts, SAS could not overcome its main problem: a lack of profitability. Only by selling old planes was SAS able to produce a total profit. In the late 1970s, one fourth of its revenue derived from selling planes. As in the previous decade, 80% of all traffic revenue came from passenger traffic whereas cargo still counted for 15%, only. The forecast that cargo would grow to the same level of importance as passenger traffic never materialized.

The 1970s The Organization

The overall introduction of the second generation of jet planes, the expanding production and traffic, and an even greater expansion of related fields of travel in a growing number of subsidiaries and affiliated companies put an increasing amount of pressure on the SAS organization.

SAS continued its organizational efforts of the 1960s, but even more systematically and determinedly. The primary object of planning was to have as many passengers and as much cargo as possible fly with SAS. Furthermore, SAS sought to meet increased competition from the charter traffic and the low profits of scheduled airline services by expanding its activities in a growing number of subsidiaries and affiliated companies relating to its core air transport service. Those included hotels, catering, charter flights, and forwarding. Accordingly, the SAS Group grew rapidly and called for more planning.

During the 1960s, SAS started to develop a comprehensive system of planning at head office that was fulfilled by the early 1970s, including 10-year plans for the next decade, company plans for three years ahead, and the budget for the next year. Ten-year plans had been part of traffic investment planning since the 1950s. From 1970, specific plans for SAS' computer and organizational development were added to the complex of management planning

---

122 This is clearly reflected in: Hagrup, *LUFTFARTEN og fremtiden*, pp. 128-130, and passim.

tools.[123] Around 1970, head office and strategic management was further strengthened, including centralized planning of maintenance.

SAS management tried to tighten its hold on an increasingly more complex organization. Only in the airline did these efforts seem to have some success. A matrix-like project organization was introduced to cover all main functions. It was closely tied to the computer organization and plans for computerizing all main functions within SAS to reduce costs of personnel and improve efficiency. Project organization was a new way of doing things across the traditional functional and hierarchical structures of SAS. Projects were ad hoc units and did not change the basic organization, but they introduced a first experience of doing things differently to the SAS bureaucracy.

Much of these organizational efforts of the 1970s were linked to a wide introduction of computer systems covering vital parts of all main functions of the airline. The reservations, check-in, and load control systems of the 1960s were being further developed during the 1970s to meet growing demands of capacity and service and a need to automate more functions within and around these basic systems of SAS. The accounting system was renewed, too. Since the early and mid-1970s, a number of additional large computer systems were implemented, covering traffic planning, cargo, revenue accounting, operations control, crew, maintenance, and salaries. All these systems were based on a thorough analysis of the information flow of separate functions and there interrelations.

In one respect it caused a deeper understanding of activities and the information basis of the SAS organization. On the other hand, productivity was improved within this framework. Furthermore, the pre-processing structure of planning was widened to extend the management grasp of the organization. These organizational efforts revealed the poor quality of the information basis of productivity measures and controls of SAS, however. As each system covered only one function, the introduction of computer systems bound SAS even more to the traditional structures of a multi-unit and bureaucratic organization.

SAS looked for other ways of reducing costs, too. Cooperating with other airlines was one of them. In the late 1960s, SAS, Swissair, and KLM established a shared technical maintenance system for the wide-body B-747. In vain, SAS tried to extend this cooperation to include computer systems for technical maintenance. Negotiations with American Airlines concerning a common booking system came to nothing, too. Each airline wanted to follow plans of its own. A potential "outsourcing" (although this expression still had to be invented) of Data Services as a subsidiary of its own was also considered, but

---

123 Unfortunately, these plans have only been preserved to a small degree.

abandoned because Data Services was not thought capable of dealing with the world outside the airline. Although these plans remained unfulfilled, they indicate the wide range of problems SAS tried to handle to improve its grasp of a still more complex and unprofitable organization.

In the late 1970s, SAS prepared a new strategy to overcome the overall problem of poor profitability. An economic crisis crossed these plans before they could be implemented, however. Shortly afterwards SAS was radically transformed to turn an unprofitable business into a profitable one.

The 1970s The SAS Group

While fighting to keep the airline profitable, the SAS Group of subsidiaries and affiliated companies kept on growing within a number of travel fields: hotels, restaurants, catering, charter, travel agencies, and so on.[124] This was a means of compensating for the poor earnings of the scheduled air service. With probably less than 1,000 employees in the early 1960s, the number of employees in businesses outside the airline increased to 2-3,000 in 1970, 4,000 in 1975 and 7,000 in 1980. During these years, the level of personnel at the airline stayed almost the same, about 15,000, until a gradual rise began from the mid-1970s.

Since the early 1960s, expanding charter traffic from Scandinavia had made SAS extend its business to include the low-price market of tourists and related services. New activities were organized by way of subsidiaries or affiliated companies, and during the 1970s, the number of such businesses surpassed 20. As a whole, this complex was called the SAS Group. Still, the airline remained its core business.

In 1961, SAS started the Scanair Consortium, a charter-company that flew tourists to sunny Southern Europe. SAS had to join the charter business to meet the growing competition. The charter traffic was not regulated to the same degree as scheduled air services, and from the early 1970s the Scandinavian governments and the large charter businesses pressed still harder to weaken the borderline between charter and scheduled flights. In the late 1970s, however, charter traffic was still restricted to flying closed groups.

Charter traffic was one line of expansion hotels were another. Scandinavia was short of hotels, so in 1960 SAS started building hotels for a growing number of tourists and passengers, especially from the USA. The hotel business reached a high level during the 1970s. Similar growth was seen in the cater-

---

124 SAS, *Annual Reports*, 1960 to 1980. SAS, *Yearbooks*, 1967 to 1980.

ing division, which ran an increasing number of restaurants and cafeterias, besides serving planes.

In general, SAS aimed at covering still more areas of the travel chain from the late 1960s. In addition to hotels and meals, during the 1960s, SAS moved into travel agencies such as Vingresor and Star Tours, and into Nyman & Schultz/Nordisk Rejsebureau, a specialized agency for businessmen. SAS became one of five large travel agencies in Scandinavia. Furthermore, SAS engaged in other travel activities such as car rental, insurance, and provision of conference facilities.

By the late 1970s, SAS was no longer just an airline business. It had turned into a company covering most of the travel activities related to air transport. The airline remained the core business, but the foundation was laid for the travel company of the late 1980s.

SAS IT

The 1950s Preparations

During the 1950s, growing production, traffic, and personnel made the volume and complexity of SAS information processing increase to such a degree that it caused serious information problems.[125]

Unlike many other businesses, an airline was faced with urgent demands of information processing during every second of the day. Making reservations, issuing tickets, handling passengers, cargo, airplanes, and crew in and out of airports throughout the day created an enormous pressure on information processing. By the end of the 1950s, there were bottlenecks of information and as a result, problems increased in handling traffic and servicing customers properly. Furthermore, jet planes were about to turn these bottlenecks into a true crisis of transactions and revenue.

Booking or reservations made up the SAS lifeline to customers. During the 1950s, SAS established 12 booking offices throughout the world, including London, Paris, Frankfurt, New York, and the Scandinavian capitals. To make this booking system work, SAS had built a communication system of its own by way of hired telephone lines and teleprinters. Communication was based on a telegram traffic that centered in Copenhagen and Copenhagen was also the center of booking.

Before computer systems were introduced, booking worked in the following way. Each of the Scandinavian capitals was given a certain quota of seats for every route. Being the center of SAS international traffic, most seats were allotted to Copenhagen. If the quota was spent, you could ask for additional seats at the Booking Center in Copenhagen. Every sales office had a table showing destinations on one axis and flight data on the other, and where the axes met you could see whether seats were available or not, red for booked and green for vacancies. The sales offices booked seats via telex, informing the Booking Center of destination, time, and the name of the passenger. When a flight was sold out, every sales office was informed by the Booking Center.

The quota system created much competition between the sales offices. Each office stuck to its quota causing many potential customers to be left be-

---

125 Interviews: *Torsten Bergner* and *Arne Hansen*. Berthelsen, *Et liv i luften*, pp. 85-93.

hind. As a consequence, SAS produced many dissatisfied customers and even worse, it lost important marginal revenue.

As traffic increased during the 1950s, these booking problems grew. The Booking Center in Copenhagen became a true bottleneck, although more than 120 people worked here at the late 1950s. Forty women forwarded 15,000 telegrams each day via 210 teleprinters, ticking 24 hours a day. Eighty percent of the telegrams concerned booking, whereas 15% dealt with matters of operation, such as traffic control, and 5% with administration.

The approaching jet age of the late 1950s promised even larger problems of information, as traffic was about to accelerate in numbers and speed. To stay profitable, SAS had to ensure that everybody wanting to fly with the airline was given a seat. The existing booking system had reached its limits and to cope with future demands a new kind of system would have to be developed.

In 1957, a working group was formed with representatives from the communications and booking departments, amongst them, Arne Hansen. They had to come up with a solution to the booking problems. As a result, the first plan was developed to computerize the booking system.

The 1960s Reservations, Check-in, and Load Control

1961 The First Computer System: SPAS, RAMAC, and ZEBRA

The first SAS computer plan aimed at automating vital parts of the reservation and check in/load control systems.[126] Step one was to automate halfway the incoming flow of telegrams to the Telegram Center in Copenhagen, by way of punched cards. Next, the first SAS computer, SPAS (Space Availability System), was built to automate the flow of telegrams from sales offices to the Booking Center in Copenhagen. Instead of the quota system, in a few seconds the salesman could be informed via SPAS whether seats were free or not on a certain flight. SPAS started in 1958.

A kind of terminal, so-called "agent sets", were built to enable the sales offices to communicate with the Booking Center in Copenhagen. The salesmen just pressed the "ASK" button to get in contact with SPAS. Within the next few years, the availability system spread to Scandinavia, Western Europe and the USA. Booking confirmation and the name of the passenger still had to be communicated by way of telegram, however.

---

126 SAS, *Data Management*, 15/11, 18/11, 20/11 1962, 7/1, 15/1, 28/2, 26/4 1963. SAS, "International Inquiry Answering Service", in *Data Processing*, July-September 1961. Interview: *Arne Hansen*.

A second computer, the IBM 305 Ramac, replaced the punched card system of the Booking Center in Copenhagen, forming the third step of the computer plan. The Ramac stored all bookings of all flights for the following 70 days. Punched cards were still used for input. Bookings and cancellations were fed into the computer continuously, being updated with the number of sold and free seats on any flight. Whenever the booking cushion was reached, a message was issued and immediately encoded into the SPAS so that the sales offices could be updated of the booking situation. A few hours before departure, the punched cards for the flight were removed in order to compile a complete passenger list. The Ramac began working in 1960.

The fourth step of automation concerned the check-in and load control functions in Copenhagen airport, followed later by Oslo and Stockholm. SAS chose to computerize check-in and load control, too, in order to avoid bottlenecks in airports and to improve passenger service at the other vital customer interface, reservations having been the first one. For that purpose, a third computer system was constructed, the Zebra. Just like the SPAS, it was bought from the German firm Standard Elektrik.

The Zebra computer contained the timetable of the traffic program and the rules of weight and balance of the planes. Agent sets, similar to those of the sales offices, accumulated current information about passengers and luggage. By way of telegrams from other departments, information on cargo, fuel, catering, crew, and flight was added to that of passengers to produce a load sheet for the captain. The Zebra started working in 1961, but it took two years before the old system was closed down. The three dedicated computers communicated by way of telegram messages.

The new booking/check-in/load control systems helped to reduce costs of personnel and increase productivity. Furthermore, they limited previous problems of over- and under-booking, improved customer service and consequently, produced more revenue for SAS.

The new computer systems did not lead to a new way of organizing the functions of booking, check-in and load control. The former was still part of the Marketing Department, and the latter of the Technical and Operation Department. However, capabilities were improved.

1965 The Second Computer System: RESCO

Long Range Data Processing Plan
When SAS applied for loans in the USA in 1959 to finance its transition from propellers to jet planes, the American lenders required an investigation of the SAS organization by the Standard Research Institute (SRI) – a leading consulting company. SRI did so well that SAS hired it to investigate the benefits of a

more general introduction of computer technology. In 1960, the SRI presented a "Long Range Data Processing Plan" concluding that SAS had much to gain from computer technology. SAS decided to acquire an IBM 7020 to run a number of computer systems. The line functions started hiring personnel to carry out the plan, but the following year the jet crisis made SAS cancel all these plans.[127]

The Long Range Plan became a guide for the future computer development of SAS, however. The plan also showed the vital importance of the reservations system, presenting primarily the stages of a new and more sophisticated booking system. The Long Range Plan had 8 steps. The first three steps covered the concluded systems of the SPAS, the Ramac, and the Zebra. Steps 4 and 5 aimed at producing an integrated and enlarged system of the first three computers, enabling agents and sales offices to make bookings on their own. The agent set had been prepared for such a "BOOK" function. Steps 6 and 7 extended the system to all Scandinavia, and step 8 rounded off by automating the message switching system connecting SAS' Teletype net with the reservations system. Apart from these 8 steps, the Long Range Plan did not seem to include a general computerization plan for SAS functions. Above all, it was important to get a new reservations system to cope with the expanding traffic of the jet age, and additional computer systems had to be built around this the core reservations system.

RESCO

The computer plans were suspended only a few months caused by the jet crisis of 1961. By request, IBM proposed the layout for a new, integrated reservations and check-in system, called Reservation Computer (RESCO). RESCO was based on IBM's new computer 1410, a second-generation computer working on transistors. Negotiations made slow progress for a long time, however, and among other things, Univac was asked to present an alternative proposal. In the end, it was decided to follow the recommendations of SRI and in March 1963, SAS management entered into a contract with IBM to build the RESCO system.

During the period from 1963 to 1965, IBM, SAS, and some foreign specialists joined forces to produce the pioneering RESCO system. RESCO constituted steps 4 and 5 of the Long Range Plan. The system was based on two IBM 1410 computers, the second one meant for fallback and for doing batch systems. The software for the system and the interface to the Teletype net was

---

127 SAS, *Data Management*, 15/11 1962, 28/2 1963. Interview: *Torsten Bergner.*

designed by a growing number of SAS programmers. A new communication concept drew on foreign expertise.

First and foremost, RESCO enabled agents and sales offices round the world to make direct bookings. Next, the three old dedicated systems were merged into one integrated system. Furthermore, capacity and speed multiplied. While the old system could only store bookings for 70 days, RESCO was able to keep that information for 300 days. RESCO delivered updated information about the booking situation on all flights, at any time. Finally, RESCO contained some new facilities. If all seats were booked, the system automatically suggested an alternative flight. The electronic name register, another new facility, would prevent double booking and incorrect cancellations.

RESCO also included check-in and load control, just as its predecessor had. Besides the traffic program and rules of weight and balance, like the old system, RESCO had some new check-in facilities. While the flight was being prepared for departure, the computer could present immediate information on the weight and balance situation. Automatic comparison of booked and checked-in passengers enabled SAS to give "last-minute-passengers" a better service. "Remote-controlled" check-in from all of Scandinavia rendered a second check-in superfluous for passengers transferring to a flight in Copenhagen.

The chief purpose of RESCO was to make the reservation system available to all agents and sales offices. By the mid-1960s, there were hundreds of agent sets throughout Scandinavia, the rest of Western Europe, and the USA. Information was collected concurrently from all agents and sales offices to produce a quick and updated state of booking. RESCO did not just improve the level of service to passengers, SAS was able to gain a better load factor, too.

Modern booking and check-in/load control started at SAS with RESCO, and the following systems and changes built on these pioneering efforts. Just like its predecessor, RESCO exchanged telex information concerning a number of other functions: cargo, the traffic control center, catering, fuel, and crew – functions that were still based on manual or mechanical systems.

RESCO was implemented in 1965 and operated from the new computer center in Copenhagen, called SAS Computer (SASCO).

RESCO 1963

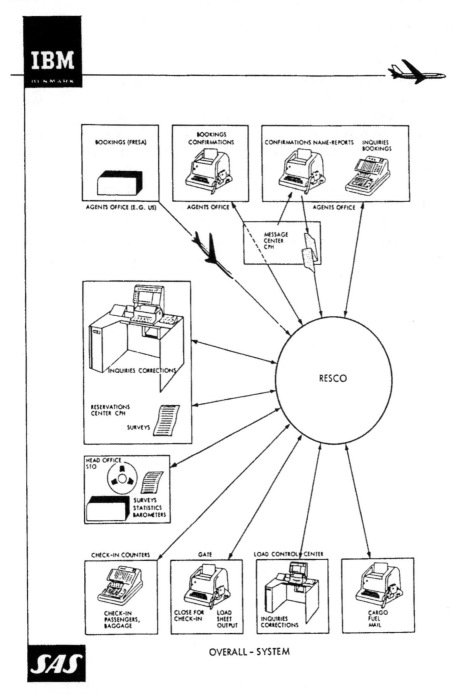

Source: SAS, *Data Management,* 19-20/6 1963.

1970 The Third Computer System: RES

Traffic increased so much and so fast that a year after starting RESCO capacity problems could already be predicted in the near future. A third generation computer, Univac 494 (U494), was bought to replace the IBM 1410.[128]

The RESCO systems were reprogrammed and Univac's operating system was developed to meet the specific demands of SAS. Many problems delayed the implementation of the new system, once more a pioneering project. In 1970, RESCO was finally closed down and the Univac system started. It was known as Reservations System (RES) and Load Control System (LOCS).

Essentially, the new U494 system did not differ from its predecessors, even though a few facilities were added during reprogramming. Increased integration of RES, LOCS, and some of the new emerging systems was an important feature. Primarily, U494 was meant to produce a much larger capacity, however, and to prepare the way for increasing computerization. The communication system was automated further, but sales offices and agents still applied agent sets, in several hundreds.

128 SAS, *Data Management*, 1/7 1966, 29-30/1, 1/3, 1/7 1968, 8/1 1969, 2/1 1970. SAS, *Yearbook*, 1970.

The 1960s Data Organization and Infrastructure

SAS IT Statistics[129]

	1960	1970	1980
Costs in mill. SEK	10	60	250
% of total SAS	1	4	4
Personnel	50	500	500
Annual mill. transactions	3	15	150
Terminals	100	1,000	7,000

Sources: SAS, "International Inquiry Answering Service", in *Data Processing*, July-September 1961; SAS, *Data Management*, 2/1 1970; SAS, V-81; SAS, *Annual Reports*.

Data Services

The first programming group headed by Arne Hansen grew quickly in numbers, reaching a couple of hundred by the mid-1960s and approximately 500 by 1970.[130] Three groups of specialists made up the first SAS computer department in 1963: programmers (including line function analysts, although there were still only a few of them), technicians from the communications department, and operators. Analysts, programmers, and operators were recruited from the line departments, as were the people who programmed the first systems around 1960.

Data Services included operations, programming, and systems. Systems development hardly existed as a field of its own, it was just an analytic dimension of programming. At first, Data Services was divided into two parts. An online part, covering the booking system, formed a subsection of the communications department at head office, and an offline part, dealing with batch systems such as revenue, accounting, traffic statistics, and salaries, belonged to the finance department. The early Data Services organization seemed much inspired by IBM.[131]

Data Services was reorganized in 1965. The online and offline part was joined in one organization, at first under the president's office, and then from 1968 until 1980 as a subsection of the new Administrative Department.[132]

---

129 Figures for 1960 are estimates. Terminals include agent sets, printers, and display data terminals.
130 SAS, *Data Management*, 1/7 1966 and 2/1 1970.
131 SAS, *Data Management*, 10/6 1963.
132 SAS, *Yearbooks*, 1967 and 1968.

From 1963/1965, SAS had a central computer department at head office with an operation center (in Copenhagen), a programming section (in Copenhagen), and a systems group (in Stockholm). National departments were established in all the three capitals, although the units in Stockholm and Oslo were much smaller than the main center in Copenhagen and dealt with a growing number of regional batch systems.

The SAS Computer Operation Center in Copenhagen: SASCO

The SAS computer operation center, known as SAS Computers (SASCO), opened in Copenhagen in 1965. It worked on two IBM 1410 machines, second-generation computer based on transistors.

While SPAS, Ramac, and Zebra were dedicated computers, the IBM 1410 of SASCO was intended to operate not only the reservations and check-in/load control systems, but also a number of other applications that were to be developed. In 1965, SAS had already outlined a computer plan for all its main functions.[133]

Very soon, lack of computer power stopped those plans. Traffic increased so fast that the reservations and check-in/load control systems exceeded the capacity of the IBM 1410 in a few years. Primarily, the reservations system took up the most capacity and pressed for more. IBM could not provide the needed computer power, however. Furthermore, SAS wanted to computerize all the other main functions of the company. Looking around the USA, a working group found a new third generation computer, Univac 494, which fulfilled the needs of SAS.

U494 was a third generation computer based on integrated circuits and an operating system. As with the IBM 1410, the second U494 was a fallback machine to be applied for batch operations. Compared with the IBM 1410, the U494 multiplied capacity and speed. It was 70 times faster than the IBM 1410 and multiplied its storage capacity. From 1965 to 1970, transactions increased from 3 to 4.8 per second, from 1970 to 1975 to 16 reaching 70 in 1985. After many problems, the U494 finally took over in 1970. The new computer center was called SASCO II.[134]

---

133 SAS, *Data Management*, 3/5, 16-17/5, 10/6, 19-20/11 1963; 21/10 1966; SAS, *Yearbooks*, 1967 and 1968. Interviews: *Arne Hansen* and *Torsten Bergner*.
134 SAS, *Data Management*, 13-14/10 1966; 5/3, 1/7 1968; 8/1 1969; 2/1 1970; 26/5 1975; 22/5 1986. Interviews: *Arne Hansen* and *Torsten Bergner*

The Computer Based Teletype Network: MESCO/DASCO

To exploit fully the potential of the electronic booking system, the SAS communication system had to be enlarged and automated. In part, RESCO automated communications between the Booking Center and the Telegram Center in Copenhagen and the many sales offices and agents throughout the world. Telegram traffic was still considerable because every booking had to be confirmed in Copenhagen. In 1965, 300 agent sets in 21 cities in 13 countries and 4,000 teleprinters communicated with Copenhagen via relay sets.

To handle the growing flow of information and make use of the multiplied speed of U494, communication between the booking offices throughout the world and the Booking Center in Copenhagen had to be fully automated. A Univac 418 computer was put in place to automate the telegram traffic. It was called "the Message Computer" (MESCO) and began its use in Scandinavia in 1966, eventually covering the whole world. In 1968, a second U418 automated the switching function between booking offices and the Booking Center. This was the so-called "Data System Computer" (DASCO). The U418s of MESCO/DASCO worked as front-end to the online systems in order not to drain capacity, particularly from the booking system. The switch over to the U494 systems of SASCO II in 1970 enabled SAS to utilize the advantages of MESCO/DASCO. The Teletype network was still based on the telephone system.[135]

Accordingly, in 1970 SAS had an automated booking, check-in/load control and communication system.

Systems Development

Staff from the line functions, such as traffic, accounting, technical, cargo, and personnel, produced the punched card systems of the 1950s. They were self-taught, although they had taken courses from IBM (who had delivered the machines). Programmers of the first booking and check-in/load control system of the late 1950s and early 1960s had the same background. They were familiar with the functions for which they developed systems. Programming demanded much knowledge of the machines because coding was done directly into the machine. Assembler and programming languages lay ahead. Without any operating system, the machines had to be instructed about all routines and activities.

The new computer department of 1963, Data Services, concentrated all

---

135 SAS, *Data Management*, 1/7, 13-14/10 1966; 1/7 1968; 7/1 1970; SAS, *Yearbooks*, 1967 to 1970. Interview: *Henning Andersen*.

RESCO programmers in Copenhagen. As a result, the programming department of Data Services remained in Copenhagen. Many programmers from Stockholm and some from Oslo went to Copenhagen the following years.

Assembler language was used for programming RESCO. Programming and programmers were the only names used at that time. Every system was based on a kind of "system description", but RESCO did not include "systems development" as such. Only in 1965, was a specialized systems department, different from programmers and using analysts from the line functions, formed at head office in Stockholm.

Systems analysis was a new field of expertise, with IBM holding its first systems development courses in Stockholm in 1964. Systems development was a matter of specifying the content of the systems that the programmers afterwards had to produce. The problem of documentation was discussed, too. The Systems Department prepared a set of rules concerning the information and documentation that should be specified before programming took over. This was the beginning of the SAS systems development method and the extensive work of development, which took place from the mid-1960s.

In 1965, the first general plan was presented to develop computer systems for all main functions of SAS, covering passenger, cargo, stations, traffic control, crew, technical maintenance, accounting, and salaries. Besides the booking and check-in/load control that were computerized through RESCO in 1965, the system analysts of Stockholm in cooperation with knowledgeable SAS personnel from the three Scandinavian capitals, started mapping the information flow of the company. Next, knowledge of the information flow was prepared for an outline of computer systems.[136]

From the very start, an important part of systems development was to make an economic calculation of the planned system. What would the system cost and most importantly, what could SAS gain from investing in a computer system. A decision to develop a computer system was based on estimations of its profitability and its importance, compared with other airlines and the customers of SAS. As a rule, a system was considered profitable if it reduced personnel and increased productivity within a few years.

---

136 Interviews: *Torsten Bergner* and *Arne Hansen*.

Data Services Organization 1968

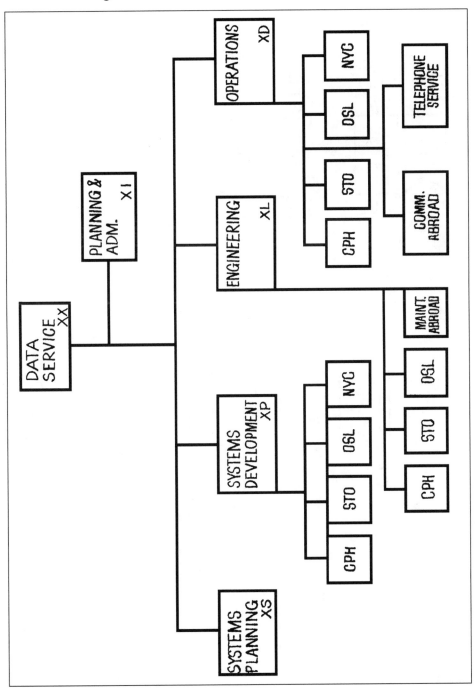

Source: SAS, Data Management.

SAS Communications Network 1969

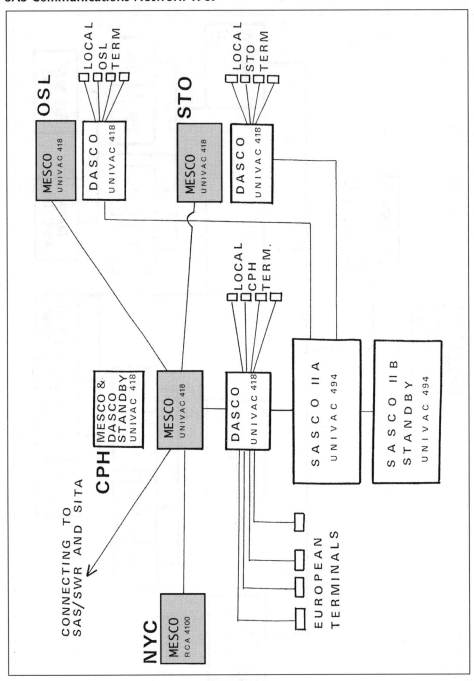

Source: SAS, Data Management.

Data Services and SAS

RESCO, MESCO, and DASCO made up the first and central part of a general introduction of computer systems in SAS. In 1965, SAS management decided on a whole program to improve the efficiency of the company, the so-called "Efficiency Driven" project. Costs were increasing, especially salaries, while revenue lagged behind. To speed up a rise in productivity, SAS had two organizational tools. One was to increase systematic management of the activities (i.e., a higher degree of structuring of the work and information flow by way of rational planning, so-called pre-processing). The other one was automating through computer technology. Management chose automation as its most important tool, bearing in mind that systematic management was also promoted by the spread of computer technology. Consequently, the "Efficiency Driven" project dealt mainly with computer plans.[137]

The first plan to computerize SAS was presented in 1965. A year later, the plan had materialized in a number of named systems:

LOCS: Load Control System
CRU: Crew Planning System
CARGO: Cargo Handling System
MOPS: Maintenance and Overhaul Planning System
OPS: Operational Control System
RES: Reservations System
TRAPS: Traffic Planning System
CATS: Catering System
ACS: Accounting System
TRASST/OPSST: Traffic and Operational Statistics System
PASAS: Sales and Revenue Statistics Systems
RECS: Revenue Control System
MATS: Material Supply and Inventory Control System
CTF: City Timetable and Fares
PERS: Personnel Systems.[138]

Soon, the plan proved to be too ambitious, at least to be implemented in the near future. It would be a very expensive project and furthermore, SAS was short of qualified people and computer capacity. Reprogramming RES and the Load Control System (LOCS) demanded many man-hours, and new online systems had to wait for the new U494 to be installed in 1970. Besides the ac-

---

137 SAS, *Data Management*, 1/7 1966. Interview: *Torsten Bergner*.
138 SAS, *Data Management*, 24/10 1967.

counting system, ACS, and the technical stock system, MATS, the other
systems of the general plan were postponed until the 1970s. During the
1960s, the three regional organizations had developed batch systems on the
IBM 1410 and later on the 360 for accounting, traffic, and so forth.[139]

SAS' First Information Systems Plan 1965

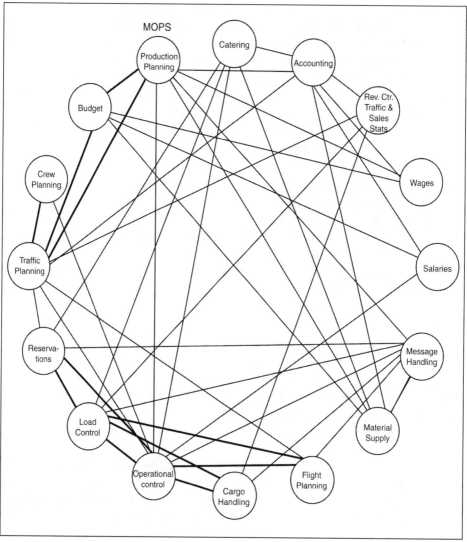

Source: Torsten Bergner.

139 SAS, *Data Management*, 1/7 1966, 2/1 1970.
140 SAS, *Data Management*, 2/1 1970.

The 1970s Data Services

Organization

From 1965 to 1968, Data Services organized the whole SAS IT field under the president's office, from 1968 to 1980 under the Administrative Department. Head office included the president, C. Reuterskiöld (1963-1970), followed by T. Korsvold (1970-1980), a staff unit for planning and administration, and the line units: systems planning, systems development and programming, maintenance, telecommunications, and operations. The three Nordic capitals and New York had local units for systems development, maintenance, and operations.

In 1970, Data Services was reorganized. Head office functions were directed more towards strategic long-term planning, while enlarging the four regional centers. The crucial position of Copenhagen as operation and development center for the large online systems and communications was stressed even more. The other centers faced marginalization, leaving local data processing to external data services. It was not until the late 1970s that the creation of the Maintenance and Overhaul Planning System (MOPS) initiated a new start for the Stockholm center, followed by Oslo.

Total Data Services personnel did not increase during the 1970s. A staffing level of 500 had been maintained since 1970. Three-quarters of the personnel was located in Copenhagen.[140]

Data Services Organization 1971

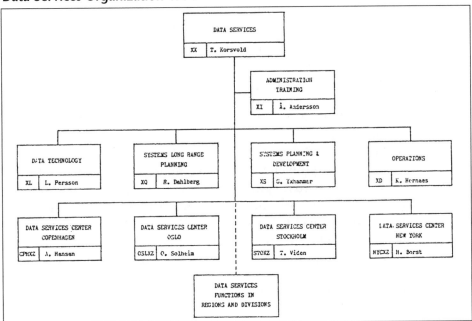

Source: SAS, Data Management.

Capacity Problems

Since 1970, online systems, especially the largest one RES, were operated by the new U494. The U494 had a much bigger capacity than the IBM 1410, but forecasts showed that its capacity would run out by 1975, even if a third U494 were included. As a matter of fact, Data Services acquired two extra U494 before 1975. Still, the problem of expanding operation demands had to be solved, particularly since a new and more powerful Univac operating system was not in sight. In 1972, management had already found the solution in building a second computer environment with IBM.

To start with, much of the batch operations on the IBM 360 in Oslo and Stockholm were outsourced to external data services, which reduced the local Data Services centers in those cities to very small units, and concentrated almost all computer activities in Copenhagen.

A third way of solving both capacity and cost problems was to cooperate with other airlines. In 1970, SAS tried to extend the technical maintenance cooperation with Swissair and KLM to include computer development in this field. SAS also looked to American Airlines for cooperation in reservations system. Both plans came to nothing. Swissair and KLM wanted to develop systems of their own and contrary to SAS, American Airlines' SABRE system had no integration with the check-in system, and SAS would hardly accept to run its reservations under the premises of American Airlines.[141]

Capacity problems were especially urgent around the middle of the 1970s. Online systems grew by 20% each year, and frequently experienced many interruptions of service. The fourth way to address the problem was to get more hardware. First, a fourth U494 was acquired. At the same time, the IBM center was started, with one 370 in 1974 and another in 1977 being used for interactive programming in Stockholm. The IBM center was located in Copenhagen, but systems development continued to be done in both Stockholm and Copenhagen. The first and most important project to be developed and operated on the IBM 370 was the large MOPS project, the first system founded on database technology.

The introduction of mini computers from the late 1970s offered a fifth approach to solving capacity problems of the big computers. They contained some intelligence and could be used for local preprocessing of data, especially in sales offices, reducing the pressure on central processing. This was the so-called Data Registration and Processing in Remote Organizations (DRAPRO) system.

A growing number of information systems, expanding traffic, and increasing information-processing tasks resulting from a growth in data terminals

---

141 SAS, *Data Management*, 24/2 and 27/7 1970.

transactions, rules and regulations, kept on producing problems of computer capacity, however. A special problem arose when Univac announced a halt in the production of the U494. After much consideration, it was decided to get the U1100, another Univac machine, and gradually emulate RES and other online systems on the new computer during the early 1980s. The new technique of emulation allowed for a transfer of systems from one computer to another without reprogramming the systems. Emulation made the system believe it was still running on the original computer.[142]

Databases and Data Models

SAS used enormous amounts of data, or rather information, every minute of the day and in the late 1970s, computer systems handled much of its information processing and storing. Often, the same data were reproduced on several systems, which was irrational. Furthermore, the file-based data organization made it practically impossible to utilize the information from the computer applications for more than just operational functions and simple statistics. As these first generation systems were being introduced, a growing number of cross-links between the systems only complicated the SAS information systems structure. Whenever systems were integrated, it was done to solve ad hoc problems rather than being part of a general integration plan. Besides, the technology of the day hardly permitted any overall logical integration of information systems. Every single application lived a life of its own, creating an organization of sub-optimal units.

During the 1970s, Data Services had already begun to wonder how SAS management, increasingly pressured by falling profitability and the problems of running an ever more complex organization, could benefit more from information from the computer systems. Data models, databases, and database management systems were the new tools produced by the 1970s computer industry to fulfill such intentions.

By 1969, Data Services had developed the first general SAS data model. It contained all the planned systems of the "Efficiency Driven" program of 1965-66. The data model had two horizontal perspectives, sales (timetable, reservations, etc.) and production (crew and maintenance), and two vertical dimensions that measured economy and traffic on the one hand and corporate planning on the other. At the center of the model, Data Services placed a common data bank, where all systems could get information as required. The data bank was probably inspired by the idea of Management Information Systems (MIS), a popular concept in computer circles around 1970.

---

142 SAS, *Data Management*, 2/4 1980.

Ideas of MIS or a data bank had no practical use around 1970, however, as the proper technology to execute such plans was still awaited. This changed from the mid-1970s, when the new IBM database management system, called Information Management System (IMS), was being used for the large MOPS project. At the same time, preliminary studies of database systems to replace existing file systems began in the other SAS functions, including crew, check-in and load control, traffic operations control, technical supply and inventory, personnel, and revenue accounting. However, economic stagnation and crisis caused many plans to be delayed or postponed.[143] Thus file systems prevailed until the 1980s.

In the late 1970s, a planning group at Data Services developed a new data model for SAS, namely, SAS Data Models (SASMO), which included several models for the company's main applications.[144] SASMO was based on the fundamental resources of SAS: aircraft, passenger, cargo, station, workshop, material, staff, and capital.[145]

There were several relationships between these objects and the most important were connected with transport: first was the aircraft to passenger relationship and next, that of aircraft to cargo. The following relationships were important in terms of production: passenger to station (checked in); cargo to station (received/dispatched); aircraft to station (operated, loaded, unloaded); and aircraft to staff (flies). Maintenance relationships consisted of aircraft to workshop (supplied tools and premises); aircraft to material (replaced used material); and aircraft to staff (maintained). The production of transport created relationships between passenger and capital (paid) and cargo and capital (was paid). Capital led to relationships between capital and aircraft (bought); capital and staff (salaried); and capital and material (bought).

All data units of the SAS business could be connected to one of the resources of SASMO, creating a general view of the data processing in the applications. Data Services wanted to standardize the data units of each resource to ensure an efficient use of data. Although principles such as objects and relations, later the foundation of relational databases, were deployed, the database systems of the 1970s and 1980s were all based on hierarchical technology, primarily IMS of IBM. Information retrieval across hierarchical databases did not come easily, however. Still, by 1980 such strategic perspectives of information resources were yet to come.

---

143 SAS, *Data Management*, 26/6, 28/9, 30/11 1978. SAS, *Data News*, Feb., March, May, June, Sept., Nov. 1978; Nov., Dec. 1979; March, Aug., Oct., Dec. 1980.
144 Unfortunately, these individual models seem to have vanished.
145 SAS, SASMO, *Data Management,* 1980.

SAS Data Model 1978

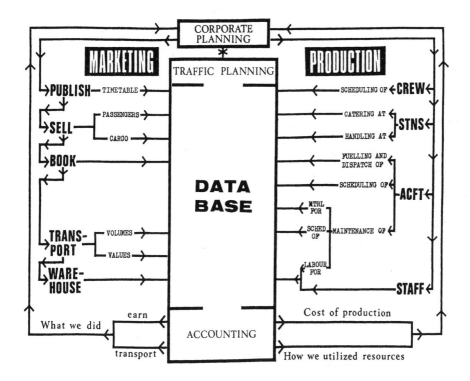

Source: SAS, Data Services, 1978.

Data Services and SAS

During the 1970s, most of the systems of the 1969 data model were implemented. The computer plans also became part of SAS planning and as a result, the activities of Data Services and SAS were becoming more integrated. Already in 1965 and 1966, SAS presented its first plan for computerizing the organization. It was called "Efficiency Driven" and in 1970 was renamed the "Efficiency Development Plan". A few years later it was called the "Company Development Plan" and was made an integrated part of the three-year forecasting company plans. Separate long-range plans for computer development were established from 1970, too. The so-called "Electronic Data Processing Long-range Plan" (ELOP) was added to SAS' general long-range plans.[146] Annual budgets, three year-plans, and 10-year long-range plans formed the com-

---

146 Unfortunately, these ELOP plans have vanished.

puter systems' integrated planning system for the SAS organization during the 1970s. Except for new airplanes, all planning aimed primarily at cutting costs and improving efficiency by replacing personnel with computer systems.

To match the SAS organization, Data Services built a similar structure of functional areas. During the 1970s, 12 such areas were established followed by master plans, namely:

1. Corporate Planning.
2. Finance and Accounting.
3. Traffic Planning.
4. Passenger.
5. Cargo and Mail.
6. Operations.
7. Maintenance and Overhaul.
8. Flight Operation/Crew.
9. Stations.
10. EDP and Communications.
11. Personnel.
12. Offices and Office Services.[147]

Project organization, a new ad hoc cross-functional way of organizing activities, supplemented the basic structure of line and staff. All computer systems were developed as projects, based on cooperation between the Data Services and SAS within the area in question. In practice, Data Services was the driving force of these projects, however, monopolizing computer expertise. The use of area and project organization displayed the intention of the 1970s to make computer technology a vital part of the SAS strategy. Finally by the late 1970s, a Data Agreement was reached, stating that users should be a cooperative part of developing new systems, too.

As a consequence of the development of first-generation information systems and the growing needs for SAS to meet pressure on profitability with increasing productivity, the information flow of the airline was being more intensively analyzed. The information flow analysis disclosed a faulty foundation in the company's measure of productivity. Neither manual and punched card systems, nor first-generation computer systems were built to produce information for management. By and large, they all reproduced patterns of the original SAS organization, which involved processing data for carrying out basic functions.

The introduction of databases and data modeling made the first and im-

---

147 SAS, *Data Management*, 24/2 1975; 26/5 1976.

portant break with traditional ways of organizing and employing data. The pre-processing ways of organizing technical maintenance in particular, paved the way for a systematic management approach to information handling, too. New concepts, such as "Management Information Reports'" to improve internal control and "Corporate Intelligence" to produce knowledge of trends in the outside world, were far ahead of contemporary practical technology and management strategy, however.

During the 1970s, many options were investigated to cut costs and improve productivity, including external cooperation with other airlines in computer development and outsourcing Data Services, but none of them was ever implemented.[148] Data and information were studied as a vital part of implementing the strategy of SAS, too, preparing the way for the strategic and technological changes of the 1980s.

The 1970s IT Infrastructure

Computer Operations

Univac

Compared with SASCO I, SASCO II of 1970 multiplied capacity and speed of transactions. Most of the pressure came from the large and expanding reservations system.

Soon, however, SASCO II also became short of capacity. Before the mid-1970s, the ever-growing RES, together with a number of new applications, forced SAS to acquire two more U494s.[149] By the late 1970s, Data Services prepared to replace the U494 with the U1100.

IBM

In spite of increasing Univac capacity, it did not suffice. Already in the early 1970s, management realized that the U494 would be unable to meet the demands of the planned computer expansion. It was therefore decided in 1972-73 to build a supplementary IBM environment in Copenhagen to run the large MOPS system complex in the first instance. The first IBM 370 was introduced in 1974 and a second in 1977, among other things to handle interactive programming from Stockholm. A number of batch systems were converted to the IBM 370. One of these was the accounting system, ACS, which made more room for the online systems on the U494. Other batch systems

---

148 SAS, *Data Management*, 6/9 1974.
149 SAS, *Data Management*, 26/5 1975.

were taken back from external data services in Stockholm and Oslo to be operated by the 370, too.[150]

After the mid-1970s, the combined Univac and IBM solutions created more space to meet the rising capacity demands. RES and the other large on-line systems never stopped growing, however, urged by new computer applications and thousands of data terminals spreading throughout the organization. The IBM center grew in time with the introduction of MOPS modules and in the early 1980s, it had reached the size of the Univac center.[151]

Communications: Telcon

Having introduced MESCO/DASCO in the late 1960s, management soon started preparing for a successor. According to estimations, data communication activities would expand rapidly to exceed the capacity of MESCO/DASCO by 1974. Instead of hundreds of agent sets, thousands of true data terminals were to be moved into the SAS organization.

The new communications system, Tele Communications Network (Telcon) started in 1974. It was centered in Copenhagen, like its predecessor, and used a front-end computer in Copenhagen and remote-end computers in Stockholm and Oslo. The system was bought from Collins Radio, UK, and adjusted to the needs of SAS. While the old Teletype system worked at low speed, Telcon operated a medium speed system, creating a considerable rise in capacity. The new Saab Alfaskop terminals were built in series of eight around a control unit and in order to cope with the growing demands of communication, new coaxial wires replaced old copper.

Primarily, Telcon substituted for DASCO, while MESCO continued to do telegram communication traffic. Still, SAS communicated with its small routes, with other airlines, and with international organizations, such as IATA, by way of telegrams. During the following years, Telcon gradually became worldwide, meanwhile leaning on the networks of Swissair, Thai, and SITA.[152]

The new structure of Telcon – computers, data terminals, control units, and coaxial wires – paved the way for a communications revolution in SAS. The number of terminals grew much faster than expected and already in 1977, the network had to be extended to what was called Telcon 2. The expansion of data terminals did not stop, however. Shortly after implementing Telcon 2, SAS started preparing for a new and larger system, Telcon 3.[153]

---

150 SAS, *Data Management*, 21/4 1972; 20/2 and 10/10 1973.
151 SAS, *Data Management*, 6/8 1979. SAS *Yearbooks*, 1975 to 1980. SAS *V–1981*.
152 SAS, *Data Management*, 7/7 1972; 10/10 1973; 22/3 and 7/11 1974. SAS, *Yearbooks*, 1974 and 1975. Interview: *Henning Andersen*.
153 SAS, *Data Management*, 26/5 and 25/11 1976; 15/6 1978.

SAS IT Concept 1978

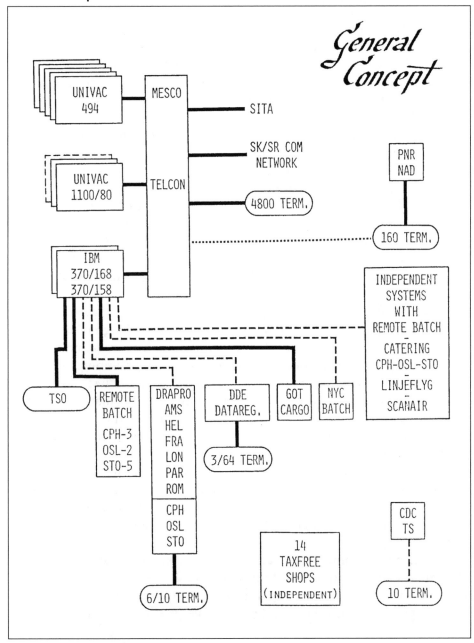

Source: SAS, *Data Services,* 1978.

Systems Development: The Classical Method

Around 1970, a structuring and formalizing process of systems development took place that was to be normative for the next two decades or more. Long-term planning of SAS and Data Services pressed for a coherent systems concept. The systems concept had two sides. One was the economic calculation, which was crucial to a decision on investing in a system. The second was the analytical basis of programming.[154]

The economic calculation included the cost of computers, systems development, communications, transactions, storing, development, test, and operation, on the one hand. On the other hand, benefits of the system were calculated, including reduced personnel.

The actual systems development process of an application included the following steps. First, a systems concept was prepared, called the "systems outline". This covered the purpose and main contents of the system. The next phase was called »systems requirements", and it specified the functional contents of the system. "Outline" and "requirements" formed the basis of the economic calculation. The third step, "decision", was crucial to the future of the project. If the proposal was approved, the fourth phase started, called "systems development". Systems development included design of the system according to the specifications of step two, and the actual programming. Programming was now being based much more on true programming languages, particularly Cobol but also Fortran. The final steps included "test" and "maintenance". Later on, the project was completed by "after calculation" comparing plans and results, undoubtedly the most precarious part of all.

This structure of systems development prevailed from the early 1970s right up until the 1990s.

The System Planning unit of Data Services managed systems development activities. During the 1970s, systems development worked according to a kind of organizational matrix, organizing all the main SAS functions in so-called "development areas". As mentioned above, 12 such areas arose during the 1970s.

A permanent committee led each area, with a chairman at vice-presidential level. The organization was, thus, anchored by top management. Below the upper level, a hierarchical structure existed from the EDP Steering Committee to project groups. Eventually, each area produced a so-called master

---

154 SAS, *Data Management*, 26/5 1976. Interview: *Curt Ekström*.

plan, a concept being introduced by way of MOPS and imported from American Airlines and IBM. The master plan improved management's grasp of the project. Master planning did not change the method of systems development, however, it just integrated method and computer technology even more into the SAS organization.

The structure created around 1970 came to influence SAS in other ways.[155] First, a divide arose between users and producers of computer technology. The first generation of computer specialists was mostly recruited within SAS. Increasing demands of computer development and knowledge meant that from the 1960s, a new generation of computer specialists was recruited externally. They were especially trained to deal with computers, but contrary to the pioneers of computing in SAS, they lacked any knowledge of the airline business. Accordingly, the computer specialists at Data Services and the employees throughout the airline grew apart.

A second divide was seen within Data Services between the planners in Stockholm and the hands-on people in Copenhagen. Computer operation, development and programming were centered in Copenhagen and were attached to maintenance and development of the large online systems. General systems planning took place mainly at head office in Stockholm. Finally, head office was developing a love affair with IBM while Copenhagen had strong feelings for Univac. Accordingly, a clash of interests and culture arose to mark the next two decades.

155 SAS, *Data Management*, 1/11 and 30/11 1978. Interview: *Curt Ekström*.

The 1970s Information Systems

SAS Information Systems Development Plan 1971

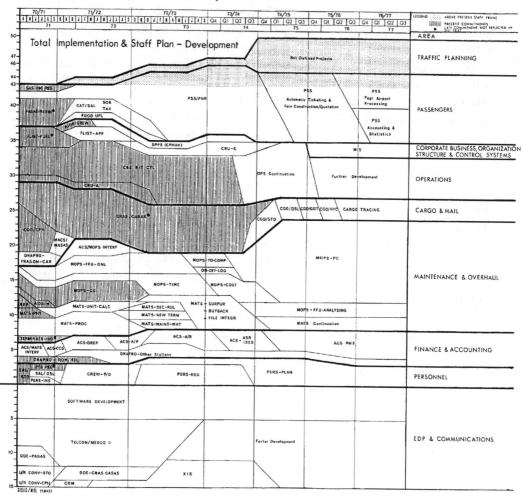

Source: SAS, *Data Management.*

Corporate

Until 1980, new aircraft technology was of the utmost importance to the SAS strategy. At the same time, decisions concerning new aircraft were major ones and were binding on the company for many years. Therefore, long-range airline investments planning made up a vital part of corporate management. Such strategic decision-making was based on traffic statistics and carefully prepared forecasts of general economic and traffic growth, the advance of aircraft technology, the plans of other airlines, and the estimated trends of SAS' own routes.

No computer system applied to overall planning of airplane investments, at that time. SAS management collected external information from various sources, such as IATA, national governments and statistical departments, aircraft manufactures, and major airlines. Information on internal affairs came mainly from traffic statistics and accounting, based on the two batch systems, Traffic Revenue Statistics (TRAST) and Accounting System (ACS), of the late 1960s. Since the mid-1970s, the Traffic Planning System (TRAPS) made these planning activities more sophisticated.[156]

Traffic

Until 1980, traffic program planning was part of the Marketing Department and exclusively a head office activity.

Traffic planning and the preparation of traffic programs was a complex process. Planning built on a number of factors that SAS was often unable to change, at least in the short run. External factors, such as the capacity of airports, international rules of pricing, technical standards, and national laws and rules of authorities, were crucial. Significant internal factors included the existing route net and airplanes, personnel requirements, including collective agreements, and the fact that the airline's product could not be stored. Since its very beginning, SAS had produced traffic statistics. Since the 1960s, these had been based on the batch computer system TRAST and since the 1970s on the more sophisticated TRAPS. TRAPS was a statistical program measuring load factor, revenue, costs, and so on, of the SAS routes and by way of a supplementary system, TRAPS could select a number of traffic programs for further investigation.[157]

156 SAS, *K-71*. Interview: *Stefan Andersson*.
157 SAS, *Data Management*, 5/3 1970; SAS, *Yearbooks*, 1967 to 1980.

Within these boundaries, SAS prepared two programs each year, a summer program and a winter program, or "timetable" as it was (and is) normally called. To book a ticket, the outside world needed to know when and where SAS flew. Inside SAS, airplanes and crew, booking, check-in, traffic control, and all other functions of the airline worked according to the timetable. The timetable was the basic tool of running the day-to-day operations of SAS.

During the 1950s and 1960s, the timetable was prepared manually. Information was communicated by telex to the different parts of the organization and published for the benefit of agents and sales offices. In the early 1970s, a computer system, Traffic Timetable Program (TTP), was developed on the Univac mainframe in Copenhagen. This file system could be used for editing the timetable on a data terminal, but its simple technology caused many errors in handling current changes.[158]

Finally, Traffic Operation Statistics (TOPST) was introduced during the 1970s, for measuring punctuality.[159]

Passenger

Until 1980, Marketing & Sales, including booking, was a subsection of the Marketing Department, whereas accounting and revenue belonged to the Finance Department. Regional functions of Marketing & Sales took care of daily activities, and revenue was solely a matter for head office.[160]

Marketing & Sales

Naturally, Marketing & Sales were SAS activities from the very start of the company. The jet age increased the need for Marketing & Sales to secure a satisfactory load factor for a growing capacity. Cargo and tourism also became important targets of traffic during the 1960s and 1970s.

Computer systems were of no direct importance to marketing, and only mattered to sales. Sales were recorded from the start of SAS in the accounting department. It was a slow and complex manual process. Interline revenue and commissions of agents had to be calculated and deducted from the recorded sales before the actual income and profit of SAS was known. Punched card accounting systems of the late 1950s and a general accounting computer system of the late 1960s improved information processing of sales.[161]

---

158 *Inside SAS*, no. 8, 1972. Interview: *Stefan Andersson.*
159 SAS, *Data Management*, 13/1 1977.
160 SAS, *Yearbooks*, 1967 to 1980.
161 SAS, *Yearbooks*, 1967 to 1980. Interview: *Eric Berggren-Lindberg.*

Reservations

The reservations system formed the core of sales as it did of the whole SAS organization. In the early 1970s, the SAS reservations system, RES, had reached its third step (1961 and 1965 being the other two steps), although still being a first generation piece of software. Increasing capacity and integration of the booking system with other systems, including agents and sales offices, characterized the booking system during the 1960s.

PNR

Just a year after implementing RES on the U494 in 1970, it was decided to introduce automatic name recording. SAS called the revised system Passenger Name Recording (PNR) and linked it with Telcon, the new communication system based on data terminals.[162] PNR was introduced in 1974, and during the remainder of the 1970s it spread throughout the organization. By then, most other leading airlines had already introduced all three dimensions of the reservations system: availability, inventory, and passenger name.[163] PNR was a fully automated reservations system, including name recording and archiving.

The terminal screen was the panacea of the sales staff. It showed:

- the timetable and gave information on available seats and alternative flights
- information on departure and about services onboard
- booked seats and cancelled bookings
- whenever a ticket was to be issued
- information about hotels, car rental, sightseeing tours, and other services attached to the routes of the airline.

The central computer in Copenhagen executed the following main functions:

- storage of information about seats, timetables, etc.
- processing and display of information on request
- receipt, processing, and storage of passenger recordings
- production of out-going telex messages
- receipt and processing of incoming telex messages from other airlines and from SAS offices not directly connected to the computer system
- production of messages to users of the PNR-system when manual handling was demanded.

---

162 SAS, *Data Management*, Sept. 1971, 7/7 1972.
163 SAS, *Yearbooks*, 1974 to 1980.

When a sales person wanted information about a flight or a combination of flights, he keyed in the "by-par" in question (by-par meaning the departure and arrival cities for the intended journey), date, and approximate time. In less than five seconds, the desired information was shown on the screen. By keying in the line number of the chosen flight the reservation could be made. In cases of no availability, the system would automatically present alternatives on the screen. Whenever the system had accepted a booking, it would automatically update the stock of seats and make sure that booked seats were not booked twice.

PNR made up the first step in a line of passenger-oriented extensions of the booking system: automatic ticketing, automatic sales recording, followed by new systems for check-in and load control, revenue, and statistics.[164]

The pressure of other airlines and growing personnel costs compelled SAS to go on automating.

TICS

The passenger information stored in the archive of the reservations system could be made available for other purposes. If you had the name of the passenger, you could print the ticket by adding its price. That was what happened next.

Automatic ticketing, Ticketing Computer System (TICS), became an integrated part of the PNR-system in 1975. On request, the system would show the salesperson all ticket prices between two cities, and a price could be selected.[165]

PAS

The fundamental idea of the Passenger Accounting System (PAS) was to use the stored information of the PNR- and TICS-systems to automate sales recording from the sales offices to the central accounting system, thereby avoiding double revenue accounting. Information to PAS for tickets other than those issued by TICS would be added manually. PAS was implemented in 1980.

During the first half of the 1980s, PNR, TICS, and PAS spread globally to the sales offices and agents of SAS.[166]

---

164 SAS, *Data Management*, 18/3 1974.
165 SAS, *Yearbooks*, 1975 to 1980.
166 SAS, *Yearbook*, 1980; SAS, *Data Management*, May 1978, July 1979.

RES on U1100

By the late 1970s, Univac advised that it had stopped producing the U494 and it was to be replaced by the U1100, and SAS had to find a substitute. In the end, SAS chose the U1100. SAS also considered a new reservations system, such as Univac's coming standard system, USAS-RES, but being in the middle of an economic crisis, it had to give up the idea of changing its core reservations system. Instead, a new technique of emulation was used so that information systems could be converted from the U494 to U1100 without reprogramming.[167]

During the 1970s, RES integrated with a growing number of computer systems (LOCS, OPS, CRU, etc.), added the important automation steps of PNR, TICS, and PAS, and introduced data terminals instead of agent sets. The fundamental structure of the RES did not change, however. RES was still built on the foundations of 1965 and 1970.

Revenue Accounting

Interline accounting made it possible to fly any number of airlines between two distances on only one ticket. Since the 1950s, IATA had organized an international system by way of a central clearing office in Geneva.

Until 1980, interline accounting was a SAS head office function, organized under the Finance Department in Stockholm, and split into two, for passenger and cargo. In 1967, the Revenue Accounting Department moved to the new office building in Copenhagen.

At an early stage, the enormous interline accounting paperwork called for technical assistance, by SAS as well as by IATA, first punched cards machines, replaced by IBM 1401 in 1963.[168]

During the 1960s, SAS had introduced a small IBM batch-computer system based on punched cards. When converting to the U494 in 1970, the batch-system was reprogrammed and extended under the name TACS (Ticket Accounting System). The system was still based on files and used punched cards for input.

TACS worked during the 1970s. To cover the whole revenue accounting process, the Inter-airline Debit Information System, IDIS, and the Passenger Sales Statistics System, PASAS, had to be added to TACS. Accordingly, doing revenue accounting was a slow and personnel-intensive field of information processing, and it took a long time before management knew the actual state of income.[169]

---

167 SAS, *Data Management*, 9/3 1982; June 1982.
168 *SAS Nytt*, no. 7, 1961, no. 37, 1963.
169 SAS, *Data Management*, 1/1 1968; 17/ 1974; 26/5 1976; SAS, *Data News*, Sept. 1980.

Cargo

Like passengers until 1980, the cargo organization was divided between the Marketing Department (sales) and the Finance Department (accounting) with regional sales functions.[170]

Handling

Handling of cargo in the airport terminals was based on the airway bill. Already in the middle of the 1950s, SAS developed a punched card system for cargo handling in Copenhagen. Stockholm and Oslo got a similar system and during the 1960s, cargo handling in SAS used the punched card system.[171]

The 1965-66 plan to computerize SAS also included a computer system for cargo handling. The information flow of handling was mapped in 1965 and Data Services started working on a system to be implemented in 1967, especially in SAS' main Copenhagen center where a large sophisticated terminal was being built. For various reasons, the plan did not hold, however. Pressed by too many projects, top management fixed an order of priority that did not include cargo. For the time being, the existing punched card system was considered adequate for the needs of SAS and cargo computer plans stopped, at least until after the inauguration of the new Copenhagen terminal.[172] Lack of manpower and long-term problems in implementing the new terminal in Copenhagen and the new Univac computer system in SASCO caused further postponement.[173]

Although cargo was the most expansive field of SAS during the 1960s, a cargo computer system was obviously not considered as necessary or as profitable as passenger systems.

In cargo accounting of the 1960s, the preparatory processing at the regional level was done by small batch computer systems on the IBM 360 in Oslo, Stockholm, and New York, and in Copenhagen on the IBM 1410, subsequently replaced by the U494.[174]

CAREX

Finally, in 1971, Cargo Export (CAREX), a system for handling exports, was implemented in Copenhagen. The system focused on export because of the extensive transit freight going through the Copenhagen terminal. CAREX operated on the new U494 and as the first application in SAS, it used data ter-

---

170 SAS, *Yearbooks*, 1967 to 1980.
171 Interview: *Torsten Bergner.*
172 SAS, *Data Management*, 10/6, 19-20/6 1965; 1/7, 25/11 1966; 1966/67.
173 SAS, *Data Management*, 1/7 1968. Interview: *Torsten Bergner.*
174 SAS, *Data Management*, 14/9 1970.

minals as the medium for input and output. A similar system was installed in Oslo and Stockholm in 1973. CAREX could handle export and transfer (i.e., all out-going cargo) but not incoming cargo.[175]

CAREX worked in the following way. When a plane left Stockholm, for instance, to fly to Copenhagen, a telegram was sent to Copenhagen with information about the cargo on board. Before landing in Copenhagen, the cargo personnel would know which cargo was to remain in Copenhagen or be stored for transport by another plane, and which would eventually continue with the same plane. When the plane landed, the computer in SASCO was told where the various collies were stored and that the corresponding cargo documents had arrived at the Copenhagen office. In the case of transit cargo, the computer sent an information sheet to the personnel who were to transfer the cargo to the plane in question. At the same time, the cargo office was informed at its data terminals which airway bills should be sent with the plane. An hour before departure, a message was issued to the load control system and the load men on the ground took over. A telegram was sent to the destination so that cargo personnel there knew what was on board well before the arrival of the plane. In the case of delivery in Copenhagen, the computer issued a message to the cargo agent that the shipment had arrived and where it was stored. Finally, when the agent had filled out customs papers and received the goods the computer compiled the basic information of the airway bill.[176]

CAREX left a number of processing holes in the information flow of cargo. Import, as well as bookings and statistics, not to mention accounting, were lacking. By request of SAS management, a broader cargo computer program started. The contemporary world economic crisis and ongoing internal competition of investments caused a delay once more, however. Furthermore, the Univac computers were short of capacity and SAS was short of qualified analysts and programmers.

Since the mid-1970s, things finally began to happen. A simple statistics system, Cargo Import Export (CAIMEX), had functioned since 1975. In the late-1970s, a statistical sales system, Cargo Sales Statistics System (CASAS) was developed. A cargo booking system followed in 1977. Cargo Booking (CARBOOK) was just an additional booking module to CAREX that could say yes or no on request. In practice, CARBOOK never became important, because of the long-lasting surplus capacity from about 1980.[177]

---

175 SAS, *Data News*, April 1971; SAS, *Yearbooks*, 1977 and 1978.
176 SAS, "Computer Systems", *Data Management*, 1974.
177 SAS, *Data Management*, 26/5 1976; 20/12 1977; June 1982; SAS, *Data News*, Feb. 1976.

CARIN

In 1977/78 resources were concentrated on finishing a new and complete handling system, called Cargo Information (CARIN) that was implemented in late 1978. Unlike CAREX, CARIN covered the whole handling area. It was an online system developed on the U494 and written in assembler language. The system was file-based.[178]

As with all handling, CARIN was based on airway bill recording. CARIN took care of import, export, and transit, and gave status information to agents via teleprinters or data terminals. Just like CAREX, CARIN had a booking module where agents and sales offices could book via data terminals and teleprinters. CARIN gave information on available room and weight for every flight. Based on this information, shipments could be booked until the capacity cushion was reached. CARIN was able to write the cargo manifest, too, a list of all the cargo items in a flight, but not the airway bill. CARIN also told agents when the cargo had arrived at a destination. Finally, CARIN communicated with the departments of invoicing and cargo statistics and the IATA clearing house.

CARIN replaced CAREX, except in Copenhagen where CAREX was connected to CARIN, but it was not actually converted until 1995.

During the 1980s, CARIN spread to all SAS' commercial centers throughout the world, reaching about 60. From local data terminals, sales offices and agents could key in airway bills and the information basis of invoices to the central systems.

CARIN communicated with a number of computer systems, including OPS, LOCS, TTP, and ACS.

Revenue Accounting

International prorating via IATA

Until the early 1970s, most invoicing and prorating were done manually, supported by punched card machines.[179] The flight manifest constituted the foundation of prorating between different airlines and between different flights of the same airline involved in a transport. Manually, a calculation was made for every flight and prorated between airlines. Tracing of missing documents was partly carried out manually, partly by way of punched card

---

178 SAS, *Data News*, March 1978; Jan. and May 1979. Interviews: *Niels Bloch, Jørgen Herz.*
179 *SAS Nytt*, no. 7, 1961. Interview: *Kjell Ivarsson.*

systems. Prorating was a rather slow process until the 1970s. During the 1970s, standards and rules were established and the leading airlines introduced revenue accounting systems to pave the way for computer-based interline prorating via IATA. A Multilateral Proration Agreement and IATA's Clearing House in Geneva with its Interline Revenue Accounting System handled interline prorating. Clearing took place each month. This was established around 1980.[180]

CRAS

In the early 1970s, Data Services and Cargo Accounting started developing a prorating system, called Cargo Revenue Accounting System (CRAS). CRAS was developed in three phases during the 1970s and early 1980s. Phase 1 was a balance module, and phase 2 a kind of tracing (of missing documents) and prorating module. A true balance module and a proper tracing system did not come until phase 3 in the early 1980s. CRAS was developed on IBM machines, first on a 360 and later on a 370. It was a batch system programmed in Cobol.

Since the late 1970s, a number of decentralized systems were introduced for data recording and pre-processing to ease the pressure on the central computer systems and deal with the growing problem of gross and net prices. In 1979, the Cargo Sales Statistics System (CASAS) was implemented to measure sales.

The information flow was as follows. CRAS received flown information from CARIN/CAREX through the flight and transfer manifest. Sold information came to CRAS as documents (i.e., airway bills), and from 1980 from various decentralized electronic systems. CRAS and IATA carried out interline prorating. Finally, sales were posted in SAS' accounting system, ACS.[181]

The Mail Revenue Accounting and Statistics System (MACS/MASAS) was introduced during the 1970s too. It was a small system, which corresponded to the cargo systems CRAS and CASAS.[182]

---

180 *SAS Cargo Manual*, 1993. Interview: *Kjell Ivarsson*.
181 Interview: *Kjell Ivarsson*.
182 SAS, Data Services, *Data Management*, 1978.

Cargo Handling System 1978

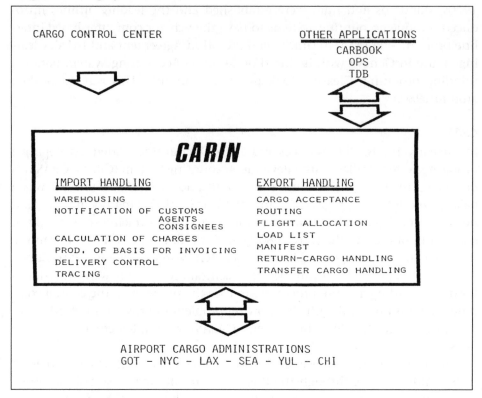

Source: SAS, *Data Services,* 1978.

Station

Until 1980, station was a subsection of the Technical and Operations Department at head office, with regional sections performing the work at airports.

Check-in and load control were basic activities from the beginning of SAS. Check-in and load control of passengers and cargo, including information on luggage, fuel, catering, crew and flight all met at the load sheet. During the 1950s, this was all done manually.

From Zebra to PALCO 1

The first computer-based system on the Zebra machine in 1961 automated some of these functions, namely the writing of a passenger list and, particularly, the load sheet. The Zebra contained the timetable and rules of weight and balance.

The next check-in and load control system was part of the RESCO project on the IBM 1410 that was implemented in 1965. Unlike its predecessor, RES-CO was an integrated system and furthermore, it had some new facilities. The system could present online information on the weight and balance situation much closer to departure than before. Automatic comparison of booked and checked-in passengers enabled SAS to give "last-minute-passengers" a better service. "Remote-controlle" check-in from all of Scandinavia rendered a second check-in superfluous in case of transition in Copenhagen.

With the transition to the U494, the RESCO check-in and load control system was reprogrammed and somewhat extended. Nevertheless, the system continued to be based on the rules of weight and balance and the timetable, including current information on passengers and cargo, while writing the passenger list and the load sheet. LOCS, as it was called, was a file-based system that integrated with RES and OPS (Operations Control System).[183]

In 1978, when the PNR reservations system and data terminals were introduced, LOCS was changed and renamed Passenger Load Control System (PAL-CO). Data terminals replaced the agent sets in the airports. A few years later, PALCO was emulated from the U494 to the U1100. PALCO 1, as it was called later on, had the following improvements:

- Improved communication from station management to personnel
- Automatic order of priority for standby passengers
- Automatic communication from crew system
- Mechanical load control of B747 Combi
- Improved security concerning load control work
- More stations could join PALCO.

Structurally, PALCO 1 did not differ from LOCS. It was still a file-based system, but it automated some more functions.[184]

---

183 See above, *The First Computer System.*
184 SAS, *Data Management,* 26/6 1978, 9/3 1982.

Load Control System 1978

Source: SAS, *Data Services,* 1978.

Operation

Operations Control and Crew made up part of the Technical and Operations Department, until 1980. Regional crew bases were centralized under head office in 1970. The Operations Control Center was a head office function located at Copenhagen Airport.[185]

Operations Control

The 1950s and 1960s
SAS had an Operations Control Center in Copenhagen from its very start, renamed the Movement Control Center by the late 1980s.

The Operations Control Center never closed.[186] Its primary function was to watch the movements of the SAS fleet minute-by-minute. In the 1960s according to the timetable, a SAS plane took off or landed somewhere in the world every fourth minute. If a SAS plane did not notify the Center of its take-off or landing within 15 minutes of the scheduled time, the Center took action. In case of irregularity in the timetable, the Center was responsible for solving the problem. The responsibility for all timetable changes 3 days or more before scheduled operation rested with the Center. It decided on all possible cancellations and changes of aircraft type, timetable, and routing, and could order extra flights. Orders were communicated by telex to all affected SAS stations over the airline's global network.

The Operations Control Center had all current information on the planes: position, traffic situation, crew lists, and periods of service. The Center surveyed the accumulated flying time of each plane between maintenance and periodic checks, according to the rules of the Technical Department and aviation authorities.

While Flight Watch monitored movements of the planes and took care of communications a particular section, Flight Dispatch, prepared the complex intercontinental flight plans. More than 40 specialists handled functions such as: aircraft movement control, traffic scheduling, aircraft scheduling, crew scheduling, weather surveillance, radio contacts, and load control. As a consequence of all these activities, the Operations Control Center communicated with many other SAS functions.

---

185 SAS, *Yearbooks*, 1967 to 1980.
186 SAS, *Yearbook*, 1967.

OPS/TOPRO

Essentially, operations control did not change over the years. The information load grew larger and more complex, however, as speed and number of movements increased. Operating the center was so important, that SAS soon took an interest in developing a computer system.

The first computerized Operation Control System (OPS) was implemented in 1970 on the new U494.[187] For more than fifteen years, OPS formed the basis of operations control.

OPS was a file-based system that changed much throughout the years. In the beginning, it contained just the timetable and recorded and updated current information on the movements of the airplanes. Before long, supporting systems were added, including integration with other systems that used information from OPS. LOCS got technical information on planes and information on crew from OPS. MOPS received information on flying times. Finally, OPS integrated with the crew system, CRU70, the cargo system, CAREX/CARIN, and the system concerned with punctuality, TOPST.[188]

When emulating from the U494 to the U1100 around 1980, OPS was somewhat changed. The revised system, called Traffic Operations Procedure System (TOPRO), included a few new facilities, such as automatic notice of irregularities. Otherwise, it remained unchanged, however.

In general, most activities concerning operations control were automated halfway or done manually in the time of OPS/TOPRO. OPS/TOPRO had no graphic interface (i.e., no visual display of the movements of the planes). It was drawn manually on paper. The timetable, technical information on the planes, and crew plans formed the information foundation of OPS/TOPRO. On the basis of the timetable, the people at the Operations Control Center devised a system with typical weeks drawn into the timetable, and for current changes they used a calendar system.

Daily, the edited current traffic program was outlined on a map hanging on a table in the center. Movement information for the day in question could be written to produce a "traffic state of affairs" at any time. Telegrams poured in all the time, informing of the movements of the planes. The information on takeoff, landing, delays, and so on, was put on the map. Delays of more than two minutes called for potential action and the map was used to see potential rearrangements. Many people participated in carrying out all these processes.[189]

---

187 SAS, *Data Management*, 2/1 1970.
188 SAS, *Data Management*, 24/10 1967; 8/8 1974; 30/11 1978; 4/2 1981; 9/3, June 1982; 14-15/10, 19-20/11 1985. SAS, *Data Services*, 1980, pp. 76-78. SAS, *Yearbooks*, 1967 to 1980.
189 Interview: *Bent Lund*.

Flight Dispatch

The authorities required flight plans on intercontinental routes. Preparation of flight plans was undertaken in the Flight Dispatch function of the Operations Control Center. A flight plan was also a significant kind of support during the flight. Optimizing fuel consumption was part of the flight plan, too, being an important element of airline economy. However, a computer system to support flight planning and fuel optimizing did not come until the 1980s.[190]

Operations Control System 1978

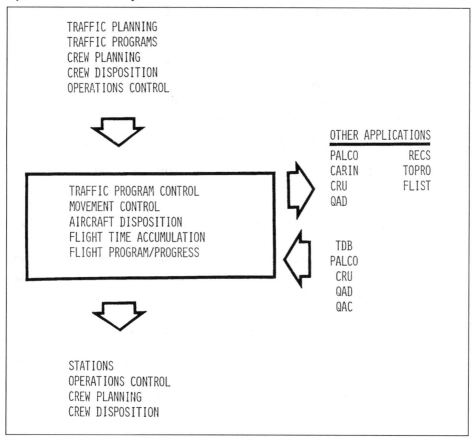

Source: SAS, Data Services, 1978.

---

190 SAS, *Data Management*, 9/10 1980.

Crew

Before CRU70

Basic crew planning took place at head office, while regional functions selected the personnel to fill in the plans and the Operations Control Center
handled current disposition of traffic. Crew covered the two functions: cabin
(cabin attendants) and deck (pilots). From the 1950s, crew planning had three
time perspectives, before Operations took over.

The long-term planning, or master planning, combined flights and crew
for weeks to optimize crew employment, also called pairing. The timetable,
the comprehensive system of rules concerning collective agreements and security regulations, was the basis of pairing. Compared with other airlines, SAS
had a particularly large system of rules. On the one hand, Scandinavian employees were widely organized in unions, and labor relations were much more
regulated by way of collective agreements than in other countries. On the
other hand, SAS had to apply the legislation of three countries.

Medium-term planning, scheduling, provided the plans with personnel.
Five weeks passed from schedule release until the first activities were carried
out (i.e., crew knew their schedule 5 weeks in advance).

Short-term planning dealt with scheduling changes required as a result of
illness or other unplanned events during the last fortnight before the job was
done.

The last couple of days before implementation, the Operation Control Center took over crew "disposal".

Increasing traffic and costs and a downward trend in prices drew attention
to a more rational use of crew. Current re-disposal of crew in case of irregularities was also a problem to be taken care of in a more rational way.

The coming of jet planes encouraged SAS to introduce computer technology on a broader scale. During the 1960s, plans were prepared for a crew planning system to reduce personnel. In 1970, parts of a batch system were finished but were far from covering all the wanted functions.[191] Only after the
implementation of the U494 system, did SAS start to develop a true and more
comprehensive Crew Planning System, called CRU70.

---

191 SAS, *Data Management*, 19-20/6, 21/8 1963, 1/7 1966, 1/7 1968, 1/2 1970.

CRU70

CRU70 was developed during the first half of the 1970s and implemented in 1975-76.[192] It consisted of the following subsections:
CRU Control controlled all crew activities in the short run. It had a batch part and an online part. The system:

- Continuously updated crew data, such as flight times and changes of schedule, and automatically fed crew bookings into the reservations system
- Transmitted historic data concerning crew to a crew statistics system
- Dealt with automatic check-in and checkout of crew
- Provided online access to all crew data.

CRU Statistics gave statistical information on:

- Control and estimated use and efficiency
- Calculating salaries
- Other personnel statistics.

CRU Roster produced crew slings from economic and other point of views.
CRU Assignment automatically created crew scheduling.

As a result, CRU 70 had three central dimensions. The first created crew-slings (i.e., pairing crew with the movements of the flights in the most optimizing way), the second calculated the crew needed, and the third divided production among the available persons. The main purpose of CRU70 was to reduce personnel by increasing information control and planning.

CRU70 included functionality for all three time perspectives of crew planning. Most effort was concentrated on planning at the master level, with less at the schedule and disposition levels.

---

192 SAS, *Data Management*, 18/5 1973, 22/11 1974, 26/5 1976. SAS Data, *Profil*, no. 23, 1990. Interview: *Allan Sørensen.*

Crew Control System 1978

CRU *Crew Control System*

```
CREW PLANNING/SCHEDULING
CREW DISPOSITION
CREW BASES
CREW TRAINING
```

```
LONG-TERM CREW PLANNING
CREW PAIRING/ROSTERING
CREW ASSIGNMENT
14-DAY SCHEDULES
SEAT RESERVATIONS
HOTEL RESERVATIONS
CREW CHECK-IN/CHECK-OUT
DUTY TIME REGISTRATION
QUALIFICATION FOLLOW-UP
```

OTHER APPLICATIONS
```
OPS
QCA
```

```
PNR
```

```
CREW PLANNING/SCHEDULING
CREW DISPOSITION
CREW BASES
CREW TRAINING
```

Source: SAS, Data Services, 1978.

Technical

Until 1980, technical maintenance was an important part of the Technical and Operations Department. Maintenance planning was a head office activity, based on regional workshop bases.[193]

Punched Cards

By and large, the information basis of technical maintenance remained the same through the years. The flight time recordings of the Operations Control Center, the captain's flight log, the workshop's fault recordings, repairs and replacement of components, and the basic information about planes and spare parts provided by aircraft manufacturers produced the information for maintenance planning.

Technical maintenance was a systematic and comprehensive activity. Each airline was programmed for different types of maintenance checks, ranging from walk-around inspection at every ground stop to a thorough overhaul control every one or two years. As a result, maintenance was a highly structured process of labor and information, and soon the growing activities of SAS called for technological support. At least, that was the case from the 1960s.

However, in the early 1950s, SAS had already started fault recording on the basis of flight log and workshop information. Gradually, a system was developed, which remained almost unchanged for the next decade. In the mid-1950s, a punched card system was implemented to handle fault recording, the Failure Follow-up (FFU) system.[194] This covered three activities. It organized flight log information in a uniform and clear way; collected fault recordings of the workshops on replaced components; and analyzed the information collected concerning security, regularity, and economy.

MOPS

Preliminary Studies 1965-1969

In 1965, a working group was formed to start preliminary studies of a computer system for maintenance planning. The studies were based on a new perspective on maintenance.[195]

Up to that time, the objectives of maintenance had mainly been a matter of doing current repairs to make the planes work. A different perspective of

---

193 SAS, *Yearbooks*, 1967 to 1980.
194 SAS, *Data Management*, 1/10 and 22/10 1965.
195 SAS, *Data Management*, 4/10, 13-14/10 1966

maintenance replaced the old mechanical one. In the future, the airplanes and their parts would be made to work in as effective a way as possible. Maintenance should not just repair faults that had occurred. Instead, with regular maintenance checks and investigations based on knowledge of the reliability of many parts of the planes, faults could be anticipated and avoided.

The Operations Control Center and flight logs on the one hand, and the comprehensive controls, measurements, tests, repairs, and replacements by the workshops on the other, produced the information needed to substitute mechanical repairs with forecast maintenance. Maintenance became much more a matter of management rather than operations. This change of view and the fast growing flight activities of SAS called for computer systems to secure reliability and safety when processing the large amount of information, and to reduce costs by preventing an increase in personnel. This was the foundation of the new maintenance system known as Maintenance and Overhaul Planning System (MOPS).

The analytical work of MOPS was started in 1966 by its Steering Committee (Hagrup, Bergner, and Reuterskiöld, among others). MOPS was meant to be a large project that would run for a number of years, until the mid-1970s. The increased computer capacity of SASCO II would make such a big project feasible. Mapping production planning, preparing a master plan, and analyzing the sub-projects took place during the winter of 1966-67, including training of the engineers. It was meant to be coordinated with an on-going reorganization of the workshops. Economic calculations showed the benefits of the new systems.

MOPS intended to produce an all-embracing and integrated computer system to minimize costs of maintenance in the workshops and optimize the employment of the working force and the investments in airplanes and equipment. Full efficiency gains of MOPS would only be obtained if the most important adjoining functions were also computerized, for instance stock management, operations control, traffic planning, and accounting. MOPS would be introduced gradually so that personnel could familiarize themselves with one subsection before introducing another.

While preparing for MOPS, plans for a stock management system, Material Supply and Inventory Control System (MATS), were further advanced.[196] MATS was a simpler project than MOPS, and was planned to be implemented in the three Scandinavian capitals in the late 1960s. MOPS and MATS were to be developed and run on the U494 in Copenhagen.

---

196 See below, *MATS*.

A general plan of MOPS was outlined in 1967 and a master plan the follow-ing year. Master planning in the modern sense of the word had to wait for the coming of IBM in 1972. The 1968 master plan had the following contents:[197]

1. Technical demands and regulations as a foundation of work at the work-shops
2. Work planning
3. Work and reporting at the workshops
4. Collecting, preparing, and presenting statistics of faults and work time
5. Book-keeping and reports of work and material costs
6. Recording the state of affairs for airplanes, engines, and components
7. Long-term planning of airplane and engine maintenance, calculating ca-pacity need of the workshops, simulating alternative solutions
8. Fifty-one functions concerning MOPS and its connections to other systems:
   - TRAPS (traffic program; connected to no. 1 and 7 above)
   - ACS (cost reporting, budget, invoicing; connected to no. 5 above)
   - PERS (time spent on work; connected to no. 4 above)
   - MATS (delivery and demand of material; connected to no. 2 and 3 above).

MOPS 1969-1973

Phase 1 of both MATS and MOPS was implemented in all four Scandinavian workshops in 1969-70. In principle, it was a matter of transferring existing routines or local punched card systems to a common computer system.

In 1970-71, the first two subsystems, MOPS-TO (Technical Order) and MOPS-FFU (Failure Follow-Up), were introduced. They controlled the issuing of technical orders; the degree to which they were implemented on airplanes, engines, and components; and the kind of repair and maintenance work that was done on the planes. In 1972, MOPS-CC (Component Control) was imple-mented. This system watched the movements of components from their first appearance in SAS until they went out of operation. Furthermore, MOPS de-veloped an interface to the accounting system ACS.[198]

In 1970-71, SAS tried to extend the maintenance cooperation with Swissair and KLM in the KSSU group to include computer systems. SAS wanted to share the large development costs with the other airlines but Swissair and KLM turned them down. These airlines seemed to be less sophisticated than SAS in computer development of maintenance, but they did not want to be

---

197 SAS, *Data Management*, 13-14/10 1966; 6/11 1968.
198 SAS, *Data Management*, 11/11 1971; 5/2 1972. SAS, *Yearbooks*, 1970 to 1973.

dominated by the SAS systems and plans and preferred to follow plans of their own.[199]

In 1972 the MOPS project took a new direction when SAS contracted with IBM.

MOPS 1973-1980s

The start of U494 and SASCO II in 1970 almost evicted IBM from SAS. The following year, IBM decided on a market plan for a comeback at SAS. Now, IBM had something to offer, namely, the 370 computer, and especially, the new database system, Information Management System (IMS). The MOPS Steering Committee liked IBM. Previously, a SAS group had been to the USA to study American Airlines (AA), at that time considered the leading airline in computer applications for technical maintenance. AA had also developed its system in cooperation with IBM and accordingly, IBM was found well prepared for a similar project with SAS. AA used modern master planning, and SAS decided to do so, too. The master plan would make management capable of controlling purpose, contents, and costs of the MOPS project, including planning, monitoring, and coordination of the many tasks concerning development and implementation.[200]

All functions and departments of the four workshops and SAS head office were studied, including wishes and ideas of the many people who were interviewed. Sixty-four segments proposed for subsystems were described, analyzed for interdependence, calculated for costs, and put into order of priority for the final master plan that was adopted by the SAS board in the autumn of 1973. The MOPS Steering Committee was authorized to carry out Phase 1, consisting of 26 segments to be developed before 1977/78.[201]

The new IBM MOPS was a databased online system. At the workshops, information could be keyed into data terminals connected with the mainframe system 370. The data registers should contain current information that could be accessed through the data terminals at any time.

Systems development and programming started. The three existing systems on Univac, TO, CC, and FFU for managing orders, faults and components, and a fourth system, Engine Log, controlling replaced engine parts at the Linta workshop in Stockholm, were all converted to the IBM system and implemented in 1974.

---

199 SAS, *Data Management*, 9/10 1970; 26/1 1971.
200 SAS, *Data Management*, 1/12 1972.
201 SAS, *Data Management*, 1/11, 10/11, 12/12 1972; 10/5, 10/10 1973. SAS, MOPS Information, *Data Management*, July 1974. SAS, MOPS Manual, *Data Management*, 1977. Interview: *Mindor Lundström*.

The world economic crisis from 1973 delayed the project, however, and the fulfillment of the whole plan was postponed until 1979/80, later to be further postponed until 1983/84. On the basis of accumulated knowledge, the 26 segments were reorganized into 17 segments, according to the MOPS Master Plan 2 in 1975.[202]

The initial systems aimed at building a database. The first system was the so-called "Reliability System" (RELS), containing all information on irregularities recorded in the flight log. This information was recorded in the database, based on various criteria. According to certain fault indicators, you were able to predict occurrences (i.e., it would be possible to forecast the probable time of a fault in an instrument, so that it could be replaced before the fault actually happened).

The second system was called "Rotables Control" (ROCO) and watched over the current state of all components. ROCO had a tree structure with four levels, from the airplane at the upper level to the smallest components at the lower level. That corresponded to the hierarchical structure of the IMS databases.

The third system was called "Modification Control" (MOCO) and managed all changes during the entire lifetime of each plane. Finally, the "Linta Production System" (LIPS) was used at the Linta workshop to manage the working process of each order compared with the time planned. These four systems were implemented from 1976 to 1978.[203]

The project was delayed several years for lack of economic resources, however. Accordingly, a third Master Plan, MMP 3, was adopted in 1979. The first four systems had created the foundation. The following systems, which were meant to improve on that foundation, were divided into modules that could be implemented separately.[204]

"Bill of Work Aircraft" (BOVAC) was a very large field, seeking to manage the overall division of maintenance jobs between the SAS workshops. The project had to be reduced and this fifth MOPS system, a reduced BOVAC, was finished in the early 1980s. A sixth system, "Maintenance Requirements" (MRS), dealing with the basic demands of maintenance for the Technical Department, was also finished in the early 1980s.

A large cost management system was being prepared, called COST.[205] The first part of it was finished, but it was never really implemented. The follow-

202 SAS, *Data Management*, 29/10 1974; 28/1 1975; 31/5 1976.
203 SAS, *Data Management*, 27/2, 17/10, 11/12 1975; 12/5 1976; 28/11 1979. Interview: *Mindor Lundström*.
204 SAS, *Data Management*, 28/11 1979.
205 SAS, MOPS COST System Overview, *Data Management*, 1978.

ing parts of the system were frozen when the technical area faced reductions during the 1980s. What was left was the interface to ACS. A project for result control within Light Maintenance (RLM) suffered the same fate around the mid-1980s.[206]

The MOPS-project ended with the following six systems: RELS, MOCO, ROCO, LIPS, BOVAC, and MRS.[207]

MATS

The first phase of the Material Supply and Inventory Control System (MATS) was implemented in 1969-70 as an online system on the U494.[208] The system was introduced in all four workshops, replacing local systems. Phase 2 was planned to be a comprehensive project of 30 subsections and was not expected to be finished until the 1980s.

Phase 1 had the following facilities:

- It recorded and updated current transactions of material in and out of the stock
- It specified decision rules for issuing orders of purchase
- It contained a list of all spare parts in the stock
- It managed a number of currently updated online registers.

Thus, Phase 1 formed the backbone of MATS. It was a file system. MATS had an Item-Master file (information on every single spare part), a Supplier-file (information on all suppliers), an Ord-file (recording all SAS orders), and so on.[209] From the early 1970s, MATS interfaced with the Accounting System (ACS).

The development of Phase 2 started in 1971. It was a comprehensive complex of analytical and supporting systems. The project had three parts. The first part was to automate the watching and reporting of orders. The second part would collect information on time and price of supplies to evaluate the quality of suppliers. The third part should contain offers from suppliers.[210]

No part of Phase 2 was ever finished. The only addition to Phase 1 was the introduction of data terminals from the mid-1970s. SAS lacked resources, and MOPS always had first priority.

---

206 SAS, *Data Management*, 31/3 1982; 2/12 1985.
207 SAS, *ROCO, RELS, MOCO, MRS, BOWAC, LIPS System Handbooks*, 1975-1986.
208 SAS, *the MATS System*, 1969.
209 SAS, *Data Management*, 1/7 1986.
210 SAS, *Data Management*, 24/10 1967; 15/4 1971; 6/4 1972; 29/9 1978.

Rotables Control System 1978

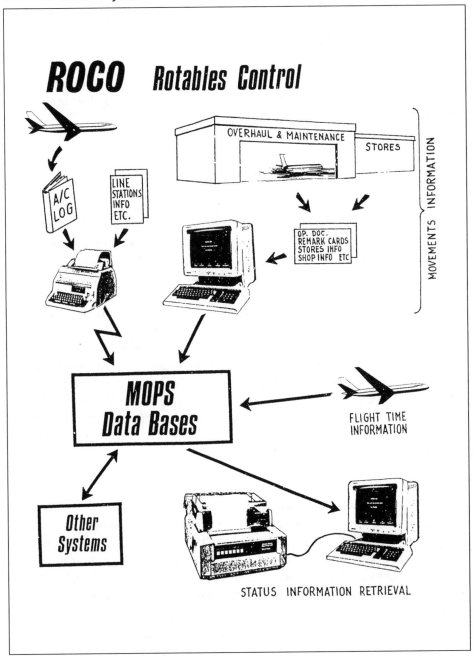

Source: SAS, *Data Services*, 1978.

Accounting

Until 1980, Accounting was part of the Finance Department at head office, with regional offices in the three Scandinavian capitals. The basis of accounting lay in the regions.

Since the mid-1950s, Accounting had used three regionally-based punched card systems, the results of which were combined to form the annual accounts.[211]

ACS

The Univac System

Led by the Finance Department and Data Services, a 16-member project group was formed in 1966 to devise a computer accounting system for the whole of SAS. The system was written in Fortran on the new U494 computer in Copenhagen and implemented in 1967, but was troubled by the technical problems of making the new Univac work. It was a batch system, called Accounting System (ACS).

ACS included chief accounts, res-contra (i.e., files of customers and suppliers), and revenue accounting. Furthermore, it calculated results at cost unit level for the various parts of the SAS organization. ACS was the first Scandinavian system to be built and the main accounts were based on a well-known Swedish account plan, that of "Mekanförbundet". At first, punched cards were used as input, replaced later by tape. Output took the form of tape and paper on monthly lists. Input and output was done in Copenhagen. From 1971, New York had its own system, called North American Division Accounting (NADAC).

The IBM System

Management in Stockholm wanted ACS transferred from Univac to IBM, to make more room for the large online systems on Univac and because of general plans to create an IBM environment. In 1971, a project group was formed to reprogram ACS to IBM, in Cobol. The new system was introduced the following year. During the first years, ACS was operated by DATEMA, a data service company. After the mid-1970s, ACS was transferred to the IBM 370 in SASCO.

---

211 SAS, *Yearbooks*, 1967 to 1980. Interview: *Agneta Peyron-Malmquist* and *Per-Erik Jegbert*.

The functionality of ACS did not change in the conversion from Univac to IBM.[212] A number of advantages were gained by reprogramming, however. First, programming and writing out reports (i.e., the monthly lists, including changes in reporting) became less arduous. Secondly, The IBM system had a more modular base than its predecessor. Last, but not least, the system ran by using parameters. By stating a parameter, you had direct access to the function in question, such as direct access files and sequential files. It was still a batch system based on files, using punched cards as the input medium until the 1980s. Only the Linta engine workshop introduced data terminals.

The structure of ACS was built on so-called "accounting units" which followed the main departments of SAS. For example, 01 was head office, 02 Denmark, 11-89 international offices, and 90-99 subsidiaries. All consolidated in 00. This structure was established in 1972 as a computer system and as a new accounting system. It excluded Linta, which formed a unit of its own. SAS used ACS as the basis for its accounting until the late 1980s.[213]

Personnel

Just like accounting, Personnel had a rather small head office function but strong regional offices. Its main task was salaries. Line departments took care of all other human resources' tasks, including collective agreements and training.

A growing number of personnel and increasing rules in the shape of collective agreements and authority regulations made salary systems more and more complicated. Modern technology was needed to ensure correct payments. In the mid-1950s, each of the three regional offices had already developed a punched card system of its own. National differences were clearly shown in matters of personnel, as a consequence of three separate labor market systems.[214]

The punched card systems worked until the early 1970s when three batch computer systems were implemented, on the Univac 494 in Denmark and the IBM 360 in Norway and Sweden.[215]

---

212 SAS, *ACS System Handbok (system handbook)*, 1973/1977.
213 Interview: *Agneta Peyron-Malmquist* and *Per-Erik Jegbert*.
214 SAS, *Data Management*, 2/1 1970. Interview: *Torsten Bergner*.
215 SAS, *Data Management*, 9/10 1987. SAS, *PERS/PINS Rutinhandbok*, 1983. Interview: *Lars Nilsson*.

The First IT Paradigm: Beginnings

The first general structure of IT and applications of the 1960s and 1970s created modal forms of technology and ways of doing things. This might be called the first IT paradigm, or at least the first part of the paradigm, with the second and final part coming in the 1980s. The set of production means that were installed established the system of central computer and communications operation that came to dominate information processing until the 1990s. Mainframes and central operating systems handled all information processing and storing. From the mid-1970s, terminals were added for input and output operation. Systems development worked according to a fixed flow of steps and processes from the initial idea to final implementation. Much "handicraft" work was needed in systems development. As information systems spread throughout the organization, systems developers became a central and powerful group within SAS. IT production was a proprietary system made to fit the particular needs of SAS.

The general structure and strategy of SAS was not changed as a consequence of IT developments in these decades. The IT department was just added to the other departments as a new functional activity and organization. A great part of this new group of professionals was internally recruited and trained, although an increasing number of people were externally recruited. As a separate department it developed a technology culture of its own, resulting in quite a strong identity. In some ways this was similar to any other department of SAS, and for that matter any corporation. The IT department was part of a general IT culture, too, marked by the revolutionary character of this new technology and the greater flow of IT people between corporate IT departments than by people from different professional cultures.

The IT applications of SAS were all created in-house, just as any other corporation did in these days. While mainframe computers formed one part of the first IT paradigm, in-house application development formed the other part. Users of the organization depended completely on the knowledge of programmers and systems developers in producing and using information systems. Normally, users took part in specifying the requirements of new systems and revisions of existing ones. By the late 1970s, this was even codified as a rule by SAS, in a so-called Data Agreement. Furthermore, users came in contact with central computers by way of terminals from the mid-1970s. However, computing was always done centrally by IT professionals on mainframe computers.

Application systems did either batch or online processing. Accounting systems, and other systems that did not depend on constantly updated information, normally used the less complicated batch technique, whereas on-line systems were introduced in areas such as reservations and technical maintenance, which required immediate updating. Online systems grew in numbers and importance, whereas batch systems might already be considered legacy systems by the late 1970s.

A final aspect of the beginnings of the first IT paradigm was the organization principle of systems. In the beginning, they were all file systems (i.e., they were organized pretty much in the same way as the manual files of old archive systems). Data access was not easy in such systems. From the early 1970s, file systems were complemented by database systems, structuring the way data was organized in the information systems. Databases were organized according to the so-called hierarchical principle (i.e., in separate tables). That made data access much easier, at least within the individual system, whereas easy cross-system access and processing was left for future relational databases.

By 1980, the value chain of activities forming the SAS business was largely affected by computer-based applications. Reservations, check-in, and load control could not work without IT applications, and even ticketing, revenue and accounting were automated. Computer information systems had been installed for traffic planning, cargo handling, accounting, crew planning, technical maintenance planning, and salaries. Increasingly, these systems integrated to combine the value chain of SAS. It must be noted, however, that only part of these processes of labor and information were automated. Furthermore, systems affected only levels of operation and functional planning.

III · THE 1980s
TRANSITION

Environment

Business Development

From the early 1970s to the early 1980s, hyperinflation, high unemployment, and low economic growth ravaged Western countries.[216] Furthermore, Western corporations suffered from lack of competitiveness towards expanding Japanese corporations. Then slowly things began to change. Economic growth and the rise of productivity remained low, but deflation replaced inflation and oil prices started a permanent process of decline. The power of the OPEC cartel was broken as Western countries developed new oil resources.

Having solved the problem of hyperinflation, governments turned to the fundamental problem of regaining competitiveness in their leading corporations. Towards the mid-1980s, radical changes in government policies appeared. The U.S. government indicated the line of development by deregulating the telecommunication and airline sectors during the late 1970s. American deregulations continued during the 1980s, and West European governments and the EEC also joined the move towards liberalization of their economies. The EEC announcement in 1985 of an open European market by 1992 symbolized the changing tides, or rather the preparations for change. During the late 1980s, the Uruguay Round of the General Agreement on Tariffs and Trade (GATT) prepared for a new global setting of liberal trade conditions that was carried out during the following decade. Governments planned for economic recovery of business by creating more markets and more competition.

A second new trend indicated radical changes, too. Since the mid-1980s, all Western governments had organized and invested in R & D projects to accelerate development and the use of new technologies, particularly information technology, but also such fields as biotechnology and materials technology. Information technology was the superior and crucial technology, however, because radical changes of the other technologies depended on advanced IT applications. Focusing on technologies, indicated revolutionary changes in the field of R & D, too. R & D was traditionally considered a separate department of scientists and engineers developing new products. IT and

---

216 Maddison, *Monitoring the World Economy*, pp. 78-87. UN, *World Investment Report 1993*, pp. 91-110. Kaplinsky, R. (1984), *Automation. The Technology and Society* (London: Longman, 1984), pp. 2-35. OECD (1989), New Technologies (Paris: OECD). Porter, *The Competitive Advantage of Nations*.

innovative trends started a process of breaking down old barriers of science and technology and creating new combinations of knowledge, based not on traditions and institutions but on related knowledge from different fields. Radically improved business applications of scientifically based knowledge by way of new technologies, that was what was needed and looked for. Still, these developments did not surpass a preparatory stage.

Liberalization and application of new technologies prepared for an economic policy that substituted protection towards national industries with a liberal framework of innovative measures. Corporations, not governments, created competitiveness and rising productivity. That was the new and emerging approach. On the one hand, the tools of recovery were more markets and competition created by governmental policies, and on the other, new technologies deployed by private business.

Western corporations began to prepare for a comeback, too. For almost a century these large firms and their followers had dominated the domestic and international economy. They had built organizational capabilities that enabled firms to overcome wars, economic crises, and challenger companies. Their inability to recover from the crisis of the 1970s gradually made Western management realize that more fundamental measures had to be taken.

According to Fordist principles, which still ruled business organizations, the ways to improve competitiveness were by decreasing costs and, if necessary, marketing new products. Forced by Japanese success on Western markets, leading American corporations of the most challenged industries, the automobile and electronic industries, such as GM and GE, started to strike back, followed by West European leaders in the same sectors. Billions of dollars were invested in computer technology to create automated factories, and more market-oriented products were also being developed.

Basically, these investments did not change the structure of organizations and the philosophy of management. Everything happened within the framework of Fordism. One exception, however, was a growing understanding of the need to adjust to the needs of markets and customers instead of the traditional means of marketing that tried to make people accept what they were offered. Whereas computer technology investments were meant to increase productivity, they also created preconditions for more flexible means of production. Without such automated tools of production, the reorganization and recovery of the next decade would never have happened. By the late 1980s, however, management found that heavy investments in new technology did not bring the rise of productivity and competitiveness they looked for. This seeming paradox made management understand, finally, that Fordism had to be replaced by a different and more flexible kind of organization to make the potentials of new technologies come true.

By the late 1980s, Jack Welch, the CEO of GE, stated the problem this way. "At the beginning of the decade, we saw two challenges ahead of us, one external and one internal. Externally, we faced a world economy that would be characterized by slower growth, with stronger global competitors going after a smaller piece of the pie. Internally, our challenge was even bigger. We had to find a way to combine the power, resources, and reach of a large company with the hunger, agility, spirit, and fire of a small one".[217] The CEO of ABB put it this way: "ABB is an organization with three internal contradictions. We want to be global and local, big and small, and radically decentralized with centralized reporting and control. If we resolve those contradictions, we create real organizational advantage".[218] An organization was looked for that combined the strengths of the bureaucratic hierarchy with the strengths of an entrepreneurial organization, managing both speed and complexity. Making such new forms of organization come true would require a new IT approach, too.

Expanding manufacturers of the automobile and electronic industries were such large and vital parts of Western economy that they greatly affected all other sectors. Computer technology vendors were heavily influenced by increased demands for new and more sophisticated digital technology, including the core technology of microprocessors. During the second half of the 1980s, such American companies as Intel and Motorola began to overcome the setbacks of Japanese competition. The rapidly increasing capacity of microprocessors was crucial to increased deployment of new technologies.

Signs of recovery were seen from the mid-1980s. Foreign direct investments increased rapidly between the dominating Triad of the world economy: USA, West Europe, and Japan. American companies invaded Western Europe, while West European companies upgraded their investments in the USA. Japanese corporations invested aggressively in both economic centers, while keeping most Western capital out of Japan by means of sophisticated institutional and cultural trade barriers. Still, Japanese multinational firms profited from a lead in productivity as a result of flexible ways of organizing production.

By the late 1980s, Western corporations still had not caught-up with the productivity level of Japan, and Fordism kept on dominating organizations. However, the great organizational capabilities of American giants, in particular, had been set in motion and begun the process of upgrading. And the enormous innovative potential of American IT firms and business cultures pre-

---

217 Applegate, "Managing in an Information Age", p. 17.
218 Applegate, "Managing in an Information Age", p. 17. See also, Womack, J. P, Jones, D. T., Roos, D. (1990), *The Machine that Changed the World* (New York: Rawson Associates).

pared to reap the profits of a changing economy, followed by West European companies in a secondary place.

In manufacturing, American industries stopped dominating the home market and many foreign markets. From the mid-1970s to the late 1980s, large industrial sectors were ousted by an invasion of foreign companies and products. In one sense, this reflected a state of crisis and lack of profitability. Otherwise, it indicated a move of investments towards more profitable and knowledgeable fields of business, including business services and IT. American capital interests sensed a change in the air.

A restructuring of the American economy was slowly being prepared, to be followed by Western Europe and other advanced regions of the world. Generally speaking, this development inaugurated a new international division of labor and business. The industrial economies started to move from being fundamentally national economies to economies focused on international relations.

The Aircraft Industry

By 1980, the aircraft industry had reached a temporary climax. The second airplane generation of the 1970s marked the end of a dominating technological trend. Since about 1950, the leading aircraft manufacturers of Boeing and McDonnell Douglas produced several airplane generations that continuously upgraded the technological capacity in terms of speed and volume. This development reached its peak with the huge wide-body planes of the 1970s, such as the Boeing 747 and DC10. These supertankers of the air matched the mass-production strategy of postwar airlines.

The airline crisis of the late 1970s and early 1980s brought this technological race to an end. Airlines stopped buying new planes and changed their strategies to serve specific segments of the market, particularly businessmen. For financial reasons, and because there was little market for used planes, airlines just renovated their existing fleets.

During the second half the 1980s, however, expanding air traffic and years of continuous profit made airlines invest in new planes. Aircraft manufacturers had prepared for a third jet generation during the slump of the first half of the 1980s, and by the late 1980s, Boeing, McDouglas, and Airbus launched their new aircraft.[219]

---

219 Selling, *Legend and Legacy. The Story of Boeing and its People*. WWW: Boeing homepage. 'McDonnell Douglas History'. Ceruzzi, *Beyond the Limits: Flight Enters the Computer Age*.

The third generation of aircraft, which was much improved during the next decade, fitted the new market-oriented strategies of the airlines. Speed did not change, having reached the limits of technology, and volume was flexibly adapted to the different airline markets. Real changes occurred in fuel consumption, noise, exhaust, and control technology. For environmental reasons, engines developed to save fuel and reduce the external influences of air traffic, a trend that was much reinforced during the 1990s.

Finally, aircraft manufacturers introduced the age of digital technology "for real". Although the second generation of jet planes had introduced integrated circuits, it was the emerging third generation that made computers the core technology of aircraft. From the late 1980s, these planes were gradually being turned into flying computers, a trend that escalated during the 1990s.

The Airlines Industry

In 1981, SAS launched its successful businessman's airline strategy. SAS management reorganized its activities and resources to focus on servicing one specific customer group, the frequently traveling and full-price paying businessman. Instead of competing with costs and price reductions, SAS moved 180 degrees to become a market-driven company. The successful businessman's strategy made all leading airlines of the world rush to copy it. As a result, a crisis-ridden industry regained its lost profitability and kept it until 1990. It started a revolutionizing development within the airlines industry that even conduced to a change of attitude within the business world, in general.

By the mid-1980s, all leading airlines had reached the same level of competitiveness, and new upgrading strategies were introduced.[220] Using strong distribution systems, such as SABRE of American Airlines, large American airlines began to invade Europe in order to expand their markets. Even some Asian airlines focused more on Europe. That invasion forced the European airlines to cooperate and to adopt a policy of open distribution systems, leading to the two large distribution systems of AMADEUS and GALILEO by the early 1990s. Furthermore, the EEC decided on a policy of gradual liberalization of air transportation, starting in the late 1980s and to be fulfilled during the 1990s. As a

---

220 OECD (1993), *International Air Transport* (Paris: OECD), pp. 21-73. IATA, *World Air Transport Statistics*, 1980 to 1990. The American development since deregulation in 1978 is covered in: Morrison, S. A., and Winston, C. (1995), *The Evolution of the Airline Industry* (Washington, D. C.: The Brookings Institute). For Europe see: Dienel and Lyth, *Flying the Flag*. The growing FDI and liberalization in the airlines industry since the mid-1980s is discussed and listed in UN, *World Investment Report 1993*, pp. 79-82.

consequence, European airlines prepared for a near future of open markets.

The American development influenced European airlines in other ways, too. The deregulation of American air transport made concentration around a few large corporations even stronger, while many smaller domestic airlines were reduced to commuter traffic to and from traffic centers of the leading airlines. Some European airlines thought that a similar concentration would happen in Europe when the open market was introduced. Consequently, medium-sized companies such as SAS started to prepare for future mergers, while larger airlines took other measures or just waited to see what would happen, leaving smaller airlines to an uncertain future.

Furthermore, leading European and Asian airlines strengthened their grasp of central hubs by starting to feed these hubs from a larger periphery. As a result, small regional airlines or commuter companies of the large airlines were developed or linked to create increasing feeder lines to traffic centers, in a so-called hubs-and-spoke system. In Europe, such centers or hubs included Frankfurt, Paris, London, Amsterdam, and Copenhagen. The airports of these hubs were all being modernized and upgraded to attract more passengers and traffic in order to remain in a leading position.

Finally, accelerating foreign direct investments throughout the world and increasing international competition caused all leading airlines to create global traffic systems to serve their most important group of customers, the businessmen. As mergers turned out not to be an option because of governmental ownership, cooperation and purchase of shares were deployed to improve global services in a number of fields, including hotels.

Nevertheless, by the late 1980s, European air traffic worked in a regulated world, keeping prices high and allowing airlines to reap an extraordinary profit by way of their strategy of targeting businessmen.

World Statistics of Passenger Scheduled Services[221]

	1980	1985	1990
Total no of passengers, mill.	645	786	1027
Share international passengers, %	25.0	24.3	26.9
Share USA, %	45.6	47.2	45.2
Share Europe, %	20.0	19.5	21.1
Share Asia, %	16.5	17.7	20.4
- share Japan, %	7.0	6.5	7.4
Share, ROW, %	17.9	15.6	13.4

Source: UN, Statistical Yearbook.

Passenger Statistics of International Airlines[222]

	1980	1985	1990
Air Canada	13.0	10.9	10.3
American Airlines	25.7	41.2	73.2
Continental Airlines	-	16.0	35.2
Delta Airlines	-	-	65.9
Eastern Airlines	39.5	41.8	-
Pan American	-	13.0	17.5
Trans World Airlines	20.6	21.1	24.5
United Airlines	32.8	38.2	57.8
Varig	4.4	4.8	6.9
Air France	10.9	12.5	15.7
Alitalia	7.3	12.7	18.2
British Airways	16.1	16.9	25.2
Iberia	13.8	13.1	16.2
KLM	3.8	4.8	6.9
Lufthansa	13.0	14.6	21.6
SAS	8.3	10.9	14.9
Swissair	6.0	6.2	7.8
Thai Airways	-	-	8.2
Japan Air Lines	13.3	14.6	23.5
Qantas Airways	2.0	2.5	4.2

Source: IATA, World Air Transport Statistics.

---

221 World figures still exclude the Soviet bloc and China. Soviet Aeroflot remained the largest airline of the world, transporting 104 million passengers in 1980, 112 million in 1985 and 137 million in 1990 (UN, Statistical Yearbooks).

222 In million passengers.

The IT Industry and Applications

The arrival of the PC in 1981 made practically all writers on the 1980s IT development call this decade the age of distribution and end-user computing.[223] By the late 1980s, millions of PCs were spread throughout corporations in the industrialized world, providing thousands of people with hands-on computing experience that would finally erode the dominance of central mainframes. Applications grew beyond operational activities, too, as managers began to see the opportunities and become involved in the deployment of IT. Low entry cost and knowledgeable user groups of managers and professionals spurred a rapid IT development that was also fueled by pent-up demand for service among users.

From the mid-1980s, PCs began to be linked in LANs, and new packaged software eased and expanded the usability of PCs. As a result, IT strategies changed to stress end-user computing and networking and to produce systems for improved planning and decision making, including back-office word processing and internal communication systems. IT was increasingly seen as a tool to increase competitiveness by other means than just replacing personnel and increasing work productivity. Increasingly, business-run IT considerations challenged the production-oriented strategies of past decades. Even systems development was being offered new tools, such as CASE or other 4GLs to speed up the slow developments of 3GLs.

That is the picture presented. It is true that millions of PCs were introduced and that strategies changed to stress the importance of business-driven computer applications. During the 1980s, business functions were also being continuously automated, including management activities. As for the rest, it is not true. The PCs were there, some new tools and software were there, and certainly the visions of the infinite potential of the computer inspired anybody who looked for change. Realities were different, however. Something new was in the air, the computer industry, the telecommunications industry, the business world in general, and governments all prepared for change and longed for change, too. Things were in a stage of transition, but new structures had not yet materialized.

Throughout the 1980s, business functions were automated to a much higher degree than before, by way of new systems. These systems had not much to do with PCs. They were practically all mainframe systems, based on

---

223 Cortada, *Information Technology as Business History*, pp. 81-99, 176-180. Zoboff, B. (1988), *In the Age of the Smart Machine* (Oxford: Heinemann), is more attentive to the changing character of information systems.

hierarchical database management systems, such as the IBM IMS. Further-more, they were developed in-house by data department professionals, or as an exception, developed as customized systems by software consulting com-panies. No "mission-critical" system, to use a modern term, was bought in the marketplace. For one thing, the package software industry was still rather small and undeveloped by the late 1980s. By the early-1990s, 9/10 of all exist-ing software applications were estimated to be in-house products leaving only 1/10 for a commercialized packaged software market.[224]

That the greater part of applications were in-house developments and therefore not visible in the marketplace, may account for this rather distorted picture of the 1980s.[225] Most software tools, such as operating systems and database management systems, were developed and sold by hardware vend-ors, while applications were in-house developments. Outside these leading software sectors, a small industry of packaged software emerged. Some pack-aged software products were developed for PCs, including word processing, probably the most widespread product, spreadsheets for accounting, and some fancy systems for advanced workstations, including CAD and simula-tion. Some packaged software aimed at mainframe systems, including deci-sion support systems. For example, the R/2 of German SAP was meant for mainframes, and only in the early 1990s, did SAP refocus on PC packaged software.

Considering these facts, it is no wonder that IBM kept on focusing on the mainframe market. Mainframes, operating systems (OS), and database man-agement systems (DBMSs) were sold in great numbers. And their utility rose as IBM and other vendors benefited from the increased capacity of micropro-cessors. Microsoft grew by way of its DOS that became almost a standard PC operating system. But although DOS and PCs were sold in millions during the 1980s, their usability in mainstream business was rather limited. They were not linked to the databases of mainframes, except for entering and presenting data (i.e., they worked pretty much like terminals). True information process-ing on PCs took place in isolated islands throughout the organization, par-ticularly in back-office word processing, including LANs of PCs.

Two technology barriers reduced the use of PCs. One, microprocessor cap-

---

224 IDC (1996), *1996 Worldwide Software Review and Forecast*, p. 10.
225 Various aspects of the 1980s are covered in: OECD (1997), *Information Technology Outlook* (Paris: OECD). Forester, T. (1993), *Silicon Samurai: How Japan Conquered the World's IT Industry* (Oxford: Blackwell). Lebow, I (1995), *Information Highways and Byways. From the Telegraph to the 21st Century* (New York: IEEE Press). OECD (1991), *Convergence between Communications Technologies* (Paris: OECD). Generally, the 1980s are poorly analyzed and understood.

acity was too small and increased too slowly during the 1980s to handle anything but simple package software. Only numbers and letters could be processed, whereas other communicative means, such as pictures, movies, and
talk were excluded, except for very advanced and expensive workstations.
Two, communications were still based on analog telephone systems. All large
multi-national corporations had created global telephone systems, and just
like their computers these communications systems were dedicated. Consequently, each business unit formed its own technological island. Although
satellites spread around the globe and telephone companies worked on digitalizing and expanding the capacity of their networks, this was all in a phase
of preparation. Digital wide area networks were yet to come. An overall electronic infrastructure did not appear in the 1980s, neither did open standards
of any considerable size. An IT industry, in the strict sense of this term (i.e.,
integrating computers and telecommunications), had to wait for the following decade.

A third barrier towards technological transformation of end-user computing might be attributed to the attitudes and practices of IT departments. IT
managers, and particularly computer professionals, disliked PCs and fought to
keep them out of their corporations. PCs posed a threat to the established IT
organizations, their mainframe applications, and the considerable power of
these people, because so much depended on their technical expertise. By the
late-1980s, it was clear, however, that they had lost the battle and business
management took the lead in technology. They were ordered to support what
came to be the client/server revolution that moved the central point of computing from in-house development to purchased packaged software for PCs,
although not making the existing mainframe systems superfluous. This
caused the end of craftsmanship as the basis of computer professionals, to be
replaced by industrialized packaged software traded in the marketplace. But
by 1990 this was yet to come.[226]

The nature of this clash of interests between computer professionals and
users of the late-1980s might be illustrated by some Danish observations.[227]
The basic characteristics of Danish computer professionals were a strong tra-
dition of craftsmanship and unionism, few computer scientists, and a high
concentration of computer people in large organizations, in addition to a high
level of "job-hopping" and high demand for people with computer skills.

---

226 Cortada, *Information Technology as Business History*, p. 234.
227 Borum, F., et al (1992), *Social Dynamics of the IT Field: The Case of Denmark* (Berlin:
    De Gruyter), pp. 191-223, and passim. It is also telling that Friedman in his book
    on systems development still saw no structural changes in IT departments by late
    1980s, see Friedman, *Computer Systems Development*, pp. 271-305.

Craftsmanship was the cornerstone of the strategies and culture of Danish computer people. Unionism worked to protect the working conditions and continuation of craftsmanship and to produce a barrier towards management interference in these fundamentals. In addition, subcultures of various departments and groups developed to make the computer people of IT departments create some kind of fortress around their towers of technology. The basics of this culture was the fact that computers had come to mean life and death to large organizations, and that computer professionals were the only people capable of handling this technology. This position and culture developed and strengthened during the 1960s, 1970s, and 1980s, because it fitted well into the Fordist paradigm of organization and business.

When business management enforced its will by the late 1980s and started a radical process of reorganization, turmoil followed, including conflicts between computer professionals on the one hand and end users and business management on the other. Next, a process of reorientation and re-qualification started to prepare for the transformation of the following decade.

Airlines IT

During the 1980s, IBM and Univac[228] kept on being the dominating vendors of computer technology to the airlines of the world. Still, communications technology, based on analog techniques, was part of the telephone complex of tele-companies and vendors of tele-equipment. Although tele-companies had started their long-term project of digitalizing the networks, convergence of computer and communications technology awaited the 1990s to be fulfilled. The only exception was the small emerging market of LANs for PCs.

The dominant IBM and Univac hardware and systems software of airlines were still based on mainframes.[229] PCs spread in rising numbers, but this did not affect the core transaction systems. They were linked to 'dumb' terminals and PCs mainly did word processing in isolated 'islands'. Systems developers and programmers dominated personnel and costs of the IT departments, producing and maintaining in-house the airlines' software applications. The IT department's share of total airlines costs averaged about 2.5%, with SAS at a somewhat higher level.

---

228 Renamed Sperry and finally Unisys.
229 *Airlines Greybook*, 1985.

Airlines IT Cost Share of Total 1983[230]

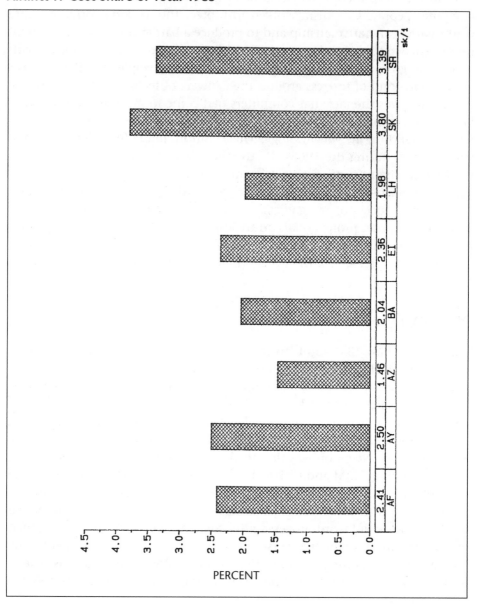

Source: Airlines Greybook, 1985.

230 AF=Air France, AY=Finnair, AZ=Alitalia, BA=British Airways, EI=Aer Lingus, LH=Lufthansa, SK=SAS, SA=Swissair.

Computer Systems in Airlines 1983[231]

TAP
No	
IBM	3/158 — 1
	3033 — 1 a)
	2
	2 a) lease-1

Swissair
IBM	360-20
	360-158
	3033
	3083 B

SAS
IBM	370-115-2 — 2
	3081-624 — 1
	4341-2 — 1
SPERRY	1100/84 — 3
	DCP-3760 — 4
	DCP-40 — 3
	1
AMDAHL	5860 — 1
	1
COLLINS	C-System — 3
PDP	11/05 — 24

Lufthansa
IBM	S/7 — 2
	370-138 — 2
	3081 K — 2
SPERRY	494
	1100/82
	1100/83
	1100/61
AMDAHL	470-V/7
	5850

KLM
IBM	3031 — 2
	3033 — 1
	3081

Iberia
IBM	4341/M02 — 1
	4341/L01 — 2
SPERRY	494 — 3
	1100/84 — 1
	1100/82 — 1
	DCP-3760 — 14
	DCP-40 — 2

Finnair
IBM	4341-2 — 1
	S/7
SPERRY	1100/62
BASF	7/65 — 2

Brit. Airways
IBM	3084 — 1
AMDAHL	470-V6 — 1
	470-V8
DEC	2
KL 10	2
KI 10	2
NAS	3
AS/9060	2
AS/9000	
ICL	1906S — 1

Alitalia
IBM	3033 — 1
	3083/B — 1
	3083/J — 1
AMDAHL	V7/B — 1
	1
	1

Air France
IBM	3032 — 3
	3033U
	3081
SPERRY	1100-44
	1100-60
	1100-84

Aer Lingus
IBM	3031

Source: Airlines Greybook, 1985.

---

231 By 1987, SAS estimated reservation systems of IBM and Unisys to cover 70 % and 10 % of the world market, respectively: SAS, *Data Management,* 2/3 1987.

SABRE

The deregulation of the American airlines business in 1978, reinforced the trend to transfer the reservations function from the airlines' own offices to travel agencies. Price competition caused the carriers to multiply the variety of fares and frequency with which they were adjusted and as passenger inquiries changed from simple seat availability to price comparison-shopping, interaction with travel agents and schedules and fares of the carriers became indispensable. In this competitive environment only the reservations systems of the largest carriers could participate.[232] United Airlines' (UA) APOLLO and particularly, American Airlines' (AA) SABRE had created industry-wide distribution systems that covered the whole of the USA. SABRE became a "cash cow" for AA and a tool of competitive advantage. It received revenue from every booking made by airlines subscribing to SABRE, putting AA in front of the screen of travel agencies.

During the 1980s, several airlines, the Civil Aeronautics Board (CAB, the American airlines association), and the US Justice Department tried to take anti-trust measures towards the anti-competitive practices of SABRE and Apollo. No anti-trust law was enforced against these powerful systems, however, but instead CAB drafted a set of rules in 1984 to eliminate display bias and discriminatory fees. Although some discriminatory practices were eliminated, during the 1980s SABRE and APOLLO's distribution systems did not change into open systems and kept on favoring their parent companies.

By the mid-1980s, SABRE was enhanced with Travelocity, which linked travel agents to SABRE. Furthermore, SABRE developed a sophisticated yield management system that enabled AA to maximize its revenues. The world of reservations systems was in a stage of transition during the 1980s. SABRE and AA targeted the large European market and compelled the European airlines to prepare for international and open systems of distribution.[233] During the 1980s, all other airline functions and IT systems went through a process of increased automation, too.

British Airways

During the 1980s, the IT department of British Airways (BA) prepared for radical changes. Its main activity continued to be the maintenance and develop-

---

232 McKenney, *Waves of Change*, pp. 97-136.
233 Generally on reservations systems, see Copeland, D., and McKenney, J. (1988), "Airline Reservations: Lessons from History", in *MIS Quarterly*, 12, no. 3, pp. 353-372.

ment of its mainframe applications and more functions were continuously being automated based on database technology. From the mid-1980s, a few thousand PCs spread throughout the organization and introduced end-user computing, particularly in word processing and decision support. By then the IT strategy of BA changed to become an integrated part of a global market-oriented airline business.

The BA reservation system, BABS, was fully developed by the late 1970s. During the 1980s, several trends were added to BA's IT portfolio.[234]

First, a build-up of IBM/IMS database systems occurred throughout the decade. This was an important IT development, although not a very illustrious one.[235]

Second, the number of fares and fare changes exploded. During the 1960s, a fundamental marketing change evolved among the international airlines. At the beginning of this period, there was a simple product structure based on class of travel, each class of travel having a clear distinction in seating comfort and standards of service. The fare structure was straightforward, based on class, time of travel (seasonably variable) and of course distance.

However, the advent of the jumbo jet and the growth in the package tour market created the necessity for a more flexible approach. With the surplus capacity created by the switch to the B747 in the early 1970s, the problem for the airlines was not in handling peak seasonable loads, but in filling the aircraft in the off-peak periods. Thus began fare discounting and promoting to flourish in the 1970s and erode the traditional concept of class travel.

During the late 1970s and early 1980s, a new online fare system was developed. It replaced the batch support system with a large database for real-time work, providing fares for up to 32 segments. This fare system was sold to other airlines, including Qantas, Delta, KLM, and Nippon. In the mid-1980s, marketing success and the impact of deregulation in the USA caused an explosion of fares. By then, the BA database had grown to 5 million fares and the requirements of neutral central reservations systems would increase the fare database to 20 million. Accordingly, a new system was called for by the turn of the decade.

Third, yield management was established. The airline crisis around 1980, and the introduction of the SAS concept of the businessmen' airline in 1981, made it crucial to BA to optimize its revenue. Furthermore, it was clear that in view of the widely differing yield being obtained, the current system of controlling seat inventory was inadequate. Consequently, a yield management

---

234 Harris, *BABS, BEACON, and BOADICEA*, pp. 285-338.
235 It hardly caught the attention of the historian of BA IT.

system was developed during the early 1980s. The fares and yield systems were fundamental parts of BA's new business approach and inaugurated a growing market and business orientation by the IT department.

Fourth, open distribution systems appeared. The original reservations systems were developed to provide terminals for the airline's own telephone sales agents. But in the UK a major part of the airline's sales effort was carried out through travel agents, rather than through direct selling. It was therefore desirable to enable the major travel agents to interface with them. In 1976, a company named Travicom was formed. It was jointly owned by UK airlines (BA and Caledonian), providers (Videcom, and ICL), and agents, who all formed a users association. Its aim was to develop a Multi-access System for Travel Agents, with costs being shared between airlines and agents.

The system went live in 1977, and all major airlines flying to the UK became members. It became a huge success with travel agents, and the number of sets connected increased into hundreds and then thousands of sets. The concept caught on overseas too. The agents started to ask for more than basic airline bookings. That included integration of business and leisure travels, and facilities for the back office to help them control their business. During the 1980s, some of these facilities were introduced. With the take over of British Caledonian in 1987, BA took 100% control of Travicom, making it a vital element of the BA distribution strategy in the UK.

The growing demand for open travel services had allowed in the competition. American Airlines' SABRE system, currently the largest terminal network in the world, had become dominant in the travel industry in the USA, and was keen to extend to Europe. Its arrival in the UK was to have a profound impact on airline thinking about travel agency support.

The arrival of the SABRE agency system brought the European airline community to realize that control of the means of distribution was fundamental for their business. Individually, they could not withstand the onslaught of the American giant. Their response was to create two European systems: AMADEUS, the Unisys group (Lufthansa, Air France, Sabena, and SAS) and GALILEO, the IBM group (led by BA, KLM and Swissair). GALILEO represented a major strategic step for BA and provided three major advantages: an effective worldwide distribution channel; a major global player by influencing the way the electronic channel developed; and bargaining power for negotiations with major US and international carriers. GALILEO was also an outstanding example of the way in which, during the 1980s, IT in BA came out of the back room to become a major part of the airline's global business strategy.

Fifth, distributed computing spread by way of thousands of terminals and

PCs used to enter and present data, and for some local pre-processing of book-keeping activities to reduce pressure on the general ledger.

Office automation was the most popular area of PC applications during the 1980s – or rather the only one. Word processing became popular in back-office and customer relations, followed by internal electronic communication, since the mid-1980s. They were local systems, however, and a company-wide system did not appear until the early 1990s. Word processing worked first as a stand-alone system, which was then linked in local area networks (LANs), outside the basic mainframe applications. Users became acquainted with computing and pressed for the introduction of real end-user computing, however. From the mid-1980s, follow-up and planning systems were added to mainframe activities.

Sixth, during the 1980s, the business reorientation of BA pressed for a change of strategy in the way IT was used.

In 1983, Stanford Research Institute (SRI) consultants carried out a review of the IT department. Their report stressed the technical expertise and skills of the staff and its awareness of technology trends. SRI felt that there was too big a divide between users, management, and IT professionals, however, and that the IT department lacked business understanding.

A seminal paper by Peter Keen of the IT department followed the SRI line of thinking even more closely, considering fundamental changes of business and IT in the field of airlines. BA had strong IT systems for management and control, but lacked a clear set of business criteria for developing the next generation of systems. He highlighted two main categories of issues: those surrounding electronic distribution, and those concerned with obtaining and managing customer data. He identified a number of American examples where aggressive use of technology had produced significant competitive advantage. The threat of their extension to Europe was very real in his view, and the airline could not delay. He recommended enterprise data modeling to create a company-wide IT architecture for the business of the nineties. What Keen did was to introduce the strategic IT and business approach.

Through 1985-86 the effect of the SRI report and the Keen analysis began to make an impact, but the top manager, John Watson, found the change had not penetrated sufficiently into the fabric of the organization, and wanted the process of change to go much further.

In 1986 a study group in the IT department was given the task of developing a new technical architecture. A year later in 1987, IBM announced its Systems Application Architecture (SAA) that developed the same theme. In 1988, a new set of principles for the technical architecture appeared, with immense ramifications for the department and the airline:

- Data should be treated as a shared corporate resource, accessible to all authorized users
- Processors, whether mainframe, mini, or micro should interact cooperatively on a peer-to-peer basis
- Data communications network should be treated as a transparent utility and should offer no constraints on data or program flow
- User interface via terminals should be consistent in its presentation and mode of interaction
- Software should aim to be portable across the network.

The development of an IT business strategy was to prove a more difficult endeavor, however. It started in 1985 with setting up a business systems unit, reorganized in 1987 into business centers, and was strategically fulfilled towards 1990. New business-oriented managers were appointed and a major program for reeducation was undertaken to realize a culture change. Thereafter, the evolution of IT long-term plans proceeded in close cooperation with those of the airline. A strategic perspective was developed for IT during the early 1990s. For the IT department, market conditions were introduced which made changes inevitable.

A user/customer education program was enforced to qualify the airline managers for involvement in managing IT, which, in turn, enabled them to make it benefit the airline's commercial success. This went on from the late 1980s and was an ambitious attempt to change the whole airline culture. As a result, a much wider ownership of the IT issues emerged within the airline.[236]

In 1990, a semi-independent division was set up, Speedwing Technologies, trading primarily with the external marketplace. That included sales of software and services.

By the early 1990s, the BA IT staff surpassed two thousand and its central computer operation did 500 million instructions per second. The worldwide network embraced 40,000 BA terminals and PCs, and over 200,000 external terminals. The total IT investment was estimated at 500 million pounds with an annual budget of 200 million pounds, making it one of the largest computer enterprises in the UK, indeed in Europe.

---

236 As we shall se below, SAS went through a similar and simultanious process.

SAS Business

Planes and Routes

For SAS, the crisis of 1979 to 1981 brought to an end a decade-long strategy of mass-production. In 1981, when Jan Carlzon was appointed the new president, a revolutionary change of strategy occurred.[237] To regain profitability, SAS was completely reformed. Instead of low pricing, the whole company turned its focus on the businessman who flew frequently and paid full price for his ticket. A market-oriented business emerged.

Based on a thorough analysis of the corporation, the airline industry and market, SAS' traffic program was rearranged. Unprofitable routes were closed down, nonstop and frequent services were introduced, and punctuality tightened to meet the demands of businessmen. Retraining programs stressed the importance of having service-minded frontline personnel and aggressive marketing targeted the core segment of the businessman. No longer would discount and full-price passengers sit side-by-side to be equally served. The latter were placed in the front section of the plane and given special service, while the back of the plane and standard service were reserved for the former group. From now on, discount pricing became part of a marginal strategy to utilize surplus capacity without requiring additional resources.

Unlike the pre-1980 period, however, the aircraft fleet was not renewed. Management had the ageing DC-9 planes freshened up with a modern external and internal design that matched the new corporate identity of the businessman's airline. SAS simply could not afford investments in new airplanes and as the aircraft manufactures had not presented any new technology, no true benefits would spring from buying new planes.

Previously, intercontinental routes and cargo were the "flagships" of the SAS routes. Since 1980, both had lost ground because they could not be made sufficiently profitable to support the SAS business. Several intercontinental and freight routes were closed down and these two sectors much reduced. The SAS core business moved from intercontinental routes and cargo to the European and Scandinavian markets.

SAS EuroClass was the new basic product for the reformed airline that clearly told of its intentions to capture the European market. While fierce

---

237 SAS, *Annual Reports*, 1980 to 1985.

price competition on the intercontinental market made it very hard to create profitable routes, the regulated European market promised much better prospects. From the early 1980s, the European routes became its main source of profit and for some years, SAS even gained an edge over all other European airlines. Scandinavian and domestic routes improved income, too, as a result of a growing share of full-price paying passengers.

The new program became a tremendous success. SAS' load factor increased and most important, its share of full-price paying passengers grew considerably, making SAS a very profitable airline. Indeed, SAS was so successful that the whole airlines industry rushed to copy their businessman strategy.

During the first half of the 1980s, SAS profits and revenue kept on growing. When the world economy started to expand again towards the mid-1980s, SAS traffic grew, too. In order to meet the demands, SAS had to buy more airplanes and increase personnel. Furthermore, the businessman strategy soon lost its unique character in the market and several new trends in air traffic pressed SAS to take new initiatives to stay profitable.

Traffic patterns began to change from the mid-1980s.[238] To expand their feeding lines to traffic centers and to keep on developing these crucial airports, large European airlines built commuter businesses. These included KLM around Amsterdam, Lufthansa around Frankfurt, and British Airways around London. Such a hub-and-spoke system, first developed in the USA, gradually changed the traffic patterns of Europe. It began to threaten the traffic foundation of SAS, too, because centers of neighboring airlines extended their feeding lines into Scandinavia.

To meet this challenge and secure its traffic basis, SAS started to build an expanding commuter business for Scandinavia and Northern Europe, primarily around Copenhagen. At the same time, Copenhagen Airport was enlarged and modernized, including extended attractions of tax-free sales, to help retain its position as a main European gateway. To remain an independent and competitive airline, it was crucial to SAS to build a strong Scandinavian traffic system.

Increasingly, information and distribution systems equalized the importance of traffic systems, too. Until the early 1980s, information and distribution systems were integrated parts of the monopoly of airlines within their respective regions. Then a process of separating reservations and distribution began, to which SAS also had to adapt. Scandinavian Multi-Access Reservations for Travel Agents (SMART) was formed as an independent Scandinavian distributor of travels.

---

238 SAS, *Annual Reports*, 1985 to 1990.

The large American airlines with their enormous combined reservations and distribution systems, such as SABRE of American Airlines, started to focus on the European market, too. To meet this threat and challenge, the leading European airlines joined in two projects to produce the common distribution systems, AMADEUS and GALILEO. Along with Lufthansa, Air France and Iberia, SAS took part in developing AMADEUS during the late 1980s and early 1990s.

In general, the development of distribution mirrored a growing commercialization of information. New information products kept on being marketed, such as credit cards that were being turned into a big business in the USA. SAS had to follow suit and bought Diners Club Nordic.

Open competition was on its way in Europe, including air transport. In the mid-1980s, the EEC decided on a program for an open internal market by 1992 and SAS started preparing for open competition. A strategic perspective for European airlines was presented that learned much from the American experience. Deregulation in the USA had caused a stronger concentration among airlines around a few traffic centers, with a number of smaller airlines feeding the centers with passengers from the periphery, and SAS management thought that the same concentration would happen in Europe. As a consequence, SAS introduced the slogan "One of five in 1995", indicating that the 22 European airlines would merge into just five, and that SAS wanted to be part of one of those five leading airlines in 1995. This scenario dominated SAS management until 1993.

Alone, the Scandinavian traffic basis was insufficient to make SAS one of the five lead companies. Therefore, SAS management wanted to organize a strategic cooperation or merger with other airlines to gain the needed strength and traffic foundation for future existence. During the second half of the 1980s and the early 1990s, SAS management was increasingly preoccupied with building the foundation for being "one of five in 1995". To prepare for that future, SAS had to create gateways elsewhere in Europe and on the other continents to produce a global traffic system. Through buying shares and through cooperation, SAS managed to establish an outline of a global traffic system, which included Swissair, Finnair, and British Holdings in Europe, Continental Airlines and Canadian Airlines in North America, LanChile in South America, and Thai Airways and Nippon Airlines in Asia.

Since the mid-1980s, SAS had felt the pressure of growing competition from other European airlines and the giant American Airlines, United Airlines, and Delta Airlines of the USA, including some rapidly expanding Asian carriers, such as Singapore Airlines and Cathay Pacific. The competitive edge of the early 1980s, stemming from the introduction of the concept of the businessman's airline, had been lost to other airlines that copied and improved on the SAS concept. To gain and even improve its position as the lead-ing businessman's airline, SAS had to try and make another great leap for-ward. Therefore, SAS stepped up integration and efficiency between the Com-mercial Division and the producing divisions. In addition, SAS introduced a new concept of "the global travel company" to include all subsidiaries of the Group.

The idea of the travel company was to utilize the synergy effect of the many units of the SAS Group. All businesses in the group were to focus on the businessman, in the same way as the airline did. While the airline just handled air transport, SAS wanted to extend its services by way of the group to all parts of the travel chain, from beginning to end. Furthermore, SAS marketed the travel company product throughout all Europe, turning gradually into a Euro-pean company.

As part of the travel company strategy, SAS concentrated much effort on hotels and in 1989 the company bought a large share of Inter-Continental Hotels. Including its other hotels, the purpose of this expansion was to be able to offer hotel facilities to businessmen at all important destinations through-out the world. Each of the various business units of the Group that entered into this widened businessman's airline strategy, still had to make its living as a business of its own. Actually, the subsidiaries were being reinforced to create stronger business units, such as SAS Leisure for travel agencies and charter, and SAS Service Partner for catering and restaurants. The original strategy of decentralized profit centers remained unchanged.

The SAS Group aimed at being the best alternative to the frequently traveling businessman, and at helping to create better business for the travel-er. Travel services were considered a value creating process to the customer. SAS took the same view of cargo. Cargo was not just a matter of transporta-tion but should be seen as part of the logistics of the customer-company. A total value-adding concept was a new way of looking at the business world and the basis of competitiveness that was radically to alter the world economy of the next decade. The previous strategy and philosophy of a mass-produc-ing and supply-driven corporation was being turned upside down. Competi-tiveness was no longer based only on low costs and prices, but more on the capability of the company to create value for its customers as an integrated part of their business activities. SAS management had captured the new emerging business trends, although they were not so easily put into practice.

The new SAS strategy was intended to secure the survival of the company in a future that promised radical changes. A scenario of a few large airlines competing openly with global travel systems dominated the strategic efforts of SAS management.

The Organization

SAS Statistics[239]

	1980	1985	1990
SAS Group			
Revenue/bill. SEK	9.3	19.8	31.9
Personnel/000	24.1	29.7	40.8
SAS Airline			
Revenue/bill. SEK	7.3	15.4	21.6
% Traffic of Group	68	64	57
% Passenger of traffic	81	86	91
% Cargo of traffic	16	13	7
Passengers/mill.	8.4	10.7	15.0
Personnel/000	16.8	18.8	22.2
% Traffic and Sales	19	31	48
% Crew	20	18	22
% Maintenance	24	21	19
% Others	36	30	11

Source: SAS, Annual Reports. IATA, World Air Transport Statistics.

The businessman strategy was linked to a new kind of organization.[240] Market orientation became the key word of all activities, based on the idea of decentralized responsibility for economic results. SAS was reorganized into divisions. The Commercial Division planned and marketed the products and was responsible for the traffic program and the profitability of the routes. The

---

239 The figures show the continuous spreading of SAS revenue from traffic to an increasing number of income sources of the SAS Group. The market orientation of SAS was seen in the increasing share of traffic and sales personnel, mainly at the expense of the back office (others). The figures of 1980 are not quite comparable with 1985 and 1990 because of some regrouping, but the trend seems clear.

240 SAS, Annual Reports, 1980 to 1985. See also, Carlzon, J. (1985), Riv pyramiderne ned! En bog om chefen, lederen og det nye menneske (Copenhagen; Gyldendal) (tear down the pyramids).

route sectors consisted of Domestic Routes in Scandinavia, European Routes, Intercontinental Routes, and Air Cargo. Each route made up a business unit of its own. The route sectors were the profit centers of SAS. All other divisions were cost centers, supplying the products needed by the route sectors. The producing divisions were managed by way of cost and service levels.

The Traffic Division took care of most of the customer service programs in airports and on board the planes. The Operations Division was in charge of crew and traffic control. The Technical Division was responsible for technical maintenance, while the Administrative Services Division undertook account-ing, salaries, real estate, and procurement. Finally, The Data Services Division handled computer operations, communications, and systems development. In many cases, the producing divisions sold services externally to other airline companies, too, such as check-in in the airports.

A market economy approach was introduced in internal relations, too. This was the most difficult part to carry out, however, as the market ruled only in-directly. To make sure that the new strategy materialized, a new controller function was introduced into all result units. Just like the airline, it was stressed that all other parts of the SAS Group should be profitable business units of their own, such as hotels, catering and restaurants, and leisure.

Moving from a philosophy of production to that of the market also re-quired a mental revolution for the SAS people. A comprehensive retraining programmed was introduced, and management strove to make employees de-velop a new way of thinking about their company, a so-called "business-minded culture". The importance of the frontline personnel in meeting the customers – "the moment of truth" – was stressed, as was the need for every-body to act according to the demand of customers, and not according to the needs of the organization.

This "culture revolution", as it was called, only succeeded partially. A re-direction from technical operations, which had been of the utmost import-ance during the previous decades, to delivery of customer value caused many controversies and conflicts as a consequence of a clash of two cultures. The change only came gradually, also because corporate cultures were embedded in broader national cultures.

The new strategy included stronger efforts to increase the efficiency of the organization and the quality of the products. The great success of the businessman's airline of the early 1980s made it difficult to effect the planned growth of productivity and the cultural change of the organization. And gen-erally, the production-oriented bureaucracy did not die easily. For decades it had been the body and soul of SAS. Since the mid-1980s, intensified compe-tition had made management attack the problems in a more determined way, however. The new policy was called "the second wave".

Increased efficiency and integration between all the links and units of the company were now on top of the agenda.[241] The producing divisions that caused most problems were pressed to reduce costs and in addition, were forced to live up to the best standards in the market. In some cases, management outsourced units that did not fulfil the goals of efficiency or income and made them exist on the premises of the market. As a consequence, tax-free sales and cash management became business units of their own in 1988, operating as SAS Trading and SAS Finance. The pressure to increase efficiency was particularly strong in SAS because of the high level of costs in Scandinavia.

The structural foundation of SAS, laid out in the early 1980s, did not change.[242] It was just the market orientation that was being enforced more directly on all units of the SAS Group. Quality measures of security, punctuality, and the like, were introduced, seeking to link the working processes to the content of the products, and not to the needs of bureaucracy. Local responsibility for profit increased and management systems were developed to plan and follow-up on performance. Horizontal ways of organizing labor were tested to soften the domineering vertical structure of the bureaucracy, too, but these remained at a premature stage.

Some corporate divisions simply had to adjust their activities to a diminished demand, such as the Technical Division where internal heavy maintenance and external maintenance jobs for other airlines declined considerably from the mid-1980s. Furthermore, Linta, the SAS motor workshop, was outsourced in 1988 to be a company of its own.

The producing divisions never fully lived up to the goals of increased efficiency and although the pressure to do so grew during the late 1980s, it did not result in drastic measures to overcome inadequate results or to direct resistance within the organization. Once more, solid profitability crossed radical organizational changes. A successful organization did not change easily. Furthermore, no other leading airline, or for that matter any Western corporation, had carried out any fundamental transformation of its organization, during the 1980s. The Gulf Crisis should alter that.

---

241 SAS, *Annual Reports*, 1985 to 1990.
242 This is seen from, *The SAS Airline Business Model*, that covered the main functions and processes of the business, see Figure.

SAS Group Organization 1982[243]

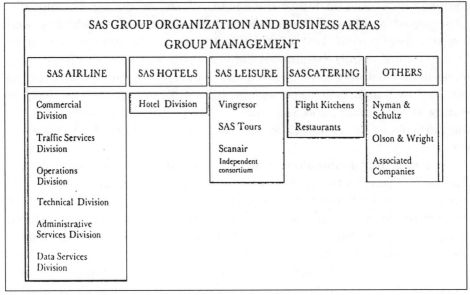

Source: SAS, *Annual Report,* 1982-83.

SAS Group Organization 1988

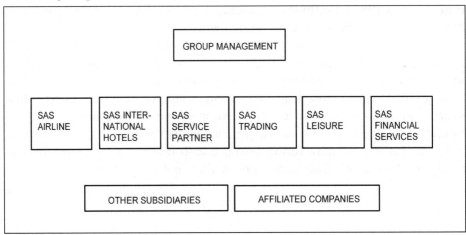

Source: SAS, *Annual Report,* 1988.

---

243 This organizational structure remained unchanged during the 1980s except for the
Administrative Services Division, which was reorganized into the Business Services Division in 1985. The Commuter Operations Department was added in 1985
and the Data and Distribution Division in 1988 (see SAS, *Annual Reports*).

SAS Airline Business Model 1988

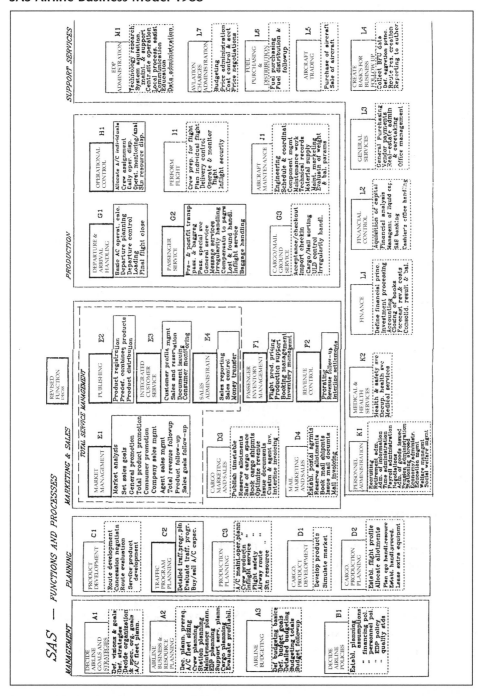

Source: SAS, "Airline Business Model", *Data Management.*

SAS IT

SAS IT Statistics[244]

	1980	1985	1990
SAS			
IT costs in mill. SEK	300	700	1,400
% of total	4.1	4.5	6.5
Personnel	50	100	200
SAS Data			
Revenue in mill. SEK	250	600	800
% of SAS total	83	85	57
Personnel	500	700	800
Annual mill. transactions	150	500	1,200
Terminals	7,000	17,000	25,000
PCs	-	300	2,000

Sources: SAS, *V-81, V-85, ARP-90.* SAS, *Data Management,* 11/5-1981; 14/5-1985; 26/6-1986. "SAS' strategi för dataverksamheten" (SAS' IT strategi), in *Nordisk DATANytt,* 1, 1985, pp. 10-15. SDD, *Vi er her (1989)* (we are here).

1980-1985 New IT Strategy and Organization

SAS Data Division

By the turn of the year 1980/81, the new chief executive, Jan Carlzon, and his new strategy had swept through the SAS Airline organization like a storm. It hit Data Services right away.

By January 1 1981, Data Services, the IT department, was transferred into a corporate-like company within the SAS group of Associated Activities and re-named SAS Data.[245] A Steering Committee was formed to take a "board-like" function. It was led by the leader of Associated Activities, Frede A. Eriksen, and

---

244 Figures are rounded.
245 SAS, *Data Management,* 1/4, 19/5, 24/6 1981.

included the manager of Data Services, T. Korsvold. Korsvold remained in charge of the new SAS Data until the early summer 1981, when he was simply dismissed and put into a minor position until pensioned off a year later. Radical and non-bureaucratic initiatives for change topped the agenda of SAS' new leadership.

During the spring of 1981, the Steering Committee accepted the new SAS Data goals. A small knowledgeable group of people, including T. Bergner, C. Ekström, A. Hansen, and an external consultant, transformed new ideas into a strategy plan. According to this plan, SAS business would be responsible for systems development, including contents, investments, and results. Consulting, analysis, and resources might be obtained from SAS Data at various stages. SAS internal customers were allowed to use and buy development resources, computers, and operation by external vendors. In the case of external vendors, SAS Data must always be asked for its bid first, except for strategic systems, such as reservations and check-in that were excluded from having external vendors. SAS Data could sell its services to external airlines as long as this did not conflict with the needs and wishes of SAS system owners. External services would be priced according to market prices, whereas a discount should be allowed to internal customers. These principles guided SAS Data during the following decade.

According to the new strategic plan, SAS Data, like its predecessor, should be able to cover the whole field of services ranging from the creation of an idea at one end to operation and maintenance of systems at the other. Furthermore, as a consequence of changing customer demands and new technologies, SAS Data would have to cultivate new areas, such as distributed computing, user computing, and office automation. It was predicted that microcomputers would increase in importance at the expense of mainframes. Such developments would make the Telcon communication network even more crucial to SAS and SAS Data.

A few days after these overall and concrete goals were presented, the Enator consultant submitted his proposal for a new organization to the Steering Committee.[246] It was a rather provocative proposal, inspired by the radical winds that swept SAS in those days. He proposed simply turning SAS Data into a consulting business, similar to Enator and other consulting firms, led by a business-minded manager. Furthermore, SAS Data should hire externally a new group of organizational and business-minded people to run the business for SAS and other customers to come. As a consequence, system developers and programmers would be pushed into the background to perform operative activities only, under the guidance of these consultants. The consultants

---

246 SAS, *Data Management*, 18/5 1981

should take over responsibility of customer-relations, including overall plan-ning of development projects, pre-studies as a basis for customer decisions, and the continuity of development projects.

Suggesting that the IT dominating groups of programmers and systems analysts should be subordinated to a new group of business-oriented consul-tants with no professional knowledge of computing hit right into the heart of SAS Data and its people. By that time it was unacceptable and also unrealistic to relegate some of the most powerful groups of SAS employees into a second-ary position.

Promptly, SAS Data management and employees reacted with total rejec-tion. It was stated that the capability of SAS Data lay in its functional compe-tence and the functional systems of SAS. While stressing the weak side of SAS Data (i.e., its lack of market orientation), the proposal of the consultant left out this fundamental and strong basis of SAS Data. Consequently, the Steer-ing Committee did not adopt the proposal and left it to a new manager to take care of the organizational development of SAS Data.

In SAS Data turmoil ruled during the spring and summer of 1981, until Curt Ekström was installed as a provisional leader, at a stormy meeting in Co-penhagen in September 1981.[247]

During the following months, reorganization of SAS Data began. An advis-ory SAS Data Development Group was formed to make employees and unions a part of the decision-making process – a procedure that was also applied by other SAS divisions.[248]

By November 1981, it was decided to organize SAS Data as a separate re-sult and market unit under the SAS Consortium, but still as a subsidiary that reported to the chief of Associated Companies. SAS remained its primary mar-ket, and resources and competence would continue to be built around the needs of SAS. SAS Data was defined as a supplier of IT services, but SAS could not leave tasks to external vendors without first letting SAS Data put forward a proposal. Any external contract had to agree with the general technological principles laid down by SAS Data, and strategic systems (such as reservations and check-in) could not be handed over to external companies.

By January 1 1982, C. Ekström was made permanent executive of SAS Data. He was asked by the Steering Committee to produce a three-year plan for the computer needs of the divisions.[249]

This three-year plan laid out a new SAS Data strategy that supported the businessman's airline strategy. SAS Data was to cooperate closely with its cus-

247 SAS, Data Management, 15/9, 16/9, 18/9-1981. Interview: Torsten Berger.
248 SAS, "First Minutes of Meeting", Data Management, 21/10 1981.
249 SAS, V-82.

tomers, fulfilling the role of a supplier to SAS. Computer processing must be user-friendly and data considered a strategic resource. SAS Data resources should be designed according to the needs of SAS, and new techniques and methods introduced to improve service quality. Computer operations were to aim at maintaining an appropriate number of operating environments based on standards of operating systems and equipment, allowing for a flexible adjustment of capacity.

The objectives of the communications strategy were to reinforce surveillance of operations, preserve an all-terminal concept, and use industry standards in order to make the user feel that he communicated directly with his application. The development strategy had a number of goals. The concept of "information resource management" should be introduced and data models employed. The strategy aimed at a reduced number of development environments and whenever profitable, software packets should be used.

Generally, a move towards distributed data processing and information centers was intended to put the user in front. At an early stage of systems development, users or customers should be a basic part of the development process. Large systems had to be divided into modules that were developed independently and project management reinforced.

To carry out these plans, production capacity must be extended. Just to cover an annual performance growth of 20% would require a continuous expansion of IT capacity and to create a market-oriented organization, competence and efficiency of personnel would have to be upgraded, too. Equivalent to other SAS divisions, SAS Data had to produce a 20 % increase its productivity by 1984.

During the strategic and organizational activities of 1982, the importance of SAS Data to SAS Airline became obvious and by October, it was made a division alongside the other airline divisions it served.[250]

By the early 1980s, SAS Data employed more than 500 people, 60% in Copenhagen, 30% in Stockholm, 6% in Oslo, and 4% abroad (mostly in New York). Annual revenue reached approximately 300 million SEK, of which operation and communication comprised 50%, development and maintenance 45%, and administration 5%. Ninety-three percent of the SAS Data revenue came from SAS Airline, 7% from SAS subsidiaries, while external sales were almost nonexistent (0.3%). By then, almost all SAS IT costs went to SAS Data.[251]

The new SAS Data was based on two principles of organization: market and result units on the one hand and production cost centers on the other.[252]

---

250 SAS, *Data Management*, 8/3, 11/5 1982. SAS, *Annual Report*, 1982/83.
251 SAS, *V-81* and *V-82*. See also in the text, *SAS IT Statistics*.
252 SAS, *Data Management*, 30/11 1981. *V-81*.

Market relations used four organizational sub-markets and units, primarily SAS Airline divisions, with revenues in brackets: The Commercial Division (150 million SEK), Traffic Services Division and Operations Division (60 million), Technical Division (35 million), and the Administrative Division and Associate Companies (40 million). About 250 people were allocated to these four markets, based on several expert groups for each of SAS' large systems, and similar groups to take care of operation and communication.

Two of the market units were located in Stockholm (Technical and Administrative Divisions). Thereby, management indicated that it wanted to reduce the IT concentration on Copenhagen. Central operation of SAS computer systems and communication system remained in Copenhagen, however. Oslo and Stockholm had just started to build mainframe centers on Tandem, but mainly they dealt with domestic computing on IBM systems. From 1980, Oslo and Stockholm in particular, expanded relatively compared with Copenhagen.

Production systems were cost centers, divided into computer operation, communications, and technology and methods, which dealt with tools and planning of information, databases, development tools and so on. Finally, three staff units were established, namely a controller (like any other part of the Consortium) to develop the new management systems of the businessman's airline strategy, including decentralized responsibility for result, a second unit for personnel, and a third one for security.

By and large, this organizational structure remained unchanged until 1987-88.

During 1982, managers of market and production units were installed and began to work out the new organization and its strategy.[253]

During 1983, SAS Data further developed its management systems, including an economic steering system, pricing of products, and individual market and production plans. To increase strategic planning efforts, a chief of all market units and one of all production units were also installed. Furthermore, a new staff department of long-term technological and strategic planning was set up. Finally, SAS and Enator formed a new company, Scanator, hoping to sell SAS computer systems on the external market[254]

However, the new strategy had not been rooted in the organization and management had to push harder to create the change that was looked for. To strengthen its position and confidence with customers, SAS Data management focused on four targets: improved stability of operation, improved productivity, improved management of SAS Data and SAS relations, and increased distributed and end-user computing.[255]

---

253 SAS, *Data Management*, 8/3 and 11/5 1982.
254 SAS, *Data Management*, 10/1, 15/1, 7/3, 25/4, 1/8 1983.
255 SAS, *Data Management*, 9/12 1983.

Such initiatives were needed. Operation stability failed during the early- and mid-1980s and SAS customers and users expressed a general dissatisfaction with SAS Data, which was also fueled by prolonged development of new systems.[256]

SAS Data Organization 1983

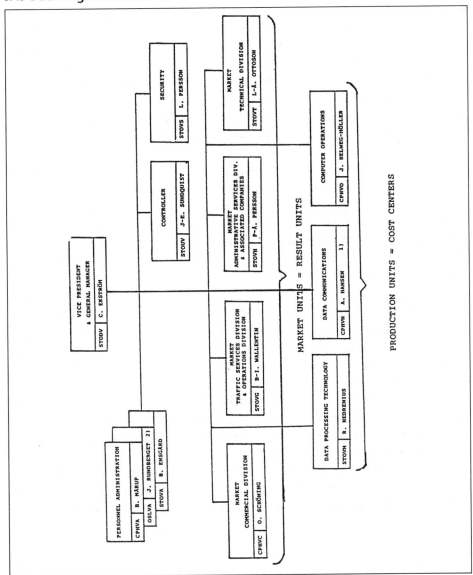

Source: SAS, Data Management, 1/12 1983.

---

256 SAS, *Data Management, 26/8 1983.*

SAS IT Plan

By 1983-84, the other divisions and headquarters were sufficiently reorganized and established to start developing IT strategies of their own. So far, the divisions had done little to fulfil their new role as a driving force of computer development. It was business as usual, leaving computer technology to SAS Data, although smaller groups of computer professionals appeared in most divisions. To meet growing competition, SAS was preparing a more aggressive strategy that implied the growing importance of IT. In cooperation with the other divisions, SAS Data presented a proposal for SAS' first data policy in early 1984. Data division plans that were being developed at the same time were integrated into this overall strategy anchored at division and corporate level. The SAS "Information Processing Strategy Plan" was agreed upon by spring 1984 and communicated throughout the organization during the following months.[257]

By 1984, the objective of information processing by SAS was to get "relevant information to the right individual at the right time to give SAS a competitive advantage".[258] "The employees are SAS' most important asset! Information is the individual's tool and is therefore the second most important asset. Individuals with information create innovation, three cornerstones in SAS' future progress and success". As a consequence, "SAS will offensively monitor, influence and take advantage of advances in information technology to provide the customers with excellence in service, give all employees the possibility of taking more responsibility, improve resource utilization, improve control and rationalization of business".

Consequently, the strategic direction of IT would change. "Information processing activities shall better support SAS' business development. Every individual shall be enabled to access computerized data and manipulate it. DP (Data Processing) will gradually be transferred to the various airline divisions. Coordination of information processing activities is performed by a strong central DP-unit (SAS Data). SAS' DP activities will be further adapted to industry standards. DP vulnerability will be reduced by stricter security measures and risk dispersion". To implement this strategic change, SAS would have to invest approximately 200 MSEK in IT during the second half of the 1980s. As a matter of fact, investments of this period turned out to be much more.

---

257 SAS, *Data Management*, Feb. 1984, 10/4 1984. Ekström, C. (1985), "SAS' strategi för dataverksamheten" (SAS' IT strategy), in *Nordisk DATANytt*, 1, pp. 10-15.
258 SAS Group, "Information Processing Strategy", *Data Management*, 1984.

At the same time as SAS Data was developing its strategy and an informa-tion-processing strategy for SAS Airline, SAS hired an external management consultant firm to review the SAS Group from the point of view of an infor-mation-processing strategy. SAS prepared an extension of its businessman's airline strategy to include all affiliated companies of the SAS Group in a new total travel concept. This strategy would require an increased rate of innov-ation of travel products and customer services. IT would play a critical role in supporting and marketing new customer services, because the airline was highly dependent upon its computer information systems for efficient oper-tions and looked to new IT to increase competitiveness. Accordingly, SAS management was faced with the challenge of integrating IT with the intro-duction of new services to realize its business objectives. The external report specifically addressed these issues. Furthermore, the strategy of a total travel concept required necessary changes for more appropriate integration of SAS Data and SAS.

In the report, the IT function was seen to consist of three generic compon-ents: applications systems development and maintenance, communications network facilities, and computers and associated peripheral equipment and operating systems software. This should be a primary frame of reference for SAS management for monitoring and controlling the IT function.

Similar to application systems development, it was recommended that a steering committee be installed for overall control, supported by prioritized master plans within each division and affiliate, and a regular review of new application project proposals and the mix of applications being proposed. This review would help ensure that development work was in concert with SAS business strategies.

Furthermore, the applications development process should be strength-ened by changing the relationship between SAS Data and the business units, strengthening the role of business unit managers in the process of defining application requirements, and clarifying the proper role of users in the devel-opment process. The report did not recommend a genuine transfer of systems developers and programmers to the user side, only that some system analysts should be transferred to take care of preliminary studies and to ensure a closer realignment of the two sides before, during, and after systems development. It had to be taken into consideration, too, that they represented different cul-tures and that SAS Data would have to uphold its competence.

The SAS communications network was critical to worldwide airline oper-ations and the need to interface with other passenger reservation systems and communications networks. Two factors impacted the network strategy. One was the growth in volume of the airline's business. The second was the need to accommodate new communication requirements resulting from SAS' total travel business strategy. The report found SAS Data's short-term communications strategy appropriate, but recommended that a long-term strategy study, involving airline management, be initiated. In addition, it was recommended that more emphasis be placed on network control and monitoring facilities, particularly because of the mixed environment of Sperry, IBM, and Tandem mainframe computers and a variety of terminal types.

The airline operations were dependent upon the large mainframe computers in Copenhagen. Effective computer capacity planning was required to maintain terminal response and an overall service level, accommodating the growth in volume of transactions from existing and new applications and the increased use of computers for management planning and control. The concept of distributed processing to handle the airline's needs was supported, but the report recommended a long-term capacity project to prepare for the next decade.

Concerning additional changes and innovation, the report looked at new technologies, user computing, and office automation. Other airlines were introducing competitive technology (e.g., American Airlines passenger self-service terminal). For SAS to maintain its competitive advantage in marketing and customer services, its was recommended that it increased monitoring, evaluating, and piloting new IT. User computing with PCs and network terminals would add the flexibility needed to meet the demands of decentralized management that traditional centralized systems lacked. An implementation strategy by SAS Data was recommended for user computing. The Administrative Division and SAS Data prepared to take advantage of advances in office technology, including word processing, e-mail, and archiving. Better coordination was recommended and that the office automation strategy be pursued separately from the user computing strategy. As for SAS Data, it was recommended that a more detailed analysis of costs affecting application development, communications, and computer operations be undertaken to ensure that they were based on business needs.

The most important success factor in SAS strategic planning and management of information processing was stated as effective senior management participation. At the applications development level, the most important success factor was the involvement of managers and staff from the business units sponsoring new applications. As for SAS Data, the strategic directions were supported, but these strategies should be developed into specific plans and project proposals, which included defined objectives with anticipated business benefits, costs, and implementation plans. Then, senior management should evaluate each project to make sure that it was consistent with business objectives. A review of the applications underway in 1984 estimated that 1/10 improved customer service, 1/3 improved operational planning and control, and the rest aimed at increased productivity.

Although SAS Data had made progress in adjusting its strategies of 1981, the SAS IT plan looked for a stronger business involvement by SAS Data in the business entities it served. In particular, the development staff needed to change its culture, while the operations staff was challenged by technical innovations ahead and the increasingly demanding service needs of SAS.

Markets and Capabilities

Although SAS and SAS Data were reorganized and both aimed at fulfilling the new strategy of the businessman's airline, the functional knowledge of the airline organization and its computer systems remained basically unchanged.[259] And they had to, because functions must be carried out every second 24 hours a day. The core of the four market units was the expertise organized around the basic computer systems of the divisions. Each large system was developed and maintained by a group of specialists in that particular system. With the Commercial Division it was reservation, cargo handling, and traffic statistics systems. With the Traffic Services Division it was the check-in and load control systems. With the Operations Division it was systems of movement control and crew planning. With the Technical Division it was systems for maintenance of planes and materials control. With the Administrative Division it was accounting and salaries systems.

Things were similar in the production units. Just as in the 1970s, computer operations mainly dealt with the continuous problems of an annual transaction growth of 20%. A major task during the first half of the 1980s was the emulation of the systems on the U494 to the larger U1100. These included reservations, check-in and load control, cargo, and materials control. For IBM, capacity problems required it to move its systems from the 370 to the new and more powerful generation of IBM 3000 and Amdahl 5000. The high-speed Telcon 3 was being prepared to substitute for the medium-speed communication systems of Telcon 1 and 2, and was to include a new "intelligent" terminal, the T80, to allow for word processing and so on. It was all a matter of more capacity and speed.

So during the first half of the 1980s, the technology of the divisions did not change in any new direction. What were called markets on the one hand and

---

259 See below, *Infrastructure* and *Information Systems*.

products on the other, did not differ from the past structures of departments of SAS and departments and areas of Data Services. The basic systems were developed to automate further functions in their fields, although generalizing the technology of databases. Only, the yield management system of passenger traffic pointed in a new direction, that of optimization. The alignment of SAS Data and SAS Airline was pretty much the same as that of the 1970s. Both kept on working along functional lines. As a result, the competence of computer and communications technology running the information processing of SAS remained by and large the same. And so too did the competence that ran the functions of the airline. Finally, no new and mature IT was available to enable organizational changes to be enforced, for such reorganization took place nowhere in the business world.

What changed was a longing and pressure for change that slowly began to be based on a new business environment and a new emerging technology. However, as with any other contemporary firm, the market business strategy was far ahead of the organization, the technology, the institutional framework and the people of SAS. Data based systems, a few hundred PCs, and thousands of terminals created a well-functioning system that brought users somewhat closer to the information of the large systems, but did not cause any radical change. The PCs, with no true connection to the mainframe systems, introduced word processing, first and foremost. Primarily, the whole idea of these "distributed" systems was to increase productivity by reducing personnel and by improving tactical planning of the use of resources, rather than to improve strategic decision-making or the competitiveness of the company.

Nevertheless, the PCs gave hands-on experience to the users, as did the thousands of terminals used for the input and output of information. They included local microcomputers for preprocessing accounting documents for the central accounting system. Furthermore, the databases created the idea of information as a management resource. Together they paved the way for a conceptual change in computer technology. Computer technology began to be called IT, because it was the information of the systems that mattered and because the technology was meant for those who used it and, in the end, should be run by people of the business, not those of the computer department. Turning Data Services into a division and defining a new strategy, based on the business' premises, signaled a change of tides. At least, there was a vision of a new structure.

1985-1990 IT Change and Upgrading

Change Wanted

Since 1985, liberalization and competition increased on SAS' main European markets. Other European airlines acted more aggressively and in addition, American airlines, with giant distribution systems, determinedly targeted the European markets. To prepare for future radical changes, SAS developed new strategic goals. Three areas of development were given top priority: efficiency and excellence in services; advanced information, distribution, and booking systems; and a global traffic system. SAS continued to focus on the businessman, but the Businessman's Airline was extended to include all companies of the SAS Group in the "Travel Company" strategy, servicing the passenger during all stages of the travel.

Information technology was crucial to the implementation of all aspects of these new strategic goals, including improved productivity and services, expanded distribution facilities towards customers, and increased relations with SAS subsidiaries and with other airlines. Furthermore, IT would be needed even more to provide management with tools of planning and follow-up, to help them maneuver through the troubled waters of increased competition.

In 1985, SAS laid out an upgraded IT-program for the next five years. It was estimated to require hardware investments of 1,200 million SEK and software investments of 500 million SEK. Income was expected to increase three times the amount of money invested.[260]

In principle, business relations ruled between user divisions and SAS Data, and SAS was free to contract externally, except for strategic systems. Divisions were supposed to be the driving force of IT developments in SAS, too. To that end, they were preparing long-term IT-plans and strategies and strengthening their IT-competence, supported by small divisional groups of computer people. Likewise, SAS Data was seeking to improve its business competence, establishing a department for "Business, Information, and Technology" in 1985. An "Information Resource Management" perspective emerged that stressed the importance of having easy access to the huge amounts of data stored in large systems. "Information Centers" were introduced to support the new PC-technologies that spread among users, followed by a "Front Office" function and a department for "Distributed Services". Still, SAS Data took care of central systems and communications, policies of standard, methods and IT training.[261]

---

260 SAS, *V-85*, *V-86*; SAS, *Data Management*, 19/11 1985, 21/2 1986.
261 SAS Data, *Data Ventilen*, no. 10, 1986.

While strategies pressed for a closer marriage of IT and business and separating the roles and relationship of SAS and SAS Data, little happened in practice. The IT competence of the divisions grew slowly, and SAS Data did no better in increasing its business competence. Divisions continued to rely on SAS Data for development, maintenance, operation, and communication, and SAS Data was primarily occupied with running and developing central systems and technology. Furthermore, top management strove more or less in vain to "tear down the pyramids" of a bureaucratic legacy.

SAS Data Distribution Division

By late 1986, SAS top management decided to do something about the wide gap between theory and practice in the IT field. A working group pointed out the essential problems that had to be taken care of. First, the division of roles and authority must be made clear. Divisions owned and SAS Data administered the systems. Second, the computer competence of the divisions needed to be much upgraded to fulfil their role as the driving force in computer development. Commercial relations should be enforced between divisions and SAS Data and the divisions should be free to choose any supplier they found best.

Concerning technology, the working group noted that systems development since the reorganization of 1981 kept on working along the traditional line of separate functional systems, and in addition, a growing number of links between the systems created a spaghetti-like pattern for SAS' information applications and resources. Furthermore, decentralization of business and the coming of the PC had added a touch of anarchy to it all.

Another investigation dealt with the need to coordinate the development of core information systems. "Information Systems Business Follow-Up" (BFU) was established as a cooperative project to ensure the efficient development of the product namely, "flight". From new-year of 1986/87, a process started turning this project into a line organization, including all the reources and systems of the field of "flight". All these systems had one thing in common: Most divisions and routes used them. Furthermore, the changing character of travel distributions towards open and global systems would require determined and strong efforts by SAS to ensure its dominating position in the Scandinavian markets. Finally, the new line organization should see to it that result accounts and reporting systems were developed by all divisions and business units, including follow-up systems on traffic and quality.[262]

In 1987, a central unit was formed to carry out strategic changes in the IT-

---

262 SAS, *Data Management*, 8/1, 20/2 1987, 12/2 1988.

field. A line organization, a division, was established and a staff unit was formed under the president. SAS Data was also linked to this division. Coming from an IT management position at L. M. Ericsson, Björn Boldt-Christmas (BBC) became the new leader of both departments and the chairman of SAS Data. In 1988, the line organization included SAS Data, the large systems of reservations and distribution, named "the automated chain of sales", and the staff unit "Information Systems Strategies" (ISS). ISS was an advisory unit for the divisions and sought to map out an overall IT strategy and order of priority for SAS, produce common methods and standards, and review the IT-plans of the divisions. Externally recruited, L. Swärd was established in a new controller function as well as being in charge of ISS. The new line organization was called the "Data and Distribution Division" (DDD).[263]

To strengthen computer competence and cooperation, separate computer departments were established within each division. The computer departments were to prepare IT-plans to be integrated into the process of budgeting for the next year and ARP-plans for the following three years. It was clearly stated that divisions owned the information systems and that they were just administered by SAS Data. An advisory council, consisting of the leader of DDD, the ISS-controller of SAS, and IT controllers of the computer departments of the divisions, took care of cross-company coordination.

As a consequence of this reorganization in 1987-88, the divisions took over responsibility for their information systems and upgraded IT competence. SAS Data and the large and strategic IT-systems of SAS, such as reservations and communications, were united in the new DDD. By way of large IT investments and organizational coordination, DDD was intended to be the dynamic force of upgrading the fields of flight and distribution. L. Swärd of the ISS staff unit started preparing a framework for an IT infrastructure, including standards of technology and an information strategy for SAS Airline.[264]

Generally speaking, business considerations replaced those of technology, and IT was made a much more important strategic resource of the company. What was carried out in 1987-1988, however, was actually just a reinforcement of what had been stated for some years to be the case. Yet, plans had not materialized. The gap between plans and practice would have to be narrowed. Having reorganized the SAS IT field on the basis of a total review by the consulting firm Programator, IT plans were anchored in SAS' annual budget and three years ARP-plans of Divisions and routes.

---

263 SAS, *Data Management*, 15/4, 6/7 1988; 16/1 1989. SAS, *ARP-88*. Interviews: *Björn Boldt-Christmas* and *Lars Swärd*.
264 SAS, *Data Management*, 12/2, 15/4, 30/5, 6/7 1988; 16/1 1989. SDS/SDN, *UPTIME*, no. 2-3, 1988; SAS, *ARP-89*.

SAS Data and Distribution Division 1988

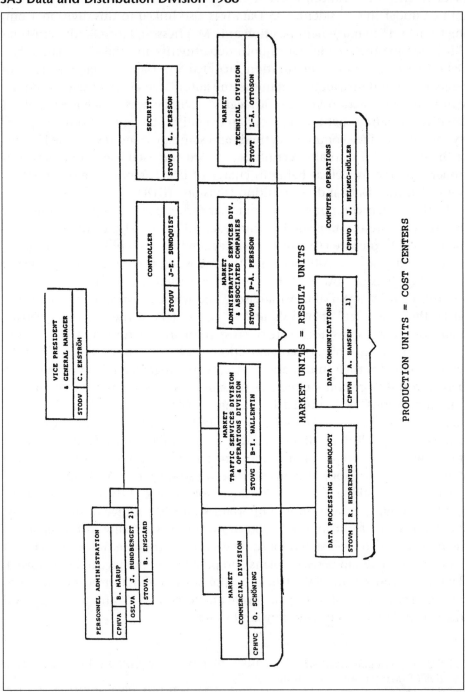

Source: SAS, Data Management, 1988.

IT Strategic Management

In late 1980s, much analyzing and planning took place to make IT a strategic weapon in SAS' endeavors to cope with increasing competition.

An Information Technology and Management (ITM) unit in SAS Data carried out a mapping of the main functions of SAS Airline and identified 28 functions that were combined into 12 areas of master planning. During 1988 and 1989, these 12 areas were intended to produce master plans for future IT initiatives. Shortly afterwards, the activities of the ITM unit were transferred to the new staff unit ISS. On the basis of this review of the 12 areas, ISS created SAS' first Airline Business Model.[265]

Like the models of the late 1960s and 1970s, the data areas of the late 1980s corresponded to functional structures and processes laid out in the business model. Unlike previous models, however, these data areas were market and management oriented. The SAS organization was no longer considered a production machine, but a business that had to adapt to the demands of the market. Each area of the model was analyzed stepwise, moving downwards from strategic management to the operative functions. The model contained 12 areas covering the following main fields, similar to those of previous data models:[266]

- Corporate planning, policies, and follow-up
- Passenger
- Cargo and Mail
- Traffic
- Crew
- Technical Maintenance
- Personnel
- Accounting and Financial Follow-up
- IT.

The data areas as well as the business model worked exclusively as tools of analysis, surveying a market- and strategically oriented company. The decentralized structure of SAS made it impossible to authorize an overall model to be followed by management of the 12 areas.

---

265 The model demonstrates the close relationship of information systems and business activities of the value chain, see Figure above, *SAS Airline Business Model*.
266 SDS/SDN, *UPTIME*, no. 5, 1988.

As a result, the following "Information Systems Policies" (ISP) of SAS Airline were only guidelines and a framework for the directions of work.[267] Standards followed afterwards, specifying and implementing these policies. The purpose of ISP was to prepare SAS for the future, and it mainly addressed decision-makers, IT specialists, and user representatives. ISP covered general procedures and methods of planning, development, operation, maintenance of information systems applications and databases, management of information systems resources, and quality and security. It was stressed that all information systems activities should respond to business demands. Initiative, planning, implementation, and follow-up were the responsibility of each business unit. The units had to have personnel with the relevant qualifications prepare an annual information-systems plan as part of the whole business plan of SAS and ARP. They also had to calculate the effects of the information-systems activities of the preceding year. The controller of the IT staff monitored coordination of the information-systems plans of the divisions that were presented to top management.

First, in ISP, software categories and interfaces were defined. All applications should offer an easy-to-use and standardized dialogue. Second, information-systems (IS) methodology was determined that comprised planning, development, and operation. IS activities should be initiated in response to the needs and requirements of business activities. IS development work should promote solutions that satisfied quality, flexibility, and a corporate view, as well as operational availability through adoption of operational service levels.

Third, Information Resource Management (IRM) was defined. The general purpose of IRM was to make the information in SAS' information systems more suitable for, and more easily available to, business activities. In helping to ensure that IRM's intentions came to fruition, the significance of a corporate wide or "global" view of data was stressed. The planning and design of information resources needed to be consistent with SAS' business model and a global data model, global meaning corporation-wide. Standardization was required, and a responsible body should exist for every data element classified as global. Global data should be documented in a coherent data dictionary that was generally available within SAS, pointing towards the future technology of data mining.

Fourth, the technological infrastructure was outlined. The hardware covered four levels from individual, via local and regional to global, leaving standards to be stated in another document. SAS communications should em-

---

267 SAS, "Information Systems Policies", *Data Management*, 1989.

ploy open-system standards and function as one logical structure. International OSI protocols and IBM Systems Network Architecture (SNA) were recommended for the future framework of communication, while IBM Systems Application Architecture (SAA) was chosen for software applications. Industry or de facto standards were to be used for all processing hardware and basic software when developing, testing, operating and maintaining applications. All applications would use standard tools for storage and retrieval of data.

These general guidelines for IT policies were followed by detailed procedures and recommendations of security, standards of technology (databases, PC hardware, PC operating systems, PC networks (the SOFIE project), and methods of systems development (Reflex).[268]

IBM SNA and SAA were chosen as part of a general plan to move all SAS applications onto an IBM platform.[269] Accordingly, Unisys (as Univac/Sperry now was called) and its large systems (RES, PALCO, etc.) had to be phased out and converted to IBM. One reason for this strategic decision was the fact that Unisys had not presented a new generation of technology to replace the U1100 and for reasons of capacity, SAS had to do something. Furthermore, distributions were being separated from RES and made part of the AMADEUS international distribution system that was being developed for implementation in the early 1990s.

Instead of just making a conversion to IBM, it was decided to produce a new reservations system, called TERESE, which would cover the inventory part of reservations. It was estimated to cost 250 million SEK. Management figured that if only four airlines purchased TERESE the investment would be earned. New systems for check-in, load control, and cargo on IBM would also have to be developed to complete the phasing out of Unisys.

The IBM plans, especially TERESE, got out of control and costs reached gigantic dimensions.[270] During the Gulf Crisis of 1991, it was decided to stop TERESE as well as the plans to replace Unisys with IBM. Only developments of check-in and load control were carried out. Meanwhile, Unisys had presented a new computer generation to solve the capacity problems of SAS.

New strategic plans for communications were presented, too, based on the technology and business premises of the late 1980s, including TERESE. The

---

268 SAS, *Handbook of IT Policy and Standards within SAS Airline*, 1990. On methods, see below, *Systems Development*.

269 SAS, *Data Management*, 21/9 1987, 15/3 1988. SAS, *ARP-88* and *-89*. SDS/SDN, *UP-TIME*, no. 9, 1988.

270 SDD, *Profil*, no. 9, 1991. Interviews: *Arne Hansen, Dan Sjølund*, and *Bjarne Karpant-schof*.

spread of distributed data processing throughout SAS and not least, the coming of international distribution systems, pressed for a de facto standard, suggesting IBM's SNA. When TERESE was closed down in 1991, a new strategy was needed for communications. At the same time, another strategic project was stopped for financial reasons. An alternative IBM center was being built at Häggvik near Stockholm to reduce the risks of having all information systems operated from Copenhagen. This was closed down in 1991, too, when an airline crisis called for drastic reductions in costs.[271]

Reorganizing SAS Data

By 1987, radical changes of SAS Data had started, too. In March 1987, SAS Data management agreed on a number of strategic fields of development to improve its support of SAS and its strategies:[272]

1. Increase the quality of products as experienced by customers,
2. Improve customer access to stored information and the availability to process this information for the benefit of decision-making (IRM),
3. Help develop a new distribution system to communicate SAS' products to an open market,
4. Make sure that SAS Data reached its economic goals, defined its products, and kept agreements with customers,
5. Develop the competence of employees to fulfil the strategies of SAS Data.

In addition, a sixth strategic area might be mentioned, namely that of office automation and user computing (word processing and LANs) and internal electronic communication (InfoMail) supported by Information Centers.[273] A technology change of particular interest was the digitization of the telephone exchanges of Scandinavian airport centers during late 1980s.[274]

The SAS Data organization was adjusted to cover these new strategic areas.[275] The combined responsibility of market and production was divided to cultivate customer relations in the market sector. Systems development was made a production unit and computer operations and communications split into two separate units. Finally, a customer center was established to support

---

271 SDD, *Profil*, no. 9, 1991.
272 SAS Data, *Data Ventilen*, no. 2-3, 1987.
273 SAS Data, *Data Ventilen*, no. 1 and 3, 1986, no. 3, 1987.
274 SAS Data, *Data Ventilen*, no. 2, 1987. SDS/SDN, *UPTIME*, no. 1, 1988.
275 SAS Data, *Data Ventilen*, no. 3, 4, 5 1987. SDS/SDN, *UPTIME*, no. 2, 1988.

customers in making their electronic working place.[276] These strategies were all intended to create clear goals and measurable results. To improve the quality of products delivered to the SAS customer, a crucial point, methods of systems development and project management were improved, and the problems of availability to the strategic systems, such as RES and PALCO, were specifically targeted.

The main idea of this strategic reinforcement was to strengthen the SAS Data support of SAS' business goals. While the SAS Data executive, C. Ekström, was appointed president of AMADEUS, the new European distribution system project, BBC was installed as the new vice-president of IT at SAS. Some minor changes in the SAS Data organization were introduced by October 1 1987, dividing responsibility of market and production to create greater flexibility.[277] But shortly afterwards, more fundamental changes occurred.

BBC intended to end the unclear roles and relations between SAS Data and SAS. Commercial responsibility was anchored completely and clearly by the divisions, whereas the IS staff unit was given an advisory role. SAS Data was left to be a vendor of computer systems and services, only. Furthermore, SAS Data was thoroughly reviewed by external consultants to create a basis for a true market orientation.[278] By June 1 1988, SAS Data was transformed from a division of SAS into two corporate-like companies led by a board and management of their own. SAS Data STO/OSL (Sweden/Norway) appointed Lars-Åke Ottoson as their leader, and SAS Data CPH (Denmark) appointed Mogens Meisler. BBC was chairman of both boards and for the time being, they remained part of DDD, but worked as independent units in terms of their results.[279]

SAS Data no longer played an overall strategic role in SAS. It was just an IT vendor if SAS chose to buy its services. SAS Data stopped being an internal SAS department or division and had to prepare for survival in a world of competition. Yet, SAS Data was not completely on its own. It was a joint-stock-like business and internal debiting still ruled SAS Data–SAS relations. Matters of personnel and finance remained parts of SAS Airline, too.

So far, SAS Data had been one organization with three regional sub-units. Now two such organizations had to be built, one for Denmark and one for Sweden/Norway, soon to split into three national units.

---

276 SAS Data, *Data Ventilen*, no. 4, 1987. SDS/SDN, *UPTIME*, no. 1, 1988.
277 SAS, *Data Management*, 12/3, 30/4 1987.
278 SAS, *Data Management*, 30/6-1987, 12/2 1988.
279 SDS/SDN, *UPTIME*, no. 6, 1988.

SAS Data Holding 1990

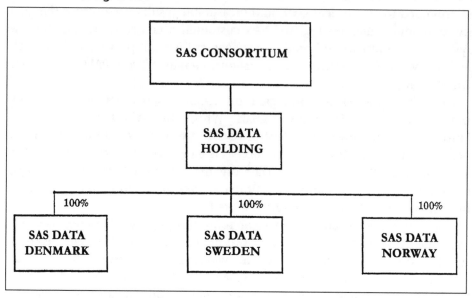

Source: SAS, Data Management.

SAS Data Denmark

In 1988, managers, representatives of employees, and other resource persons started a process of laying out the framework of the new organization of what was finally named SAS Data Denmark (SDD). They agreed on an organization made up of five units: Sales and marketing, Systems Development, Operations, Communications, and Support and in addition, staff units such as Accounting and Personnel. During 1989, staff expanded with the addition of quality and security units, areas that were upgraded. A new unit of distributed information processing was also established.[280]

By autumn 1988, line managers and staff were installed. During the winter of 1988-1989 managers of sub-departments were recruited, personnel reorganization implemented, and goals and strategies agreed upon. SDD of 1989 occupied almost 500 people and earned almost 550 million SEK, out of an SAS Data total of approximately 800 employees and a total revenue of about 800 million SEK[281]

The overall idea of SDD was stated this way: to help SAS improve its com-

---

280 SDD, *Forandring af en dataafdeling* (Changing an IT department), 1990. SDD, *Pro-fil*, no. 13, 1989, no. 13, 1990.
281 SDD, *Vi er her* (we are here). See, *SAS IT Statistics*, above.

petitiveness by delivering reliable, efficient, and future proved products of IT. The SDD business idea was to be an IT service business with a broad knowledge of information processing and expert competence within a number of fields. Those included global computer communications, mainframe computer operations with high availability and high volumes of transaction, central surveillance of local computer installations, central computer administration, development of information systems for the travel service chain, and distributed information processing.

Consequently, it was SDD's strategy to be the preferred IT vendor of SAS, while external sales should be marginal (i.e., selling only surplus capacity). To make that happen, SDD would have to become a competitive business unit in a competitive environment, where SAS was free to choose its IT services. Just like SAS, SDD wanted to decentralize business responsibility for the individual fields of business throughout the organization. Market orientation, flexibility, and development of personnel were made strategic targets.[282]

Since early 1989, SDD had chosen the following parameters of measurement for improving its capabilities: 1. Level of profits and revenue of market activities. 2. Quality of operations of RES and PALCO and of delivery of systems tasks. 3. Productivity: particularly of the systems development unit. 4. Personnel: annual interview of all employees, and reduced amount of overtime. 5. Change: joined 24-hour unit of operations and communications, sales and marketing in place, releases of modifications, job profiles in place, and a Unisys plan of competence.[283]

During 1989, the process of organizational development was aimed at creating a matrix organization based on separate responsibility of products and production. This separation of responsibility was considered a key factor in creating business units. By late 1989, communications and computer operations introduced separate responsibility, while still working on upgrading the systems development unit to a high level of consulting activity. Functions of sales and marketing, personnel, finance and other aspects of administration remained cost center staff units.[284]

Generally speaking, SDD aimed at aligning its business closely with that of SAS Airline. Furthermore, this process of organizational change was performed in a true Danish or Scandinavian way, characterized by cooperation between management and employees and an open and assertive information policy.

From 1988 to 1990, SAS Data stayed in an intermediary position. Invest-

---

282 SDD, *Vi er her* (we are here), 1989. SDD, *Profil*, no. 13, 1989.
283 SDD, *Profil*, no. 22, 1989.
284 SDD, *Hvidbog* (white book), 1989.

ments and personnel had to follow the rules and strategies of SAS Airline, and legally SDD was not an independent entity. SAS management saw this as an unsatisfactory state of affairs, making the pressure for change less strong than they wanted. SAS Airline management moved aggressively to run a market-oriented organization during these years, including outsourcing some of its affiliates. At that time some large corporations in Scandinavia and elsewhere even prepared for outsourcing their IT departments.[285]

The decision to turn SAS Data into joint-stock companies crystallized during the second half of 1989. It was a radical step that caused much anxiety and turmoil among personnel. Already by mid-1989 when SAS top management first launched the idea of outsourcing SAS Data, the main cooperative unit of management and employees at SDD started a process to prepare for a possible decision to make SDD a joint stock company.[286]

By autumn 1989, SDD laid out the preconditions for a transformation into a joint stock company.[287] That included an outline of SDD's business idea, stressing SDD's competence within operations and management of computer systems and communications, its knowledge of international travel activities, and in particular of SAS, and indicating that SDD wanted to remain the main IT vendor of SAS. First and foremost, SDD stated its goals, business ideas and strategies to make money. It aimed to be less dependent on SAS and to increase its external share of revenues to 10% by 1995 (1% by 1989) and 30% by the year 2000.

A number of preconditions were stressed as crucial to making the business idea a success. Most crucial were the following: SDD wanted total freedom of action to be able to perform in a business-like manner. It wanted to buy all business areas and production means that it was in charge of at the time. It wanted total ownership of products for which it was responsible (InfoProducts, including InfoMail and MESCO), and the rights of sale and co-ownership of applications for which it was responsible (such as the reservation and check-in/load control systems). Finally, SDD wanted a five years framework agreement that covered its position as operator and manager of systems and communications of SAS Airline, and staff compensation should be no less than by SAS Airline.

No vital disagreement seemed to exist between the three units of SAS Data and SAS Airline and SAS Data was legally put under a common holding company, owned 100% by SAS. A plan for cooperation between the three units of

---

285 SDD, *Profil*, no. 25/26, 1989. SAS, *Inside*, no. 22, 1989.
286 SDD, *Profil*, no. 38, 1989.
287 SDD, *Hvidbog* (white book), 1989.

SAS Data was agreed upon. A common SAS Data Group (SDG) was formed between the three units, headed by BBC, with the intention of coordinating internal and strategic activities.[288] At the same time, M. Meisler stepped down as chief of SDD. Ole Skyt Johansen was acting chief until the installation of a new chief in October 1990. By 1990, the three companies were in place with a total of 800 employees and revenue of 800 million SEK, of which SDD covered almost two thirds.[289]

Employees were in many cases very hesitant and even unwilling to accept the break with SAS. It took months before all had signed the letters of engagement with the new company, and some decided to leave at that time.[290] For decades, hundreds of computer professionals had enjoyed the privileges of monopoly. Within a few years or even months, commercial conditions were forced upon them, challenging their influence, competence, and mentality.

When SAS Data converted to joint stock status a renaming was required. The firm SAS Institute claimed its exclusive right, except for the airline, to carry the name SAS. SAS Data was renamed Scandinavian Airlines Data, Denmark, Sweden, and Norway respectively.[291]

SAS Data Sweden and SAS Data Norway

The reorganization of the two other regional units into a "joint-stock-like" company of Sweden/Norway (SDS/SDN) in 1988 seemed less dramatic than the Danish organization.[292] The Swedish part was less than half the size of SDD in personnel and revenue (some 200 people and a revenue of about 250 million SEK), whereas Norway only reached one-tenth the size of SDD (about 50 people and more than 50 million SEK in revenue). For the time being, Norway was made a fourth unit of the Swedish organization, except for market, systems, and production. Norway had its own departments of production and systems. By January 1989, the new organization and strategies of SAS Data Sweden/Norway were ready. Much pressure was put on the new organization.[293]

During 1989, a new economic system was developed and installed to make SDS/SDN an independent economic unit by January 1 1990.[294] It took most of the first half of 1990 before true invoicing and reporting began to

---

288 SDD, *Profil*, no. 39, 1989, no. 2-3, 5, 14-17, 20/21, 1990.
289 SDD, *Profil*, no. 24-26, 1990.
290 SDD, *Profil*, no. 28, 1990.
291 SAS, *Data Management*, 4/7 1990. For the sake of convenience, we shall keep on calling it SAS Data.
292 SDS/SDN, *UPTIME*, no. 8, 9, 10, 1988.
293 SDS/SDN, *UPTIME*, no. 10, 1988, 1-2, 1989.
294 SDS/SDN, *UPTIME*, no. 3-4, 1989.

work properly, just about the time when SDS/SDN was turned into two separate organizations.[295] By January 1, 1990, Sweden and Norway split into two economic units and by July 1, 1990 into two joint-stock companies.[296]

While SDD was based on operating the central strategic systems and communications of SAS, SDS and SDN were much more locally oriented. Furthermore, SDS benefited from being situated close to head office, developing competence particularly in technical maintenance and administration. Close relations with head office and the lack of large central computing made SDS focus even more on the new technology of distributed computing and the introduction of software packages.

Technologically, SDS and SDN had developed Tandem as a platform of central and distributed computing since 1980. In many ways this strategy had failed and by 1988, SAS decided to phase out Tandem, just as Unisys would be phased out and replaced by IBM. SAS cancelled the agreement of full service to the four systems run on Tandem by January 1 1990.[297] Furthermore, SAS top management had decided to build a large IBM center near Stockholm at Häggvik to reduce the risk of having all strategic systems run in the Copenhagen center.[298]

During the second half of 1989 and during all of 1990, Häggvik computer operations were established and a number of systems moved from Copenhagen to the new center. It was impossible to make Häggvik a profitable business, however, and it ran at a deficit all through 1990. As a consequence of the Gulf Crisis, its was closed down in 1991 and systems moved back to Copenhagen. Plans to give up Tandem were cancelled, too.[299]

Markets and Capabilities

By 1985, 90% of SAS Data's revenue came from SAS Airline and the rest from subsidiaries and associated companies in the SAS Group, including external customers (less than 1%). Major markets were divisions of SAS Airline. A number of second-generation mainframe systems were being developed during the 1980s, mainly based in Copenhagen (reservation, cargo, check-in, stock material, movement control and partly revenue accounting and crew and personnel) and Stockholm (technical maintenance, and partly traffic, accounting, load control, crew, and personnel).[300]

---

295 SDS/SDN, *UPTIME*, no. 5, 1990.
296 SDS/SDN, *UPTIME*, no. 5, 13, 1990.
297 SDS/SDN, *UPTIME*, no. 8, 1988.
298 SDS/SDN, *UPTIME*, no. 3, 1989.
299 SDS/SDN, *UPTIME*, no. 4, 1989, no. 1, 9, 12, 14, 15, 17, 24, 1990, no. 10, 11/12, 1991.
300 SAS, *V-85*.

At SAS Data in Copenhagen, between 75 to 100 persons worked annually on maintenance and development of passenger and cargo systems, 4/5 with passenger systems and 1/5 with cargo.[301] During the second half of the 1980s, plans and preparations for a new distribution system, which included a new cargo system too, became a major new strategic field. During the period from 1987 to 1991 much manpower was occupied in developing the international distribution system AMADEUS and the new reservation system TERESE, until TERESE had to be stopped in 1991 for financial reasons. Supported by the consulting firm Programator, SAS Cargo tried in vain to develop a completely renewed cargo system during the late 1980s until this project was also closed down in 1991.

During the late 1980s, a new traffic statistics system and a new flight follow-up system improved planning of the timetable. The timetable system, TPTS, was given additional follow-up and planning facilities during the second half of the 1980s. These additions to timetable planning were bought externally.

The new CRU80 was installed in 1985. During 1986 to 1988, the new Operations Control System (OPUS) for movement control was implemented. Thirty to forty people worked continuously on maintaining these systems.

Traffic Services Division shocked SAS Data when an external vendor was engaged to develop a new mainframe system for load control in the late 1980s. This was Palco Aircraft Handling (PAH), which followed the new passenger check-in system (PCI) of the mid-1980s. Later SAS Data had to take over systems development to make sure that the new system was completed, however. Thirty to forty people worked on these systems.

Technical Division (TD) tried to develop a few new modules of MOPS and a new MATS, but were unable to do so. Technical documentation was automated and 30-40 persons by SAS Data worked continuously on maintenance and development of TD's systems.

Business Services Division (BSD) developed three new mainframe systems during the 1980s. The personnel system PERS/PINS was developed in three national versions, but development plans had to be reduced. Fifty to sixty staff members worked on development and maintenance of these systems. Furthermore, SAS Data and BSD cooperated in developing office automation throughout SAS. This included PCs for word processing, spreadsheets, and communication.

---

301 SAS, *V-85*. SAS, *Handbook of IT Policy and Standards within SAS Airline*.

A new accounting system, General Ledger Millennium (GLM), was developed and installed during 1989-1992. Once more SAS Data saw an external firm take over development of a new mainframe system, although SAS Data had to assist in finishing the project.

Finally, SAS Data developed and implemented a new revenue accounting system of passengers, IMPALA, by the early 1990s.

In 1985, SAS Data kept about 700 people occupied, with about 100 computer professionals employed in other SAS divisions.[302] By 1990, the number of personnel amounted to approximately 800 with SAS Data and about 200 throughout the divisions. In addition, more than 100 external consultants were working on SAS computer projects at that time. While SAS Data covered about 85% of all SAS IT expenditure by 1985, that share had fallen below 60% by 1990, indicating the radical changes in SAS-SAS Data relations during these years. Projects, such as AMADEUS, TERESE, GLM, and PAH counted for much of the increasing external costs during the second half of the 1980s. Follow-up systems added to the mainframe systems made up a minor but increasing external purchase of software, including package software to PCs, during the same period. Total revenue of SAS Data increased from approximately 600 million SEK in 1985 to approximately 800 million in 1990, while all SAS IT costs amounted to 1.4 billion SEK in 1990, twice as much as in 1985.

Still, most SAS Data revenues came from operating and maintaining systems and communications, and systems development made up a large but declining share by 1990. SAS Data Denmark took care of all central computer and communications operation, except for a short period when some central systems were moved to Häggvik near Stockholm until it was closed in 1991 and they returned to Copenhagen. Central systems development was divided between SAS Data Denmark and Sweden. Some development took place mainly in Copenhagen (reservation and cargo) whereas other developments focused on Stockholm (technical and administration) with traffic and operations more equally divided between the two units of SAS Data. The Norwegian unit stuck to local activities.

The functional knowledge of SAS and central systems operation and planning of these functions made up the core competence of SAS Data and the computer professionals throughout the divisions. Whether they did preliminary studies, systems development, programming, maintenance, or operation, all capabilities were built around these basic functional systems. Since the mid-1980s, strategic efforts increased to make SAS Data more business- and market-oriented and the divisions capable of taking over responsibility

---

302 See, *SAS IT Statistics*, in the text.

for IT planning and development. The computer professionals of SAS were made aware of the strategic transformations and requirements of SAS, but in practice little happened. However, the strategic IT reforms of the late 1980s no longer left SAS Data practice unchanged.

The pressure for change was most directly felt by the core group of systems developers, especially in Copenhagen; a group that for decades, had been the center of SAS' mainframe systems.[303] Systems development was made a production unit, separated from market units, while area-responsible market consultants took care of customer relations. A new department of distributed processing was formed, too, to support local customer computing on PCs. Systems developers were trained in business perspectives and project management, some being retrained to become consultants and others to deal with distributed developments. Furthermore, a new model of development was introduced to meet customer demands of business alignment and faster developments.

System developers and programmers represented very strong cultures and groups that only reluctantly adopted new development tools, such as 4GL, to improve productivity and were even more hesitant about PCs and the ideas of distributed data processing. Their competence and influence was based on developing and maintaining mainframe systems, particularly in SDD, whereas SDS/SDN were perhaps more open to PC-systems and packaged software because they did not run the central systems of SDD. Furthermore, the declining SAS Data share of SAS IT projects and a growing number of external consultants at SAS also pressed for radical actions. Finally, deeply rooted mentalities were strongly resistant to true change when SAS management turned technical and functionally oriented units into business-minded organizations.

It must be considered, too, that SAS kept on being completely dependent on its central systems and that new central systems were being developed right up until the early 1990s. SAS divisions had profound problems in getting rid of old bureaucratic ways. Furthermore, by the late 1980s no mature technology really existed to replace the second-generation mainframe systems of SAS. Accordingly, what radical changes of technology and business orientation actually meant remained a bit unreal to most people. Things and people were on the move during these years, but it took the break with SAS in 1990, the subsequent Gulf Crisis and determined reorganization of SAS, and an emerging client/server technology of the early 1990s to make changes come true.

---

303 SDD, *Forandring af en dataafdeling* (changing an IT department), 1990.

IT Infrastructure

Computer Operations

The main task of computer operations was to have sufficient capacity to keep the large online systems running and ensure operation stability. Since the early 1980s, demands for capacity grew, as a consequence of the Businessman's Airline strategy, the reorganization of SAS, and the spread of the new generations of IT applications and communications.

Still, central computers situated in Copenhagen dominated computer operations. Since the late 1970s, some mini-computers were installed for local data processing, including tax-free and bookkeeping processing in major European offices, transferring information to the central accounting system by way of tape and punched lists.

During the first half of the 1980s, the U494 was replaced by the U1100 and by the mid-1980s, IBM 370 computers were replaced by the new 3000 generation and the IBM compatible Amdahl 5000.[304]

Besides Univac (later Sperry and finally Unisys) and IBM, Tandem was introduced in 1980 as a third standard to deliver combined central and distributed systems. During the first half of the 1980s, fruitless efforts were made to develop new cargo and load control systems on Tandem. By the late-1980s, only four systems ran on Tandem. These were a new Station Resource Planning System (STREPS) for ground services in Copenhagen, FATIS for airport information in Oslo and Bergen, Decentralized Accounting Processing (DAP) for local customer invoicing and so on, and CASH for airport shops. 20 persons worked with Tandem at SAS Data, divided between the three countries.[305]

The IT upgrading efforts from the mid-1980s also affected computer operations. On the one hand, with all computer systems in Copenhagen, management wanted to reduce the risks of a breakdown. On the other hand, management aimed at creating a uniform and solid technological platform to secure future development. Risks were connected with SAS' total dependence on computer technology. If there were to be a breakdown, SAS would stop functioning in a few weeks. It was discussed whether risks should be reduced by utilizing the potential of the new system of distributed computing or by set-

---

304 SAS, *Data Management*, 17/11 1980. SAS, *Handbook of IT Policy and Standards within SAS Airline*.
305 SDS/SDN, *UPTIME*, no. 8, 1988.

ting up a new center in Stockholm. Top management wanted the latter solution.[306]

In the late 1980s, an alternative center was being built at Häggvik outside Stockholm. The project proved to be more costly than expected and technically it was also difficult to transfer jobs from Copenhagen to Stockholm. From the start, the center proved unprofitable and during the Gulf Crisis of 1991 it was closed.[307]

The largest project of the late 1980s, however, concerned plans to phase out Sperry/Unisys and move all systems to IBM technology.[308] Sperry/Unisys had difficulties in producing a new generation of mainframes to replace the U1100 that soon would run out of capacity. At the same time, management wanted to make IBM an overall standard as IBM was considered the most reliable future partner. Consequently, SAS decided to phase out Tandem, too.[309]

Converting all systems to IBM was no simple task, however. Large systems, such as RES, would have to be reprogrammed. As the international distribution system AMADEUS was being developed at the same time, reducing RES to just an inventory, it was decided to use this opportunity to develop a new reservation system in cooperation with IBM, called TERESE. The TERESE-project expanded enormously, costing probably hundreds of millions SEK. It simply ran out of financial control. Finally, it was closed down during the Gulf Crisis in 1991. So, nothing came of it all and SAS was left with the three technologies of Unisys, IBM and Tandem.

Still marginal, emerging technologies of office automation, decision support systems, and distributed computing had little influence on computer operations of the 1980s.

---

306 Risks had been considered since the early 1980s (SAS, *Data Management*, 5/10 1981), and more determinedly by the mid-1980s (SAS, *Data Management*, 19-20/11 1985).
307 See above, SAS Data Sweden and SAS Data Norway.
308 SDD, *Profil*, 1989 to 1991. Interviews: *Arne Hansen* and *Björn Boldt-Christmas*.
309 SDS/SDN, *UPTIME*, no. 8, 1988.

Peak Transactions for Reservations on Unisys

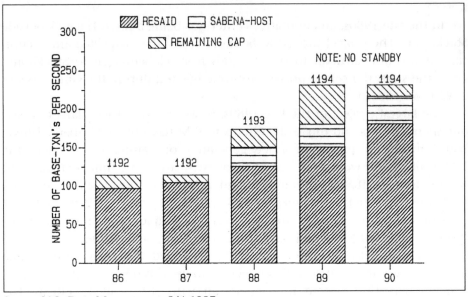

Source: SAS, Data Management, 3/4 1987.

Peak Transactions on IBM

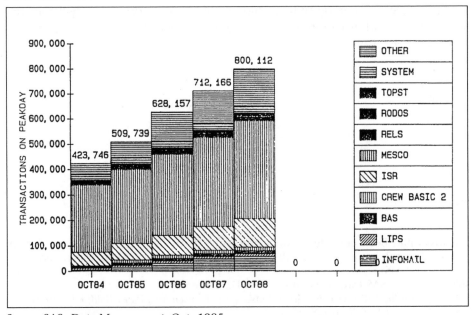

Source: SAS, Data Management, Oct. 1985.

Communications

Since the 1970s, the new Telcon structure paved the way for a communications revolution in SAS. The number of terminals and transactions grew so rapidly that a third and much improved version of Telcon, Telcon 3, was being prepared from the early 1980s.[310]

So-called Data Communications Processing (DCP) computers were introduced at front-end and remote-end. Telcon 3 was built in modules, being easily extended to cover expanding communications. Capacity and speed were much increased, going from medium to high speed. By way of new software, Combine enabled the user to reach Univac and IBM applications from the same terminal. Telcon 3 had three Scandinavian centers revolving around the Univac computer in Copenhagen. At each center, Telcon was connected to regional computers and terminals. To cover the growing number of terminals, and waiting for Telcon 3 to be fully developed, Telcon 1 and 2, were still employed until 1990 when Telcon 3 was ready to take over all communication traffic.

Just after implementing Telcon 3 in 1984, a new and more sophisticated terminal was taken into use, the T80.[311] T80 was more than an input/output terminal. It had a small "intelligence", allowing work with local applications, including mini-systems for local data and SAS InfoMail. LANs of PCs introduced package software for communication, such as MS Mail, but these were still small compared with InfoMail.

Since the 1980s, increased competition and commercialization in the airlines business prepared for strategic changes in communications. The coming of open and international distribution systems and SAS' increasing cooperation with other airlines revealed the limits of a dedicated communications system. The spread of PCs and LANs of different standards throughout SAS also called for an open and common standard.[312]

---

310 SAS, *Data Management*, 17/11 1980; 14-15/9 1983; 21/12 1984. SAS, *V/ARP*, 1981 to 1990. Interview: *Henning Andersen*.
311 SAS, *Data Management*, 21/12 1984.
312 SAS, *Data Management*, 14/4, 20/11 1989.

Systems Development

Although the new top management behind the Businessman's Airline strategy in 1981 wanted to get rid of classical systems development, considered a bureaucratic reminiscence, this method survived. The reorganization of SAS into decentralized result units, including SAS Data, and the coming of a supplier-customer relationship between SAS Data and SAS started to loosen the application of defined systems methods, however. But generally speaking, development and maintenance of mainframe systems did not change. During the 1980s, the development of a number of second-generation mainframe systems preoccupied SAS Data. Management wanted to speed up systems development to cut costs, but little happened in that respect during the 1980s.[313]

Growing competition increased the interest of management in introducing follow-up and optimizing systems. External software firms, familiar with a business approach to systems development that was alien to SAS Data, produced most of these systems. For the same reason, some divisions even left the development of mainframe systems to external companies in the late 1980s. Business considerations gradually replaced those of functions as the basis of systems development, but little changed at SAS Data.

Information Systems

Corporate

Corporate management took care of overall planning.[314] It formulated goals and strategies, including aircraft investments, and planned preconditions of resources application, did budgeting and laid out policies for SAS-functions. These overall planning activities could be seen in the "sky" of the business model.[315] In the middle of the model followed the proper business of passenger transportation, from product marketing to flight performance and destination service, including cargo. Operative planning of airport, crew, and

---

313 SAS, *Data Management*, Sept. 1982. SAS, *V/ARP*, 1981 to 1990. Interviews: *Torsten Bergner, Curt Ekström, Mogens Kischovsky*.
314 SAS, *Handbook of IT Policy and Standards within SAS Airline*.
315 See Figure, *SAS Business Model and Information Systems*, which is an illustration of *The SAS Airline Business Model*, see the text above.

maintenance supported the transportation business. A number of staff-units took care of accounting, revenue, human resources, fuel, and so on. The business model included all the many information systems that made the various SAS functions work.

Budgeting was an important short-term activity of corporate planning.[316] It was based on information from several sources and information systems, such as traffic program, revenue, fuel, charges, and route results, before detailed budgeting and follow-up could be carried out and consolidated in finance. The Online Budgeting System (OBS), and its improved successor, OBS2, helped to coordinate the flow of information in producing a budget. Business follow-up became an important part of all SAS functions and systems during the second half of the 1980s.[317] The results and information production of all these systems were aggregated (in BFU Data) to enable business follow-up for each flight and highly improved the basis of current corporate planning and decision-making. The business follow-up picture also indicated the enormous complexity of integrated systems that had developed during the 1980s.

---

316 See Figure, *Airline Budgeting*.
317 See Figure, *Corporate Business Follow-Up*.

SAS Business Model and Information Systems 1989

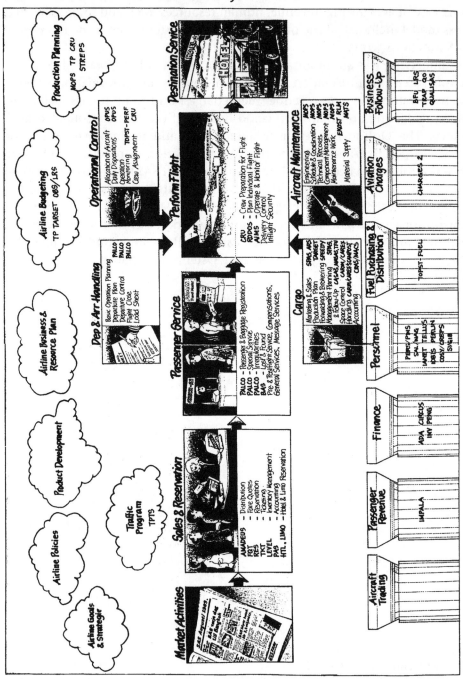

Source: SAS, Handbook of IT Policy and Standards.

Airline Budgeting 1989

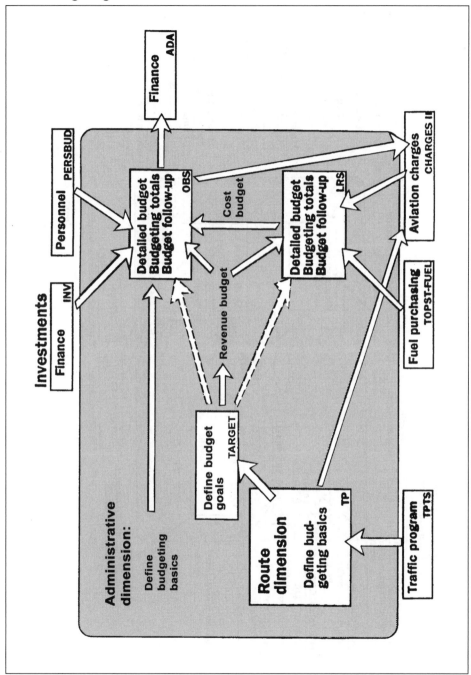

Source: SAS, Handbook of IT Policy and Standards.

Corporate Business Follow-up 1989

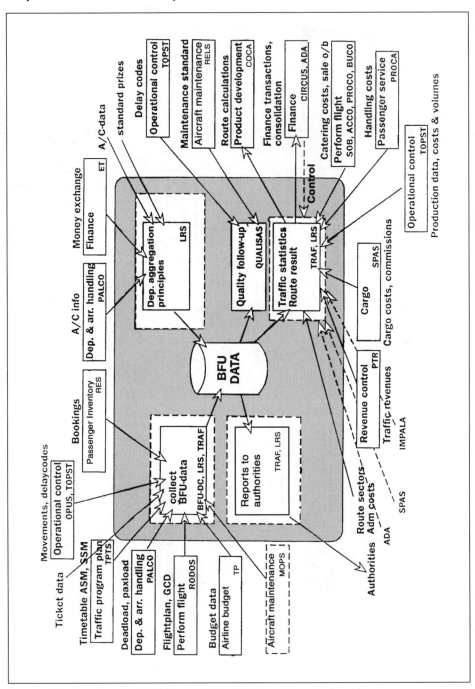

Source: SAS, Handbook of IT Policy and Standards.

Traffic

During the 1980s, Commercial Division covered all passenger and cargo traffic planning, product development and marketing. Through its products, Commercial Division strove to make customers fly with SAS (being a customer involved having booked at ticket). The route sectors of Domestic, Europe, Intercontinental, and Cargo joined with production divisions to produce a traffic program for summer and winter, respectively. The traffic program, or timetable, formed the basis of all airline planning and activity. Europe was the most important and profitable route sector of all.

Since 1988, the large passenger systems, including RES and Revenue Accounting belonged to the new Data and Distribution Division. Fundamental traffic and technical production systems were part of the Traffic Services Division and Technical Division. The Administrative Division, from 1985 renamed the Business Services Division, covered several back-office functions, including personnel/salaries and accounting.

Traffic planning and follow-up used a traffic statistical system, TSST/-TRAPS, and a line route result system, LRS.[318] While the statistical system was older, the line result system was introduced as a consequence of the businessman airline strategy of the early 1980s. By the late 1980s, improved follow-up systems of traffic statistics and route results were introduced, the Traffic Planning System (TRAF) and International Route Information System (IRIS).[319]

Second Generation Timetable System

By the late-1970s, development started on a new sophisticated timetable system on IBM, based on the IMS database and data terminals.[320] This Timetable Planning Traffic System (TPTS) consisted of a number of modules being gradually developed and implemented.

The first module, the Aircraft Rotations System (AROS) was implemented in 1979 and involved automatic updating of the timetable information, a function missing in the old system. AROS had a slinging function, too, which optimized the use of flights within the timetable framework. A second Timetable Distribution module automatically distributed all timetable changes to other systems using this information (i.e., to most SAS systems). Keying-in a desired route, a third system, Schedules Control (SCOL), would process the timetable and present the flight route. Fourth, a system was developed for

---

318 SAS, *Data Management*, 27/1 1983.
319 SDS/SDN, *UPTIME*, no. 3-4, 1989. Interview: *Stefan Andersson*.
320 Interview: *Stefan Andersson*.

timetable publishing. Fifth and finally, the functions were united in one system, TPTS, in 1983-84.

TPTS was the first step towards a flexible and market-oriented system. Until 1980, to create a traffic program required only that a timetable be laid out and statistical reports be sent to management every sixth month. TPTS moved traffic planning and editing onto a higher level that included concurrent adjustments to market demands according to the Businessman's Airline strategy.

Follow-up Systems

From the mid-1980s, a new dimension was added to traffic systems. Management wanted to follow-up on traffic development to optimize profit and as a consequence, a new kind of system appeared in SAS. In 1984-85, a budget and forecast system, Traffic Projection (TP) was added to TPTS. That was followed in 1987 by BCDC (Business Cooperative Data Collector), which produced statistics by retrieving information from various databases. In 1988, TRAF was implemented, the important statistical follow-up traffic system. Since 1989, COCA (Common Calculation System) calculated costs and income of different alternatives. IRIS produced flight results from 1990-91, combining TP, TRAF, costs and income. In addition, some smaller support systems were developed, such as a preliminary system timetable, simulating slings based on mathematical optimizing.

All these follow-up systems were based on statistical trends, producing monthly reports for management of routes and divisions, previously issued quarterly.

By 1990, traffic planning had the following chain of systems and information: traffic program and timetable, budget and forecast, traffic follow-up, and follow-up and calculation of profitability.[321] During the 1990s, these follow-up systems were transferred to the new client/server technology.

---

321 See Figure, *Traffic Program Planning.*

Traffic Program Planning 1989

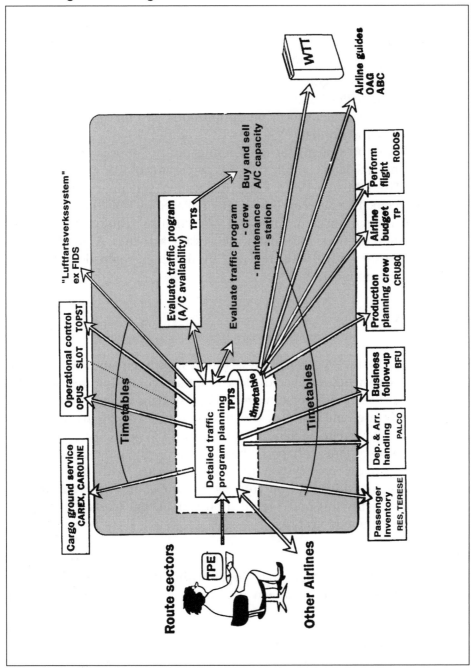

Source: SAS, Handbook of IT Policy and Standards.

Passenger

Marketing & Sales

From 1980, sales used the following systems: the reservations system PNR and its two integrated system functions, TICS for issuing tickets and PAS for automatic transfer of sales figures to the central accounting system ACS, and the Passenger Sales Statistics System (PASAS). The business traveler's airline strategy of 1981 made management focus on optimization and follow-up on profits. PAS made it easier to do that.[322]

Proper follow-up systems for route results did not appear until the mid-1980s. BFU and LRS, later combined in IRIS, were parts of SAS' reinforced market strategy. From the mid-1980s, Cargo had its own systems, especially SPAS. SOB was developed for sales on board, later replaced by SOBOB.[323]

An increasing number of fares and fare changes required a computer system to handle all these information-processing activities. A simple system was used from the early 1980s, replaced by the more sophisticated system "FARE QUOTE" around 1990.[324]

Reservations

RES/PNR

From the mid-1970s, SAS' RES/PNR reservation system remained by and large unchanged. A growing number of data terminals communicated with the system, and the second-generation mainframe systems of the 1980s created an increasingly large and complex structure of integrated systems around the basic reservation system, including the follow-up systems. Furthermore, a growing number of fares enhanced the pressure on the reservation system. Reservations was the core system that communicated with practically all other SAS systems, which kept on growing in number and size.[325] To replace this huge and highly integrated reservation system that worked 24 hours a day would be a tremendous task.

TERESE

Since the early 1980s, radical changes began within the business field of reservations. Distribution had so far been an integrated part of reservations, being

---

322 SAS, *Data Management*, 31/8 1983.
323 Interview: *Erik Bergreen-Lindberg*.
324 SAS, *Handbook of IT Policy and Standards*.
325 See Figure, *Sales and Reservations*. See also Figure, *RESAID System Environment 1991*, below in the text.

monopolized by SAS and its agents in Scandinavia. New technology and systems allowed travel agencies to break SAS' monopoly, manifested in the establishment of Scandinavian Multi-Access Reservations for Travel Agents (SMART) in 1984. Reservations and distribution started a process of separation that was reinforced by the expansion of large American airlines and distribution systems in Europe. To match the Americans, the European airlines responded by starting two great projects of building international distribution systems, AMADEUS and GALILEO. While preparing to move its distribution to AMADEUS, SAS decided to replace the old RES with a new reservations system or rather inventory system for the 1990s, called TERESE.[326]

Just like any other leading airline, SAS' reservation system was old, and both hardware and software needed replacement. More important, management wanted to make a strategic move to IBM. Since 1970, RES had operated on Univac/Sperry/Unisys mainframes and as Unisys had difficulties in producing a new generation of technology, SAS decided in 1987 to phase out Unisys and move all mainframe systems to IBM. Instead of just reprogramming RES, management took the opportunity of developing a new system from scratch. The SAS travel company strategy, which required new computer functions, was a further motivation for a new system. And finally, SAS management counted on selling a new system to some of the other large airlines that needed a replacement just as much as SAS did. Calculations showed that by selling the system to four airlines, the investments would be paid off.

While leaving the distribution part to the AMADEUS project, SAS and IBM started the joint TERESE project, based on the IMS database. A huge project organization was formed.[327]

The project did not develop according to plans, however. IBM seemed unable to master the technology for such enormous numbers of transactions and users kept on requiring new or changed facilities. Eventually, the project became more or less unmanageable, and expenses broke all budget limits.

By 1991, design and systems development were almost finished and they were about ready to start coding. Then, the Gulf Crisis undermined the economy of SAS, compelling the airline to make drastic cost reductions. As a result, the TERESE project was closed down in 1991.[328]

---

326 SAS, *Data Management*, 19-20/11 1985. SAS, *V/ARP*, 1984 to 1990. Interviews: *Arne Hansen, Göran Pettersson.*
327 SAS, *Data Management*, 21/9 1987. SAS, *ARP*, 1987 and 1988. Interview: *Arne Hansen.*
328 SDD, *Profil*, no. 43-44, 1991. Interview: *Arne Hansen.*

Distribution

SMART

During the 1970s, the PNR-system, data terminals, and more sophisticated tools of communication created the technological foundation of new relations between airlines, other conveyors (railroads), and travel agencies. Distribution used to be an integrated part of the airline's reservations system and in Scandinavia SAS had a de facto monopoly. The new technology gave travel agencies and agents the chance to break this monopoly. "Multi-access" was the international name for a new principle of distribution that began to spread in Western Europe and the USA. Multi-access meant that travel agencies could freely, and on a neutral basis, choose between a number of airlines, railroads, and so forth, offering alternative transportation in the area where the customer wanted to travel.

SAS disliked multi-access, because it undermined its monopoly and in order to remain in control, it offered travel agencies a connection to TICS/PAS and PNR, including financial follow-up and invoicing.[329] The Scandinavian travel agencies declined this offer, however. Travelers wanted multi-access and in the end, SAS had to comply with the principle.

SAS, SJ (the Swedish railroads), and a little later the airline Braathens SAFE of Norway, took the initiative to develop a new distribution system. Still, SAS tried to channel all information through PNR, but as the travel agencies stuck to their demand of having a neutral solution, SAS finally had to give in. A non-profit enterprise called SMART (Scandinavian Multi-Access Reservations for Travel Agents) was formed, covering all business expenses. SMART started in 1984.

SMART pressed SAS to reform its distribution strategy to allow competitive relations.[330] Being the leading Scandinavian airline, SAS wanted to make sure, that its booking system was found by all domestic agents. International studies showed that 90% of all sales were based on the first display. SAS products should not only be leading but also be visible. In the future, airlines had to compete, system-to-system and product-to-product instead of through the old distribution monopoly. Increasingly, SAS turned its attention to the marketing of products through a more open distribution system.

Since 1984, SMART has been the leading travel distributor in Scandinavia. In 1992 it was linked to AMADEUS.

---

329 SAS, *Data Management*, 15/11 1977; 8/7, 15/7, 24/10, 30/10 1980; 11/11 1982; 29-30/9 1983.
330 SAS, *Data Management*, Oct. 1983.

AMADEUS

More than anything else, the arrival of open distribution systems caused radical changes at SAS.[331]

Distributing travel services was vital to airlines as well as travel agencies. It included:

- Information about timetables, prices, and so on, for flights, hotels, and rental cars
- Making bookings
- Issuing tickets and other documents,
- "En-route" service during the travel,
- Invoicing and administration of payments for services performed,
- Follow-up on costs of travel undertaken.

During the 1980s, new IT technology undermined the information monopoly of airlines and made it much easier and cheaper to extend the communication networks outside the individual airline.

Furthermore, new partners entered the distribution market of travel services. These included:

- Integrated reservations and distribution systems of airlines (American Airlines-SABRE, United Airlines-APOLLO, etc.)
- Electronic publishers (e.g., Dun and Bradstreet, the Official Airline Guide/OAG, Reed International/ABC)
- Credit/payment card companies (American Express, EuroCard, etc.).

All these partners had one thing in common, they wanted to make money from information, including bookings, document delivery, and payment arrangements. Their systems used modern IT and they were user-friendly to the benefit of firms, passengers, and travel agencies. Furthermore, the systems often included a wide selection of airlines, hotels, car rental companies and so on. Finally, suppliers and customers were offered attractive prices on transactions.

Accordingly, SAS was challenged to such a degree that it had to come up with a comprehensive strategy for distribution to ensure its commercial existence under changing premises. That included heavy investments in new technology and enhanced expenses for new distributors, particularly the international distribution systems SMART and AMADEUS, the new reservation system TERESE, Diners Club Nordic for electronic payments, and later on

---

331 SAS, *ARP*, 1986.

automatic ticketing and boarding. Through these initiatives SAS fought to keep its dominant position in the Scandinavian market.

SMART signaled a growing trend in international airlines business towards open and competitive distribution. From the mid-1980s, the pressure of American airlines, having already been deregulated, was clearly felt in Europe. Prospects of direct competition from the huge integrated reservations and distribution systems of these companies (SABRE, APOLLO) pressed the national airlines in Europe to prepare for open and international solutions.

In 1985-86, the 22 airlines of The Association of European Airlines (AEA) tried to agree on a joint system, but failed as a consequence of differing systems and interests. On the ruins of this attempt, two international distribution system projects arose. An IBM group, including Swissair, KLM, British Airways, Alitalia, and a few smaller airlines, started to develop a system called GALILEO. At the same time, a Unisys group, including Iberia, Lufthansa, Air France, and SAS, began to develop AMADEUS.[332]

The Unisys group bought System One of Eastern Airlines as a basis for further development (curiously enough, an IBM system). In 1987, a large and growing project group was formed in Miami to outline specifications and requirements, including all changes needed to satisfy the airlines involved. It took 2 1/2 years of "dogfights" between these multiple interest groups before specifications could be signed and the Miami group closed down.

The AMADEUS project moved to Europe for final development. The operation center was located in Munich, the development center on the Riviera in France, headquarters in Madrid Spain, and the president came from SAS (Curt Ekström). This huge, multi-national project group worked for the next couple of years bringing together System One and the specifications developed in Miami in a new system called AMADEUS. Not surprisingly, the project became extremely expensive, breaking all budget plans. In 1991, the Gulf Crisis made SAS give up its joint ownership of AMADEUS for financial reasons. AMADEUS came into operation in 1992.

These revolutionary changes in distribution and airlines business were backed by internal initiatives of the SAS organization.[333] In 1988, upgraded distribution activities became a vital part of a new division, the Data Distribution Division (DDD). The objectives of DDD were to make SAS products visible in all major markets and to ensure that technical and resource limits never prevented SAS from carrying out its market strategy, including, in the long run, reduced costs of distribution.

From 1989, DDD, reorganized into the Marketing Automation Division (MAD) in 1990, focused more directly on creating an automated sales chain of reservations, distribution, and stations, soon to be the start of the large Automated Ticketing and Boarding (ATB) project of the 1990s.

Sales and Reservation 1989

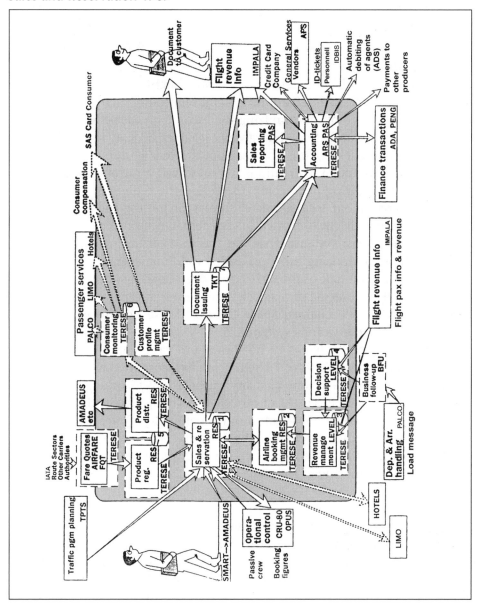

Source: SAS, *Handbook of IT Policy and Standards.*

---

332 Interviews: *Arne Hansen, Göran Pettersson.*
333 SAS, *Data Management,* 13/2, 1/6 1988; 16/1 1989; 31/5 1991. SAS, *ARP,* 1988 to 1990. Interviews: *Göran Pettersson, Björn Boldt-Christmas.*

Yield Management

Booking and Overbooking

From the early days of SAS, Space Control existed as a function within the Market department. In the beginning, it was simply equivalent to booking, a function that manually registered the sales on archive files. Having introduced a computer-based reservations system, registering might also be automated, even to the point of optimizing the income on each flight.

No-shows and cancellations had always troubled SAS, as they did all airlines. SAS used an overbooking strategy from the very start, but based this on experience. The computer reservations system solved some of these problems, but to meet the growing price competition and the economic stagnation of the 1970s management took a greater interest in raising the load factor. A system for overbooking was devised to counterbalance no-shows and cancellations (i.e., a forecast system). That was the start of turning the registering function into an optimizing function, called yield management.

During the second half of the 1970s, two overbooking systems were developed to fight the problems of no-shows and cancellations.[334] As a result the Booking function was renamed Space Control. These systems were an integrated part of the reservations system RES.

The extent of the problems of no-shows and cancellations may be seen from figures of the early 1990s.[335] Then, no shows amounted to 9% of 15 million passengers, and there were as many cancellations as tickets sold (i.e., all seats were actually sold twice). Most cancellations happened in charter travels. For instance, Spies would book seats months before departure, often based on too optimistic a forecast of demand. The first two components of a yield management system sought to compensate for such problems, trying to sell the seats at the right time and at the right price.

LEVEL

True optimizing did not begin until the start of the Business Traveler's Airline strategy in 1981, when Space Control became part of the Commercial Division.[336] Seats were separated into two classes, business and economy. The primary target of the strategy was to get as many full-price paying business people on every flight as possible. As a consequence, optimizing was most important, also because businessmen often booked at short notice. SAS optimized on two classes only, but in 1988 it expanded to one business class and

334 SAS, *Data management*, 30/8 1977.
335 Interview: *Helge Rasmussen.*
336 SAS, *Data Management*, 14-15/10, 19-20/11 1985. SAS, *V/ARP*, 1981 to 1990.

four economy classes. In 1990, the number of classes was extended to 12, including two or three different products of the business class, and even more on intercontinental flights. During the 1990s, open competition made the number of products explode.

The first true optimizing system, Departure Level Control System, LEVEL, was implemented in 1982.[337] LEVEL was a so-called "leg" optimizing system, a leg being the smallest operating unit of a plane, namely flying from one city to another. A flight going from Oslo, via Copenhagen to Madrid would have two legs. The next level of unit was a "segment", meaning the product that was sold, such as the journey from Oslo to Madrid. Often passengers flew by way of more than one plane to reach their destinations and in case of price differentiating, optimizing would be insufficient. Not until the 1990s, was a system developed to cover the whole journey.

Revenue Accounting

Second Generation System: PADOCS

Plans for a successor to TACS, Passenger Document System, PADOCS, started in 1978. During the first half of the 1980s, PADOCS was developed in phases on the IBM 370 and the IMS database, to be implemented in 1985.[338] On the basis of small samples, the first system phase enabled the revenue accounting department to give the most accurate revenue accounting of tickets between SAS and other airlines. In order to optimize the use of resources, manual calculations were partly replaced by a number of simulating models in the second phase. A third phase, which registered all passenger documents eliminating uneconomic double registering, formed the database of future revenue accounting systems. Furthermore, other systems could access all document information in this data bank.

In 1980, a provisional system, PADOCS Interims, substituted for the worn out punched card systems in many areas until the true PADOCS was implemented. PADOCS Interims ran partly on a mini-computer in the revenue accounting department in Copenhagen and partly on the large IBM system.

Unlike TACS which it replaced, PADOCS covered the whole field of revenue accounting. PADOCS was built on a statistical model and included sampling and estimating to create an interim monthly report. PADOCS received its information on SAS' sales and cash flow from PAS. Clearing information concerning other airlines was obtained from IATA.

---

337 Interview: *Helge Rasmussen.*
338 SAS, *Data Management*, 15/1 1983; 19-20/11 1985. SAS, *Data News*, Sept. 1980. Interview: *Arne Hansen.*

A New Second Generation System: IMPALA

While PADOCS was being developed, SAS introduced its new businessman's airline strategy. Market orientation and service improvements towards this segment added to and changed the demands of information access and processing. Although PADOCS was data based and processed information much faster than TACS, it did not suffice to meet the new business demands nor did it provide sufficient forecasting. Primarily, inaccuracy was caused by the fact that calculations were based on flown tickets, instead of sold tickets, causing much delay before information was presented to management. That is why the revenue accounting department, having just finished developing PADOCS, started planning for a new system.

In 1986, a revenue accounting system was bought by KLM to form the basis of a new SAS system. This was the beginning of the great IMPALA (Information Management Passenger Line Accounting) project, which continued until 1992.[339] The first phase of IMPALA, implemented in 1989, made up the fundamental part of the system, which concerned ticket revenue accounting and statistical information. The second and final phase improved revenue accounting towards other airlines, including a sub-system to produce a general view of income for individual flights and to calculate agent commissions. In 1992, the second phase concluded systems development and implementation of IMPALA. Like PADOCS, IMPALA used IBM and IMS

While PADOCS worked on the basis of flown tickets, IMPALA was based on sold tickets. This difference was one main reason for developing a new system. Management received relevant information much more quickly than before, because a long time might pass from buying a ticket to the actual flight. Now, information was caught at the moment of sale, calculating much earlier the share of the price that SAS was entitled to get.

Compared with PADOCS, the forecast system formed the other essential improvement of IMPALA. IMPALA could predict the result of all alternatives where the ticket had not yet been flown. Quickly, this facility gave sales and marketing knowledge on the results of individual marketing campaigns. PADOCS had similar tools of analysis, but IMPALA could follow information right down to the level of an individual ticket and produce very accurate information, on the basis of comprehensive data processing in the enlarged database. Finally, the forecasting sub-system was made much bigger than before to cover many more segments of the market. As a consequence, the IMPALA database was much enlarged compared with PADOCS.

---

339 SAS, *Data Management*, 19-20/11 1985. SDD, *Profil*, no. 14, 17/18, 1989, no. 22/23, 1990, no. 10, 1991, no. 2, 1992. Interview: *Mogens Meisler*.

Revenue Information 1989

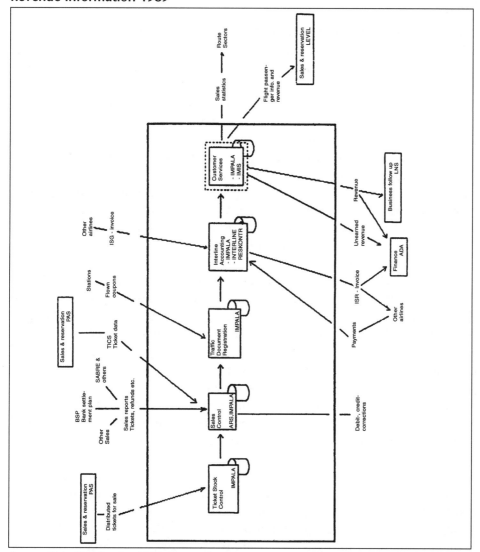

Source: SAS, Handbook of IT Policy and Standards.

The flow and processing of revenue information was based on input from the sale of SAS tickets and on sales reports of other airlines.[340] Interline accounting was done to show actual SAS sales. The resulting revenue information of SAS sales on various routes and total sales were then transmitted to the many users of revenue information, including Sales and Marketing, Route Sectors, Finance, Business follow-up, and Yield Management.

---

340 See Figure, *Revenue Information.*

Cargo

Plans for a Second Generation System: CARINA/CAROLINE

As a consequence of the SAS reorganization in 1981, SAS Cargo became a result unit within the Commercial Division. The introduction of the businessman's airline strategy affected SAS Cargo deeply.[341] All non-profitable routes were stopped, which greatly reduced Cargo activities. The important cargo sector of the past became a downgraded business that was paid little attention by top management.

While downgrading Cargo, growing competition from other airlines operating in Scandinavia, particularly Lufthansa and KLM, and from new transporters specializing in air cargo, stepped up pressure on SAS Cargo. Consequently, competitors took over much of its market. Having had half the Scandinavian air cargo market in 1980, its market share was more than halved during the 1980s. Under such circumstances, planning and developing new computer systems was no easy task.

CARIN was implemented in the late 1970s and its revenue system during the early 1980s. In spite of the crisis and reduction of cargo activities at that time, SAS Cargo, and particularly the cargo group in SAS Data, started to prepare for a new handling system based on a database management system and further automation of functions and relations.[342] Increased market orientation and competition urged SAS Cargo to improve its data services towards agents and customers, including management reporting.

In 1982, KLM and Swissair, for instance, had market-oriented systems functions such as booking, space control, airway bill capture, issuance, and rating, and Lufthansa and British Airways planned to introduce these facilities in the near future, too. Technically, other airlines were able to put data terminals with some built-in functions with Scandinavian agents. Cargo could foresee open distribution and competition on its Scandinavian home market, just like Passenger. According to a market survey in autumn 1980, most Scandinavian agents were strongly interested in automated data communication with SAS, especially in matters of booking and airway bills. SAS Cargo chose to include these functions in a new system, taking into account that agents sold about 90% of its freight.

From the time of implementation of CARIN in the late 1970s, Cargo considered the character of a next generation system. Cargo reviewed the Univac

---

341 SAS, *Data Management*, 26/3 1982. SAS, *V/ARP*, 1981 to 1990. SAS, *The First Fifty Years*, pp. 60-62.
342 SAS, *Data Management*, Sept. 1981; 26/3, June and Oct. 1982. Interviews: *Jørgen Herz* and *Niels Bloch*.

and IBM systems, but found them insufficient to cover a number of local demands. Instead Cargo decided on a Tandem databased system, called CARINA (Cargo Information Application).

CARINA was a total cargo system covering all major handling functions, some converted from CAREX/CARIN and others that were new. CARINA was based on ordinary data terminals, but contained some sophisticated presentations. Starting in 1981-82, the project was planned to finish in 1985-86. SAS Data took care of systems development.

Besides the basic functions of CARIN (export, import, transfer), CARINA would include several new functions. First, sales offices, agents, and customers would make reservations through data terminals. Second, it would offer space control. Third, there would be automatic data collection and issuance of airway bill on SAS stations, by agents, and customers. Fourth, a joint database, storing and applying the information of airway bills during the whole process of transportation. And fifth, improved management reporting according to decentralized result responsibility of the businessman's airline strategy. As a result, CARINA targeted enhanced automation, integration, and reporting. Finally, SAS Data and Cargo counted on selling CARINA or its modules to other airlines.

During the summer of 1982, the consulting firm Enator evaluated the comprehensive and costly CARINA project, to clarify its foundation and economic potentials.[343]

CARINA was designed as a functional system. Enator wanted the project to be based on a business and organizational view that aligned with the business traveler's airline strategy. To make that come true, it was recommended that SAS Cargo management should take over the lead of the project, having so far left most initiatives to SAS Data.

Enator helped SAS Cargo formulate a new strategic perspective on CARINA. SAS Cargo's first information systems policy was linked to the new system and included the following considerations:

- Operative activities
- Product development
- Sales
- Optimizing the business
- Information exchange within the total transport chain from sender to receiver
- Satisfying centralized as well as decentralized wishes
- Minimizing transaction costs.

---

343 SAS, *Data Management*, 16/9, 4/10, 7/10 1982.

Furthermore, the CARINA functions were seen from a market point of view:

- Booking via terminal
- Space control
- System wide access to status information
- Transfer of import data to agents and customers
- Module structure to improve possible sales to other airlines
- Compatibility with O & W Doris (the SAS forwarding company)
- Data capture at source.

To stress the reorientation of the project, its name was changed to CAROLINE (Cargo On-Line). The project was developed according to a plan laid down by Enator. First the export module would be made, then the import module in 1986, completely replacing the old CAREX/CARIN systems. CAROLINE aimed at being a distributed system with much local data processing, still based on Tandem, including the new booking and issuance of airway bill functions of CARINA. In 1984-85, the export module was partly implemented at some Scandinavian stations.

The project was drawn out, however, and costs increased above budget. Finally, Cargo management lost patience in 1985, closed down the whole project and stopped cooperating with SAS Data. As a result, everything was washed out, leaving Cargo with CAREX and CARIN.[344]

The failure of the Caroline project may be understood from various angles. First, it included a shift of technology platform from Unisys to Tandem. Second, it intended to substitute a database management system for a file system. Third, Enator convinced SAS Cargo management that the functional CARINA system of SAS Data should be replaced by a market-oriented system. Fourth, by the early or mid-1980s, nobody had any real experience with a market-oriented system. Fifth, new functions had to be added to the existing CAREX/CARIN system (i.e., programmed from scratch). Sixth, during the project, SAS Cargo was changing requirements. Seventh, SAS Data had little experience with Tandem. To conclude, too many changes had to be carried out at the same time. The move forward was too ambitious. No wonder the project failed.

---

344 SDD, *Profil,* no. 9-10, 1984. Interview: *Jørgen Herz.*

CAROLINE II

Since the mid-1980s, Scandinavian air cargo competition intensified and the SAS Cargo market share kept on falling. As a consequence of SAS' new expanding strategy of 1985, SAS Cargo was required to upgrade its competitiveness. A comprehensive and market-oriented computer system covering cargo fields became an important part of this offensive.

In 1988, a project was started to develop a new, total cargo system.[345] Cargo management had lost faith in SAS Data and chose Enator as its new system supplier. Enator started all over again. A completely new cargo system was designed, not only covering handling but also revenue and even mail. In cooperation with users, and even a few specialists from SAS Data, Enator carried out a comprehensive analysis, preparing requirements and specifications for programming the system. The new system was called CAROLINE II, wanting to build on the basis of the Caroline project of the early 1980s.

CAROLINE II contained the following facilities:

- Cargovision: linking agents, customers, customs, and so on
- Booking and space control: flight profile, booking and capacity control, follow-up on capacity use
- Cargo handling: document free transports, control of cargo carriers, historic information
- Cargo accounting information: supporting cash booking on local cargo offices, invoicing, calculating net income, reports for results and statistics, supporting income optimizing routing
- Air mail information: modules for planning, handling, and mail revenue accounting, supporting mail services handling at airports and integrated with the space control system of SAS Cargo to make better use of capacity
- Handling revenue accounting between SAS and the post office.
- Providing historic information.

CAROLINE II was meant to support SAS Cargo strategies for cost efficiency and increased profits and competitiveness. In keeping with the new one-technology platform strategy of SAS, it was recommended that CAROLINE II be developed on IBM and its IMS database.

Specifications were ready in 1989 and SAS Cargo invited tenders for the task of systems development and programming. Cap Gemini was chosen as head supplier and SAS Data Denmark as sub-supplier.

---

345 SAS, *Data Management*, 1988. SDD, *Profil*, no. 11/12, 40, 1988.

The project was much too expensive, however, costing more than one hundred million SEK.[346] Top management let Cargo know that the project could not be continued unless two or three partners were found. In spite of intensive marketing directed at many airlines throughout the world, nobody wanted to buy CAROLINE II. At the time, two standard cargo systems dominated the airline business. One group of airlines employed Unisys USAS Cargo developed around 1980. Another group of airlines had an IBM standard system, the Fast System, originally developed by Alitalia in the 1970s. Some had systems of their own, such as SAS.

Although all cargo systems were old, no airline wanted to enter into business relations with SAS, probably because of the intensified competition of the time. In the end, SAS Cargo made an agreement with Alitalia, however, to develop a new cargo system called COLUMBUS. Alitalia and SAS saw big business opportunities in a successor to its old cargo system, which was marketed by IBM and had been bought by more than forty airlines. As a result, COLUMBUS ended up being based more on the Alitalia system than on CAROLINE II. IBM was to produce the new system. This was just before the outbreak of the Gulf War in 1991.

The Gulf War brought all cargo projects to a halt. Once more, SAS was left with its systems of the 1970s, as were all other airlines. Again, SAS Cargo had surpassed its capability. From a low level, SAS Cargo had wanted to move too many steps ahead at one time.

During all these troublesome plans and failures, SAS Cargo kept on running its business and information flow.[347] It started at one end with SAS corporate and traffic planning. It continued via SAS Cargo business planning and external relations with agents, customers, customs, and other airlines, to internal relations with flight departure and arrival. Finally, business follow-up and financial consolidation ended the Cargo circle of information and activities.

---

346 Interviews: *Jørgen Herz, Robert Skoog.*
347 See Figure, *Cargo Information.*

Cargo Information 1989

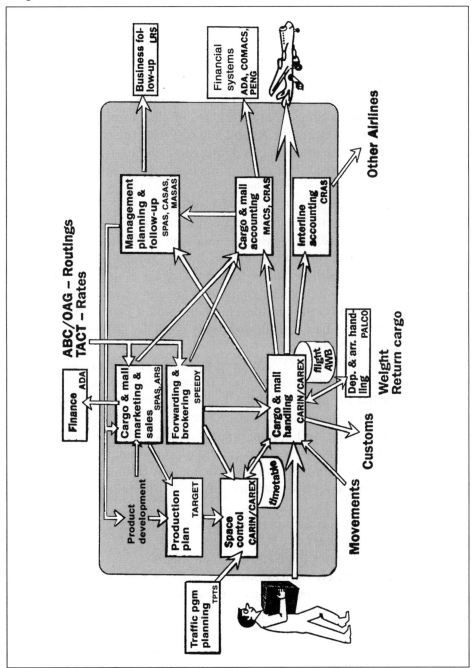

Source: SAS, Handbook of IT Policy and Standards.

Station

Second Generation System for Check-in: PALCO 2

More than any other division, Traffic Services Division (TSD) took care of customer services, receiving and sending passengers to the planes in the airports, loading and unloading planes, and doing some booking and ticket service, including services onboard.[348] Furthermore, TSD handled station activities in Scandinavia for other airlines, making up 1/3 of all station activities in the first half of the 1980s. During the second half of 1980s, the large airlines took over station handling themselves, competing more and more with SAS, while only handling of smaller airlines in Scandinavian airports was left to TSD.[349]

In 1982, it was decided to start developing a data management-based successor to the old file-system LOCS/PALCO 1, called PALCO 2.[350] To hasten fulfillment, plans were divided in two, concentrating on the more important check-in part first. Increased service demands of the businessman's airline strategy called for an improved system, the old one going back to 1969. PALCO 1 could not offer such special services to customers as quick check-in and seating. Furthermore, offering seat guarantees or sales of empty seats would increase sales. Generally, product development would benefit from greater flexibility. Finally, SAS had to introduce new check-in facilities because its main competitors had done so.

The requirements for PALCO 2, dictated by the businessman's airline strategy, were set up jointly by TSD and the Commercial Division. Furthermore, the system needed to integrate with all other systems that communicated with stations, such as reservations, revenue accounting, movement control, cargo and mail, catering, and ground operations. Primarily, daily activities of check-in and PALCO 2 were based on information coming from the reservations system and with some information being sent from OPS/TOPRO, too. The following essential services were to be fulfilled by the system:

- Servicing all passengers with particular demands, for instance food
- Pre-booking a fixed seat
- Seating of all passengers in all classes on all flights
- Informing crew of passenger information, such as names, special food requests and transfer information, to improve services on board
- Paving the way for a future self service check-in system
- Enabling a gradual extension of functions and capacity to adjust to future commercial demands

---

348 See Figure, *Station Handling Information.*
349 SAS, *V/ARP*, 1981 to 1990.
350 SAS, *Data Management*, 1/6, 3/6, 20/10 1982.

• Allowing for distributed data processing (in Copenhagen, Oslo, and Stockholm) to reduce the risks of being affected by external disturbances.

PALCO 1 met only a few of these requirements, as did the systems sold by IBM and Univac. As a consequence, TSD and SAS Data joined to create the specifications for a new system that could provide the required services and would build on experience and knowledge of the existing system.

PALCO 2 was developed in modules and implemented in 1984-85.[351] Contrary to most new second-generation systems of the 1980s, which chose IBM and IMS, PALCO 2 was a Univac system based on Univac's database management system, DMS (Data Management System). PALCO 2 stuck to Univac because of close relations between check-in and reservations.

PALCO 2 improved the capabilities of TSD and particularly its station activities that made up a vital direct link to customers. With the introduction of PALCO 2, check-in was highly automated, too.

Second Generation System for Load Control: PAH

PALCO 2 covered check-in, only. In 1987, a project started to modernize and add new functions to load control, including a new seating system that for various reasons was found in the load control system.[352]

Unlike the check-in system, the new load control, PAH (Palco Aircraft Handling) was developed on IBM and IMS, in accordance with the general plan of converting to IBM. Plans were developed to convert the check-in system to IBM, too, but were given up for want of resources. TSD followed the new IT strategy and by way of tenders, left it to the market to decide who should develop the new system. The Swedish software and consulting company Programator won the contract for the PAH project.

For the first time, SAS Data lost a mainframe systems development project, one of the shocks of the late 1980s that made SAS Data realize the radical change of tides. Programator could not cope with the task, however, and with its extensive knowledge in the field of load control, SAS Data had to take over. The project was finished in 1991, but it did not stabilize until a couple of years later. Having implemented PAH, the check-in system was renamed Passenger Check-In (PCI).

What PAH did was primarily to automate many more functions than its predecessor. The user just had to make a few inputs for each flight, because most information was entered automatically. PAH received information from a number of adjoining systems.[353]

---

351 SAS, *Data Management*, 14-15/10 1985 and 19/11 1985. Interview: *Anders Eriksson*.
352 SAS, *Data Management*, 21/9 1987. Interview: *Anders Eriksson*.
353 See Figure, *Station Handling Information*.

RES sent bookings, passenger and booking forecasts came from LEVEL, timetable information was based on TPTS, OPUS informed on which planes were to fly the individual flights, RODOS ran fuel information, and CRU80 provided information on crew. PAH also sent a great deal of information to other systems.

PAH received booking forecasts at an early stage, a couple of days before departure and then projected load, weight, and balance of the plane. PAH could project right up to departure, updating as check-in, crew, and fuel information arrived. PAH proposed load planning, too. Just before departure, forecasts and reality met in a load sheet.

PAH aimed at automating as many functions as possible, including sophisticated forecasting, to save personnel and improve security—load control being a vital part of plane security. As in the case of all previous load control systems, producing a "load sheet" was an important part of its functionality. The load sheet contained all information on who and what was onboard the plane (passengers, crew, cargo and mail, fuel, luggage, etc.), and where it was found onboard (its location in different parts of the plane).

The production of a load sheet was based on a number of technical and security rules, apart from the current information on passengers, cargo, and so on. PAH had all basic information on planes and their loading structure originating from the timetable system, TPTS. Being informed of the type of plane by Movement Control, OPUS, the night before departure, PAH was able to use the relevant information for load control, because many rules were based on plane types, sometimes including individual planes. To process incoming information, PAH contained a very large register.

PAH was divided into two parts, one part contained master data, the other part aircraft handling data. Master data was the basic data needed to handle the individual flight, with aircraft handling data being the operating part. Carrier data made up a large field, covering all rules specific to the various airlines. Aircraft data contained all the rules, depending on which plane type was flying. Finally, Route data decided which way to fly. Information on each station was located into Station's data.

When planning PAH, a 3rd generation system with a DB2 relational database and distributed data processing was examined as a possible preference to the hierarchical IMS database. No stable database was found that ensured full uptime, however, and PAH had to be working and accessible all the time. Finally around 1990, Station did not have functions that motivated a PC system.

Station Handling Information 1989

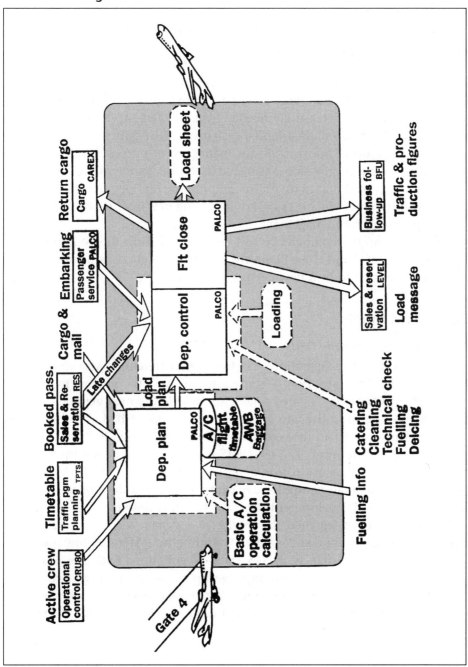

Source: SAS, *Handbook of IT Policy and Standards.*

Operation

Primarily, Operation Division (OD) included Crew and Operations Control. OD's information systems integrated with a number of other systems.[354] By the mid-1980s, OD developed its first IT strategy.[355] The strategic goals aimed at improving efficiency of flight security and in-flight service. To fulfill these goals, rational data production had to be ensured. Quick and reliable statistical information was increasingly needed for management decisions. Existing functional and operationally oriented systems made it difficult to achieve statistical data and other information for management purposes, however. Furthermore, relevant information was stored in several systems (CRU, TPTS, PAL-CO, RES). Hence, OD had to invest in computer technology to improve information, communications, and support, including new mainframe systems and follow-up systems for management.

Whereas computer competence had developed within the departments of Operations Control and Crew Planning, overall strategic considerations at division level seemed to be a new perspective for OD.[356]

Operations Control

Second Generation System: OPUS
In the early 1980s, the Operations Control Center (renamed Movement Control Center by the late 1980s) started to prepare for a new mainframe system.[357] Univac/Sperry seemed unable to provide the next generation computer technology, so in the late 1970s SAS management had already decided to replace Univac with an IBM database system, following MOPS in technical maintenance. Furthermore, the 1981 SAS strategy change urged the business side to play a more dynamic role in computer development. At the Movement Control Center a small computer department that had developed since the late 1970s prepared development plans for the new system.

At first, the group searched the world for a system to buy, and for some time a Canadian system was considered. Finding no system usable, it was decided to develop a system with SAS Data. Negotiations with the Canadian company had qualified the computer group to define its requirements. It pressed SAS Data to produce a system that would meet these requirements and would be based on a fixed price and time of delivery, with SAS Data be-

354 See Figure, *Operation Control*.
355 SAS, *V/ARP*, 1981 to 1990.
356 SAS, *Data Management*, 25/2 1986.
357 Interview: *Bent Lund*.

ing used to set the premises itself. The new system based on IBM and its IMS database was called OPUS (Operations Control System).

OPUS intended to automate all important information activities of the Movement Control Center. The computer group prepared the analytical basis of the system. To integrate all sides of traffic operations in a process of automation, all activities were thought of as a matter of flying, including ground and special operations, such as technical maintenance that was handled manually. Looking at all activities from the same point of view, it was possible to achieve automatic slinging or flight-rotation, combined with assignments of particular planes and ground operations. It was all managed from the database that did the updating, including issuing telegrams to relevant parties concerning flight disposals. Still, the timetable formed the foundation of information, including technical information and rules of technical maintenance. Systems analysis was facilitated by the fact that all links in the process were fixed.

Developments began in 1982 and programming in 1984. OPUS was developed in modules, which were implemented one at a time to allow users to see the results. OPUS had five modules. The first module, the "weather" module, was introduced in 1985. Two modules followed the next year, one a "flight" data module that contained the timetable for handling such important data as when to do maintenance and two, a "flight progress" module. The two final modules, a "simulation" module and a "report" module were implemented in 1988. A graphical interface dialog to the mainframe computer was developed to indicate different activities and states by way of colors.

The old OPS/TOPRO system kept on operating while the OPUS modules were gradually being implemented. Parallel operations went on for some years, until OPUS finally took over and OPS/TOPRO closed down in 1988. As a result of automation, all manual procedures disappeared, including the large overview table.

The automated OPUS functions reduced personnel demand and increased the speed of information flow. Furthermore, it made up a much better planning tool than its predecessor. OPUS predicted the time of maintenance of the planes and based on the timetable, OPUS could create an updated and improved planning of flight operations for the following ten-week period. At the same time, planning data and reported movements of planes were crucial to other SAS systems, especially technical maintenance, crew planning, check-in and load control, cargo, and reservations. A number of complex validating routines were therefore introduced to make the OPUS information as accurate as possible. Opus integrated with more than twenty systems, primarily in the role of information supplier, in a very complex system world.

The statistical operations system, TOPST, was linked to OPUS, too. It became the key to ensure the highly upgraded punctuality of the 1990s. TOPST worked in a special module in order not to disturb the operation of OPUS.

Flight Dispatch

Since mid 1980s, RODOS (Route Documentation System) handled Flight Dispatch information.[358] RODOS was a system that combined maps, technical manuals, routings in the air, weather forecasts, load control information on load and weight of the plane, rules of fuel, and so on. All these incoming data were being changed all the time, even during the flight. To produce an optimized intercontinental flying route, RODOS made millions of calculations.

Crew

Second Generation System: CRU80

CRU70 was implemented in 1976, but soon pre-studies started for a successor, called CRU80 (Crew Planning System). One reason to plan for a replacement of CRU70 was that Univac had not presented a satisfactory substitute for the U494. Another reason was plans within the Technical and Operations Department for a general move from Univac to IBM, following the road of the MOPS project that was based on the IBM MVS operating system and the IMS database manager. Furthermore, the new Operations Division and SAS market strategy in 1981 pushed for a better crew planning system.

CRU80 analysis and development continued during the first half of the 1980s.[359] CRU80 was divided into several modules: pairing, schedule, disposal, vacation planning, meetings, resources (of production, stand-by, vacation, leave, illness—for both planning and disposal) and legality (collective agreements, rules of security, etc.). A Basic part made it possible to build detailed elements of data, to be deployed in the succeeding phases. These data elements contained information reported to SAS for the benefit of all functional demands. The Basic part improved planning capability and thereby reduced costs of the pairing system.

CRU80 automated many more functions than its predecessor, including check-in and checkout and automatic production allotments to crewmembers. The disposal module improved the potential for re-disposal of plans and

---

358 SAS, *Data Management*, 9/10 1980. Interview: *Bent Lund*.
359 SAS, *Data Management*, 30/3 and 3/6 1982, June 1982.
360 SDD, *Profil*, no. 23, 1990.

alternative schedules. In general, CRU80 reduced personnel in crew and crew administration.

Daily, CRU80 was an indispensable tool that managed all the rules of manning and collective agreements, authority rules, and SAS' security demands. Phases one and two of CRU 80 contained 110 functions, updating all information on every crew member, flight services, working hours, training, and the complete SAS traffic program, including all data on manning rules. CRU80 was prepared for gradual extensions.

As its predecessor, CRU80 was still a mainframe system based on data terminals for simple input and output. Besides increased automation, CRU80 had a much bigger legality module of rules than the old system. Many of the legal issues dealt with collective agreements with seven crew unions. By the mid-1990s, for example, the legality module made up 40 % of the whole system. While CRU70 concentrated on master planning, CRU80 focused more on disposal to improve handling of often changing flight operations.

CRU80 was implemented in 1984-85 with CRU70 operating in parallel until 1990, however.[360] The main users of CRU80 were:

- Crew base offices
- Crew disposal offices
- Crew scheduling offices
- Crew resource planning
- Scanair crew management.

Far more than its predecessor, CRU80 integrated with other systems as follows:[361]

TPTS: CRU80 had a database of all timetable disposal information that was being continuously updated. Changed information of disposal, such as cancellations of flights, delays, etc., was taken from CRU80 to see its consequences, including re-manning for a new type of plane. In case of re-manning, a warning was sent for that purpose.

OPUS: CRU80 received information of flight movements from OPUS (i.e., every landing, departure, and deviation from the timetable). In case of deviations, for instance delays, CRU80 checked the legality module for any rule-related manning problems.

---

361 SAS, *Data Management*, 25/2, 6/3 1986. SAS, *Data News*, August 1985. SDD, *Profil*, no. 23, 1990. Interview: *Allan Sørensen*. See Figure, *Operation Control*.

RES: Fifteen days before departure, seats needed to be available for crew-members transferring to their destinations (these bookings were made on RES). In the early 1990s, automatic Express Check-in was introduced for crew.

PALCO: CRU80 was integrated with load control, providing information on the total number of pilots and cabin attendants on board the individual plane.

Per Diem: Per Diem obtained all its information from CRU80 and calculated per diem payments and allowances for the personnel. From 1990, personnel, using pin codes, were able to draw money from automatic tellers, which were connected to the salary system and the individual's bank account.

CRU-S was an improved version of an old statistical system of CRU70. It generated the same files as CRU70, but was extended to cover more rules and internal reporting. The reports provided information on flown kilometers and average productivity. Working hours were measured 'from push back to on block', too.

CRU80 meant to be a system for the 1990s. However, when CRU80 was being implemented in 1985, the view of information systems in SAS had already turned in a more strategic and market-oriented direction. Primarily, CRU80 automated a number of functions and enlarged the logical rule base. In a world of hierarchical databases built around separate functional areas, it was difficult to do cross-information processing of the individual applications for purposes of decision-making. So when management wanted combined information to meet increasing competition, the limits of CRU80 became obvious.

Operation Control 1989

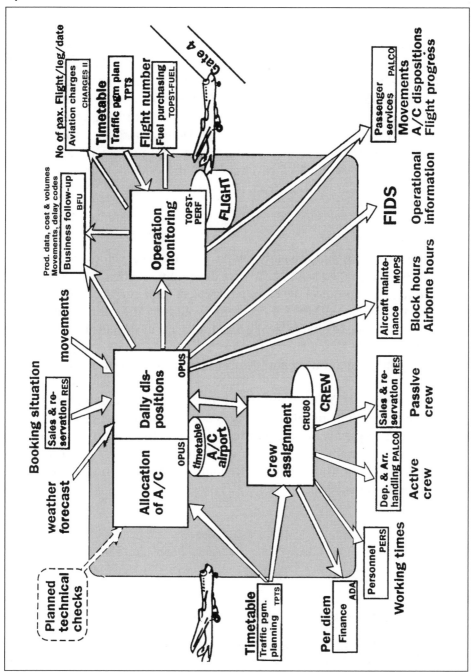

Source: SAS, Handbook of IT Policy and Standards.

Technical

Second Generation System: MOPS

Implementation of the large MOPS project finished by the mid-1980s and included the six subsystems of RELS, MOCO, ROCO, LIPS, BOVAC, and MRS.[362] Plans for other subsystems, especially an economic system had to be given up. During the late 1980s, Technical Division (TD) was reduced and rationalized when heavy maintenance was outsourced and light maintenance adapted to a new generation of Boeing and McDonnell-Douglas airplanes that needed less maintenance. Furthermore, growing competition pressed TD to reinforce its efforts to reduce costs. As a consequence, the once dominant technical field within SAS lost ground. Instead, IT investments were directed at market-oriented systems.[363]

Plans of MATS 2

During the late 1970s and the early 1980s, TD tried to develop a modernized successor to MATS, called MATS 2. To save development costs, SAS, Iberia, and Univac joined in a common development project for a new data-based system to replace the file-based MATS 1.[364] Iberia would do the programming and have the system free of charge, while SAS took care of systems development, and Univac was free to sell the system on the market. Iberia was not capable of handling the programming part, however, and the project had to be abandoned.

In 1986, Technical Division and SAS Data took over programming.[365] SAS Data worked on MATS 2 in the following years, but the project collapsed again for reasons of complexity, for want of resources, and insufficient management priority, and was finally closed down during the Gulf Crisis in 1991.[366] So, MOPS and MATS continued to run the maintenance information linked to several other systems.[367]

---

362 SAS, *MOPS Information Handbook*, 1980-1987. See also, previous chapter on Technical.
363 SAS, *V/ARP*, 1981 to 1990. Interview: *Mindor Lundström*.
364 SAS, *Data Management*, 29/9 1978, Sept. 1978; April and Dec. 1983.
365 SAS, *Data Management*, 27/6, 1/7, 29/12 1986.
366 SDD, *Profil*, no. 22-23, 1989, no. 40, 1991.
367 See Figure, *Aircraft Maintenance*.

Aircraft Maintenance 1989

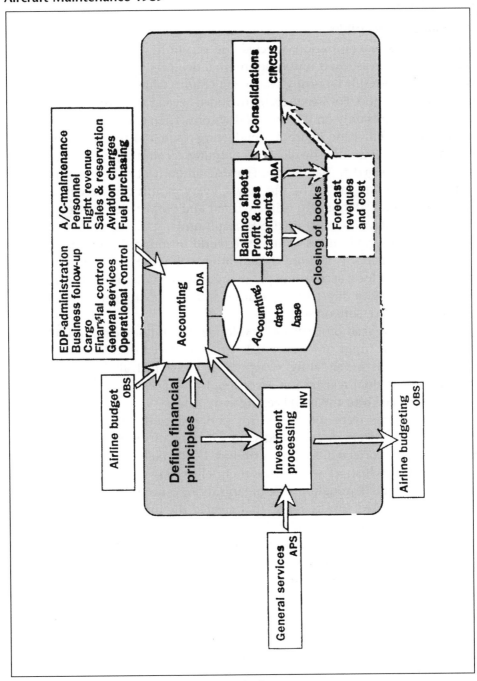

Source: SAS, *Handbook of IT Policy and Standards.*

Accounting

Additions of the 1980s

The 1981 SAS reorganization affected the accounting system little.[368] Divisions were set up as result units and internal debiting was introduced. Nevertheless, official result reporting was made countrywide and just extended to cover divisions, too. For instance, 02 included several areas that would be aggregated to results only on the level of divisions. Then corporate management used aggregated division figures for budgeting result and cost management of the individual divisions. The old ACS computer accounting system of the late 1960s still managed to handle the growing amount of data and number of transactions during the 1970s and 1980s. Every month the account was balanced and it took 48 hours to validate input and output. Results were printed in a couple of days and sent to all SAS result units.

Around 1980, SAS offices around the world introduced the Data Registration and Processing in Remote Organization (DRAPRO) – a mini-computer-based system for local accounting pre-processing and entering. With DRAPRO, figures could be sent directly to validating and final booking in ACS, reducing the processing pressure on ACS.

In 1983-84, a head office group developed the Online Registration System (ORS), an online input system for ACS, which replaced the old punched card system. ORS was a validating system.[369] It controlled all booking of pre-systems and manual registration according to the accounting system, before input was locked into the bookkeeping system.

Data terminals were substituted for punched cards. At the time of the punched cards system, users would send a list of faults to the accounting department to be corrected. Having introduced ORS, fault lists were sent to the line departments instead, where users themselves were responsible for producing correct input. Throughout the organization, central ACS was based on a number of so-called "pre-systems" that created the information entered into ACS. For instance, the files and disks of salary-systems were read into ORS via control programs, before entering the bookkeeping system. Once every month, data were delivered to central accounting. The number of pre-systems grew in time with SAS computer expansion.

---

368 SAS, *Data Management*, 26/4, 5/9 1983. Interview: *Per-Erik Jegbert, Agneta Peyron-Malmquist*.
369 SAS, *Data Management*, 26/4, 5/9 1983.

In 1982-83, the divisions started developing accounting systems of their own to complement the central system. The systems were intended to manage costs and customer revenue, creating a superstructure to ACS.

Second Generation System: GLM

Pre-studies for a new budget and accounting system started in 1983, when the consulting firm WM-data presented a description of functions and goals of a new system. The project was delayed, however, until ACS was replaced by a new system General Ledger Millennium (GLM), also called Airline Decentralized Accounting (ADA), in 1989.[370] GLM was not completely implemented until 1993, however. At the same time, SAS introduced a new accounting plan.

Technically, ACS worked well but just like all mainframe systems of the first generation, it was production oriented. Having introduced the Business Traveler's Airline Strategy in 1981, SAS reorganized on the basis of decentralized result units. Furthermore, as data-based systems were introduced in all line divisions, it became obvious that the ACS file system would not be a proper foundation for result management. Then, the intensified efforts from the mid-1980s to improve SAS' competitiveness made the Business Service Division (a reformed version of the Administrative Division) introduce a new accounting system to substitute for ACS.

Business Services Division had lost faith in SAS Data in matters of large systems development and decided to buy a standard system on the market to be adjusted to the needs of SAS. It sounded easy, but proved extremely difficult, time-consuming, and costly to carry out. The GLM system was bought from Dun and Bradstreet. Redevelopment and adjustment carried on during 1988, with implementation set for January 1 1989. Something began in 1989, but the new system had many problems of transition.

Even if you bought an application system on the market, it needed more than just pushing the button to make it work. About 60 pre-systems produced information for the central system, and integrating these systems into GLM required major adjustment.[371] A great number of users had to change their working procedures, too. On top of it, a new accounting plan was introduced, implying new codes all along the line. All this was costly, and SAS hardly profited from substituting GLM for ACS.

---

370 Interview: *Per-Erik Jegbert, Agneta Peyron-Malmquist.*
371 SAS, *GLM Systemforvalter Handbok* (system management handbook), 1993.

The crisis of the early 1990s, the SAS reorganization in 1991 and 1993, and the radical move to a functional Scandinavian organization in 1994 created recurrent problems of adaptation. Whenever SAS reorganized, the accounting department was compelled to remove the blocks that made up the system and that functioned almost as self-contained systems. In particular, when SAS abolished its regional structure in 1994 it caused much bookkeeping alteration and retraining of personnel.

In which way did GLM differ from ACS? First, there was a new accounting plan. The previous plan contained accounts and cost centers, whereas the new system measured an extended number of costs, including projects and products. That made it more difficult to apply the new accounting plan.

The new accounting system and plan demanded greater specification in line departments. Instead of just filling in cards of accounts and cost centers of the old system, basic data work in the new system grew more complicated and demanded greater accuracy and knowledge. Furthermore, the decentralized structure of SAS until 1994 seemed to hinder uniform practice. Because filling in figures of accounts and cost centers was controlled it was always done, whereas accounting and organizing according to products failed because of different practices through out SAS. Each division had its long-established way of accounting for products, varying from division to division. Therefore, a uniform standardized approach to product accounting was not implemented until after the 1994 reorganization.

Why did SAS acquire a new economic system? The organizational reasons for a change of accounting plan and computer system based on the principle of decentralized result units was a result of the new 1981 strategy and new economic model. Secondly, SAS wanted to replace a batch accounting system with a data-based online system. ACS had no balancing database with online access. Everybody could do online registration by way of ORS, but no one throughout the organization was able to go online into the system, because ACS was based on files and not on a database.

Nevertheless, management bought a halfway batch system, originally a batch system based on sequential registers modified with special facilities for online running and parameters. By the late 1980s, the market for standard accounting or economy systems was still at an early stage, as were systems of distributed data processing and relational databases, such as DB2. Furthermore, the Business Service Division did not want to develop a system from scratch. GLM was what could be obtained. After years of implementation problems, where plans for introducing standard packets for res-contra and suppliers had to be given up, GLM did finally work adequately since 1993.

Systems Overview

GLM was a system located somewhere between the first and second generations of information systems, not being based on a true database. On the other hand, it contained facilities close to those of a database system. ADA was made up of an accounting system, GLM, and a recording system, ORS. OBS was deployed for budget recording.

The ADA pre systems were made up of various administrative, technical, salary, sales, and production systems, about 60 in total.[372] The bookkeeping transactions of these pre systems were read into GLM via ORS that was adjusted to fit GLM instead of ACS. In 1989, a revised OBS 2 for budget registration was implemented that was also used for updating GLM with budget values. In principle, budget was on the level of a center account. Technically, GLM, ORS, and OBS2 ran on different SAS Data operation environments, including Customer Information Control System (CICS), IMS, and DB2.

GLM was divided into six blocks that represented different units of SAS. Before the reorganization in 1994, these units consisted of the three Scandinavian countries, the rest of the world, the individual divisions, and subsidiaries. From 1994, only the divisions existed and in principle, each block constituted a GLM system of its own.

Although GLM was not a true data-based system, it contained many database-like facilities. Each GLM block contained several functions, such as reading routines, registers, and reporting. Registers formed a kind of database, consisting of tables, such as control and codes that allowed direct and quick online system updating. Both batch and online reporting was included: partly permanent reporting of control, balance, and result, partly ad hoc facilities for extracting certain kinds of information.

GLM worked like this.[373] When data were entered in the main numbers of the accounting plan (i.e., by divisions and subsidiaries), they came together in a consolidating system for all of SAS Airline and its subsidiaries and produced one total result. Under ACS, the consolidating system was CCS (Centralized Consolidation System), under GLM replaced by BM (Business Manager).

---

372 SAS, *GLM Systemforvalter Handbok*. Interview: *Ulla Edlund*.
373 See Figure, *Accounting Information*.

Accounting Information 1989

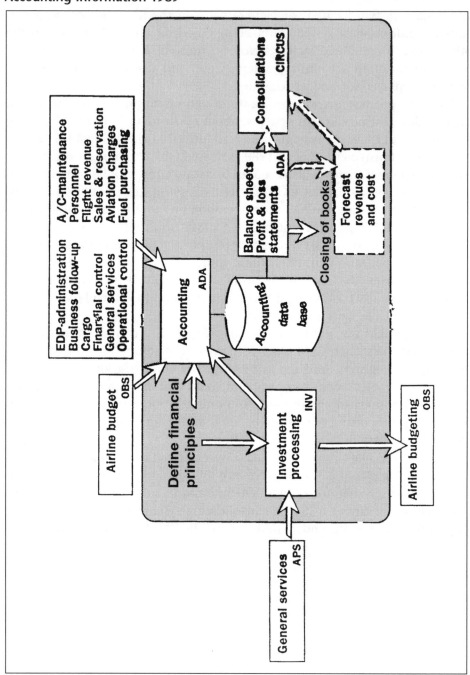

Source: SAS, Handbook of IT Policy and Standards.

Personnel

Second Generation System: PERS/PINS

During the second half of the 1970s, Data Services Area 11 (Personnel) and small newly formed computer groups in the three national departments of personnel, took the initiative to develop second-generation salary systems to be based on a common database. A kind of Scandinavian master plan was formulated in 1976-77 and from 1978, a development project was carried out in the three countries.

This was the so-called Personnel Registration and Planning System/Personnel Insurance System (PERS/PINS), which included both salary and insurance administration.[374] PERS/PINS was based on the same technology as MOPS, namely IBM and its database tool IMS. Developing new salary systems made up the major part of the project.

By way of a joint definition of standardized data objects in the database, the PERS/PINS project aimed at creating as many common elements as possible. It was a Scandinavian project to be implemented in phases. Because of different national SAS personnel departments, different strategies of development were deployed. The PERS/PINS plan consisted of two main phases followed by two additional phases. The two main phases included basic personnel and salary administration, divided into six functions or modules.

The management module, the first module, was to include such pre-structuring information as collective agreements, authority rules, and so forth. To handle a growing number of new and changing laws and rules and to give users quick access to updated information, the management system had to be online.

Personnel register was the second module, a database that contained all basic information on the individual SAS employee, such as name, age, sex, position, and length of employment. It was planned to include all SAS employees and replace the many different personnel registers throughout the organization, covering for instance workshops, airports, and crew. Users would swiftly get updated information on any employee by way of online access.

The insurance part made up the third module. This PINS function included all the complex rules of pensions and insurance. It would be kept up to date through direct connection to the insurance companies, and would be available online for systems maintenance and users.

Modules four and five planned to take care of salary administration. Module four was to ensure that concurrent salary payments were done correctly.

---

374 SAS, *PERS/RINS Rutinhandbok* (system handbook), 1982-83. Interview: *Lars Nilsson.*

Every month, SAS made huge numbers of transactions to banks and employees, transactions that should be registered in a batch-system that did corrections and updating by way of data terminals. Module five was concerned with calculating salaries. It included all calculation programs through which salries were calculated. Furthermore, it initiated salary operations and stored information on salaries paid. Module five formed the management part of salary administration.

Module six was the reporting module. A great number of statistics and reports were sent to authorities and trade organizations and were included in productivity measuring, in budgeting, salary negotiations, and so on. Users would enter data to be used for statistics and reports in data terminals. This too was a batch system.

Such were the plans for the two main phases of the project. Phase one was carried out more or less according to plan, in three versions based on some common data objects in IMS. Phase one included that part of the management module that handled basic personnel information and the personnel registration module, including the whole insurance module. The Danish system was implemented in 1981, the Norwegian system in 1982, and the Swedish system in 1983.[375]

Developments made slow progress, however. National differences were strong obstacles, and a common development depended on the goodwill of the individual personnel departments. The complicated rules and laws in the field of wages formed the greatest obstacle of all. Not only did the number of rules and laws rise radically from the 1970s, but they were of three national kinds, too. A complete Scandinavian management module would be so complicated that it would be impossible to implement. Accordingly, the first phase of the project included only the least complex parts of the management module, namely a register of basic information on personnel.

Unlike the first phase of the project, the next phase encountered difficulties when dealing with salary administration.[376] The common Scandinavian development project had stopped by the mid-1980s. In Denmark the personnel department went on and developed a salary administration system alone (i.e., phase two). A Danish PERS salary system was implemented in 1987. Collective agreements still formed the basis of the system, while position codes made up the foundation of the whole salary and personnel system. The system included parameters, which meant that the new rules for each em-

---

375 SAS, *Data News*, Sept. 1981; July 1982; April 1983. SAS, *PERS/PINS Rutinhandbok*. Interview: *Lars Nilsson.*
376 SAS, *Data Management*, 9/10 1987, April 1988. Interviews: *Lars Nilsson, John Schmidt-Hansen.*

ployment category could be entered, whereupon the system would update for the individual person. Formerly, much work was required to reprogram changes for each employee. From 1987, the Danish personnel department had more or less fulfilled the plans of the late 1970s to produce an integrated system of salary and personnel, which provided information on name, address, wage, pensions, department attachment, matters of organization, and so on.

In cooperation with Sweden, the Norwegian department developed a simplified version of the PERS salary system. It contained the same basic information as the Danish system but did not use parameters and was therefore less flexible.

The Swedish personnel department started to develop the second phase of PERS/PINS, too, but the project was stopped in 1987 for financial reasons. Instead, management decided to buy a standard salary system, called PA (Personnel Administration).[377] PA was finally implemented in 1990 and included salary calculations and transactions.

In 1990, the first and second phase of the PERS/PINS project was more or less finished, consisting of three national systems of basic personnel information, insurance administration, and salary administration.

PERS/PINS had plans for a third phase, too. It was to be called LINE-PERS and was to start in 1985.[378] LINE-PERS was intended to cover personnel according to the new 1981 divisions. However, because of the drawn-out nature of the development of the salary component of PERS, LINE-PERS was never implemented. Plans for a time registration system for technical departments suffered the same fate.

In 1990 there were three different personnel and salary systems.[379] They contained some common data objects, but the basic management module was expressed in three different national versions. Plans for a common database for all personnel were never fulfilled.

The three PERS/PINS systems were integrated with several other systems, such as technical, stations, crew, and sales.[380] All main SAS areas, divisions and subsidiaries, had personnel systems of their own that were applied for matters such as staff planning and training. PERS made up only the first step of a true personnel system.

---

377 SAS, *PA-Systemets Använderhandbok* (the PA-System User Handbook), 1993.
378 SAS, *Data Management*, 15/1 1983; 9/10 1987.
379 SAS, *Data Management*, April, 1/11 1988. SAS (1993), *PA-Systemets Använderhandbok*. Interviews: *Lars Nilsson, John Schmidt-Hansen.*
380 See Figure, *Personnel Administration Information.*

Personnel Administration Information 1989

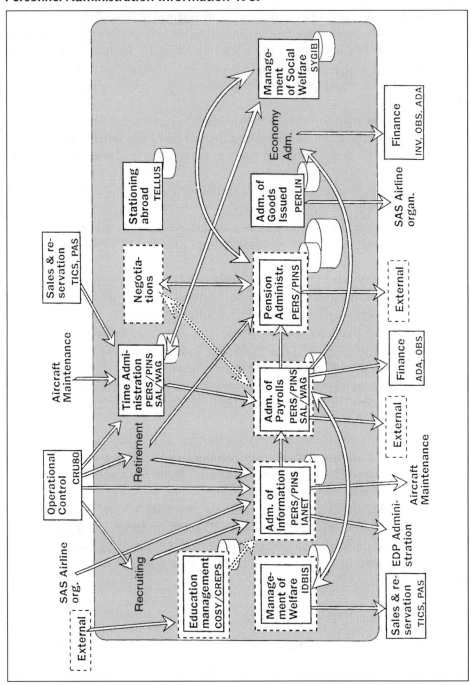

Source: SAS, Handbook of IT Policy and Standards.

The First IT Paradigm: The Peak

The first IT paradigm, starting in the 1960s and the 1970s, was greatly extended during the 1980s. The 1980s remained within the structure of the first paradigm, still based on mainframes, central operating systems and in-house application development. As was the case before 1980, systems development used third generation languages and required much skill in programming, maintenance, and so on. Terminals trebled in numbers and spread in thousands throughout the organization, during this decade. To meet the pressure of increasing transactions, the central Telcon communication system was upgraded from medium to high-speed level and capacity.

The vast majority of new systems of the 1980s were organized on the basis of the IBM IMS database management system. They replaced previous file systems and introduced online access and real time processing instead of batch technology. These second generation systems of the 1980s contained a much larger set of rules then their predecessors. These included collective agreements, technical specifications, legal provisions, and fares, which required greatly extended cores of logic. With the new systems, a much wider field of functions was automated, including further planning activities. Furthermore, from the late 1980s, follow-up systems were introduced to allow management to adapt to changing market conditions. Finally, links between applications kept on increasing.

By about 1990, the SAS information systems flow went like this. The information system TPTS created the traffic program, RES linked the Commercial Division to markets and customers, with TICS for ticketing and PASAS for economic transfer to accounting. From 1982, LEVEL had optimized reservations to ensure that other groups were never booked at the expense of businessmen. Cargo used its handling system CARIN and its revenue accounting system, CRAS. Since 1985, Route Result (LRS), a route sector management system had been used and had also provided a basis for traffic planning. During the late 1980s, business follow-up systems multiplied to increase optimization and adaptation to market changes. Relations with agents were based on a commission model (i.e., a percentage of revenue, including a reward for increased sales). PADOCS/IMPALA handled passenger interline accounting. CRU70 and CRU/80 did crew planning, and OPS/TOPRO and OPUS took care of operations control in airports. LOCS/PALCO handled check-in and load control. MOPS and MATS covered technical maintenance. ACS/GLM managed accounting and finance, and PERS-PINS handled salaries and personnel.

By about 1990, practically all SAS information flows of operative and tactical planning activities were automated on the basis of central IT systems and a few national systems. Systems were all functional and based on hierarchical databases that did not easily allow for cross-systems information processing. More than ever, the SAS business depended on IT applications and central computers and communications. During the late 1980s, IT was clearly up-graded to management and market orientation levels in preparation for the radical changes of the next decade. By 1990, the SAS value chain of business activities were linked to its information systems in a very high degree, and vice versa.

IV · THE 1990S TRANSFORMATION

Environment

Economic Development

The world crisis of the 1970s and the ability of Japanese corporations to defy recession by ousting Western corporations in their home-markets, forced American and West European capitalism to strike back in order to regain lost competitiveness. This was a prolonged process that required a deep restructuring to succeed. While Japan never stopped prospering, it took Western economies twenty years to recover from the crisis of the 1970s. The rate of growth and productivity was still low in Western Europe and the USA. During the 1980s, hyperinflation flattened and investments grew, however. In particular, rapidly growing international investments indicated a future prosperity. In the early 1990s, the world economy receded once more, however, aggravated by the Gulf War, which hit the airlines particularly hard.[381]

Then from 1993 to 1994, the world economy recovered in a remarkable way. The rates of economic growth and productivity increased, and Western corporations expanded their investments and trade throughout the world, fueled by liberalized trade, revolutionizing IT, the new capitalist economies of Eastern Europe, and a blooming East Asian economy. A true global economy emerged, as leading firms reorganized into Transnational Corporations (TNCs) and continuously upgraded their businesses towards knowledge-based products and activities. This global economy was very much dominated by the Triad of the USA, Western Europe, and Japan.[382]

In 1997 and 1998 East Asian economies overheated and moved into their first crisis in many years, followed by all other non-Western economies of the world. The economy of Western Europe and the USA kept on prospering, however, and leading Western TNCs regained and reinforced their dominating position, especially in the strategically important fields of knowledge and technology, such as IT and business services.

After a prolonged period of business restructuring, Western corporations had regained their competitiveness. Having reorganized into flexible global organizations, they were now able to mobilize their innovative business capabilities.

---

381 Maddison, *Monitoring the World Economy*, pp.78-87.
382 The World Bank (1994-1998), *Annual Reports*, 1993 to 1997 (Washington, D. C: The World Bank).

In contrast, East Asian economies seemed to have exhausted their competitive potential. The time had come for Eastern corporations and governments to transform according to the demanding conditions of an open and global economy. A prolonged period of Asian crisis and restructuring, including Russia's tumbling move from planned economy to capitalism, might eventually hamper Western economies. More likely however, is that Asian and perhaps Latin American economies, too, would strive hard to regain strength by upgrading their competitiveness and institutions.[383]

Globalization

Since the 1950s, international trade has increased twice as much as economic growth, but since the mid-1980s, foreign direct investment (FDI) (i.e., international production), has multiplied four times more than economic growth. During the 1990s, international production came to dominate international business.[384]

Globalization of industry referred to an evolving pattern of cross-border activities of firms involving international investment, trade and cooperation for purposes of product development, production, sourcing, and marketing.[385] These international activities enabled firms to enter new markets, exploit their technological and organizational advantages, and reduce business costs and risks. Underlying the international expansion of firms, and in part driven by it, were technological advances, the liberalization of markets, and increased mobility of production factors.

These complex patterns of cross-border activities increasingly characterized the international economic system and distinguished it from the earlier predominance of trade in finished goods. National economies were becoming more closely integrated as firms spread their operations and assets across countries. Globalization was a powerful motor of worldwide economic growth. Policies that promoted trade and investment liberalization and non-discrimination were particularly important in facilitating globalization. Globalization heightened the need for closer co-operation among governments at the international level and increased inter-linkages between different policy domains. This applied particularly to areas such as R & D and technology policies, intellectual property protection, foreign investment policies, and competition law and policies.

---

383 OECD (1997-1998), *Economic Outlook*, 1997 and 1998 (Paris: OECD).
384 Dunning, J. H. (1993), *The Globalization of Business* (London: Routledge). UN (1990-1998), *World Investment Reports*, 1990 to 1998.
385 OECD, *Globalization of Industries*, pp. 20-63.

TNCs played a leading role in the unprecedented expansion of international transactions. They built integrated, international production networks that paved the way for the increased international specialization of the production of goods and services. To compete in these international markets, companies increasingly needed technological sophistication, maximum flexibility, customized products, and extensive supplier networks. Assisted by modern information and communication technologies, this was often attained by establishing a network of affiliates operating on a global scale. But a number of other forms of cross-border co-operation, such as international subcontracting, franchising, licensing, joint ventures, R & D alliances, and other forms of cooperative agreements have become increasingly important.

As a consequence, globalization took on three dimensions. First, global industrialization and division of labor deepened. The liberalization of trade in goods and services, of movement of capital, and financial markets was a precondition for the emerging, integrated international production and distribution system. Second, to survive in such increased and globalized competition, firms had to upgrade their competence and keep on upgrading it. A precondition for continuous upgrading was a determined focus on core competence, leading to a thorough reorganization of all internal and external functions and relations of the firm. Third, reorganization was fueled by liberalization of trade, by advances in transport, including aviation, and in information and communication technologies. A network kind of organization emerged based on more permanent relations between suppliers and industrial buyers.

Services were particularly affected by this development, and became the most dynamic element of world trade, accounting for the major part of FDI. The main driver of this services revolution was the rapidly increasing demand for knowledge-based services that became essential for corporate competitiveness, as firms concentrated more and more on upgrading their core competence. More functions of the value chain were being externalized, forming the basis of separate business services such as accounting, human resources, computing, inventory, logistics, and marketing. The market was taking over an increasing number of functions that used to be carried out within the bureaucracy and at the same time, creating new fields of business as demands for knowledge and technology increased. As a consequence, the composition of international sourcing was shifting from primary commodities to intermediate products. Finally, the revolutionary development of IT and the knowledge content of products and labor processes contributed to a blurring of borders between more and more functions and fields of business. Such blurring of borders took place between computers and communications and between technology and the information content being processed, for instance IT and business services.

All these growing fields of industrialization took on the same form of organization. They became TNCs because competition globalized.

The most important changes in the competitive environment which were forcing TNCs to adopt new strategies – or to adapt existing ones – could be described on the one hand, as factors which were converging across borders and on the other hand, those which were diffusing through the international economy.

Converging factors included national policies, technologies, and consumer tastes. The convergence of these market characteristics across national borders meant that TNCs now faced larger, more homogenous markets, and that the economic distance was narrowing between countries, particularly developed countries. The second category combined those elements that were diffusing rather than converging: innovation, international competition, and production locations.

These trends pushed TNCs to seek new ways of gaining international competitive advantages. They increased their efforts to innovate and cut costs by locating abroad and by paying close attention to different elements of their value chains. The relationship between TNCs and technological change became crucial. TNCs were key actors in the development of technology, yet, at the same time, they were greatly influenced by it. In fact, technological developments were a major factor behind the growing importance of TNCs and their increasingly global strategies, which were often motivated by the need to gain control over the development and use of new technologies.

As a result of this escalating process of innovation, a notable shift occurred in the perception of the process of technology development.[386] The conventional view was that scientific innovation and discoveries were largely made in academic institutions and research laboratories. Once these were in place, firms sought to commercialize them. This view of technology development was no longer appropriate. With the emergence of information-based technologies, the increasing globalization of enterprises and growing competition in the international market place, science and technology had become more and more linked. It was increasingly recognized that a large part of technological development occurred because of actions taken by enterprises.

In addition to technology-sharing networks, powerful transnational computer-communication networks owned by single firms or groups of firms were becoming more important. In some industries (for example, banking, insurance, hotels, airlines), such electronic networks became the basis for international transactions, and access to them was therefore a crucial matter. From the mid-1990s, these proprietary networks were being rapidly changed into

---

386 OECD, *Technology and Economy*, pp. 23-45.

an open global electronic infrastructure by the advent of the Internet. The Internet opened the possibility of increasing globalization on the one hand and an even more competitive environment on the other.[387]

Reorganization

As TNCs created internationally integrated production, they adopted new strategies and transformed organizational structures to carry out these strategies. Reorganized structures defined new lines of authority, coordinated flows of resources, and established mechanisms of accountability to link together the different functional and geographical units of the firm.

A firm's various functions can be described as comprising its value chain.[388] The ability of a firm to identify and exploit those activities and linkages that mattered most for its performance was crucial to its success and competitiveness.

There was a trend among TNCs in many industries to adopt strategies and structures that involved closer integration of their functional activities.[389] To more and more firms it became clear that international production could occur at almost any point on the value chain. Complex integration strategy was based on a firm's ability to shift production or supply to wherever it was most profitable. Each operation was judged in terms of its contribution to the entire value chain.

Advances in IT that increased the capacity to process and communicate information and to reduce costs were critical in coordinating activities throughout the value chain. In rather the same way as multi-plant and mulidivisional strategies created the need for greater coordination and a bigger managerial structure in the past, so did the development of complex integration strategies increase the need for TNCs to manage their cross-border networks. IT also allowed the value chains of firms under separate ownership to become more integrated.

New IT both facilitated and required new forms of organization. The speed, ease, and cheapness of communication helped to undermine hierarchical reporting systems and increased possibilities for horizontal communications across functional and geographical lines. To take advantage of the new technologies, firms needed more flexible reporting and organizational systems.

---

387 OECD, *Information Technology Outlook*, 1997.
388 Porter, *The Competitive Advantage of Nations*, pp. 33-67. See also chapter I of the text, *Theories of the Firm*.
389 UN, *World Investment Report*, 1993, pp. 115-132.

The move towards more decentralized market-driven structures within firms and knowledge-based products also led to a major change in the organization of work and in the approach to the management of a firm's human resources.[390] Flatter hierarchies, less direct control, greater flexibility, and more employee responsibility took over, as well as demand- and value driven considerations of organization.

These new strategies and organizational structures differed significantly from previous management models, dominated by so-called Fordism in large corporations. Its major departures from Fordism consisted of:

- Adoption of networking, sub-contracting and just-in-time delivery, a basic reversal of the trend to ever greater vertical and horizontal integration which had become an important dimension of American and European Fordism.
- Reorganization of work.
- Significant reductions in compartmentalization and hierarchical organization within firms.

In combination, these three changes led to totally new levels of flexibility, while retaining the main advantages of standardization and setting new standards for quality (zero defects).

To catch this transformation, a new concept of management was born, called Business Process Reengineering (BPR).[391] Its goal was to achieve dramatic improvement of efficiency and competitiveness by focusing on cross-business processes that were crucial to adding value for customers. In contrast, traditional rationalization focused on individual departments or functions of the firm. While traditional measures of efficiency had an internal perspective, BPR was based on an analysis of customer needs and competitor activities. The time used and the amount spent must result in value-adding products, which reached the best standards on the market. The firm was what it did to its customers, compared with its competitors.

BPR was built on the following approach. First, a firm's competitiveness was defined, based on its business strategy, its core competence, and its crucial business processes. Second, based on a customer-analysis, goals for results were drawn for those vital business processes concerning time, quality, costs, and customer service. Third, business processes were reconstructed by eliminating non-value adding activities and by optimizing value-creating activ-

---

390 OECD, *Technology and Economy*, pp. 89-106.
391 Hammer and Champy, *Reengineering the Corporation*.

ities. This was supported by an innovative use of IT and most importantly, a customer-oriented organization. Fourth, results in relation to customer goals were followed up. Fifth, results and rewards of processes were being linked to the people responsible for these processes.

Since the early 1990s, all large corporations of the world that wanted to stay in business launched radical BPR projects to attack traditional bureaucracy. Towards the mid-1990s, BPR was followed by a new process-oriented innovation to create a continuous process of transformation from bureaucracy.[392]

Until the 1990s, the sequential movement of products and services – engineering, marketing, manufacturing, sales, customer service, and so forth – across business functions characterized almost every large business organization. Not only was this approach expensive and time-consuming, it often did not serve customers well. To fulfill the goals of process innovation, business must be viewed not in terms of functions, divisions, or products, operating in a sequential way, but in terms of horizontal key processes. Key cross-functional processes were selected and a gradual and continuous innovation process of cross-functional flow and organization began to develop. Furthermore, vertical layers of management control were reduced and management strategically strengthened through radical developments in IT.

During process innovation, the business organization still aimed at upgrading core competence and customer relations and its flexible adaptability towards a rapidly changing economic environment. Process innovation combined the adoption of a process view of the business with the application of innovation to key processes. Taking a process approach implied adopting the customer's point of view. Processes were the structure by which an organization did what was necessary to produce value for the customer. Consequently, an important measure of a process was customer satisfaction with the output of the process. To the organization, innovation of key processes had an enormous potential for helping any organization achieve major reductions in process cost or time, major improvements in quality, flexibility, service levels, or other business objectives.

Since the mid-1990s, corporate organizations followed a process of innovation and learning, having realized that old structures and cultures of organization and technology were not easily transformed. IT was a significant enabler of this innovation process. As a consequence, evolutionary, horizontal, holistic, and market-run views came to dominate, accompanied by radical IT developments.

---

392 Davenport, Process Innovation, pp. 5-18, and passim. Hammer, M. (1996), Beyond Reengineering. How the Process-Centred Organization is Changing Our Work and Our Lives (London: HarperCollins Business).

The Aircraft Industry

During the 1990s, the same few firms kept on dominating the global aircraft industry. Concentration even increased, as Boeing and McDonnell Douglas merged in 1996. Increasing demands for investment in the R & D needed for developing new planes made McDonnell Douglas give up and integrate with Boeing. Apart from Boeing, only European Airbus was left. Continuous innovation and high loads of IT in manufacturing and products pressed the aircraft industry to upgrade its activities to a degree and with a speed never seen before. As a consequence, the new planes of the 1990s were turned into what you might call flying computers, automating navigation, communications, and passenger services. This new third or maybe fourth generation of jet planes was more environmentally compatible than their predecessors, reducing noise and exhaust. New technologies of environmental compatibility and computerization helped airlines to meet the growing demands and pressures of a globalized industry of open competition.[393]

The Airlines Industry

Increasingly, deregulated, consolidated American airlines and distribution systems challenged the European airlines from the mid-1980s. To meet the American competition, European airlines joined to create two international distribution systems, AMADEUS and GALILEO, by the early 1990s. No consolidation of European airlines took place, however. National interests prevailed.

In the mid-1980s, the EU (former EEC) decided upon a plan to implement an open European market in 1993, which was to include the airline industry, too.[394] From the late 1980s, the airline industry was being gradually liberalized in three steps. Controls were relaxed, covering the key areas of tariff approval, market access, capacity, and the application of competition rules. Prior to liberalization, bilateral agreements between member states governed the EU market. These agreements tended to control route entry and capacity, while airlines agreed on fares by way of IATA. Many international routes were restricted to operation by only one airline of each country.

In the late 1980s, the first two EU packages of liberalization measures largely removed the single destination provisions so that any airline was able to operate and therefore compete on the major international routes within the

---

393 OECD, *The Future of International Air Transport Policy*, pp. 39-56. Boeing (1997-1998), *Annual Reports*, 1996 and 1997 (WWW).

394 EU (1997), *The Single Market Review. Impact on Services. AIR TRANSPORT*, pp. 11-25.

EU. Airlines were given greater freedom to provide capacity to match market demands and more flexible procedures for the approval of fares, including lower fares. With the third package, substantial liberalization of the EU became possible. EU carriers holding an operating license now had free access to virtually all international routes within the EU and were generally free to charge the fares they wished. Since 1997, member states' domestic markets were opened too, concluding the European liberalization process.

The dominating trend of the airline policy of international and national institutions and authorities aimed at developing a workable balance of competition being as open as possible and the removal of any barriers to a market of fair competition for all business sectors of the airlines value chain.[395] Globally, the EU led this development. Since the mid-1990s, EU-policies included plans for integrated and upgraded IT systems of air traffic management to meet growing problems of congestion in the air and airports. The EU even prepared general policies for a European integrated traffic infrastructure.[396]

While open competition spread from North America and the North Atlantic routes to Europe, the rest of the world stuck to regulations to some degree. That included the most expansive part of the world economy and airline traffic, the Asia-Pacific region. Large and expanding Asian airlines appeared more often in the European and American markets, and European and American airlines flew more often to expanding Asia, however. Thus, increased global relations tended to break down all restrictions of trade.

In the early 1990s, most airlines sustained heavy financial losses as a result of the Gulf Crisis and a short general depression.[397] Since then, growth and profitability have characterized the airlines of the world. Businessmen still constituted a large segment of passengers, but tourism was expanding. Air cargo transport also grew rapidly to meet the needs of globalized production and distribution of a growing sector of high-value commodities of intermediates. Revenues of freight traffic only made up c. 10 % of the total, however. Tourism and leisure travel was the most expansive category of travel, followed by air cargo. Businessmen made up 40-45% of passengers and tourists 55-60%.

The development of business service activities, including the geographical widening of manufacturing and services activities, influenced the long-term growth of business travel. Furthermore, such factors as increased communica-

---

395 OECD, *The Future of International Air Transport Policy*, pp. 16-23, and passim. Morrison and Winston, *The Evolution of the Airline Industry*, pp. 159-162.

396 EU, *The Single Market Review*, pp. 25-31. EU (1998), *Transport Research. Fourth Framework Programme. Air Transport VII-69*, and other publications of the ESTEEM project.

397 IATA, *World Air Transport Statistics*, 1990 to 1997. OECD, *The Future of International Air Transport Policy*, pp. 39-130.

tion by way of IT and competing fast trains transportation caused uncertainties of future economic development. Airline traffic kept on increasing, however, particularly international air transport.

The radically changing business environment of the 1990s put increasing pressure on the two main business areas of airlines, cargo and passengers. In cargo, the transformation of national small-package service operators into globalized, all-cargo express service operators/integrators, had been an important development in the airfreight market since the early 1980s.[398] After powerful growth in the USA markets, express operators developed rapidly in the international airfreight market of the 1990s. Airlines struck back by upgrading their cargo businesses. A few took to outsourcing. Most chose the road of alliances and cooperation to meet the growing competition on a global scale.

Passenger traffic was the crucial business of all airlines.[399] Since the early 1990s, open global competition and the globalized distribution systems of the 1990s undermined a stand-alone strategy. Furthermore, industries emerged wanting to take over more and more fields of the airlines' value chain. First, management met the challenges by reorganizing their firms. Next, airlines entered global alliances. Finally, outsourcing was being increasingly considered.

In the early 1990s, all leading airlines started a radical process of reorganization in order to cut costs dramatically and transform into flexible organizations, adapting to a rapidly changing market.[400] Since the mid-1990s, airlines have focused more on process innovation and revenue creating activities by upgrading their value-adding products. Global alliances were also considered a necessary step to improve competitiveness and ensure future existence, just like any other industry of the new global economic order.

Large European and American airlines formed alliances that were turned into global alliances by including Asian and Latin American airlines, for example, the Star Alliance of United Airlines, Lufthansa, SAS, Thai Airways, Varig, and Canadian Air.[401] To make it truly global, Star Alliance would most likely be extended to other airlines of industrialized and newly industrialized countries of the world. Since the mid-1990s, global alliances started a process of cooperation, covering such business activities as traffic plans, bonus programs, code sharing, and cargo in the first place, probably to be followed by

---

398 OECD, *The Future of International Air Transport Policy*, pp. 41-44. EU, *The Single Market Review*, pp. 62-63.

399 OECD, *The Future of International Air Transport Policy*, pp. 39-56. EU, *The Single Market Review*, pp. 58-95.

400 OECD, *The Future of International Air Transport Policy*, pp. 81-100. EU, *The Single Market Review*, pp. 33-48.

401 OECD, *The Future of International Air Transport Policy*, pp. 81-100. IATA, *World Air Transport Statistics*, 1990 to 1997.

operative functions of maintenance, stations, and crew. Eventually, mergers might be the consequence of this development.

Except for the passenger field, all airline functions were candidates for outsourcing, including marketing, cargo, station, crew, maintenance, human resources, and finance and accounting. Some airlines started early to outsource maintenance (BA) and even accounting (Swissair).[402] However during the 1990s, most large airlines, including SAS, chose to keep all main functions within its organization.[403] The reasons for doing so were probably that the outsourcing industries of business functions in most cases had not yet matured, and that airlines considered competence upgrading necessary before taking radical decisions on outsourcing. Once outsourced, a functional capability might be lost. Furthermore, employees also had a say in these matters that could not be ignored, considering the tight, institutionalized labor relations in most European airlines. But only as long as airlines kept on being profitable and every value-adding activity of the firms met the highest standards of the market, did transactions remain in-house. This was the new business scenario. And by the late-1990s, continuously fierce competition and maturing service industries on a global scale pressed airlines more than ever towards outsourcing and even merger.

World Statistics of Passenger Scheduled Services[404]

	1990	1994	1997
Total passengers, mill.	1,027	1,225	1,400
Share international pass., %	26.9	28.3	30.3
Share USA, %	45.2	41.7	40.0
Share Europe, %	21.1	22.3	20.7
Share Asia, %	20.4	22.7	26.4
- Japan, %	7.4	6.8	7.5
Share ROW, %	13.4	13.3	12.7

Source: UN, *Statistical Yearbooks.*

---

402 UN, *World Investment Report,* 1993, p.122.
403 SAS, *Annual Reports,* 1990 to 1997.
404 Prior to 1990, UN world passenger statistics did not include USSR and China, but Russia is now included with the European figures, and since 1994 China has been included as part of Asia. Sovjet Aeroflot used to be the world's largest airline measured in number of passengers transported annually. Since 1990, Russian traffic has been much reduced, whereas air transport in China has escalated. Figures for 1997 are extrapolations of trends from 1990 to 1994.

Passenger Statistics of International Airlines[405]

	1990	1994	1997
Air Canada	10.3	11.2	15.6
American Airlines	73.2	81.1	81.1
Continental Airlines	35.2	42.2	38.6
Delta Airlines	65.9	89.1	103.2
Northwest Airlines	-	49.3	54.6
Pan American	17.5	-	-
Trans World Airlines	24.5	21.6	23.4
United Airlines	57.8	78.7	84.2
USAIR	-	57.7	58.7
Varig	6.9	9.5	10.5
Air France	15.7	15.6	29.1
Alitalia	18.2	20.3	24.6
British Airways	25.2	30.2	34.2
Iberia	16.2	13.8	16.1
KLM	6.9	11.7	14.4
Lufthansa	21.6	30.0	35.3
SAS	14.9	18.7	20.6
Swissair	7.8	8.5	10.7
Cathay Pacific	7.5	9.7	10.0
Singapore Airlines	7.1	10.8	12.1
Thai Airways	8.2	12.8	14.4
4 China Airlines	20	25	31.1
Korean Airlines	12.1	18.7	25.4
Japan Airlines	23.5	28.8	31.8
All Nippon Airways	33.0	34.5	40.7
Qantas Airways	4.2	15.0	16.5

Source: IATA, *World Air Transport Statistics.* UN, *Statistical Yearbooks.*

---

405 In million passengers. The 1994 to 1997 leap in Air France traffic is due to a merger with two other French airlines. The leap of Australian Qantas from 1990 to
1994 is also due to a merger. Figures of the four Chinese regional airlines for 1990
and 1994 are based on estimations. These Chinese airlines are included to indicate the sharp increase and huge potential of the East Asian region.

The IT Industry and Applications

IT Markets

In 1995, the world IT market, as measured by the revenues of primary vendors of hardware, software, and services, was worth an estimated $527 billion.[406] A decade earlier, it had reached only half that size. By the late 1990s, the world IT market was probably worth $7-800 billions. Including all information and communication technology, total world production would be about one quarter more.

From the mid-1980s to the mid-1990s, the world IT market had a growth rate nearly twice that of GDP. This strong growth did little to redress the geographical imbalance in the world IT market. The OECD countries still counted for more than 90 % of the market, which was concentrated within the G7 countries. The USA stood for almost half the IT market, Western Europe for more than one quarter, and Japan for less than one sixth, leaving less than 10 % to non-OECD countries. From the mid-1990s, USA and Western Europe had reinforced their growth and positions in the worldwide IT market, while Japan has lost ground. IT vendors of hardware, and particularly software and services were very much dominated by American companies, which covered approximately three quarters of world production.

Since the mid-1980 and particularly since about 1990, the world IT market underwent a structural change involving two broad trends. The first was a downward trend in the relative importance of hardware and a corresponding rise in software/services. The second was the increasing popularity of PCs and workstations, while mainframes and other computers dropped considerably. Mainframe systems were still irreplaceable for a number of applications involving large-scale data processing (e.g., on-line transaction processing). Within the PC-market, the pace of technological upgrading had quickened considerably and rapidly reduced the life cycle of PC models. There was a general trend towards downsizing and networked computing. Another feature was the increasing convergence of PCs and consumer electronics, through joint development of hardware and specific software for use on the Internet. Computer-related communication equipment rose, however. Prices of hardware and software have dropped sharply, especially since about 1990.

Packaged software was one of the main contributors to growth in IT markets within the OECD area. From the early 1990s, the services market was the second largest contributor, after PCs, to the overall IT market growth. The

---

406 OECD, *Information Technology Outlook*, 1997, pp. 13-66.

broad increase in the services market had been accompanied by structural changes in the industry. First, as firms moved to PCs and packaged software, the relative importance of customized software declined, whereas the use of system integration services grew. Second, as the pace of internal reorganization continued to quicken, firms were increasingly turning to IT services. The increased use of consulting services indicated that firms were making major structural changes as they adapted to new technologies, entailing changes in organizational structures, working arrangements and the relations between them. Finally, in an effort to control costs, firms made outsourcing of information systems a central aspect of changes in corporate strategy.

From the mid-1980s, growth in OECD countries' IT markets was largely driven by services, and to a lesser extent by software. Several broad trends were evident: a marked increase in data communication equipment and a sharp increase in PCs and workstations; a relative decrease in systems software and utilities and a marked rise in applications tools; finally, a sharp rise in IT services. Mainframes were the only segment to have contributed negatively to market growth over the period. Since the mid-1990s, these trends seemed to continue in a slightly different way. The increase in data communication equipment slowed down in a market beginning to be saturated, only to be replaced by a sharp rise in the 1990s when the breakthrough of Internet and mobile technologies fueled and helped to integrate IT on a higher level. Markets of enterprise and client/server software kept on growing, and IT services did not stop their sharp rise.

From the mid-1980s, there was sustained growth in semiconductor demand in all major regions of OECD, escalating from the early 1990s. PCs were a major outlet of semiconductors, accounting for half the world sales. Microprocessors, the central component in PCs, became the key component and driver for semiconductor technology.

Chips

The microprocessor is the core technology of IT. Since the late 1980s and early 1990s, the processing and storage capacity of microprocessors, or chips, has escalated.[407] Capacity was doubled every 18 months. Real and potential demand for increased power was tremendous, and Intel and other leading corporations competed diabolically, investing almost half of their income in R & D to stay in business and meet the rapidly expanding markets of PCs, communications, industrial products, and so forth. Any information activity

---

407 OECD, *Information Technology Outlook*, 1997, pp. 26-32.

might be digitalized. The chips revolution of the 1990s paved the way for an industrialized IT sector that grew faster than any other part of the economy and opened up for increasingly new kinds of applications.

Networks

Telecommunications used to be an analog technique separate from computers. Since the 1980s, the national telephone companies of the world have been concerned with digitalizing telenets, a goal that was fulfilled during the 1990s. From then, all information processing was based on the same digital technique. As a consequence, computer technology and telecommunications integrated to form the so-called »information technology« (IT). Digitalization covered all links in the telecommunications system. Furthermore, the capacity to transmit information escalated. Copper cables were replaced by optical fiber cables on all main lines within and between developed countries of the world. Demand for digital communication technology exploded around 1990, and that spurred vendors of tele equipment and newly privatized tele companies to build a new electronic infrastructure during the first half of the 1990s. At the same time, governments and some huge corporations of leading industrial nations achieved a global system of satellites. Satellites also made possible a breakthrough in the new mobile communication technology in the early and mid-1990s.[408]

With fiber optic cables, satellites, digital communication, escalating chips capacity, and rapidly emerging packaged software to run communications, the field of communications as well as that of computer technology was revolutionized from the early 1990s. A global electronic infrastructure was built. Multinational organizations were enabled to reorganize into transnational corporations (TNCs) and to loosen up the functional links of bureaucracy, including relationships with suppliers and customers. Increasing competition, innovation and productivity followed this process of globalization.

The merging computer and communications technology, including the increased capacity of chips and the launching of many new kinds of software, made barriers between industries blur to an even greater extent. Besides computer and communications technology, mass media such as television programs and movies, books, magazines and newspapers, all began to merge into one complex multimedia industry with overlapping lines of business. The CD-Rom became the new medium for storing and presenting information of

---

408 OECD, *Information Technology Outlook*, 1997, pp. 32-36, 141-161. IDC (1997), *European Network Product Support Services Markets and Trends*, 1995-2001. OECD (1997), *Communications Outlook*, 1997 (Paris: OECD).

any kind, including text and numbers, pictures and movies, as well as talk. All forms of information, now digitalized, could be presented and processed with one and the same technology, the computer.

Since the mid-1990s, networked computing and business had taken one big step further, namely, the Internet breakthrough. The Internet revolutionized communications within a few years by presenting the common communication standard and medium that all businesses longed for. All internal and external communication took over the Internet Protocol made up of Transmission Control Protocol/Internet Protocol (TCP/IP).

Furthermore, companies started to exploit the Internet and its WWW software to reach customers and suppliers. Electronic commerce inaugurated a trend that might turn out to be the beginning of a new business paradigm. It might also influence social relations, since most information and knowledge of public administration and institutions, as well as most communication between businesses, between businesses and consumers, and between government and citizens were about to take place through the Internet. The IT industry rushed to serve this new field of business with software tools and applications. This might be the start of a revolution of software, too.

While local area networks (LANs) spread rapidly in organizations, a shift to open wide area networks (WANs) was seen from the mid-1990s, fueled by the Internet. As a consequence, organizations shifted from the combined mainframe and desktop environment of the 1980s to a networked architecture.

All these developments were spurred by a sharp drop in hardware and software prices.

Servers

Client/server

Until the 1980s, and in fact until the early 1990s, practically all servers were mainframes. The emphasis then shifted radically to client/server computing in networks. The trend towards client/server software influenced and fueled the new server market.[409] Servers provided services to client computers (PC-users) connected via a network. Servers were defined by their use. Most commonly they were dedicated machines that provided a range of services from basic file sharing, print sharing, and internal LAN communications to access

---

409 IDC (1997), *Vendor Performance in European IT Markets 1996*. IDC (1996), *1996 Worldwide Software Review and Forecast*. IDC (1997), *1997 Global IT Survey*. IDC (1998), *1998 Global IT Survey*. OECD, *Information Technology Outlook*, 1997, pp. 26-44.

or provision of applications such as database, e-mail, fax, and sophisticated applications such as large databases and online transactions. For this reason servers could be computers of almost any size and capability. Server platforms might be classified into three categories ranging from high-end, via medium-end, to low-end.

The high-end servers were proprietary enterprise systems. By the mid-1990s, mainframes, mainly IBM MVS and its modernized S/390 version, accounted for half the servers at the high-end, while multi-user client/server systems, mainly running Unix, counted for the other half. At the end of the 1990s, mainframes were still important because large online transaction systems still depended on them. Medium-sized servers, mostly running Unix, moved up the capacity ladder, however, and IBM and other mainframe vendors had to upgrade their servers. Companies were shifting away from IBM's MVS (and other mainframes) to Unix servers as they moved from custom applications to packaged applications built on relational database management systems (unlike the hierarchical mainframe systems). Whether this would make high-end and medium-sized servers finally emerge, was yet to be seen by the late 1990s.

Many large corporations moved slowly to replace mainframes with client/server technology. Most client/server systems in large corporations were built on top of mainframe systems, at least in the first instance. Since the late 1990s, corporations seemed to move more determinedly towards true client/server systems, which required a demanding process of reorganization, however.

High-end servers remained critical to large corporations. Enterprise-wide, it might be more correct to say that high-end, medium-end, and low-end servers made up a complex pattern of servers to be integrated if corporations wanted to reap the fruit of the new client/server technology. Since the mid-1990s, this enterprise perspective gained momentum, as further development would need a true interoperability and integration of often several platforms. That gave mainframes and high-end systems a kind of renaissance.

Super-servers or workstations comprised the midrange segment of the server market. Super-servers grew rapidly, too, owing to increasing demand for important server applications such as database, e-mail, fax, workflow, and remote access, combined with the availability of multiprocessor technology in the low-end machines. Unix also dominated this level of servers, although Microsoft NT successfully targeted these markets and reached the level of Unix by the late 1990s.

Technological innovations in microprocessor chip technology had improved performance of enterprise servers and super-servers and driven demand. Reduced instruction set computing (RISC) chips succeeded in raising power in

the high- and midrange segment. In the low-end market segment, complex instruction set computing (CISC) chips promised a similar increase in power.

At the low-end, PCs and small-scale servers, single-user or LAN servers,
provided various services to desktop computers on the network. Single-user
servers were increasing in numbers as companies continued to invest in LANs
for downsizing and in LAN-based applications. Until the mid-1990s, most
servers were proprietary systems, and Unix benefited from its dominance at
the medium-end. When large organizations moved into client/server systems
Unix also tended to dominate the low-end server market.

As Microsoft Windows spread rapidly on the PC-market, Microsoft's server, Windows NT, took hold of the low-end server operating system (OS) market in the late 1990s. Windows NT gained popularity for its multi-platform
hardware support, unlike Unix, the ability to act as applications server, and a
common interface. Novell's NetWare dominated network operating systems
for LANs, followed by Microsoft Windows and NT.

As PC LANs and e-mail systems continued to proliferate, the demand for
group-ware was increasing. Group-ware was an additional feature to PC LAN
servers. Group-ware allowed groups of users to receive and access messages,
documents and files, typically within a department or firm and sometimes beyond the company. The leading group-ware products were Lotus Notes,
Novell's Groupwise, and Microsoft's expanding Exchange. As companies
based their internal networks on the Internet, some functions performed by
group-ware and the Internet's WWW were beginning to overlap, and group-
ware became more compatible with Internet standards.

The Internet allowed organizations and individuals to communicate with
users, numbering in the millions and growing into hundreds of millions.
Many types of Internet applications ran on client/server architecture and from
the mid-1990s, the Internet revolution caused Internet server sales to increase
rapidly. Unix also dominated Web servers, owing to its traditional support for
the Internet Protocol (IP), followed by expanding NT.

The dominance of Unix-based servers has been challenged by several
trends in development since the mid-1990s. The IP was no longer confined to
the Unix world, as other computer operating systems and networking protocols were upgraded to include IP. Through its dominance of the desktop computer environment particularly, Microsoft NT threatened the position of
Unix-based servers. Furthermore, Microsoft practiced a strategy of embedding
more and more basic facilities into its operating system. As a consequence,
Microsoft Windows became the worldwide dominating base on the client side
and, by the late 1990s, NT threatened to pass Unix on the server side. Microsoft sought determinedly to take advantage of escalating chip technology to
move up towards the midrange segment of servers. However, mainframe pro-

prietary operating systems (IBM) still dominated large corporations combined with proprietary multi-user client/server systems (Unix or NT).

Recently, Linux launched its open source operating system that might create an even more challenging server environment. The outcome of this is yet to be seen.

Database Management Systems

Database Management Systems (DBMS) constituted the basic technology of client/server systems.[410] Oracle and Microsoft were the main competitors in this market, Microsoft being the stronger in the lower-end and Oracle in the upper-end. In the high-end, IBM was still an important vendor. Whether built on top of mainframes or standing alone, they were typically relational database management systems, unlike the hierarchical database management systems of mainframes. Object-oriented database management systems promised to be the next DBMS generation of the early twenty-first century.

Until the late 1990s, the market for objects was still relatively small, because existing corporate information systems were programmed and organized according to functional data. A break-through of object-oriented programming and database management systems emerged towards the end of the twentieth century, however, as business and technology transformation escalated, fuelled by globalization and the Internet revolution.

Besides these high-, mid- and low server levels and markets, so-called application servers emerged towards late 1990s. Application servers sought to break down the walls of corporate functional information systems and facilitate cross-functional information processing. Such cross-functional information retrieval was crucial to create flexible management systems adaptable to rapidly changing market conditions.

Component Software

The widespread adoption of client/server application packages alongside existing customized applications created problems of interoperability. For a radical move towards a web technology to materialize, as promised by the Internet, information systems needed to be interoperable. A new and rapidly emerging group of software technologies, component software, promised to solve that problem, thereby causing great changes in the software industry and user environments. The most important and successful commercial architecture for component software was Java.[411]

---

410 IDC (1998), *Programmer Development Tools Synopsis: 1998 Worldwide Markets and Trends*.
411 OECD, *Information Technology Outlook*, 1997, pp. 163-174.

292   ENVIRONMENT

Java was a set of technologies for writing, transmitting, and executing plat-
form-independent programs. Platform-independence was the first crucial
characteristic feature. The two core technologies were the Java language itself
(an object-oriented high-level programming language) and the Java Virtual
Machine (a virtual computer that executed Java code using the computation-
al resources available on a specific platform). Java made it possible to transfer
small applications (often called applets) across networks for execution on any
computer with a Java Virtual Machine.

Java was developed by Sun Microsystems, and was released in 1995. Since
then, scores of hardware and software vendors announced their support, including Microsoft, IBM, Apple, Oracle, and Netscape. Java was available for all
major computing platforms, including Windows, Macintosh, and Unix.

Java aimed at producing a much more flexible, open, and productive platform for software technology. First, it attempted to break conventional applications into small chunks (components or so-called applets), or at least to allow
large applications to share functions. Second, it was strongly influenced by the
growth of networks, including the Internet, and collaborative works, delivering code over networks. Third, it tried to facilitate the use of heterogeneous
computing platforms. Fourth, it had similar effects on the software industry.

Conventional software applications were organized around tasks. Today's
word-processing applications, for example, contained the functions necessary
to write documents, including text editing, spell checking and page layout, to
create graphics, tables, and equations, and even to access and create documents on the Internet. In contrast, component software, which focused on integration, was organized around functions. Instead of using a single application to write a document, it used a set of software components, each of which
fulfilled a single function. The functions could be combined to meet the user's
needs, rather than those determined by the vendor.

Component software radically altered the traditional notion of a document. So far, documents were files created by a single software application.
Documents »belonged« to applications. With component software, documents would instead be related to a common focus rather than to the program used to create them.

The Internet encouraged component software in another way. A large number of organizations wished to make custom applications available to users
with various combinations of hardware and software. Now that network
connections were becoming ubiquitous, the audience for an organization's
custom applications was growing tremendously. With network delivery of
components, the nature of documents also changed, as they could contain
content of nearly any degree of complexity without concern for the applications available to the user.

Component software would have important effects on markets and vendors, too. It diversified market opportunities for software vendors. It lowered barriers to innovation. Innovation components could be sold individually without having to support other functions. And component software should make changes less disruptive for users and technical support groups. The most important effect of component software might be to reduce the importance of hardware and operating systems, currently dominated by Microsoft and Intel in the desktop computer market. Component software could also lower switching costs for consumers. The third likely effect on the market and vendors was an increase in the importance of standards.

In many senses, component software was the next logical step in an environment increasingly centered around electronic work and collaboration, yet it would also alter nearly every aspect of conventional software, as well as the very definitions of software, data, and networks. By the late 1990s, component software was on the verge of a breakthrough. Existing information systems, however, still called for different solutions unless replaced by up to date component-software technology.

Microsoft

Microsoft had come to dominate the server software technology in an extraordinary way, almost as IBM used to do in the age of mainframes.[412] The PC operating system of DOS, followed by Windows 3, Windows 95, and Windows 98 (continuously to be followed by new versions), with a 32-bit platform, formed the basis of Microsoft's success. In the early 1990s, Microsoft moved into servers in the low-end, launching Microsoft NT. Microsoft NT clearly intended to challenge the strong position of Unix in low- and medium-end servers. By the late 1990s, Microsoft NT was moving up the midrange and had reached the strength of Unix. Furthermore, Microsoft practiced a strategy of embedding more and more basic facilities into its operating system, including net-ware, group-ware, and Internet-ware, such as its browser.

As a consequence, Microsoft Windows became the worldwide dominating base on the client side and, by the late 1990s, NT was threatening to pass Unix on the server side. NT was clearly the object of the Microsoft strategy to embed all central software in the server and to move into the midrange market. In carrying out this strategy, Microsoft sought determinedly to take advantage of advancing chip technology. Microsoft wanted to dominate the world markets of systems- and tools-software, such as operating systems, net-ware, middleware, and database systems.

---

412 IDC (1996), *1996 Worldwide Software Review and Forecast.* IDC (1998), *Programmer Development Tools Synopsis.*

While Microsoft tried to achieve a dominant position in the server market, similar to its position on the client side, strong contenders such as IBM, Hewlett Packard (HP), Unix, and Oracle did not stand still. Furthermore, the breakthrough of the Internet, emerging component software, and the blurring boundaries of software and information businesses made it increasingly difficult for one corporation to control the core technologies of IT. Finally, Linux' open source strategy increased the competitive pressure on Microsoft.

On the other hand, Microsoft contained strong organizational capabilities. These capabilities were extended by a number of alliances and shares within a growing information world, including leading vendors of applications and services.

Applications

Since the early 1990s, client/server applications have escalated. While mainframe applications covered 9/10 of applications in the late 1980s and only 1/10 belonged to client/server systems, the relationship had reversed by the end of the 1990s.[413] Instead of developing systems in-house, applications were bought in the marketplace. Packaged applications in client/server environments gave the end-user direct access to the information of the corporations' databases. The radical reengineering process of all large corporations of the world since the early 1990s was the prime mover for client/server developments and application purchases. This business process reengineering (BPR) aimed at drastic cost reductions by linking core business activities with the demands of customers and the power of competitors, while often outsourcing non-strategic parts of the business. Client/server applications were a crucial part of BPR, as they aimed at creating an improved flow of information within a reorganized business and at speeding up planning and decision-making.

Furthermore, IT enabled organizations to create a networked business. Corporations did not just reorganize to produce flexible and innovative organizations. With computerized networks they also turned their businesses into globally organized firms, including supply chains and customer links.

Since the mid-1990s, having created the basics of globalized network organizations, corporations moved to use IT applications to gain revenues. Corporate databases were activated to search for new products, new markets, and new ways of managing the business for marketing purposes, including data mining.

---

413 IDC (1996), *1996 Worldwide Software Review and Forecast.* IDC (1998), *Programmer Development Tools Synopsis.*

Packaged software may be divided into cross-industry and vertical-industry applications. Within these types of application, packaged software covered three primary markets, each containing several specialized market-niches: application development tools, applications, and system-level software. The worldwide packaged software market grew considerably from the early 1990s. From being almost non-existent in the late 1980s, the worldwide packaged software market grew to a revenue value of almost $100 billion by 1995, and was expected to reach almost double that size by the year 2000. IBM was the largest software vendor until the mid-1990s, but Microsoft took over the lead in the second half of that decade. The USA covered half the software market, and 3/4 of software revenues of the world came from American companies.

The tools market continued to be dominated by database management systems. It covered the rapidly expanding client/server systems and distributed information management in a broader sense, including the new fields of data-warehousing, multimedia support, Internet enablement, and enterprise workgroup and mobile computing needs. In the second half of the 1990s, tools were being upgraded from two-tier (client/server) to three-tier (including the Internet) to provide higher levels of utility, flexibility, and maintainability, and to include business-logic and database management.

BPR and client/server systems, globalization, and networking spurred the industrialization and expansion of the application market. The system software market changed from mainframe operating systems to a platform of client/server technology that became layered to meet the many needs of the organization and its applications. The middle-ware market continued to grow to cover the growing need to combine applications of different technologies.

Microsoft expanded in all three markets, clearly replacing IBM as the leading vendor of packaged software. It was no strong lead, however, as the packaged software industry was still preparing for a final consolidation by the late 1990s. Only the client market had a clear leader in Microsoft. Except for its office package, Microsoft had no position in industry applications, however. Its strength was based on basic software technology, not on user applications, except for office software. Industry packaged applications were the huge and expanding markets of the client/server revolution, however.

Cross-Industry Applications

Packaged applications experienced a technological transition in the early 1990s, when they moved from mainframe-based applications to client/server applications. Furthermore, applications were upgraded to integrate analysis tools, as the use of business information advanced beyond routine reporting of static information to more ad hoc, custom reporting, often used for strategic decision-making and planning. At the same time, the platform started a transition from IBM to Unix, particularly in multi-user systems. Finally, the market of packaged application grew from the rather low level of the 1980s to the multi-billion dollar business of the 1990s.[414]

During the 1980s, most applications, such as accounting, human resources, manufacturing, and distribution were in-house products. Only word processing applications, and to some degree accounting packages, were marketed. The move from custom applications to packaged applications was slow during the recessive years of the early 1990s. Economic recovery and reorganization of corporations fueled packaged applications from 1993 to 1994, however. While this happened, the leading American software firms invaded the European market and created an environment of fierce competition that pushed forward development and implementation of industrial software.

The movement to client/server applications continued to fuel growth of the worldwide applications market. The business drivers for this shift to client/server technology were the need to improve end-user access to information and the need to implement support for BPR. Enterprise client/server applications increasingly incorporated decision-support and groupware-based technology to improve end-user access to information and worker productivity. BPR moved to extend beyond the corporate walls to include business networks of suppliers, customers, and other business partners.

The breakthrough of the Internet since the mid-1990s has fueled this continued growth in the applications market and in usage. The need for globally applicable applications and the spread of packaged applications to medium-sized companies and newer markets in Asia/Pacific and Latin America spurred this market, too. Furthermore, these trends would probably cause an increased concentration of this industry around a few global TNCs, such as was clearly seen in the enterprise-wide suites of applications.

SAP (Systems, Applications, and Products in Data Processing) clearly led the market, followed by PeopleSoft, Oracle, Baan, and J.D. Edwards. Thus, in industrial applications American firms did not dominate as they did in server and systems software. SAP and others mainly led the market of large corporations, whereas many software vendors throughout the world, including such Danish vendors as Damgaard Data and Navision, addressed the growing market of small- and medium-sized corporations. SAP and other large application vendors began to look eagerly towards this expanding market, as the large corporation market became satiated.

---

414 IDC (1998), *Cross-Industry Applications: 1997 World Market and Trends*. IDC (1993), *The European Application Solutions Marketplace, 1991-1997*.

The next step in applications software that sought to form a network of inter-linked applications, covering all information flow and processing to and from users in an organization, had already been introduced and would most likely benefit TNC vendors at the expense of many small- and medium-sized companies. Vendors looked to component and object software to build the next generation of applications, and formed an increasing number of alliances with vendors of systems and tools software, including consultants and systems integrators. Since the late 1990s, this process was fueled by the breakthrough of the Internet.

Finally, the back-office focus of enterprise wide applications would probably move to front-office and customer relations as a consequence of the Internet, too.

Vertical-Industry Applications

By the late 1990s, revenues for the worldwide vertical-industry application packaged software segment reached much lower levels than that of cross-industry applications.[415]

Until the early 1990s, all leading IT vendors were also leading vertical-industry vendors that delivered hardware and basic software, such as OS and DBMS. Such vendors included IBM and Unisys, for example in the airlines industry, during the mainframe era. IBM and Unisys offered standard solutions in distribution and cargo, too, and worked as system integrators. IBM, in particular, played a similar role in all other major industries, such as banking, finance, and manufacturing.

In the mainframe era, applications were developed in-house, as a rule. However, heavy investments in automation during the 1980s created an emerging market for vertical-industry applications, at first for mainframes. Then, the client/server revolution created potentially large markets for all vertical industries, including banking/finance, manufacturing, retail, wholesale, transport, communication, and utility industries.

In the early 1990s, leading vendors of the mainframe era reorganized into service industries as system integrators that provided solutions to user organizations, including outsourcing activities. These system integrators were the first group of vendors to address the growing market of applications and solutions in industries that reorganized by way of BPR and IT to become TNCs. System integrators, like their mainframe predecessors, were never strong in applications software. Individual software firms produced most client/server

---

415 IDC (1998), *Vertical-Industry Applications: 1998 Worldwide Markets and Trends*. IDC, *The European Application Solutions Marketplace 1991-1997*.

applications packages that were bought by user organizations (i.e., by cross-industry applications vendors). System integrators served to customize or just consult on these products, according to the overall strategy and portfolio of business and information systems.

Having saturated the market of single functions by the mid-1990s, cross-industry vendors developed integrated suites of applications that aimed at being enterprise-wide. These enterprise-systems expanded strongly during the late 1990s. From the mid-1990s, cross-industry applications vendors began to extend and adjust their suites of applications to suit the vertical-industry market that demanded upgraded and integrated portfolios of applications. This "cross-verticalization" process was led by leading suite suppliers (those that currently offer general accounting, materials management, human resources management, and one or more vertical application capabilities), such as SAP and Oracle. Although declining, single-function applications remained a strong category.

By the late 1990s, leading vendors began to ship Internet-based software, preparing to move towards this higher level of electronic infrastructure. The advent of the year 2000 and the particular software problems of the millennium precipitated the replacement of corporation's legacy systems with enterprise resource planning (ERP)-solutions, too.

Services

Since the early 1990s, BPR, client/server systems, globalization, and a focus on core business had created enormous demands not only for software, but to an increasing degree also for services. At the same time, revolutionary IT developments caused a radical restructuring of software and services markets. Since the mid-1990s, corporate headquarters had targeted more determinedly enterprise-wide planning of business and IT. As a consequence, enterprise resource planning software (ERP) was being demanded on the one hand, and on the other hand, systems integration services, including management services, were sought to reap the strategic fruits of sophisticated IT, too.[416]

IT and business services markets covered a very wide field. The competitive landscape was not only influenced by the expansion of IT, but also by the blurring of barriers between computer and communications technologies.

---

416 IDC (1997), *ERP Consulting and Integration Services in Western Europe.* IDC (1997), *Riding the Wave. An Analysis of Outsourcing Market Leaders in Western Europe.* IDC (1997), *European Outsourcing Markets and Trends, 1995-2001.* IDC (1996), *Consulting and Management Services* (Bulletin). IDC (1997), *1997 European Network Management and Monitoring Services.*

Furthermore, as corporations concentrated on their core business and tended to outsource activities that used to be done within the frames of bureaucracy, the barriers between technologies on the one hand and business areas on the other, were also being blurred. New markets were created and whetted the appetite of new competitors. First of all, there was a strong move towards upgraded demands of knowledge, pressed by growing competition within IT and services, and by an increase in knowledgeable products and strategic considerations of user organizations that act on the basis of globalized competition and consumer tastes.

Many individual markets did not mature until the late 1990s (including network and monitoring services) and user organizations had to become comfortable with the concept of outsourcing. A lot of upgrading and reorganization, including alliances, were needed to qualify service vendors for the complex tasks of handling multi-platforms of large corporations in an integrated manner. Outsourcing IT was one large service market that created much interest because it challenged traditional in-house IT departments and showed the radical changes in IT and business relations.

By late 1990s, the worldwide outsourcing market reached a total of approximately $100 billion. The USA covered half the market, Europe a quarter, and the rest of the world a quarter.

Processing services represented the largest type of outsourcing service. Banking, financial services, government, and manufacturing were the dominant sectors, but outsourcing was exploding beyond these sectors, in utilities, retail, health care and communications. U.S. firms dominated the market. Major players in the IT outsourcing market included EDS, IBM Global Services, CSC, and Cap Gemini.

These trends caused growing concentration, integration, and interrelationship within corporations that served such global markets. Three types of companies were main actors on the scene of IT services.

First, consulting firms, such as Andersen Consulting, Deloitte & Touche Consulting, KPMG, and Price Waterhouse.

Second, systems integrators, such as IBM Global Services, CSC, and Cap Gemini.

Third, ERP software vendors, such as SAP, Oracle, and PeopleSoft.

Because packages required a degree of customization, there was a sizeable service component to any enterprise application integration project. In addition, and perhaps most importantly, often a significant amount of re-engineering and change management was associated with major consulting and system integrating companies such as Arthur Andersen and IBM.

In reaction to the abundant opportunities in the packaged client/server market, most of the largest integrators in the world had developed a keen interest in enterprise applications from SAP, Oracle, PeopleSoft, and others and had built up alliances with these software vendors. Mostly, software vendors focused on the product and its improvements and upgrades, and not on the integration aspect. But increasingly they tended to become more aggressive in providing consulting and integration services themselves.

Andersen Consulting

Andersen Consulting developed as a separate business from Arthur Andersen & Co.'s accounting and auditing practice. During the 1970s and 1980s, Andersen's consulting services, which concentrated on information systems, accounted for an increasing portion of the firm's revenues. As a result, Arthur Andersen and Andersen Consulting were established as distinct entities.

Andersen Consulting was the largest management and technology consulting firm in the world whose mission was to help clients change to become more successful.[417] The firm worked with clients from a wide range of industries to align their people, processes, and technologies with their strategies. By the late 1990s, Andersen Consulting had offices in nearly 50 countries around the world and employed almost 50, 000 people. Of those, probably one-third worked in Europe. The firm cooperated with approximately 1, 000 partners worldwide.

Andersen Consulting had several global industries organized under five global market units: Communications, Financial, Government, Products, and Resources. Each of the industry groups was divided into three geographic divisions: The Americas, Europe/Middle East/Africa/India, and Asia/Pacific.

Andersen Consulting's products included systems building/systems integration, change management services, technology services, strategic services, software products, and computer operations management and systems support. The company's operations in those areas covered a broad range of industry groups. These included airlines and hospitality, aerospace and defense, discrete and process manufacturing, energy, and retail.

By the late 1990s, Andersen Consulting's total worldwide revenues were almost $6 billion, of which nearly one-third came from Europe. Worldwide revenue increased rapidly, trebling during the 1990s. Systems integration revenues amounted to almost half of its total revenues, enterprise resource planning and integrating being the most dynamic part by the late 1990s.

In Europe, Andersen Consulting created a comprehensive SAP business organization, to assist clients with SAP R/3. Andersen had relationships with all the major application software vendors. SAP was the largest practice, and Andersen was one of SAP's largest and most important partners.

---

417 IDC (1997), *ERP Consulting and Integration Services in Western Europe*, pp. 13-23. Andersen Consulting (1997-1998), *Annual Reports*, 1996 and 1997 (WWW).

Andersen's main competitors were system integrators such as EDS, IBM, CSC, and consultants such as Price Waterhouse. Deloitte & Touche, and KPMG. Andersen's integration services in Europe were moving more and more towards global services due to the nature of its clients.

IBM

During the early 1990s, IBM was radically changed from being an old traditional mainframe vendor to a totally different and market oriented services industry.[418] Mainframes still made up an important business, but mainframes now became an integrated part of its much-expanding services that made IBM the largest system integrator business in the world. All leading hardware vendors were positioning themselves as solutions vendors, integrating their technological offerings with a service approach. IBM Global Services was a vital part of IBM and of growing importance to the corporation. IBM Global Services provided the full spectrum of professional services: management and technology consulting, custom software development, systems integration, facility management (FM), outsourcing, network management, training and education. IBM Global Services revenues almost trebled from 1992 to 1996, and in 1996, it employed almost 150,000 professionals.

The introduction of IBM Global Services was part of the corporate transformation process of IBM. The concept behind IBM Global Services was to transform IBM's geographic teams and line-of-service activities into a truly integrated global services business. It was the strategy of IBM to provide clients with total integrated solutions that included hardware, software, and a complete range of services.

IBM practiced partnerships with competitors and all major application software vendors. Its main competitors globally were Andersen Consulting, Cap Gemini, CSC, and other big consulting firms. In Europe, IBM also competed with local, niche-specialized firms.

By the mid-1990s, IBM focused on system-integrating services that included its server products of the high-, medium-, and low-end levels. A few years later, IBM launched its strategy of electronic business services worldwide. The Internet and its Web technology created huge opportunities for new and rather uncultivated markets. Focusing with all its organizational capabilities gave IBM a head-on start in the e-business.

At the same time, IBM reviewed its server strategy and moved to upgrade its high and mid-level servers and enter into alliances with other strong vendors, such as HP, Oracle, and Microsun Systems with its Java component soft-

---

418 IDC, *ERP Consulting and Integration Services in Western Europe*, pp. 73-81. IBM (1997-1998), *Annual Reports*, 1996 and 1997 (WWW).

ware tool. On one hand, the upgrading of e-business, its OS and a focus on the new paradigm software of Java, were all intended to capture very promising concurrent and future markets, and to avoid meeting Microsoft on its dominating client/server (C/S) battlefield. On the other hand, IBM aimed at creating an open technology platform that might undermine the proprietary world of Microsoft.

SAP

SAP was founded in Germany in 1972.[419] In 1979, SAP launched a mainframe system known as R/2 with moderate success. In 1992, however, the company launched its client/server product R/3, which became a profound success accounting for the majority of SAP sales (the »R« stands for »real-time-processing«). Both products had comprehensive business functionality; modular and integration design, providing enterprise scalability, and industry specialization. SAP was a market and technology leader in client/server enterprise application software, particularly in large corporations. Half of its staff performed services: consulting, implementation, and support. SAP was organized by operating regions: Americas, Europe, Asia/Pacific, Africa/Middle East. Total revenues were $2.4 billion in 1996; almost four times that of 1993. In 1996, 71 % of the company's revenues came from product sales. R/3 product sales represented 92 % of SAP's total sales. Europe represented almost half its global revenues in 1996. In 1996, SAP had about 11,000 installations worldwide. It employed about 20,000 professionals.

SAP provided solutions for companies of all sizes and all industry sectors, but it was particularly strong in large companies. R/3 was accepted as the standard in many industries.

SAP developed relationships with hardware partners, consulting partners, complementary software partners, value-added resellers and technology partners. SAP's customers had access to partners that provided a full range of products and services to support SAP projects. Consulting partners were business and technology consulting firms that provided assistance in all phases of an R/3 implementation project, including the largest multinational companies. Andersen Consulting was SAP's biggest consulting partner worldwide.

SAP's main competitors in the client/server arena were Baan, PeopleSoft, and Oracle. SAP's goal was to achieve a higher market share with smaller enterprises. SAP expected to grow its service and support network by increasing its partner

---

419 IDC, *ERP Consulting and Integration Services in Western Europe*, pp. 110-115. IDC (1997), *SAP's Component-Enabled Business Framework* (Bulletin). SAP (1997-1998), *Annual Reports*, 1996 and 1997.

consultants.

The core modules of R/3 were: Accounting, Human Resources, Logistics, and Workflow. R/3's architecture was three-tier with PCs at the front end, application servers in the middle, and a single database server at the back end. The integrated system allowed updates to one module to become available to other modules. Since 1996, R/3 included Internet and Intranet facilities, including Java-applicability. Version 4 of R/3 in 1997-98 opened R/3's architecture for easy integration with third-party software. The new object-based architecture was broken into components allowing customers to upgrade piecemeal to suit their needs. By then, SAP was preparing determinedly for Web solutions. Even SAP and Microsoft started a process of cooperation, as did IBM and SAP, targeting the age of web commerce.

Historically, SAP was positioned in the manufacturing sector, both discrete and process. Since then, it has expanded into most markets with is industry-wide modular service. While SAP had proven very successful in large enterprises, the company was now pursuing the SME market and had plans to partner with a number of resellers in order to help it go after that market.

The widespread adoption of client/server application packages reflected a growing trend for organizations to buy solutions rather than build them. Yet as broad as a packaged application suite might be, it was not sufficient to meet all of a company's application needs. The need to link software applications, some packaged and some custom, made ease of integration important to companies selecting a major application package. Therefore, application vendors were investing in improving their support for application interoperability, including component software. During the late 1990s, SAP focused on developing a version of R/3 that could be broken down into components. Ease of interoperability was important for extending a horizontal solution to meet specialized customer needs, including those particular to a vertical industry. In addition, as new technologies such as the Internet appeared, R/3 could be extended to exploit these innovations. The resultant broad application of a complex integrated system concept was one of SAP's strongest competitive advantages.

IT Management

Until the late 1980s, the IT department was one of a number of departments in the multi-functional organization.[420] It made up a world and culture of its own that had been cultivated for decades. Other departments developed similar islands of culture. IT development, operation and communication were centralized in the IT department, and IT professionals monopolized the knowledge for handling this increasingly important technology. As a staff unit, the IT department addressed all other functions. Furthermore, IT investments were largely based on the proposals of the IT department, seeking to obtain productivity gains from the other business functions. This was a technology driven process. Increased user cooperation of the 1980s introduced user checkpoints in systems development, but did not cause any fundamental change. Each system was developed and modernized according to individual cost/benefit calculations that continued to produce sub-optimization of each function of the corporation.

By the late 1980s, a breakthrough in a strategic perspective on IT developments occurred in large corporations. This strategic change should dominate the 1990s. Functional and technological criteria were replaced by business considerations of the whole organization. At all levels, a process of strategic alignment of IT business was introduced to meet the demands of growing competition. The center of gravity moved from the IT department to the line organization and even the level of corporate management. IT developments became a business driven field. This was stressed by a radical introduction of market relations between the two parties. Often, the IT department was turned into a company of its own, competing with other vendors in servicing its former parent company.

This so-called outsourcing occurred in varying degrees. In some cases, a break materialized. More often, the parent firm kept ownership control of the new IT company. Some corporations outsourced parts of their IT activities, usually operations. Outsourcing was intended to cut costs and put maximum market pressure on former IT departments. To survive during these radically changing conditions, the former IT departments carried out a proper cultural revolution. A technology-driven and we-know-best culture was replaced by a business-driven culture. Furthermore, a determined and continuous process was started to upgrade competence of the IT professionals so that they should

---

420 Developments of IT management might be seen from the changing content and approaches of Information Systems textbooks, see Chapter I on IT. Conference proceedings of information systems management add to this picture, for instance the IFIP and IRMA conferences.

learn to align with strategic business considerations. The dominating mainframes were being replaced by a new client/server technology, too.

The client/server technology was part of revolutionary changes in the IT field as such. The central point moved from mainframes (servers) to users (clients). IT industries emerged to offer software packages for tools and applications. Within a few years, traditional systems development from scratch more or less vanished. In-house development of applications was substituted by packages bought in the market place. Furthermore, open and 'intelligent' networks to support the PC-based client/server technology substituted for the proprietary networks of mainframes and terminals.

All these radical changes took place during the first half of the 1990s and they affected all large corporations of the highly industrialized countries. Corporations fought fiercely to remain profitable or to regain profitability during the recession of the early 1990s. Towards the mid-1990s, the strategic alignment of IT and business moved into a new phase of development. Considerations of core competence and competitiveness increased the importance of knowledge upgrading and process innovation. Furthermore, experiences of the early 1990s, made it clear that radical changes were also a matter of continuity and learning being continuously pushed forward.

These trends combined to increase corporate management's overall strategic efforts, including IT. IT was seen as a core competence field that had to be upgraded. Outsourcing seemed less attractive than just a few years before. Or rather, if former IT departments were considered strong enough to survive in a globalized economy they moved further away from their parent company and started a determined process of competence upgrading and market offensive. Otherwise, a cooperative and combined process of IT upgrading was initiated for the parent company and its former IT department. Considerations of improved core competence acquired top priority, although IT activities were still measured according to the best standards in the market. IT was considered a tool for increased integration and improved strategic management. Cross-functional and strategic systems gradually moved in to complement or replace the functional legacy systems of corporations and all hardware, software and even services were bought in the market place to be integrated into the whole corporate structure of IT and business.

Former or continuing IT departments turned into system integrators. It became the job of IT professionals to integrate the complex components of corporations that often consisted of old legacy systems and modern c/s solutions, including new networks. Furthermore, high quality operation of enterprise applications, networks, and c/s systems were left to present or former IT departments if they could match the competition of the IT services market.

Globalization added another dimension to the IT field. Large corporations reorganized on a global basis and entered into a growing number of strategic alliances to live up to accelerating demands of knowledge and investments in order to stay in business. As a consequence, information systems and networks moved up the ladder to a cross-bordering and cross-business level. This was pushed further forward by the breakthrough of the Internet and electronic commerce.

Airlines IT

Until 1990, IBM and Unisys dominated the IT airline industry. Networks remained traditional telephone systems with computer front ends. Most airlines used IBM mainframes and operating systems for their core transactional applications with Unisys in second place. All leading airlines of the world developed their applications in-house by way of large IT departments. As an exception, one airline might buy a system from another airline, mainly in cases of more complex systems, such as BA's FARES system that was sold to several airlines.

Since 1990, this old and well-established structure was challenged by a radically changing world economy and IT industry.[421] Mainframe vendors, such as IBM and Unisys, lost ground and started to transform their business into systems integration services. Client/server technology expanded dramatically to move Unix servers, followed by NT of Microsoft, to the foreground including the leading PC-Windows system. A large packaged applications and tools industry emerged, dominated by companies such as SAP and Oracle.

Around 1990, a radical change of IT strategy was carried out in all leading airlines. IT departments were turned into subsidiaries, having to adapt to market conditions, but with their parent company as their main customer. In-house developments of large systems stopped and were replaced by purchased client/server systems and increased efforts to enforce systems integration on the basis of a distributed networked IT. While being market-oriented on the one hand, the IT subsidiaries were aligned to the strategic goals of their parent firm on the other. IT moved to the level of strategic management. A few IT subsidiaries moved into the airline software market with some success, including SABRE of American Airlines and Speedwing of British Airways.

By the early 1990s, distributions were transformed from proprietary to open systems that soon were inter-linked into global systems. Proprietary net-

---

421 Little research was done on airline IT developments during the 1990s, except for some on SABRE and the early years of British Airways. SAS developments support the outline presented here.

works of airlines were turned into open networks, too. As most regulations were liberalized at the same time, airlines were left to compete under open conditions. This was further stressed by the revolutionizing breakthrough of the Internet from the mid-1990s. Proprietary IT systems no longer contained any significant competitive advantage. Networked ubiquitous IT created business potentials of huge dimensions, never seen before.

SABRE

American Airlines and its IT department, SABRE, based much of its business on massive, centralized, proprietary computer systems. The SABRE reservations systems had been of particular significance to American Airlines (AA) since the 1960s.[422]

SABRE started in the 1960s as a simple reservation system. During the 1960s and 1970s, its functionality was greatly expanded, including flight planning, maintenance planning, crew scheduling, and developing a range of decision-support systems for management. SABRE and its associated systems became the control center through which AA functioned. Since the late 1970s, SABRE had developed a dominating role as a travel-industry distribution system. During the 1980s, new services were added to the database to help travel agents (hotels, rails, rental cars) provide better service, including direct access by terminals. AA used its ownership of SABRE to lock-in customers and lockout competitors to the benefit of its own business. As a result, travel agents accounted for 80 % of all passenger tickets by the early 1990s as compared with 40 % in 1976, and SABRE contributed greatly to making AA a profitable airline.

Since 1990, radical changes had occurred. The widespread adoption of open standards in hardware, software, and telecommunications, followed by a massive acceleration in performance, made computers as ubiquitous as telephones and as easy to use. And it was all bought in the marketplace. Finally, end users took over from data processing departments. For 30 years AA had been handcrafting its computer systems. That age was over.

As a consequence, SABRE radically changed its strategy by the late 1980s. InterAAct, as it was called, was a strategy for organizational computing that was built around hardware and software provided by third-party vendors, while Sabre played the role of a system integrator. Economies of scale became more important than ever and required increased mainframe capacity. At the

---

422 Hopper, M. D. (1990), "Rattling SABRE – New Ways to Compete on Information", in *Harvard Business Review*, May-June, pp. 118-125.

same time, SABRE depended on distributed computing with increased access to information for users. PCs replaced "dumb" terminals and client/server systems were added to mainframe systems. The big databases and computer systems were to be more open to as many users as possible, and not to be the private reserve of AA, or to be systems that in any way locked in customers and locked out competitors.

InterAAct was not just a new technological platform. It aimed at being part of an organizational transformation of AA, which would increase the airline's flexibility and competitiveness. Next it wanted to turn SABRE into an IT vendor in the market, selling systems that even included AA's most vital technology, the yield management system. AA transformed its competitive philosophy to compete on the use of computer systems, not on their exclusive ownership.

Since 1990, SABRE had stopped being a proprietary competitive weapon for AA. It turned into not just a general distribution system for the airline industry, but into an unbiased electronic travel supermarket. Other airlines were no longer discriminated against to the benefit of AA. No travel agent could be locked into the SABRE system. If an agent was not satisfied with its services, another system could be chosen.

During the first half of the 1990s, AA and SABRE were transformed by innovative activities to upgrade competitiveness towards an open market.[423] As a consequence, SABRE was made a business unit of its own in 1993, called the SABRE Group, managed as an independent division of AA. In 1996, the group became an independent legal entity, but the company remained under AA control. In 1996, SABRE Business Travel Solutions was introduced to the corporate market.

During the 1990s SABRE upgraded its technology to cover client/server technology, based on relational database management systems, Unix servers, and the Windows PC interface, and the increasing demands on its capacity at its computer center in Tulsa Oklahoma to run transactions and networks. Furthermore, it expanded its portfolio of marketed information systems from engineering and operating the SABRE distribution system to cover a full range of technologies with the airlines and travel industries.

The SABRE Group's 1997 revenues accounted for $1.8 billion and employed 8,500 people. Two-thirds of its income came from distribution fees, one-third from IT solutions and services. Since 1996, it has been listed on the New York Stock Exchange as an independent company from AA. Still, AMR Corporation, as AA was now called, owned about 82 % of its equity. SABRE

---

423 The SABRE Group (1998), *Annual Report*, 1997 (WWW).

made a 10-year affiliate agreement with AA as it separated its activities fully from its parent airline. It was a transitional arrangement before total market relations were established, providing AA with certain IT services and AA providing certain management services for SABRE, including marketing cooperation, a non-competition agreement, travel agreements for reduced fares, and a credit agreement.

The core business of SABRE was its global distribution system that covered approximately 25 % of all airline traffic of the world and approximately 50 % of all North American airline traffic, including reservations for hotels, car rentals, railways, tour companies, passenger ferries and cruise lines. SABRE distribution was based on its easySABRE online system for travel agents from the mid-1980s, which since the mid-1990s has also been available for consumers over the Internet. The new system, Travelocity, provided a more powerful Internet reservation interface for consumers with simple point and click booking and browsing, instead of command driven easySABRE.

From the early 1990s, SABRE was investing heavily to cope with a changing world where proprietary IT advantages were being replaced by open market competition, further stressed by the expanding Internet. SABRE tried to diversify is revenues more towards markets for IT solutions and outsourcing deals, including reducing the importance of its largest customer AA (deriving less than 65% of its IT solutions revenue from AA in 1997). In 1996, for example, SABRE agreed upon a 25-year multibillion dollar, total IT outsourcing agreement with US Airways.

In 1997, SABRE's IT solutions operations made the transition to becoming a regional organization, putting people closer to its customers throughout the world. SABRE intended to expand worldwide, although the U.S. business remained its primary source of revenues in IT solutions. SABRE signed a growing number of global alliances with other electronic travel distribution systems, including WORLDSPAN, AMADEUS, GALILEO, and ABACUS.

The core business of SABRE Technology Solutions, the IT division of the SABRE Group, included software development, advanced decision-support systems, outsourcing, multi-host services, consulting services, and logistics solutions. Airline solutions formed the core of the SABRE IT division. It covered all basic airline-functions. These included:

- Distribution solutions.
- Flight Scheduling Solutions.
- Crew Scheduling Solutions.
- Maintenance & Engineering Solutions
- Finance and Revenue Accounting Solutions
- Airline Pricing Solutions.

- Revenue and Yield Management Solutions.
- Cargo Solutions
- Consulting Solutions.
- Airport, Hospitality, and Rail Solutions.

SABRE was the only IT-company in the world that offered a complete line of solutions for a vertical-industry, such as that of airlines. Except for its distribution system, its many IT applications and consulting activities were sold in only a few cases to other leading airlines besides its parent corporation American Airlines. Its maintenance system, for example, was sold to British Airways.

But things were changing. On the one hand, SABRE expanded its sales of IT solutions and on the other, competition was clearly increasing. Since the mid-1990s, the packaged applications industry was expanding determinedly into vertical industries. Although airlines alliances might pave the way for sales of IT solutions among the IT subsidiaries involved, the large cross-industry applications vendors moving into vertical industries might be the winners of this tough game, after all. Just as AA had done, all airlines adopted a strategy of buying third parties' solutions. For example, SAS chose SAP and Oracle when developing new systems for Human Resources and Finance respectively, and some packaged software by SABRE for Station personnel management.

SAS Business

Planes and Routes

Early 1990s Crisis and Change

The early 1990s were years of crisis and change. In 1990 and 1991, the Gulf War halved revenues of scheduled air service and of the whole travel business as such. Until 1993, all international airlines lost money and created major burdens of debt. Furthermore, the reduced traffic brought to light the cost problems of airlines. For SAS, problems were only aggravated as a result of an economic crisis in its two major markets England and Sweden. In its third large market the North Atlantic, SAS met the vicious circle of increasing competition during a period of declining traffic and prices.

SAS and the airline industry in general took drastic measures to regain profitability, cutting personnel and unprofitable traffic routes and succeeded with radical changes of strategy and organization.[424] Contrary to many airlines, SAS was financially well consolidated, however, and possessed the available capital to carry out needed structural changes. Whereas the Gulf War crisis required cost reductions, more thorough methods had to be taken to adapt to an increasingly open global competition. The profitability crisis of the early 1990s made airlines start a process of fundamental restructuring.

During the late 1980s, SAS prepared for the open competition of the 1990s. A global traffic system was built around Scandinavia and Copenhagen, based on gateways in Europe and on the other continents, by way of cooperation with other airlines. SAS even bought shares of airlines such as British Holdings. As part of its strategy, SAS merged with Swedish Linjeflyg in 1992 to consolidate its dominant position in the Swedish market. As a consequence, the number of destinations to be reached from the Scandinavian capitals multiplied and nonstop traffic doubled.

Furthermore, SAS invested billions of SEK in airlines and hotels to create a global traffic system and carry out its strategy for a global travel chain. Even more was invested in new planes, reaching 5 to 10 billion SEK, to replace the DC-10 with the B767 on the intercontinental routes and gradually to start to replace the DC-9 in Europe with the new MD80 McDonnell Douglas generation.

---

424 SAS, *Annual Reports*, 1990 to 1995.

The Gulf Crisis brought an end to these investments. All agreements of lease and purchase were critically reviewed and delivery of new planes postponed.

The second strategy to create an international distribution system by way of AMADEUS was implemented in the early 1990s. AMADEUS brought open distribution to the airlines and travel business.

The third strategy of the late 1980s that was intended to increase efficiency by 5 % each year was part of a general strategy to break down traditional bureaucracy. By 1990, management had succeeded in improving efficiency to some degree, but failed to overcome bureaucracy. Then the Gulf Crisis led to a reduction of 3 billion SEK in costs and 3,500 personnel. Next, management determinedly targeted a reorganization of the SAS bureaucracy to prepare for a business environment of increasing competition.

Since the mid-1980s, corporate SAS had looked for partners to create its vision of being "one of five in 95" (i.e., one of the five large European airlines that corporate management in 1985 predicted would dominate European air traffic by 1995). In the early 1990s, negotiations for a close alliance and eventual merger took place between SAS, Swissair, KLM, and Austrian Air. All companies were being thoroughly analyzed to prepare for a future process of integration and rational organization. During 1992 to 1993, this so-called Alcazar project was almost fulfilled, but in the end it came to nothing. Too many obstacles and differences blocked the way for such a radical change as merging these old and proud national airlines into one.

SAS management had prepared an alternative plan in case of failure of the Alcazar project. This plan, which was carried out during the winter of 1993-1994, made SAS return to its core business. SAS defined its new business idea to include air transportation and activities immediately related to that business, mainly hotels, and accordingly, the travel company strategy of covering a long chain of travel services was abandoned.

As a consequence of its new core business strategy, SAS sold out all non-core activities, such as its large holdings in Inter-Continental Hotels, Service Partner and Diners, and downsized the SAS Group to a much lower level. Just as in the early 1980s, SAS returned to its core business of transporting businessmen by air. Carlzon's ambitions of making SAS a European airline were given up and instead, SAS concentrated once more on enforcing its role as the leading airline of Scandinavia. The SAS organization and business consolidated to carry out the new strategy. Its program of drastic cuts in cost had succeeded more or less and was even continued as a consequence of growing price competition. And since 1994, world economy had prospered and traffic grown again.

This strategic reorientation came at the same time as competition increased in SAS' main markets. On the one hand, all international airlines and business in general reorganized to focus on their core business and improve their adaptability towards changing markets. On the other hand, in 1993 the EU implemented Phase 3 of its plan to deregulate European air traffic, allowing free access and free pricing for all licensed airlines. Domestic markets in Sweden had already been deregulated in 1992, followed by a deregulation of Norway in 1994, and Denmark in 1997. All European airlines prepared for open competition, although some companies were slow do so and kept on leaning heavily on the State to counterbalance continuing deficits and debts. By the late 1990s, the EU finally stopped this unbalanced competition.

Drastic changes in the early 1990s made the SAS Group shrink to cover mainly its airline and hotel business, with revenue and personnel being much reduced. From 1994, SAS was again a profitable business, and the number of passengers transported regained its growth trend.

Mid and Late 1990s Core Business and Global Alliance

Core Business

In 1995, SAS ordered 41 B737-600 and 8 MD90 planes to be delivered by the late 1990s.[425] B737 and MD90 should fly distances of short and medium length in Scandinavia and Europe, the most vital parts of SAS' route network. In order to live up to reinforced EU rules, the new planes had the best environmental performance of all planes in the market, reducing noise and exhaust pollution and saving fuel. Being environmentally compatible created a competitive edge for SAS in the airline business. Finally, the new planes were heavily loaded with computer technology in navigation, external communication, and internal services, introducing so to speak the flying computer.

According to its new Scandinavian-oriented strategy, these small- and medium-sized planes, with 100-150 seats, reflected SAS' intentions to offer many competitive flights to and from Scandinavia and all major European destinations, including an upgraded program for domestic flights. SAS also planned to buy new planes for the intercontinental market. Decisions were postponed, however, because SAS had little to offer in the intercontinental market and little profit to gain, compared with large European airlines such as Lufthansa and British Airways. By the late 1990s, SAS even considered closing its intercontinental traffic, an unlikely outcome, however, unless SAS would give up its independence and merge with other airlines. This long-term planning of size and composition of the fleet was made by way of sophisticated computer simulations, based on historic data, forecasts, wanted frequencies, slot limitations, and so on.

---

425 SAS, *Annual Reports*, 1995 to 1997.

Since the mid-1990s, increasing international trade and production has made air transport expand. Globalized production created an increasing intermediate trade and transportation of goods between companies throughout the world. Just like other nations, Scandinavians traveled more and more by plane for business and even more for pleasure. SAS Cargo grew, too, for the first time in years. During the 1980s, Cargo marginalized and its share of Scandinavian air cargo halved to about 20 % by the mid-1990s. International integrated forwarders conquered much of Cargo's main express market of smaller packets delivered door-to-door, as did large neighboring airlines, such as Lufthansa. Instead of outsourcing its cargo business, however, it was decided to improve SAS Cargo's competitiveness by upgrading its organization.

Since the mid-1990s and definitively since 1997, open competition ruled in the USA and the EU, the dominant parts of world economy. The other continents approached a similar state of affairs, but still clung to some kind of regulation. As a consequence of the arrival of open competition in the airline industry, price competition increased enormously in SAS' Scandinavian home market. Furthermore, leisure travel grew more than business travel and even businessmen began switching to low-price tickets. The full price-paying businessman remained SAS' key source to profits, however, and its bonus program was highly upgraded to keep the loyalty of this core customer. SAS could not stop a general international trend of continuous relative decline in business class travels, however, and had to upgrade its marginal pleasure travel strategy to create a higher load factor. In 1998, SAS took the consequences of this development and revised its strategy to become an airline for »business and pleasure«, often targeting the same people in two different roles.

In 1995 and onwards, SAS launched a market offensive in two directions. First, the company aimed at raising the quality of its products, seeking once more to be the best European airline, just as in the early 1980s. A number of analytical and follow-up projects were carried out to make that program come true. Automatic or electronic ticketing, Express, and TravelPass were parts of this product development aimed at lightening and individualizing the journey of the frequently traveling businessman. Since 1997, SAS and all its partners had accepted electronic ticketing. Furthermore, you could book and buy tickets by way of the Internet – a promising approach for the near future. The latter was also part of SAS' endeavors to cut agency commissions, or rather to start a process of replacing the intermediate role of agencies by a direct link to customers through the Internet. Finally, the new planes added to SAS' service improvement strategy. Based on customer evaluations and analyses, these market initiatives were part of a continuous process of product development aimed at learning from customers.

In its marketing efforts, SAS strongly benefited from its loyalty program,

EuroBonus, and from its customer database. In 1998, EuroBonus had more than one million members. SAS hotels were an integral part of these loyalty programs.

Global Alliance

While striving to upgrade its core business, a globalized economy and open competition made SAS look for alliances and partners. To remain a leading airline and to stay in business in the long term, SAS had to be able to offer a global traffic system to its Scandinavian customers. The Alcazar failure in 1993 set the stage for a more gradual strategy of cooperation then the big bang of a merger. Instead of medium-sized airlines of the Alcazar project, the success of a global alliance required cooperation with large airlines. In 1995, SAS established a strategic alliance with German Lufthansa, one of the two largest European airlines (British Airways being the other one). Furthermore, Lufthansa had one of the largest air cargo businesses in the world and a strong position in the Scandinavian market, too, which made great synergy effects with SAS possible.

In the largest air traffic market of the world, the USA, SAS formed an alliance with United Airlines, one of the three dominating US airlines (American and Delta being the other two), and with Air Canada and Varig of Brazil, the largest South American airline. In Asia, SAS' old liaison Thai Airways joined this global "Star Alliance". Other Asian partners, most likely a Japanese airline and airlines of Australia and New Zealand, including Singapore Airlines might join the Star Alliance by the late 1990s. In Africa, only South African Airways seemed a candidate for the Star Alliance. As a consequence of this global alliance, a second large global alliance was built around American Airlines and British Airways, followed by other global alliances. Just like any other industry, airlines moved rapidly towards an oligopoly structure with a few leading groups of airlines, although still not having recourse to merger.

The Star Alliance focused on business, while leaving operative cooperation to future considerations. A globally coordinated traffic system multiplied the number of destinations offered to Scandinavians, including common loyalty programs. Gradually, alliance cooperation was being developed to include cargo, code-sharing, and even initial operating activities, such as maintenance. By the late 1990s, operational cooperation was yet to come, but increasing synergy effects of the alliance were surely an integrated part of SAS' plans, including rationalizations. Still, merger was no option for SAS on corporate level. Lower levels of the individual SAS businesses and functions, such as cargo, moved in to be strong candidates for merger-like trends by the turn of the millennium.

Largest Airline Alliances 1997

	Operating revenue (MUSD)	Employees
Star Alliance SAS – Lufthansa – United Airlines – THAI – Air Canada – Varig	46,000	231,000
BA/American Group British Airways – American Airlines – Qan tas – Iberia/Aviaco and others	45,400	247,000
Air France Group Air France – Alitalia – Continental – American West Airlines	24,100	116,000
Swissair Group Swissair – Sabena – Austrian Airlines – Delta and others	23,500	96,000
KLM/Northwest Group KLM – Northwest – Martinair – Air UK and others	17,600	83,100

Source: SAS, *Annual Report,* 1997.

The Organization

SAS Statistics

	1990	1994	1997
SAS Group			
Revenue/bill. SEK	31.9	36.9	38.9
Personnel/000	40.8	28.4	25.1
SAS Airline			
Revenue/bill. SEK	21.6	32.4	36.8
% Traffic of Group	57	75	79
% Passenger of Traffic	91	91	89
% Cargo of Traffic	7	6	7
Passengers/mill.	15.0	18.8	20.8
Personnel/000	22.2	20.9	22.5
% Traffic and Sales	48	47	43
% Crew	22	22	23
% Maintenance	19	18	17
% Others	11	13	16

Source: SAS, Annual Reports. IATA, World Air Transport Statistics.

Early 1990s Reorganization

While building a global traffic system and a new distribution strategy for an open market dominated the activities of SAS during the late 1980s, the Gulf Crisis forced SAS to attend to the problems of efficiency and costs. Rationalization and automation were given the highest priority in the early 1990s. Soon, SAS began to prepare for radical changes in its organization to enable it to function in a world of open competition. Finally, income-creating activities had to be considered, too.

Automation

SAS was reorganized in 1990-91 and used decentralized responsibility in the regions and divisions as a means of carrying out the program of reduced costs.[426] The company was divided into routes and business units – separate airlines so to speak (Norway, Sweden, Denmark, International) – and into production units of the enlarged Data and Distribution Division. These were called the Marketing and Automation Division (MAD), the Technical Division, and the Operation Division. Four airlines (Norway, Sweden, Denmark,

---

426 SAS, *ARP*, 1991.

International), and two "factories" (MAD and Technical/Operation), as they were called. MAD ran the overall program of cost reductions and increased market orientation. Hundreds of initiatives were taken to cut costs throughout the organization.

During 1991 to 1992, SAS focused on reducing resource-demanding processes, including those requiring a high number of personnel, such as check-in, sales, and maintenance. Furthermore, an improved organization and system of cash flow could reduce costs and raise revenue, as would new systems of yield management and revenue accounting. Secondly, MAD and SAS prepared for individual service to customers without increasing cost and losing flexibility. Thirdly, having closed down the TERESE reservation system project and being connected to the international distribution system of AMA-DEUS, SAS had to adapt to a future with the old Unisys technology. Finally, plans were made to prepare for a new and open IT infrastructure and for information systems to increase management capabilities and customer services.

While personnel was dismissed by thousands and costs cut by billions, SAS decided to invest 600 million SEK in IT to upgrade automation, planning, and optimizing. Some were long-term projects to be developed during the first half of the 1990s and implemented in the second half of the decade. Those included plans for automated ticketing and boarding in sales and stations, the making of a new IT infrastructure for open competition and cooperation, and a new user and management-oriented application structure of information systems. The latter spread gradually throughout the organization from 1991, in the shape of so-called client/server systems that moved the chief point of IT from central systems to distributed applications of users. Many c/s systems were introduced to increase productivity as well as revenue.

Lean Enterprise

While the 1991 SAS plans mainly targeted cost cutting as an immediate consequence of the Gulf War, 1992 plans started a radical change of the SAS organization.[427] During the 1980s, SAS management had not been able to carry out a profound reorganization of the old bureaucratic organization. As a consequence of crisis and deficits and an emerging open competition, reorganization and structural changes of the working process could no longer be postponed. The whole organization was thoroughly analyzed and several projects were started under the joint name of »Lean Production« or »Lean Enterprise«. Lean enterprise might also be a name for »business process reengineering«

---

427 SAS, *ARP*, 1992.

(BPR), another catchword to describe a general trend in large organizations of the early and mid-1990s. Like lean enterprise, BPR intended to overcome an old and deeply rooted bureaucratic and production-oriented organization. It was not the end of traditional bureaucracy, but it was the beginning of quite another kind of organization, a more flexible and market-minded one.

SAS deliberately wanted to reproduce the Japanese process-oriented way of organizing work to achieve a much higher level of productivity. Unlike traditional rationalization, lean enterprise was customer run. All SAS activities were analyzed to remove tasks without customer value.

According to this analysis, cost and sales-related costs at large Scandinavian stations might be much reduced without causing a decreased level of productivity and service. This could include automation of the chain of sales and handling from booking to departure and interline prorating (i.e., reservations, ticketing, check-in, boarding, meals, and prorating). Furthermore, a New Crew Planning project would improve planning for flight deck and cabin attendants by creating a much more flexible and adjustable system. Maintenance planned to introduce a factory concept to industrialize maintenance work in order to make radical cost reductions. Foreign governmental charges were analyzed to create a basis for reform of Scandinavian charges and cash flow. Head office overhead costs also needed to be much reduced. In general, it was planned to cut annual costs by 8%.

As a follow-up on lean enterprise intentions, minor changes to the SAS organization were carried out in early 1993, making a Business Division for routes (replacing four route sectors), an efficiency unit called Support Division (replacing MAD), and a Production Division (replacing Technical and Operation Divisions). Support and production divisions should enable the business units to make SAS a profitable company. A development perspective was enforced seeking to connect any activity to a function and its budgeted results. For SAS, the benefits would be increased income (yield management) and improved efficiency (station, crew, and maintenance projects).

Within sales, plans for basic production support automation were installed (ticketing, accounting, and back office), and sales processes prepared for telemarketing and -sales, too. Furthermore, sales productivity was to be increased by way of a new IT dialog at sales offices, by developing a tool kit for telephone sales, and with a total plan for all sales channels, including agents, booking, ticketing, back office, and revenue accounting. Beyond all expectations, the Columbus customer database and its EuroBonus loyalty program turned out to be a successful income producer. On the leisure side, the Jackpot program had positive income effects, too. EuroBonus and Jackpot formed parts of SAS' strategy towards passengers, who were now able to compare all airline prices themselves through the new international distribution systems. This strategy included efforts to increase the level of service in the airports for businessmen, quick check-in, lounges, punctuality, and so forth.

A new yield management system improved capabilities of optimization, always seeking to make seats available for all full price-paying passengers who often cancelled or booked minutes before departure. It also included other measures for passenger revenue optimization. Further initiatives included projects of dynamic aircraft rotation, a review of the traffic program planning chain (traffic planning, reservation, flight production), an improved flow, and integration of related systems.

Station activities and systems were reviewed to create a holistic view of processes, including the large project to automate ticketing and boarding (ATB). A strategic project, P50, reducing all procedures by 50 %, was also adopted. Tools of day-to-day planning were introduced (rosters, gate allocation, minute-by-minute allocation of resources), including a new shift system. In cooperation with other airlines, a new luggage concept was being planned, based on active identification of passengers' missing luggage.

Although strong in its basic production, Movement Control's capability of optimizing SAS resources had to be improved. That included matters of punctuality, flight plan simulation, and delivery of status data at the right time, all of which were important to crew planning, station planning, and many other activities in airports.

Cargo had a stable plan under development, but it still wanted a new central IT system. A new IT infrastructure was being developed and c/s systems paved the way for a new information architecture and improved adaptability to market changes.

Benchmarking

During 1993 and 1994, SAS kept on fighting to reduce costs, having much trouble in keeping up with external price competition. Therefore, SAS management reinforced pressure for radical cost reductions and organizational changes. A benchmarking system was introduced to enforce cost reductions to make sure that SAS did not pay more for a service than its competitors. All costs had to be reduced to at least the lowest cost level of competitors, either by internal reductions or by outsourcing.[428]

Benchmarking worked according to the following plan. First, markets were analyzed to locate the cheapest relevant services, and then results were compared to internal costs to see if services were best done internally or ex-

---

428 SAS, *ARP*, 1993.

ternally. Results would be presented to unions and relevant personnel, allowing a reasonable period to enforce changes necessary to reach market level. If internal SAS production did not succeed in this procedure, the unit should be sold, based on a five-year contract to continue services to SAS. If a contract was not obtained, the business activities should be liquidated and an agreement reached with a third party for doing the necessary services.

An overall analysis of SAS costs showed that more than 40 % of services produced internally could be bought on the open market and therefore, they could be exposed to competitive pressure. Primarily, that included Station, Maintenance, Crew, and Cargo and to some extent, agent provisions, government charges, revenue accounting and computer support. Furthermore, this analytical approach divided activities into strategic, image-creating, and non-strategic activities to improve management knowledge of core and non-core business.

Strategic activities were defined as head office activities: market activities, traffic program, products, quality follow-up, optimization of revenue and functions (Yield management, Movement Control Center); security (flight standards, technical standards, security); crew planning and scheduling; large customers and agents.

Image creating activities included crew and frontline personnel at principal stations.

Non-strategic activities included pilots, ground services and equipment, technical maintenance, revenue accounting, Technical Academy, Flight Academy, SAS Data, and Cargo.

Thus from 1992, a profound benchmarking analysis took place to present corporate management with the tools needed to adapt its core business to a changing environment, including measures of cost reductions and outsourcing. Only unions and personnel had a say in these matters that might cross such management plans.

Functional Organization

Following the break down of merger negotiations between Swissair, KLM, Austrian Airlines, and SAS, a renewed company analysis was carried out in autumn 1993, returning SAS to its core business. The analysis showed that in spite of radical cost reductions of the early 1990s, SAS cost level was still too high to secure future profitability. More radical initiatives were needed.

In 1994, the new president, Jan Stenberg, who took over after Jan Carlzon's long presidency, carried out a historic break with the regional basis of SAS.[429]

---

429 SAS, *Annual Reports*, 1993 and 1994.

A Scandinavian functional SAS organization replaced the traditional combined structure of divisions and regions. SAS was to be one organization with all functions united in one line, leaving out the many double functions of the past. Management was reinforced to ensure that reorganization and result improvement was carried out. Many functions were redefined and responsibility made clear. Responsibility, authority, and control should be one and the same. Lack of unity in these matters often created many problems in the history of SAS. While strengthening business control at management level, the daily operations were given more attention and higher priority, too. All functions were streamlined and organized in a number of line functions and staff units. Once more, IT resources were linked to the structure and strategy of SAS.

The new 1994 organization had the following lines and divisions. For the first time, the Marketing & Sales Division combined these functions in one unit. The commercial Division of the 1980s was more or less revived in the shape of the Business Systems Division, covering Routes, Products and Cargo. The Production Division united the former Technical Division and the Operations Division (in 1996 once more divided into the Technical Division and the Operations Division). The Information Systems Division reproduced, by and large, the former Data and Distribution Division. Furthermore, new or extended staff units reinforced corporate management: Corporate Finance and Control, Human Resources, PR and Government Affairs.

In addition to a changed organization, routes and logistics were thoroughly investigated, making SAS capable of reducing its number of planes by 19 with only minor changes to its traffic. The Marketing & Sales organization was given much higher priority and a comprehensive program was enforced to upgrade personnel and to renew and improve marketing. A new strategy of human resources aimed at creating a business-minded culture and the ability to see things from the point of view of the customer. Actually, it just repeated what Carlzon had tried to effect since the early 1980s, but now the time had come for a more profound attack on leftover bureaucratic thinking and structures. Management was upgraded, too, by creating a learning perspective on organizational development. All in all, SAS launched radical changes in organization and prepared for minds to follow suit.

Mid and Late 1990s Process Innovation

Gradual Change

The SAS reorganization on the basis of Scandinavian functions would take years to fulfil.[430] Many procedures of work and information systems were deeply rooted in the old mixed bureaucracy of regions and divisions. Rebuilding all divisions into true Scandinavian organizational units began in 1994 and would continue after the turn of the millennium. As late as early 1998, the Information Systems Division was dissolved and its line functions transferred to their proper divisions. Revenue Information and Hosting went to the Business Systems Division, and Distributed Services to Marketing & Sales, leaving only a staff unit behind. This completed the functional strategy. Even the structure of stock and capital were being changed to make SAS appear on the stock market as one joint-stock company, although this had still not been fulfilled by the late 1990s.

As a consequence of this new functional organization, its core business strategy, and in order to meet increasing competition, some business units were outsourced, while others were integrated more firmly into the SAS organization. Most outsourcing happened in the mid-1990s, including Service Partner, Diners, and Leisure. Since then, market orientation by way of benchmarking and similar tools was preferred to outsourcing, at least for the time being while the SAS organization was being upgraded and many outsourcing markets were still immature. Benchmarking spread throughout all divisions, including subsidiaries such as SAS Data, and put pressure on any organizational unit to live up to the best market standard. A total quality concept was introduced as a guiding line for all activities, including the new staff units of Airline Quality Manager and Traffic Execution Department.

A recurrent problem since the introduction of the businessman's airline strategy of the early 1980s was conflicts between management and employees concerning matters of rationalization and changes of organization. Since the mid-1980s, management tried to soften and make more flexible the structure of collective agreements that outlined the working process within and between the many specialized groups of SAS. Lack of flexibility prevented management from moving employees around according to shifting peaks during the day. Conflicts were most apparent in airports and among crew. Management tried to create a system of more individual planning for each employee, while unions and personnel were reluctant to accept this, fearing a loss of their influence. More than anything else, this showed how deeply rooted historical structures continued to make barriers for change.

---

430 SAS, *Annual Reports*, 1995 to 1997.

Corporate management tried to replace the traditional division of management and employee cultures by building a new cooperative attitude. Instead of a "they-and-we" approach, a common perspective of company and customers was being created. What was good for customers was good for the company and for the employees. Only a profitable SAS could present future jobs to employees in a world that within a decade had transformed a monopoly into a global competitive actor. Company and customer attitudes were difficult to cultivate, however, because they met an old culture of union concern in which employees and employers appeared to be two contradictory parts, a culture that also stuck deeply with management. Mistrust and fear on both sides added to this state of mind during the turbulent 1990s, fueled by strikes and other conflicts that exposed the vulnerability of even large airlines such as SAS. In a world of open competition, there is always another airline available, and why fly an airline hampered by strikes and other irregularities, at all.

A learning process started on both sides, however, to upgrade understanding and practice in order to prepare for a future culture of cooperation, ruin being the only other option. Personnel qualifications, including those of management, and value-adding capabilities of the organization had to be upgraded to prepare for fierce competition in a rapidly changing globalized economy.

Total Quality Management

In addition to this program of reorganization, management started a process of determined market improvements. A Total Quality Management (TQM) program was introduced in 1995 to make SAS the best airline of Europe by 1998. First, basic quality was addressed, in such areas as punctuality and regularity of flights and luggage. Cross-divisional groups were organized to identify problems across the organization and to create identical and common quality. Basic qualities were being continuously improved throughout the organization with high cost consciousness. Several quality assessors enforced quality evaluations and annually since 1996, SAS has generally been described on the basis of quality criteria.

Customer experience of SAS quality, such as response time on telephones and check-in and comfort onboard, was regularly measured. A radical improvement of service was intended, covering the whole journey from booking to the end of the travel. To improve preconditions for better customer service, SAS started a research program on the behavior of customers. Anthropological observations were made at airports and during the journey to understand the customers' view of travel as a basis for further improvements

The basic philosophy was to give passengers control over their travel instead of just adjusting to systems, making systems serve passengers to a much higher degree. Simplicity and freedom of choice were the two key words. It should be simple to travel without having to fight a lot of practical problems, and the passenger should be free to travel as he or she preferred.

In 1997 many organizational reforms were implemented. A comprehensive program of rationalization was carried out within distribution and technical maintenance, while customer-related personnel increased in order to improve service. Furthermore, a Traffic Execution Department was erected to enforce punctuality. In 1998 SAS went more on the offensive then ever, introducing a large leisure program, new terminals in Oslo and Copenhagen, and a fleet renewal scheme.

To meet increasing competition, many new price initiatives were introduced to maintain high yield and improve cabin load. These included a new revenue management function. Improvements of quality and products were weapons to meet growing competition. Cost and productivity problems were attacked by structural changes in distribution, namely the increased focus on electronic channels of sales. SAS targeted quick and simple booking routines, including self-booking and ticketless travel as well as the Internet as a new distribution channel. Electronic ticketing was continuously being developed through, for example, TravelPass and an integrated credit card and ticket.

Global alliances gave operational benefits from joint venture operations: Germany-Scandinavia, code-share flying via partner nods, marketing and sales, customer and agents programs, passenger service at airports, cargo handling, and maintenance of airplanes. Common use of resources and continuous integration would streamline customer service while improving internal efficiency. Still, no proper operative integration was introduced.

During the late 1990s, strategic cooperation deepened, globally and regionally. Quality work was carried out according to TQM-principles. Process innovation of the SAS organization was pushed forward by all these endeavors to upgrade quality and productivity.

Changes were gradual, however, moving the large SAS organization towards market adaptability. True reorganization was a learning process, seeking to move embedded social and cultural structures in new directions. However, SAS did not have all the time in the world. Competitors did not stand still. They moved quickly and sometimes more quickly than SAS, and it became more and more difficult to gain a competitive edge. The business environment globalized and revolutionized in escalating ways that brought to light leftover barriers to organization and IT. By the late 1990s, two decades of SAS wrestling with legacy organization and systems seemed to move into its final stage.

The SAS Organization

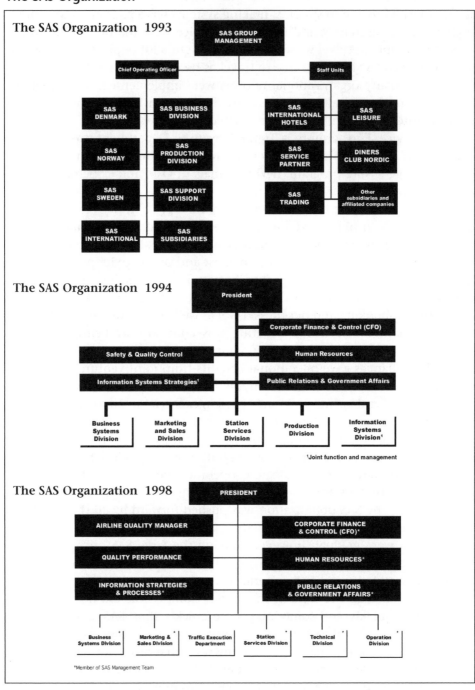

The SAS Organization 1993

SAS GROUP MANAGEMENT

Chief Operating Officer — Staff Units

SAS DENMARK	SAS BUSINESS DIVISION	SAS INTERNATIONAL HOTELS	SAS LEISURE
SAS NORWAY	SAS PRODUCTION DIVISION	SAS SERVICE PARTNER	DINERS CLUB NORDIC
SAS SWEDEN	SAS SUPPORT DIVISION	SAS TRADING	Other subsidiaries and affiliated companies
SAS INTERNATIONAL	SAS SUBSIDIARIES		

The SAS Organization 1994

President

Corporate Finance & Control (CFO)

Safety & Quality Control — Human Resources

Information Systems Strategies¹ — Public Relations & Government Affairs

Business Systems Division — Marketing and Sales Division — Station Services Division — Production Division — Information Systems Division¹

¹Joint function and management

The SAS Organization 1998

PRESIDENT

AIRLINE QUALITY MANAGER — CORPORATE FINANCE & CONTROL (CFO)*

QUALITY PERFORMANCE — HUMAN RESOURCES*

INFORMATION STRATEGIES & PROCESSES* — PUBLIC RELATIONS & GOVERNMENT AFFAIRS*

Business Systems Division* — Marketing & Sales Division* — Traffic Execution Department — Station Services Division* — Technical Division* — Operation Division*

*Member of SAS Management Team

Source: SAS, Annual Reports, 1992, 1994, 1997.

SAS IT

SAS IT Statistics[431]

	1990	1997
SAS		
IT costs in mill. SEK	1,400	2,300
% of SAS total	6	6
Personnel	200	200
Terminals	25,000	10,000
PCs	2,000	20,000
SAS Data		
Revenue in mill. SEK	800	1,400
% of SAS IT costs	57	60
Personnel	800	1,000
Annual transactions in mill.	1,200	1,600

Source: SAS, *Handbook of IT Policies and Standards within SAS Airline*. SAS Data, *Organizational Papers*.

SAS IT Strategy and Organization

Since corporate management had more determinedly taken over responsibility for IT developments in the late 1980s, SAS went through various stages of a fundamental process of transformation. It was a learning process driven on the one hand by environmental changes in business, in the airline industry, and in IT products presented by the IT industry. On the other hand, the internal structure of IT and organizational potentials and barriers formed the working ground for management policies.

1991 End of the IBM Strategy

The strategic IT decisions of 1988 dominated activities until 1991 and formed the first part of a transformation process to come.[432] Roles of SAS and SAS Data were clearly separated, making SAS the owner and initiator of IT developments and applications, whereas SAS Data was defined as a supplier of IT ser-

---

431 Numbers are rounded.
432 SAS, *Handbook of IT Policy and Standards within SAS Airline*. SDD, *Profil*, 1989-1991, passim. SDS/SDN, *UPTIME*, 1989 to 1991, passim.

vices on market conditions. Furthermore, SAS Data divided into three national units, to become three limited companies in 1990. In SAS, a strategic IT upgrading took place. The Data and Distributed Division line organization was formed in 1988 to lead SAS into a changing world of open distribution systems.

During the 1980s, IBM technology took over an increasing number of SAS systems. To position itself in an open competitive world, it was decided to move all SAS IT onto the leading market platform of those days, IBM. Non-IBM strategic systems, such as reservation, check-in, and cargo would migrate from Unisys to IBM, at the same time phasing out Unisys and the much smaller Tandem platform.

A corporate staff unit, Information Systems Strategy (ISS), was established to coordinate IT strategies and standards on a holistic corporate level. The IT strategy included plans to make IBM's new Systems Application Architecture (SAA) the foundation of emerging distributed systems. A Common User Access description of a graphical user interface for mainframe-PC interaction was of particular significance. In addition, SAA included a Common Programming Interface, a Common Communications Support, and a Common Applications Architecture. In 1990, SAA might be considered a de facto market standard in distributed systems or client/server systems, although this name had not yet gained momentum.

By 1990, no breakthrough had occurred in distributed systems, however, and nobody seemed able to foresee the importance of Microsoft and not IBM having a dominant market position in PC operating systems, namely DOS, and its graphical interface and follower, Windows 3 of 1990. IBM and Microsoft jointly developed and marketed the second most important PC operating system OS/2 and its graphical interface Presentation Manager. In 1991, IBM took over OS/2 and Presentation Manager, realizing that distributed computing or client/server systems made up a genuine alternative to its dominating mainframe position, whereas Microsoft focused successfully on DOS and Windows. Up until then IBM had still clung to its long-term successful mainframe strategy.

According to its IBM strategy, SAS chose OS/2 as a standard but allowed Microsoft systems, too, both having little importance in SAS in 1990. Within communications, IBM Systems Network Architecture (SNA) ruled for mainframes and Virtual Telecommunications Access Method (VTAM) for terminals. However, SAS' proprietary Telcon handled most communication by way of central computer systems in Copenhagen. LAN Manager and Communication Manager of IBM was the LAN standard together with Novell Netware – Novell being the most widely used technology, both in SAS and elsewhere. IBM DB2 was applied as the relational database management standard.

SAS started preparing for an intelligent communication network, too, to complement its plans for future distributed systems and to meet the demands of open distribution and increasing cooperation with other airlines.

Authority remained with line organizations, however, and they were free to choose their technology as long as they performed according to budget and did not disturb the remainder of SAS. Still, SAS was a highly decentralized corporation based on decentralized result responsibility, stressed even more by the 1991 reorganization.

All these grand IT plans were more or less abandoned because of the Gulf Crisis in 1991, however. SAS gave up the expensive move onto one IBM platform and cancelled development of a new large reservations system, too. Furthermore, IBM turned out to be less technologically sophisticated than expected and did not whole-heartedly produce the new distributed technology that SAS was looking for. By and large, SAS had to start planning all over again. From 1991, a new IT strategy gradually emerged and new technologies began to spread in decentralized SAS.

1991-1995 Client/Server Technology and Open Network

During 1991 to 1995, the second phase in SAS' IT transformation took place.[433] Previous vague plans for a new open IT infrastructure started to materialize from 1991, covering a new communications platform as well as a new client/server (c/s) applications architecture. The SAS ISS unit followed market trends in search of strong and long-lasting technology standards to guide corporate developments, not always followed in a traditionally decentralized SAS corporation, however. Furthermore, IT standards emerged only gradually in the market during the first half of the 1990s, so whether a certain piece of technology would turn out to be a true standard remained open to argument.

Client/Server

In matters of standard for the new c/s technology, IBM was still the preferred choice. This was seen in the three Scandinavian capital airports Arlanda, Fornebu, and Kastrup in 1991 to 1992. Fiber optic and software-based cabling multiplied information transport capacity and introduced digitalized and software-based communications. IBM's Token Ring was chosen for LANs and the new router multi-protocol technology for information transfer. New airport information systems applied brand new c/s technology, based on IBM's

---

433 SAS, *Savings through Standards*, 1991 to 1994. SDD, *Profil*, 1991 to 1994, passim. SDS/SDN, *UPTIME*, 1991 to 1994, passim.

OS/2. SITA's Common User Terminal Interface (CUTE) project for an international OS/2 IT airport check-in standard pushed SAS in the OS/2 direction, too. Projects on automatic check-in and boarding systems also used OS/2. Furthermore since 1991, SAS had decided to buy intelligent workstations (IWS) only, underlining its intentions to move from mainframes and terminals to a c/s structure.

During the first half of the 1990s, all major functions and units introduced c/s applications to improve productivity and revenue along the SAS value chain. They speeded up management planning and follow-up, adaptation to market changes, and revenue optimizing at corporate, sales and marketing, station, operation, maintenance, finance and personnel levels.

The c/s structure covered three levels: host server, LAN server, and client server. By 1993, host server standards were IBM MVS, UNISYS OS/1100, and Tandem Guardian. Main vendors consolidated their positions in the market and with SAS. OS/2, its Presentation Manager and LAN Manager worked as LAN server and client OS standards, increasingly pressed by the expanding multi-user Unix server (by that time, OS/2 was a single user system needing LAN Manager to make multi user system), and Windows for clients with its graphic interface. Microsoft moved into a leading position on the client side from 1993, supported by its popular office packages. Microsoft office systems, including Word, Excel and Power Point for presentations, were official standards at SAS from 1993. Novell Netware continued to dominate the LAN area, although expanding c/s systems were reducing its influence. During the first half of the 1990s, no winners appeared in immature middleware markets, where IBM DB/2 remained the preferred database management system (DBMS). By 1995, market winners seemed to be IBM in host servers, Unix in multi-user servers (with IBM OS/2 in a secondary place), and Microsoft in client servers.

Open Network

In 1991, SAS' Synthesizer project started to create a new communications platform. It resumed previous plans but on a different basis. During 1991-1993 a new platform, which replaced SAS' Telcon proprietary system and IBM's VTAM, was developed and gradually introduced during 1994-1996. Synthesizer created a simple data transport system, while support functions of DCS/Telcon and SNA/VTAM networks were put on PC-software in SAS' new c/s environment.

Synthesizer used the Open Systems Interconnectivity (OSI) data packet switching protocol, X.25, as a general gateway basis, assisted by X.400 protocols for e-mail and document transport, and X.500 for address handling.

Multi-protocol routers linked network information traffic of different platforms. The communication infrastructure included plans for network control and management, too, such as the Overture project for remote operation that made HP Open View a candidate. This included e-mail handling and other Value Added Services (VAS) for users, for instance downloading of software and new versions of software. SAS e-mail was a proprietary system within Telcon that might eventually be replaced by Microsoft's MS Mail. Structured information exchange between SAS and other companies looked for Electronic Data Interchange (EDI) standards, primarily EDIFACT for invoices and custom documents. For decades, passenger ticket and cargo invoice information had been prorated through IATA-standards of AIR-IMP and CARGO-IMP. Ericsson MD110 clearly dominated the Scandinavian market for digital telephone exchanges and this included SAS.

Gradually, internal and external communications moved towards an open and digital platform, only to be fulfilled in the late 1990s, however. By 1995, no WAN (wide area network) market standard was obvious. Although officially recommended throughout the world, OSI was never loved nor generally accepted and the Internet TCP/IP was still at an infancy stage.

During the first half of the 1990s, it was no easy task to plan and carry out a general move from mainframes and proprietary technology to c/s and open market standards in communications and applications, because such winners were only beginning to emerge in the global IT industry. Furthermore, recommended standards by SAS ISS built on no authority of enforcement. Divisions and business units did pretty much as they pleased in a decentralized SAS. Finally to keep the business up and running, existing large corporate systems had to process and communicate transactions non-stop at high speed and in huge volume.

SAS IT Costs 1992[434]

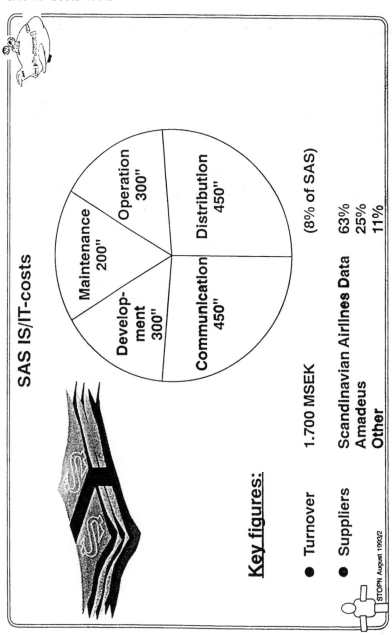

Source: SAS, *Data Management.*

---

434 A relative high IT share of total SAS costs, 8 %, was due to very low revenues in 1992.

Mid and late 1990s Strategic Alignment

Strategic Alignment

In 1994, decentralized SAS reorganized along functional and strategic central-ized lines. Where national IT applications prevailed corporate systems were planned to take over, and management systems were widely introduced. SAS Data aligned closer with SAS Airline on the basis of an account management system, following the main functional areas of SAS. The three national SAS Data subsidiaries started an integration process, being finally unified in one organization in 1997.[435]

The staff unit Information Systems Planning Group (ISPG) was upgraded from divisional to corporate level. Furthermore, Information Systems Div-ision, a line organization, restored, more or less, the former Data and Distribu-tion Division (DDD). A superstructure of divisional vice presidents and man-agement of the SAS Data Group was formed to enforce strategic IT planning on a corporate level and standards and modernization of the infrastructure were determinedly carried out. Benchmarking pressed the SAS organization and SAS Data to live up to best market practice. By 1998, Information Systems Division was dissolved and SAS Data put in a strategic position in matters of IT.

From the mid-1990s, SAS Airline and SAS Data enforced a process organ-ization strategy. Furthermore instead of being a total deliverer, SAS Data took on the role of system integrator, always looking for the best IT in the market according to the strategic goals of SAS. Gradually de facto market standards re-placed SAS proprietary systems and standards seeking at the same time to minimize the number of standards.

Since the mid-1990s, SAS IT and business aligned in a close match, while external IT and service industries moved towards maturity and put increas-ing market pressure on SAS Data, as they did on SAS line and staff func-tions.

C/S and Web

By 1995, the old IT proprietary infrastructure was not yet replaced by a new and open infrastructure. It turned out to be a long and tenacious haul during all of the 1990s. From the mid- to late 1990s, de facto IT market standards developed in most fields however, and SAS quickly adjusted to these standards, as it focused more determinedly on carrying out its IT transformation. Microsoft and Unix had conquered and dominated server positions in the c/s technology. Microsoft became a de facto standard for office packages and generally, the application

---

435 SAS Data, *Linje 1*, 1994-1998, passim. Interview: *Hans-Henrik Hedegaard.*

packages industry rose to present an overwhelming alternative to in-house systems development.

Based on market analyses, by the late 1990s SAS considered Microsoft NT to be a winner and the emerging market standard and chose NT as the new OS standard on both the client and the server side. At SAS by the late 1990s, Microsoft Windows dominated clients, while Unix followed by OS/2 and NT servers dominated c/s technology and IBM followed by Unisys and Tandem dominated host servers. All host servers were highly upgraded during the 1990s to handle the increasing volume of transactions. With DBMS, Oracle moved swiftly into a strong position compared with DB/2 that dominated at SAS, whereas SAS had no clear leader in packages, although Oracle and SAP moved in.

During the second half of the 1990s, c/s technology matured and spread throughout the corporation in matters of planning, follow-up, communication, revenue optimizing, market adaptation and customer relations. However, systems for data mining across applications lagged behind at SAS.

By the late 1990s, SAS planned once more to phase out Unisys and Tandem. Fewer standards would reduce the number and costs of technology environments. However, escalating developments of servers, networks, applications packages, and intelligent systems for information mining across different technologies kept on challenging SAS IT management with new capabilities. The IT industry moved towards solutions for enterprise-wide interoperability of applications and servers that made it easier to link old and new systems and to replace old systems with new ones, too. Although market standards materialized in most fields from the mid-1990s, IT developments took on such revolutionary directions and speed that it remained difficult to make the right strategic decisions.

Perhaps more than anything else, the breakthrough of the Internet and its open TCP/IP protocol illustrates the revolutionary character of IT changes towards the end of the millennium. SAS chose TCP/IP as the communication standard, representing the first true non-proprietary protocol in IT history. First, an Intranet was established on the basis of the Internet technology. Second, plans developed for a wide area Internet network. Third, Web technologies moved into application packages. Fourth, customer relations with other firms and with passengers took advantage of Web technologies. Finally, business and technology began to upgrade towards a mobile infrastructure. Within a few years, technology and business threatened to revolutionize the basis of strategic management. By the late 1990s, SAS had taken step one and two, prepared for three and four, and considered the mobile challenge, too.

SAS Data Strategy and Organization

Early and Mid 1990s Market Orientation

By July 1 1990, the three regional SAS Data units were turned into legally independent joint stock companies, although 100 % owned by SAS. At the same time, they had to change their name. By previous agreement with SAS, the SAS Institute had obtained exclusive rights to the name SAS as a computer company. Consequently, SAS Data was changed into Scandinavian Airlines Data, Ltd., adding Norway, Sweden, and Denmark respectively to their name. A holding company was put on top of the three subsidiaries, led by the vice president of the new Marketing Automating Division that replaced DDD. Between the three SAS Data units a cooperative agreement was reached. It did not include market sharing, however, making them open to competition towards SAS. [436]

The break between SAS and SAS Data and the determination of SAS Airline to enforce open competition on SAS Data made radical changes at the three companies inevitable. First, SAS Data had to develop strategies and organizations according to the new situation. Second, it had to upgrade its IT and market competence to match the changing character of IT, the IT industry, and the demands of SAS.

SAS Data Denmark

The organizational split with SAS caused much anxiety and animosity among personnel, particularly in Copenhagen and to some degree in Stockholm. Oslo, however, was less attached to the central activities of SAS. They were all worried about their future jobs and the benefits they used to enjoy as SAS employees, including travel. Furthermore, having just gone through a process of reorganization during the late 1980s, motivation for a restart was low, particularly in Copenhagen. Some left and it took until 1992, before the employees had signed the new agreement of occupation in joint stock companies.

At SAS Data Denmark (SDD), the head Mogens Meisler left by July 1 1990, and a new leader, John Dueholm, was not installed until October. John Dueholm was the first SDD chief of external origin, underlining the intention to create a competitive organization. During the following year, SDD concentrated on building a new profitable organization, including strategy and plans of action.[437]

---

436 SAS, *Data Management*, 4/7 1990. SDD, *Profil*, no. 26, 1990. SDS/SDN, *UPTIME*, no. 13, 1990. For the sake of convenience, we shall keep on calling it SAS Data, however.

437 SDD (1991), *Fremad mod 1995* (forward towards 1995). SDD, *Profil*, no. 3, 1991.

The new SDD organization was resolutely introduced.[438] During the winter of 1990-1991, the organization was thoroughly analyzed, following which 22 persons were sacked in May 1991 with additional cuts elsewhere. Employees went on strike, but the decision was effected. Radical changes had come to stay. Friction between management and employees and unions continued, however, and lingered until a four-year collective agreement was reached by 1992 and the employees finally signed the new company conditions of appointment.

The new strategy focused on a general quality and competence upgrading to increase SDD's capability to add value to its customers, linking every department and person to this quality goal. SDD wanted to consolidate its position as the best alternative to SAS Airline and next to the SAS Group, but primarily the new market strategies targeted a strong position on the open external market to make SDD less dependent on SAS.

The new SDD organization was ready by early 1991.[439] The line organization of production and sales of products was pretty similar to previous SDD, and included Marketing and Management Consulting, Systems Development, Systems Maintenance, Distributed Information Processing, Operations, and Communications. By way of the new Distributed Information Processing unit, SDD upgraded its focus on the expanding field of client/server systems. Management Consulting made up another new competence to be developed that was considered a crucial part of the new business strategy. On the basis of annual account plans, consultants matched each customer.

Just like the reorganized SDD of the late 1980s, systems development was defined as a production unit along with computer operations and communications. Customer relations were taken over by management consultants and systems developers would be re-qualified to introduce new and much more productive systems methods, so-called 4GL and Information Engineering, to minimize development time. Systems Maintenance expected a radical increase in productivity too, to reduce decades of heavy SAS maintenance costs.

Computer Operations prepared for modernization and increased capacity, including a Unisys revival, and taking Facility Management plans into consideration. Communications were faced with the tremendous task of turning the existing proprietary system into an open system based on industrial standards. Staff was expanded to run the new firm's activities. That included a true personal department to take care of employee re-qualification in new IT and business principles and collective agreement negotiating that used to be han-

---

438 SDD, *Profil*, no. 16-17, 1991, no. 4-8, 1992.
439 SDD, *Profil*, no. 10, 1991. Interview: *John Dueholm*. SDD, *SDD-Guide*, 1992, is a detailed description of the new organization.

dled by SAS. Accounting, Security, and so on, made up other company staff units.

In 1992, SDD strove to break through on the external market, focusing on an increased market for Facility Management (FM).[440] SDD never succeeded on the external market, however.[441] As a new contender, SDD was unable to compete with large companies such as IBM (Responsor) and Cap Gemini. The FM market at this point had not matured. Furthermore, main sectors of Danish business and government administration had for decades been dominated by large computer companies with positions within their respective sectors that were similar to those of SAS Data in SAS.

By early 1993, it was obvious that expansion plans had failed. John Dueholm left and was replaced by Tage E. Christiansen, coming from another computer firm, LEC.[442] By then, the Alcazar merger plans had collapsed and SAS Airline returned to a core business strategy. In 1994, SAS Airline reorganized along lines of increased Scandinavian integration and upgraded strategic management. As a result, SDD and the other two SAS Data companies moved closer to SAS and gave up plans for external expansion. SDD reorganized according to SAS functional lines.[443] Finally, the three SAS Data companies started a process of cooperation through the SAS Data Group (SDG), reversing a five-year period of unclear lines of competition and cooperation. Gradually, IT plans, products and infrastructure were integrated to make SAS business demands rule future SAS Data developments.

The new SDD organization corresponded to that of SAS. SDD was organized according to its key SAS customers.[444] Eight key accounts were defined, organized around two basic units each of four customers, Alfa and Bravo. Alfa covered Business Division, Production Division, Revenue Information, and SAS Denmark. Bravo covered Space Control Services, Stations and Sales, Station Copenhagen, and Cargo. A separate group was formed for external markets, including the SAS Group and customers outside SAS. A manager was appointed for each of these ten key accounts. The key account manager had total customer responsibility. A manager was appointed to each of the three groups of Alfa, Bravo, and External Market. Communications and Computer Operations remained two basic line units, which included two staff units of personnel and administration. SDD remained a legally independent subsidiary of SAS, as did the other two SAS Data companies.

---

440 SDD, *Profil*, no. 1, 1992.
441 SDD, *Profil*, no. 1, 1993. Interview: *John Dueholm*.
442 Interviews: *John Dueholm* and *Tage E. Christiansen*.
443 SDD, *Profil*, no. 16, 1993, and no. 2, 1994.
444 SDD, *Profil*, no. 3, 1994.

SDD Markets and Capabilities

Operating central SAS computer systems and networks made up two thirds of SDD's income. The remaining revenue came from systems development and maintenance. Local SAS Denmark systems were part of this structure. SAS Denmark transported about 1 million passengers every year, corresponding to about 5 % of all SAS passenger traffic. This was a minor business for SDD, contrary to the case of SDS and SDN. By 1990, external business counted for only 1 % of SDD's revenue. This SDD revenue structure did not fundamentally change during the 1990s, except that traditional systems development came to be replaced by distributed systems development, integration, and services. SDD remained a profitable business during the 1990s, occupying more than one half the SAS Data Group's (SDG) personnel and two thirds of total SDG revenue.[445]

Turbulent and radical changes started during the early 1990s. For a short time, one third of SDD's IBM systems moved to the new operation center near Stockholm, until it was closed down in 1991. At the same time, merger negotiations with three other airlines included plans for radical IT changes by SAS Data. Furthermore, the closedown of the great TERESE project in 1991, and the end of phasing out plans for Unisys computer operations called for revised infrastructure plans, too.

In central computer operations, it was decided to modernize the worndown Unisys platform as well as the IBM operation center. The Unisys platform was being modernized during the first half of the 1990s, while the IBM platform upgraded from the mid-1990s, followed by plans for a second Unisys upgrade. To cover the increasing field of c/s systems, a separate Unix center was established from the mid-1990s. Modernization and large improvements of productivity were needed to meet increasing demands of capacity and flexibility in information processing as SAS was increasingly challenged by open competition.

During the first half of the 1990s, central communications at SDD was being changed from a proprietary system to an open technology, continuously upgraded during the second half of the decade. Increasing market pressure reached its first climax in 1994 when the SDD communications center was forced into a tender for the future administration of SAS communications. SDD Communications won the tender competition, thanks to improved performance and for want of a mature IT communications outsourcing industry. Telephony went through a revolutionary digitalization process, too. By the

---

445 SDD, *Vi er her* (we are here), 1989. SDD, *Guide*, (1992). SDD, *Strategy 1994-1996*, 1993. See also in the text, *SAS IT Statistics*.

late 1990s, SAS Data communications might escape a destiny of outsourcing only by matching the best communications vendors in the market place.

Systems development including programming, the third part of the SDD business and production system, was profoundly influenced by the c/s revolution. For decades, mainframe developments and maintenance formed the core of systems development competence. Therefore, the move to c/s systems threatened the livelihood of the systems development department and group. Furthermore, the SAS business takeover of IT responsibility and the building up of local IT competence deprived SDD of most opportunities for pre-studies and systems requirement analysis. Divisions and routes hired consulting firms to carry out business analysis, while they took care of requirement analysis themselves. Finally, SAS stopped developing mainframe systems and introduced c/s systems instead. Systems development people and departments were forced into radical changes.

Changes came in a number of ways. A new department of distributed systems development was established to qualify for c/s systems. For business relations with SAS and other customers, a group of management consultants was formed. A number of system developers were retrained for these new functions. For the remaining system developers a process of re-qualifications started. That included business orientation, project management, and the use of 4GL tools for speeded up and improved systems development and maintenance. Except for continuous maintenance and upgrading of SAS' large information and communication systems, the mainframe systems market vanished and only c/s systems development remained. Since the mid-1990s, the breakthrough of an application packages industry had undermined even that part of systems development. By then, systems development had simply stopped and been replaced by systems integration only. A growing field of office application packages added to increasing service activities.

On the one hand, systems developers had to adapt to radical IT changes and particularly, to replacing a technology approach with a business perspective. Although they were quick to learn the new technologies, the barriers of a deeply rooted technology culture did not fall easily. Nevertheless, from the mid-1990s, gradually a transformation began to materialize. On the other hand, systems developers possessed a thorough understanding of systems and business functions throughout SAS that turned out to be indispensable. A reform and commercialization of IT functions and systems in a large and complex organization such as SAS could not be achieved without including this competence.

SAS Data Sweden and SAS Data Norway

By October 1990, SAS Data Sweden (SDS) appointed a new chief, Björn Lilja, who, as in the case of SDD, was externally recruited. He too faced the task of building a new competitive organization. The SDS reorganization seemed to create less turmoil than there had been in Copenhagen, although it also caused dissatisfaction and some flow through of personnel, fueled by a 10 % reduction in personnel.[446] It took most of 1991 to establish the new organization.

A particular problem was the new computer center at Häggvik near Stockholm.[447] In the late 1980s, SAS had decided to split its central computer operations in Copenhagen into two centers, moving one third of its IBM systems to Stockholm. The plan was carried out during 1990 but by late 1990, Häggvik showed signs of permanent lack of profitability. The Gulf Crisis and pressure on costs in 1991 made SAS decide to close the Häggvik center and move the systems and computers back to Copenhagen.

Unlike SDD, SDS did not determinedly target external markets.[448] First and foremost, SDS addressed SAS Sweden and SAS division headquarters, mainly Technical Division and Business Services Division – to some degree that included Traffic Services Division (PALCO), too – all data markets centered in Stockholm since the early 1980s. SAS Sweden had been a main target of SDS since the STO computing unit began its expansion around 1980. Furthermore, subsidiaries and associate companies of SAS in the SAS Group were of particular importance to SDS compared with SDD and SDN, because many of them had their headquarters in Stockholm.

SDS wanted to be business and customer focused, just like the other two units of SAS Data. Three business units of customer service-, production-, and administrative systems formed the core of the new organization. They included all links of the process from sales, pre-studies, analysis, development, to administration, and full economic responsibility for markets within the SAS Group (i.e., total responsibility). Later on, they somewhat reorganized to align with the SAS organization. Service Systems and Administrative Systems were turned into Customer Service Systems and Back Office Systems. The Production systems were renamed Traffic and Technical Systems. Systems Support took care of methods, standards, quality control, databases, and other problems of technology. Network Control Services handled communications. A Market unit intended to profile SDS towards its customers. During the early months of 1991, managers of these five units were appointed, and finally, staff units of personnel and accounting were established.

---

446 SDS/SDN, *UPTIME*, no. 14, 1990, and no. 4 and 9, 1991.
447 SDS/SDN, *UPTIME*, no. 15, 24, 1990, and no. 1, 1991. SDD, *Profil*, no. 7, 9, 1991.
448 SDS/SDN, *UPTIME*, no. 26, 1990, no. 1, 4, 1991, and no. 1, 1993.

During 1990-1993, SDS seemed increasingly to align to SAS markets, and the introduction of a key account manager system in 1994, in terms of the functional reorganization of SAS Airline, did not much change the organization.[449] Covering approximately 30 % of total SDG numbers, SDS moved from a state of 230 employees and revenues of 275 million SEK in 1990, to 275 employees and revenues of 350 million SEK by the mid-1990s.[450]

SAS Data Norway (SDN) was a much smaller organization than SDD and SDS.[451] It had about 50 employees and revenue of about 75 million SEK in 1990. By the mid-1990s, it reached 65 employees and revenue of approximately 100 million SEK. As SDN was smaller, its organization was less detailed. Its focus was in two main service areas: communications/networks and applications. By the time of the reorganization of 1994, the changing character of technology and customer demands towards distributed systems of client/servers, consulting, LANs and connections to WANs, including telephone exchanges, was clearly seen. SDN was much related to its national SAS customers, but a rather large part of its revenue came from external customers, related to air traffic, such as airports.

SDS and SDN Markets and Capabilities

When Häggvik was closed down in 1991, SDS was left with its small Tandem center. By 1992, Linjeflyg merged with SDS and a process of building a modern and much larger Tandem center was started to handle the systems of SAS Sweden. SAS Sweden was the largest SAS passenger market, annually transporting more than 4 million passengers. Furthermore, SAS subsidiaries in Stockholm, SMART and Leisure handed over computer operations of their Tandem systems to SDS. Towards the mid-1990s, the Tandem center introduced new technology and a much-increased capacity to handle growing demands of operation, including a number of c/s systems.[452]

Although a large Tandem center was built, it never created a big business similar to central operations at SDD. While the latter formed a business of about 500 million SEK, the Tandem center amounted to only one tenth of that revenue. To keep up a business with more than 200 employees, half the size of SDD, SDS had to focus even more than SDD on capturing the growing SAS markets of c/s technology. The expanding Tandem market of SAS Sweden was one part of it, and here SDS developed a strong competence and competitiveness, helped by the fact that external competitors were relatively weak in the small Tandem platform.

---

449 SAS Data, *Linje 1*, no. 1 and 3, 1994.
450 SAS, *Pressrelease*, no. 35, 1990. SASA Data, *Linje 1*, no. 1 and 3, 1994.
451 SAS Data, *Linje 1*, no. 1-2, 1994. Interview: *Knut Hallen* and *Gjermund Gullberg*
452 SDD, *UPTIME*, 1990 to 1994, passim.

SDS system developers were challenged in the same way as those of SDD and had to replace a mainframe competence with that of c/s. Furthermore, a new competence was required on SDS' second big market, networks, when the proprietary network was replaced by an open software driven network. During the first half of the 1990s, SDS participated in building a new network technology in Sweden and generally at SAS, beginning at Arlanda and at headquarters in Frösundavik. A growing number of LANs were connected to SAS' WAN, which from 1994 was being turned into an open network technology based on intelligent PCs. SDS competed openly with SDD and external bidders in most strategic c/s projects, for instance sales and station (ATB), crew (DNB), and cargo (LUCAS).

SDN determinedly targeted the new c/s and network technology markets, too. During 1992-1993, competence was upgraded to match the changing demands of its main customer, SAS Norway. The SAS Norway market amounted to approximately the same size as the Danish market, about 1 million passengers annually. SDN operated, maintained, and developed the local systems of SAS Norway. SDN did not have the capacity to take part in the general bidding of the growing number of central c/s systems, as SDD and SDS did, only 10 % of the total number of SAS Data employees being based in Oslo. From the early 1990s, its markets and competence developed during a growing number of projects for modernizing the communication technology of Norwegian airports and local c/s systems.

SAS Data Organization 1994

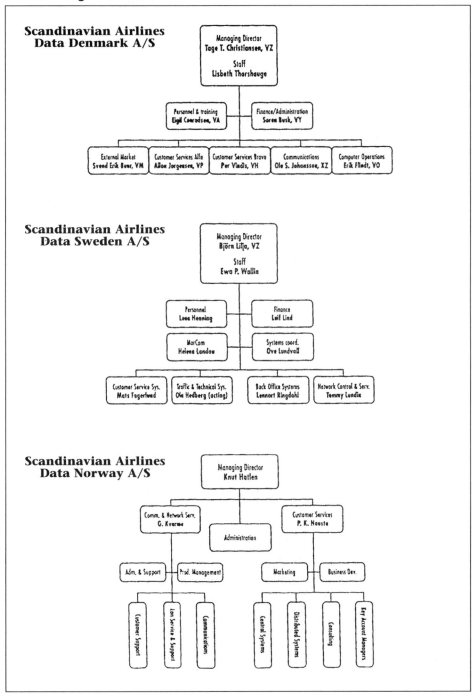

Source: Linje 1, August 1994.

Late 1990s SAS and SAS Data Strategic Alignment

Since SAS reorganized in 1994 and the three SAS Data companies adjusted to the SAS structure, cooperation between the three data units increased. Finally in 1997, they united into one organization, a business of about 1000 employees with revenues of about 1.4 billion SEK out of a SAS total of about 2.3 billion SEK IT expenditures.[453]

The three SAS Data units organized according to the principle of key account management, matching the divisions and organizational structure of SAS.[454] External customers were no longer targeted and internal competition was removed. SAS business demands defined the use of SAS Data IT resources, always seeking to remain competitive according to market standards of the IT industry. Technology was modernized and a determined process was started to enforce uniform standards throughout SAS and SAS Data.

Large investments were made to upgrade and modernize the IBM and Unisys computer centers of Copenhagen and Tandem center of Stockholm.[455] From the early 1990s, benchmarking was applied to make these centers live up to the best standards in the market. A similar benchmarking was looked for by c/s technology, communications, and systems development. From the mid-1990s, a change management project started in Copenhagen to stabilize the new Unix center and create a central operation center of c/s systems with the same stability as those of mainframes.

From the mid-1990s, network management systems were introduced, too, to handle the new communications technology. SAS' WAN was made more open by introducing the TCP/IP Internet protocol for internal and external communication. A process of standardization was started to simplify a chaotic number of different platforms. Finally, a systems development project aimed at developing a common system of methods and tools for all platforms. Telephony changed radically as a consequence of digitalization, moving it towards computer communication and blurring the old borders of these two technologies even more. A growing number of telephony value added services (VAS) appeared from the mid-1990s. At SAS Data organization, a process management system was introduced in 1996 to prepare for a continuous and integrated innovation process aimed at increased productivity and customer satisfaction. SAS Data products aligned with SAS customer needs.[456] In 1997, a common SAS Data organization was finally established, based on common

---

453 See in the text, *SAS IT Statistics*.
454 SDD, *Profil*, no. 1, 1994. See, Figure, *SAS Data Key Account Areas*.
455 See below, *IT Infrastructure*.
456 SAS Data, *Linje 1*, no. 2, 1996. See, Figure, *SAS Data Process Organization*.

principles of key account management. A determined process of shared use of resources started, replacing a structure of parallel competence.[457]

At SAS, a superstructure on top of SAS Data and the divisions underlined the new strategic alignment with SAS Data. A kind of SAS IT steering committee of divisional vice presidents took care of overall strategic problems between the two parties. An IT board of divisions (DIT) was established to deal with general IT matters, such as standards, and make sure that decisions were enforced. A staff unit, now in corporate management, administered standards and other general problems of IT. In 1998, the Information Systems Division was dissolved and a final IT structuring took place along functional lines.

Market relations between SAS Data and SAS changed, too.[458] Nevertheless, SAS Data continued to deliver on the basis of market conditions and had to live up to the best standards in the market. Increasingly, SAS Data entered into total service deals with SAS, covering operation, administration, and development. Pressed by external competitors, SAS Data managed to keep its market share by SAS, but never reached the total dominant position of the past.

From the mid-1990s, in-house systems development stopped, replaced by application packages bought in the market. Time-to-market was required of all systems, meaning quick implementation to adapt to rapidly changing market conditions and needs of optimization. Increasingly horizontal integration of systems was needed as SAS pressed for a process organization and for improved information for follow-up and planning. Often these horizontal endeavors met the barriers of existing functional systems. In search of systems to create intelligent information, new concepts of "corporate warehouse" or "data mining" emerged to try to overcome the deficiencies of old mainframe systems, but no such structures had materialized by the late 1990s.[459]

Strategies of alignment and total contracting were based on a new role for SAS Data.[460] SAS Data was a system integrator that developed IT for SAS Airline by a combination of existing systems and package software bought in the market. SAS Data was no longer an in-house developer. By the late 1990s, it was considered strategically imported to align SAS Airline and SAS Data, but only as long as SAS Data lived up to the best standards in the market, including expanding IT industries for outsourcing.[461]

---

457 SAS Data, *Linje 1*, no. 4-5, 1997.
458 SAS Data, *Linje 1*, no. 7, 1995, no. 1, 1996.
459 SAS Data, *Linje 1*, no. 8, 1995. Interview: *Poul Strand-Holm.*
460 SAS Data, *Linje 1*, no. 1, 1996, no. 1 and 3, 1997.
461 SDG, *SDG Forbedringsaktiviteter 1998-2001. Handlingsplaner (SAS Data action plans),* 1998.

SAS Data Organization 1997

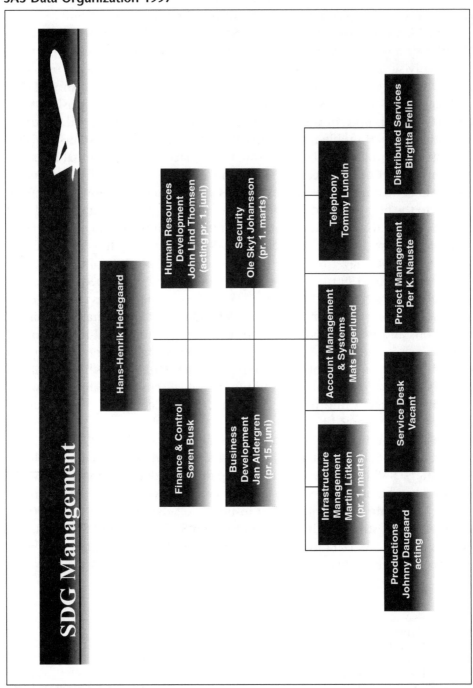

Source: SAS Data, *Organization Papers.*

SAS Data Key Account Areas 1997

Scandinavian Airlines Data

Key Account Areas

❖ **Stations & Sales: Tobias Malmgren**
  ◆ ATB C-I/Boarding, PCI, PAH, DSS, Selfservice automates, Columbus, Corporate System, SFA, EuroBonus, EDISS Sales

❖ **Technical: Terje Kabbe**
  ◆ MOPS, MOVEX, LIMBO, PAMP, HPS

❖ **Operation (incl. MCC): Poul Strand-Holm**
  ◆ CRU, Rodos, OPUS/TOPST, TDB

❖ **Business Systems (incl. Cargo & Trading): Per Vindis**
  ◆ IRIS/TRAF, BFU/DC, SAFARI, Impala, SPI

❖ **Distribution (Info Systems + Revenue Mngt. Serv.): Helle Hytting Ullum**
  ◆ RES, Amadeus, TICS, PAS, Level, ODRMS

❖ **Finance & Personnel (SAS Staff): Leif Lind**
  ◆ ORS, GLM, INV, PUSS, PERS, SAP, IDBIS, ROS, SAIAC

❖ **External market (outside the SAS Airline): Thorleif Thorvaldsen**

Source: SAS Data, *Organization Papers.*

SAS Data Process Organization 1996

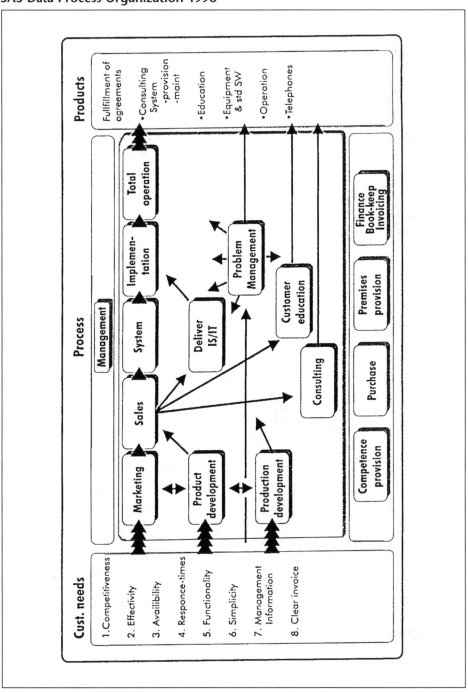

Source: Linje 1, no. 2, 1996.

IT Infrastructure

Computer Operations

The Unisys Center

When the large IBM TERESE reservation project was closed down in 1991, plans died to phase out the Unisys platform, too. Unisys computers operated some of SAS' strategic systems, for example reservation, check-in, cargo, and the Telcon communication system.[462]

In the late 1980s, Unisys finally presented its new U2200 mainframe to replace the old third generation computers of the 1960s. SAS bought a U2200 machine to meet the increasing demands for reservations system capacity, until the new IBM TERESE was able to take over.[463] By the early 1990s, program development was still carried out on terminals without use of modern tools and Unisys developments covered 15 % of all development time. When the TERESE project stopped it was obvious that a new Unisys technology would be required to fulfill SAS' business goals to halve development time and cut annual operation prices by 10 %.

During 1992 and 1993, it was decided to combine U2200 computers with Unisys' new USAS-SYS 11R2.[464] The 11R2 included tools needed to increase productivity and quality in a modern operation environment that allowed for c/s developments, too. During 1993 and 1994, a large number of people worked to adjust, test, and implement the new system software. Finally, by the end of 1994 a changeover over was made to the large reservations system, giving the SAS Data Group an updated and standardized Unisys platform.

SAS' volume of transactions kept on rising, however, and U2200 limits might be reached sooner than expected. Furthermore, it was difficult to cope with permanent demands for a 10 % annual price reduction. By the mid-1990s, SDG began to plan for new technologies.[465] Already, rapidly expanding microprocessor technology paved the way for the next generation of large Unisys computers. During 1997 and 1998, the Unisys center prepared for a replacement of the U2200 by the much more compact, powerful, flexible, modular, and less energy-demanding U4800 ClearPath technology.

By the late 1990s, a move to Unisys ClearPath was still not decided. Once more SAS and SDG had a Unisys phase-out in mind that might lead to a concentration of central systems on one IBM platform. Encapsulation of the U2200 would lighten a possible integration with other platforms.

---

462 SAS Data, *Profil* no. 2 and 7, 1992.
463 Interview: *Dan Sjøland.*
464 SDD, *Profil*, no. 5, 1993. SAS Data, *Linje 1*, no. 1, 1994, no. 1, 1995.
465 SAS Data, *Linje 1*, no. 5, 1995. Interview: *Dan Sjøland.*

There were three reasons for plans to phase out Unisys.[466] First, to reduce costs of hardware, software, personnel, and training a more simple corporate architecture was needed. Second, Unisys personnel were getting old and it seemed impossible to recruit a new group of programmers to such an unattractive platform as Unisys. Third, the future of corporate Unisys was uncertain. Just like IBM, Unisys reacted to the c/s revolution by reorganizing into a system integrating business. It kept on developing its large computers, having just launched its new ClearPath technology. Unisys remained strong in the airlines industry but in a globalized world of business, size and investment demands might surpass Unisys capabilities, seeing for instance large Tandem and DEC merge with Compaq. So far, Unisys had survived, but its future with SAS remained unsettled.

The IBM Center

MVS

In 1988, it was decided to move all SAS systems onto one IBM IT platform. At its Copenhagen center, the IBM MVS or Virtual Machine (VM) operating system, the 3000/Amdahl 5000, operated most SAS systems, including technical maintenance, crew, load control, revenue accounting, accounting, personnel, and telegram traffic. Plans were made and projects started for phasing out Unisys and Tandem systems. Furthermore to share risks, an alternative IBM center was being built in Stockholm. By 1991, the Gulf Crisis brought this ambitious one-IT-platform strategy to an end.[467]

The VM and MVS core technology originated in the pioneering OS/360 of the 1960s that introduced interactive operating. The VM/370 (Virtual Machine) of the 1970s added virtual storage, allowing for multiprogramming and parallel processing, followed by the hierarchical IMS (Information Management System) database management system. The MVS 3000 series and the IBM plug-compatible Amdahl 5000 series of the 1980s extended facilities even further. During the 1970s and 1980s, microprocessor development moved CPUs to increasing capacity heights. In the 1980s, IBM launched its DB2 relational database management system for distributed systems, too. This was the state of art by 1991.[468]

After the Gulf Crisis, increasing traffic and information integration required more capacity from the IBM center.[469] Furthermore, the IBM center

---

466 SAS, *Technical Platform Strategy*, 1998.

467 SDD, *Profil*, no. 7, 1991. SDS/SDN, *UPTIME*, no. 11, 1991.

468 SDD, *Profil* no. 7, 1992. Bertelsen, T. et al (Red.)(1991), *EDB-LEX: Det store informatik-leksikon* (IT dictionary)(Copenhagen: Gad). Interview: *Bjarne Karpanschof.*

469 SAS Data, *Linje 1*, no. 5, 1995. Interview Bjarne Karpanschof.

had to comply with radical business requirements of halving systems development times and an annual 10 % reduction of operation prices. By the mid-1990s, the IBM/Amdahl configuration of the 1980s was replaced by the IBM S/390 modernized version of the MVS operating system. S/390 had a modular CPU structure, modules being connected mutually with online fall back. Compared with its predecessor, it was much more powerful, it enabled flexible capacity extension, it used less energy and it contained improved tools for development, maintenance, and management.

By the late 1990s, IBM S/390 ran more than 150 systems and almost half of all SAS development time was used on this platform.[470] Besides investments in hardware and software, SAS and SDG focused on skills and competence development of people working on the IBM platform. The S/390 was considered a true enterprise server with high quality, scalability and reliability. IBM kept on upgrading S/390, too, and was developing facilities for a more open structure towards Unix, NT, and TCP/IP, the stars of c/s and networking technology. Online transaction support to IMS applications was not available, however, a true disadvantage considering the significance of those systems at SAS. As the best choice in the market, SDG and SAS planned to make the IBM S/390 the only platform for its large legacy applications, and even for future enterprise systems requiring the same quality and reliability. Unlike Unisys, IBM kept on being a strong company and although it made service and integration its new core business since the mid-1990s, it kept on upgrading its server technology.

Disguised as a modern server, the mainframe survived and lived well at the end of the millennium. Still, no mature technology or winners had appeared for an enterprise-wide integration of servers at the high-end, mid-end and low-end. IBM was a candidate for the high-end due to its historic dominance of mainframes. By the late 1990s, a platform strategy at SAS could only adjust to this state of the market.

OS/2

In 1990, IBM/Microsoft OS/2 was considered the future market leader of the emerging client/server technology.[471] OS/2, which IBM took over in 1991, was a single user PC operating system, and the IBM LAN Manager had to be added for multi-user applications, including IBM Presentation Manager for graphic interfaces. As SAS wanted to make IBM its only IT standard, the OS/2 complex was chosen for the first c/s systems of the early 1990s. Airports and stations

---

470 SAS, *Technical Platform Strategy*.
471 SDD, *Profil*, no. 2, 9, 1992. SDS/SDN, *UPTIME*, no. 2, 18, 22, 1993, no. 3, 1994. SAS, *Technical Platform Strategy*.

were major candidates for OS/2 because c/s came early here and also because SITA, the international communications association, based its common airport CUTE PC on OS/2 technology.

The expected IBM dominance of c/s technology did not occur, however. By 1990, IBM was not even the strongest vendor of an emerging distributing technology. Microsoft DOS and its graphic interface Windows dominated the PC world market and in LANs, Novell's Netware had become the de facto market standard. IBM marketed and developed its OS/2 complex, but the corporation did not target c/s technology in the same way as Microsoft and Novell did. Furthermore, little difference existed between IBM OS/2, IBM Presentation Manager, and Microsoft DOS/Windows, or between IBM LAN Manager and Novell Netware.

Gradually, during the first half of the 1990s, OS/2 lost ground in the market and at SAS where interest in OS/2 dwindled. Although upgraded to multi-user level by the mid-1990s, by the late 1990s it was apparently a "no future" platform, although IBM kept on updating its technology. SDG and SAS maintained OS/2 for the benefit only of a few applications, until they might be phased out.

AS/400

When SAS implemented its large customer database, Columbus, for Euro-Bonus in 1992, a new IBM platform was introduced, namely AS/400.[472] AS/400 was a modern distributed platform suitable for relational database systems and c/s. SDG had no competence in the AS/400 field, therefore leaving Columbus to be operated by a UK company. When the Technical Division decided to replace the MATS with a standard system MOVEX on AS/400, SDD began to build its own AS/400 environment. In 1995, SDG took over operation of Columbus and MOVEX.

By the late 1990s, 6 systems operated on the AS/400 platform.[473] Mainly, SDG handled these systems on the basis of facility management, whereas systems development was left to be done by external companies, and SDG had no plans for extending its competence and resources to the AS/400 platform. AS/400 had a good market penetration, it was supported by a number of independent systems vendors, and it could be integrated with other platforms by way of standard middleware. Furthermore, IBM kept on upgrading AS/400. According to strategic plans of the late 1990s, AS/400 was a platform to be maintained and only used for additional applications in cases where a standard package could not be run on one of the strategic platforms.

---

472 SDS/SDN, *UPTIME*, 12, 1992. SDD, *Profil*, March 1994. SAS Data, *Linje 1*, no. 1, 6, 1995, and no. 5, 1996.
473 SAS, *Technical Platform Strategy*.

The Tandem Center

The 1988 decision to make IBM the only SAS IT standard included a phase-out of Tandem, too. By 1990, Tandem only operated a few systems in the three Scandinavian capitals: New STREPS in CPH (planning ground services), FATIS in Oslo and Bergen (airport information system), DAP (local customer invoicing, payments and credit handling), and CASH (economy system of more than 30 airport shops).[474]

The 1991 close down of TERESE and the end of the IBM strategy gave new life to Tandem, just as it did to Unisys.[475] While CPH planned to phase out Tandem, and OSL (to a minor degree) wanted to continue Tandem production, SDS built a large Tandem Center at Arlanda (Stockholm). Tandem technology was upgraded to the most advanced level. The SAS-Linjeflyg merger gave Tandem a large work field. Furthermore, SMART (distribution in Scandinavia) and the former SAS Leisure Group (Premier, Ving, and Saga travel agencies) entrusted computer operation to the SDS Tandem center, too.

By the late 1990s, Tandem ran a number of systems, including c/s.[476] Most of these systems concerned its major customer, SAS Sweden, and included local systems for passenger, luggage, check-in, cargo, movement control, flight information, airport information and personnel planning.

In the late 1990s, a small Tandem staff handled 39 systems, covering 3% of all SDG development time.[477] In the market, independent Tandem systems vendor support was low and furthermore, Tandem merged with Compaq. Plans were being prepared to migrate applications to future strategic platforms of SAS, but nothing had been decided yet.

The UNIX Center

The new ORD yield management system in 1992 was the first SAS Unix c/s system.[478] Unix was a multi-user operating system and a more open platform than OS/2 and DOS/Windows, and right away it became popular at SAS. Originally, Unix was an American Telephone & Telegraph (AT&T) system that was free to everybody and caused much excitement and developed new knowledge throughout the college world of the 1980s. During the first half of the 1990s, IT firms began to develop and market Unix proprietary systems. Micro-Sun Systems started and led the Unix market for some time, until it was taken over by Hewlett Packard (HP), followed by other firms in second and third

---

474 SDS/SDN, *UPTIME*, no. 8, 1988.
475 SAS Data, *Linje 1*, no. 2, 1994.
476 SAS Data, *Linje 1*, no. 4, 1997.
477 SAS, *Technical Platform Strategy*.
478 SAS Data, *Linje 1*, no. 8, 1995. Interview: *Dan Sjøland*.

place. Already by the mid-1990s, the number of SAS Unix c/s applications reached a considerable level and it was becoming a de facto c/s standard at SAS as well as in the market in general.

As Unix servers of c/s systems spread throughout the SAS organization, problems of operation and maintenance emerged. In 1995, SDG established a Unix Center in Copenhagen to handle the increasing number of Unix boxes. From a low position, Unix competence and staff increased gradually during the 1990s. In the late 1990s, Unix remained the core SAS c/s system platform, although being challenged by expanding Microsoft NT.[479]

Microsoft

During the second half of the 1980s and first half of the 1990s, Microsoft DOS and its follower Windows became the worldwide dominant PC operating system (i.e., on the client side), although still a relatively small-scale technology. By the early 1990s, the SAS organization had a number of DOS and Windows servers. Corporate SAS recommended IBM standards but as a consequence of decentralized authority, each division and its sub-departments chose their own local technology as it pleased. PC DOS/Windows word and calculation packages, such as Word Perfect, Word, and Excel, were mainly used in back office functions,

The c/s breakthrough from 1991 created rapidly expanding markets for non-mainframe servers. By the mid-1990s, de facto market standards began to emerge. Unix came to dominate the server side and DOS/Windows the client side, although no clear line separated the server and client technology markets. Microsoft introduced its strategy of embedding an increasing number of facilities in its Windows product, starting with office systems. In 1995, Windows was the client standard at SAS and Unix was about to be the server standard below mainframe levels.

By the late 1990s, server markets and corporate server practice and strategy were changing. To find emerging winners, SAS analyzed the server markets.[480] Since the mid-1990s, Microsoft had moved into a strong winner position in low-end and even mid-end markets of operating systems or servers. Embedded with more and more facilities, Windows 1995 and 1998 became the indisputable client server market standard. In 1995, Microsoft launched its NT server, targeting the profitable and expanding mid-server market dominated by Unix. Just like its client technology, it was Microsoft's strategy to embed as many facilities as possible in its NT server, including files, printers,

---

479 SAS, *Technical Platform Strategy.*
480 Ibid.

network and database. With this embedding strategy, Microsoft targeted specialized markets of network and databases, which were led by Novell and Oracle.

Corporations, including SAS, looked for systems and platforms integration on all levels of servers if possible. Microsoft moved rapidly to gain and maintain a leading role in an escalating technology race. By the late 1990s, Microsoft had reached a market position that challenged the dominant position of Unix in mid-end servers. Microsoft even prepared to integrate Windows and NT to create one single server, that of NT. By the late 1990s, SAS operated about 16 NT servers. Competitors began to strike back at Microsoft, however, and furthermore, the Internet promised radical changes of the whole IT field.

Still, decisions on server standards were not as easy as SDG management would have liked them to be. At SAS, SDG tended to make Windows/NT the low-end and mid-end server platform, leaving the high-end to IBM. With few and recent skills and no NT organization by the late 1990s, it would take SDG years to convert generally to NT servers. Servers formed a complex structure that could not easily be adapted to new market standards. Finally, an emerging field of so-called "application servers" as well as the Internet revolution might change the scenario and make it much easier to link information based on different platforms.

Help Desk

Help Desk was the SAS Data fault and ad hoc service towards its customers throughout the SAS organization.[481] Faults were registered in a system called MIMER, which each day organized and followed up on faults, including MS Access, which enabled customers to create statistics themselves. A Hot Line was added to take care of acute problems. In general, SDG expanded technical services in the three capitals to support the rapidly growing number of PCs, LANs, and software packages.

One Operating Center

By the late 1990s, SDG prepared to join all activities in one central operation center that would also include communications.[482] Expanding c/s technology and a truly networked corporation called for central management and surveillance. This was needed even more as SAS management pressed continuously for productivity rises and quality improvements.

---

481 SDS/SDN, *UPTIME*, no. 16, 1992. SAS Data, *Linje 1*, no 1 1995.
482 SAS Data, *Linje 1*, no. 4, 1997. SAS, *Technical Platform Strategy*.

Communications

The Open Network

In 1991, SAS resumed its plans for a new and open communication standard.[483] Open distribution systems and increasing airline cooperation demanded open communication. The existing communication structure was based on a combination of SAS front-end computers connected to telephone systems. It was a SAS proprietary system that did not easily communicate with other airlines and external communication systems in general. The Telcon protocol, SASALFA and DCP front-end computers made up the core of this SAS communication system that connected terminals to central mainframes in CPH, assisted by an IBM VTAM 3270 protocol. In 1990, the SAS network linked more than twenty thousand terminals.

The new network platform, the »Synthesizer« project, was developed from 1991 to 1993.[484] Synthesizer created an open and »intelligent« network, based on software and high capacity connections, linking an increasing number of c/s technology systems. From 1991 to 1992, the first intelligent networks were developed in Scandinavian capitals and at headquarters in Stockholm. The pioneering Arlanda airport network at Stockholm consisted of fiber optic cabling, a local Token Ring network protocol, OS/2 for client servers at check-in connected to SASALFA and VTAM protocols, LAN Manager for communication between server and terminal/PC, Presentation Manager for graphical interface, and Nokia displays. When possible, Arlanda stuck to IBM standards. These intelligent airport networks were followed by SITA's international CUTE computer system that enabled airlines throughout the world to log in on the same airport PC. The first CUTE version came in 1989, and the second version in 1995.

By 1991, no market standards existed for data transfer between different technological platforms.[485] SAS and SDG looked for technical solutions. Gradually, standard elements of a new infrastructure emerged. Multi-protocol functions became available by so-called backbone Routers, linking different PC and terminal protocols in the new network. At LAN level, Novell Netware dominated, whereas IBM LAN Manager never succeeded. HP OpenView became the preferred network management system, although still no mature technology.

In 1994, SAS started to phase out Telcon and its DCPs and install Synthesizer instead.[486] Finally in 1996, Telcon closed down. The Synthesizer network

---

483 SDD, *Profil*, no. 7, 1992.
484 SDS/SDN, *Nätvärlden* no. 1, 1991. SAS Data, *Linje 1*, no. 1, 1995.
485 SDD, *Profil*, no. 2, 1992, no. 4, 1993.
486 SDD, *Profil*, no. 4, 1994. SAS Data, *Linje 1*, no. 1, 3, 4 1995, and no. 1, 3 1996.

made up a transport channel that used the OSI standards of the day to guide data around, X.25 protocol for packet switching, X.400 for e-mail and documents, and X.500 for addressing. Instead of a few services built into the previous proprietary network of Telcon and VTAM, a standard transport system allowed for an increasing number of software services.

During 1994, tenders were invited for SAS data communications.[487] Corporate SAS wanted to put maximum market pressure on SAS Data and make sure that communications gave value for money. SAS Data communications won the open tender competing with large market vendors. This victory and the simultaneous alignment of SAS Data and SAS did not ease market pressure on SAS Data communications, however. A P50 project in 1995 aimed at halving communications operation prices and in 1997, an agreement on Mandatory Communication Services was made to prevent SAS Data from gaining any monopoly profit. In the open market, a maturing communications management industry pressed SAS communications department still harder, too.

Synthesizer was just the first and fundamental step in developing an open communications infrastructure for a corporation that moved towards c/s technology and an increasing number of internal and external links. During 1995, SDG analyzed market trends in communications technology to come up with a future SAS communications platform. SDG management systems were mapped, too, showing approximately 200 different communication management tools. This had to be tied up. During 1996, HP Open View was implemented as strategic platform.[488]

OSI protocols never succeeded in the market, and Synthesizer was impeded by that fact. With growing speed, an alternative technology had been emerging since the late 1980s, the so-called Internet. By the mid-1990s, a true Internet revolution started, presenting a global TCP/IP communication standard that corporations jumped to use. Synthesizer had prepared SAS for open standards. Now, it moved to make TCP/IP the communication standard, externally as well as internally, so-called Intranets.[489] By the end of 1998, only TCP/IP was allowed for as the communication protocol of SAS.[490] Furthermore, SDG chose Microsoft NT as its communication server, depending on Star Alliance negotiations and SAS policies for IT and telephony networks, however.

---

487 SDD, *Profil* no. 5, 1994. SAS Data, *Linje 1*, no. no. 5, 1997.
488 SAS Data, *Linje 1*, no. 1 1996.
489 SAS Data, *Linje 1*, no. 8, 1995, no. 5, 8 and 11, 1996.
490 SAS, *Technical Platform Strategy*.

VAS

Already Telcon contained communication services to SAS employees, so-called Value Added Services (VAS).[491] InfoMail was its main service. As PCs and LANs spread, a new kind of package mail system appeared in the market. Microsoft MS Mail became the preferred system, later on replaced by HP Open Mind, because it included electronic mail, fax, and directory services as well as an applications connection. Finally, a TCP/IP Intranet was established.

Multi-Share was another VAS for PCs on LANs. It gave the user access to subscribe to a number of services, including storing room, program library, database handler, fax, printer and so on.

Having introduced the intelligent network, any software package that customers demanded on a large scale might become a service on the net. By the late 1990s, it was yet to be decided whether digitalized telephony and services should be an integrated part of the IT network or should remain separate.[492]

Telephony

During late 1980s and early 1990s, Ericsson MD110 digitalized SAS telephone exchanges.[493] Continued digitalization and explosive IT development brought telecommunication within the realm of computer technology and a growing number of value added services began to emerge. InfoDial, connecting a home PC to Telcon or VTAM communication lines, was one of the first VAS. CallCenters for EuroBonus and Direct Sales with automatic call distribution and answer applications were introduced, but early installations lacked capacity and facilities to succeed.

By the mid-1990s, Interactive Voice Response, as it was called, began to mature. Investigations of SAS telephone service, InfoLine, showed that 4 out of 10 calls dealt with questions of price and seat for leisure passengers, and that many of its primary customer group, business passengers, were lost to competitors because of blocked lines. As a consequence, a c/s voice response system was introduced during 1995, based on Alcatel hardware and developed by SDG on a Unix platform.

At the same time, SAS took the next radical step in telephony. SAS and SDG undertook pre-studies and devised requirement specifications for a new CallCenter platform.[494] A Windows computerized telephone catalogue informed on all SAS employees' competence, integrating telephony and com-

---

491 SDD, *Profil* no. 3, 1993, no. 5, 9, 10, 1994. SDS/SDN, *UPTIME*, no. 21, 1991 and no. 19, 1993.
492 SAS, *Technical Platform Strategy*.
493 SDS/SDN, *UPTIME*, no. 22, 1991, no. 10, 1992.
494 SAS Data, *Linje 1*, no. 1, 1995, no. 2 and 5, 1996.

puters. The system would help the switchboard to lead agents and other customers to the person best able to help. The system produced valuable statistics of agent calls, too. Mobile PC and telephone were also included to reduce dependence on physical employee position. Furthermore, the system enabled employees to integrate individual calendar information and answer machines into the system. The new platform was based on the MD110 exchange and a software package adjusted to SAS needs and operated at SDS Tandem.

By the late 1990s, telephony was an expanding business at SAS, producing a growing number of services throughout the net.[495] Still, telephony was based on a pretty well defined network that advocated a continued separation of telephony and IT, although one integrated network might be the outcome, too. Outsourcing was always an option to be considered for future telephony operation.

Systems Development

The First Half of the 1990s

For decades, systems developers had produced and maintained information systems that were increasingly important to the operation and competitiveness of SAS. All these systems were mainframe-based and dedicated in-house applications. Systems developers and programmers possessed a de facto knowledge monopoly of information systems' development and maintenance that gave them a powerful position in the corporation. That was the state of the art in practically any large corporation in the world.

Since the late 1980s, radical changes in business and IT industry rather quickly undermined the classical structure and conditions of systems development. Challenges were of a double kind. One was a strong and increasing pressure to replace functional criteria of technology with business considerations. Increasingly, management wanted systems for follow-up on market developments, for optimizing revenue and resources, and for creating new revenue. In 1988, SAS business divisions and routes took over IT development responsibility, putting SAS Data in a supplier's role on market conditions. Divided roles of business and IT were stressed even more in 1990 when SAS Data was turned into three independent SAS subsidiaries. By way of tenders, SAS divisions and staff began to leave systems development to external software consultants that promised greater business aligned information systems than SAS Data did. For the first time, SAS Data lost large systems development tasks such as load control, finance, and cargo systems. In-house systems development was truly threatened.

---

495 SAS, *Technical Platform Strategy*.

The second challenge to traditional systems development was the rather sudden end of mainframe systems development. By 1991, the last mainframe systems were finished (load control, finance, and revenue accounting) or abandoned (reservation and cargo). Only, maintenance of large systems was left to do. Instead of in-house development of applications on mainframes, the IT industry presented a true alternative. That was the client/server technology that moved the chief point of information development to the business user, the client, reducing mainframes to a server base. Furthermore, radical changes in networking created the electronic infrastructure that enabled the distributed systems to come true and fulfill management requirements for systems that gave competitive advantage.

This process of transformation took place during the first half of the 1990s. During these years, new software packages and tools emerged to replace in-house development and SAS' systems development strategy followed suit.

A process of re-qualification and market orientation started with system developers and programmers of the three SAS Data companies, seeking to turn a technology culture into a business culture.[496] SDD, SDS and SDN aimed at transforming traditional mainframe systems development into a c/s technology based on industrialized products, new tools and management considerations.

New tools for increased productivity of systems development were looked for in the market. Traditional systems development up till about 1990 used so-called third generation programming languages (Cobol etc.) to produce systems from scratch. From initial idea to final test, systems development worked according to classical SAS methods, although so-called fourth generation programming languages (4GL) promised higher productivity by automation and computer-based systems management.

Computer Aided Software Engineering (CASE) was such a tool, or rather it was a concept that intended to cover all phases of systems development, especially automated support to development, project management, and maintenance of systems. CASE was no mature technology. Nor had any relevant method been developed in the market to cover the whole field of systems development.

From 1990, the SAS staff unit ISS recommended such standards for systems development as the IEW CASE tool, the Project Manager Workbench, Data Manager, and the general Reflex method, used by the Swedish software

---

496 SAS, *Handbook of IT Policy and Standards*. SAS, *Savings through Standards*, 1991-1994. SDD, *Profil*, no. 28, 34-36, 43-44, 1990, no. 2, 1992, no. 9, 1993. SDS/SDN, *UPTIME*, no. 19, 1991.

consultant Programator. A project handbook or guide was developed for project manager education and guidance and training started in 1990. Later on, Navigator replaced Reflex but during the first half of the 1990s, no new general method was really enforced to replace the old SAS systems development method. DB2 became a de facto database management standard.[497] Gradually, Microsoft Windows moved into a dominant position on client technology, handling data access (SQL), and presentation, supported by for example Telon. Graphic interfaces became a natural part of the development environment. Still, it was a proprietary world, where Microsoft gained ground in client standard products and CASE in systems development.

In some cases, applications might be bought in the market, as a package or an airline product to be adjusted to SAS.[498] In other cases, people at SDD, SDS, or SDN developed c/s themselves, such as EDISS for sales offices, Cargo Monitor, automated crew check-in at airports, and the great ATB project for automated ticketing and boarding.

As market products developed and c/s competence was upgraded, SAS Data gradually moved into a position of system integrator and adapter. Of traditional systems development, only maintenance and operation was left. Distributed systems development of c/s technology used more and more of the industrial products for database management, data access, access of different platforms, graphic interfaces, systems development automation, and so on. By the mid-1990s, a new age of reorganization and systemization started to replace the confusing and learning years of the early 1990s.

The Second Half of the 1990s

SAS and SAS Data reorganization in 1994 started a new turn in systems development.[499] SAS Data aligned more and more to SAS needs and organization and at the same time, decisions on standards, tools, and so forth, were being determinedly enforced at corporate and divisional level. An increasing number of client/server systems throughout SAS, and an IT market presenting for the first time a platform of standards for the new c/s technology and networks, made SAS and SDG start looking for and preparing a true modern method of systems development. First, projects were started to develop a standardized model of methods and tools, based on experiences of other leading European airlines. Next, projects were coordinated to create a common system house for all three SAS Data units, called Common Methods and Tools (COMET).

---

497 SDD, *Profil*, no. 26, 1990. SDS/SDN, *UPTIME*, no. 19-21, 1991, no. 5-6, 8, 11, 15, 1992. SDD, *Projektlederguide* (project management guide), 1990.
498 See, *Information Systems*, below.
499 SAS Data, *Linje 1*, no. 1, 1994, no. 1-2, 4, 1995.

In support for a Total Quality Management (TQM) approach, the market was searched for tools to gain dynamic development, graphic user interfaces, and a high degree of development automation.[500] In 1997, COMET was put into practice. Servers were installed in the three Scandinavian capitals, and training in the new method started, including »project management«, »client/server development«, and »maintenance and system integration«.

During the second half of the 1990s, systems development had two goals.[501] First, it had to live up completely to the expectations and wishes of its SAS customers. Second, systems that supported new SAS products had be delivered at short notice according to changing market demands, the so-called »time-to-market« principle.

During 1996 to 1997, a »Process Concept« was carried out to optimize a customer-run process within SAS Data and between SAS Data and SAS.[502] The process concept included a Review model ensuring that the customer achieved the expected business advantages of the system and that SDG profited from the project. In addition, Account Executives should enforce TQM during the development job, ensuring that the system delivered was as faultless as possible and that the process was optimal. Finally, »benchmarking« was used to regularly measure systems development, making SAS Data live up to the best international market standards. In this way, systems development was integrated into the general process innovation approach that SDG and SAS endeavored to carry out from the mid-1990s.

Databases

Since the 1970s, the IBM IMS hierarchical database management system dominated SAS' increasing number of IBM mainframe systems. When SAS decided to make IBM its only IT standard in the late 1980s, DB2 was chosen as the new relational database handler to supplement existing mainframes in distributed systems and as a basis for new central systems. The new traffic statistics system (TRAF) was the first DB2 project, followed by a new budget system, OBS2, the Columbus customer database, and many more throughout most main SAS functions. DB2 suited distributed systems on IBM mainframes and remained standard until the mid-1990s. Then Oracle took over as the preferred DBMS on distributed systems. SQL worked as data access.[503]

---

500 SAS Data, *Linje 1*, no. 7. 1995, no. 1-2. 1997.
501 SAS Data, *Linje 1*, no. 1, 4, 9, 1996. Interview: *Poul Strand-Holm*.
502 SAS Data, *Linje 1*, no. 1, 2. 9, 1996. See, Figure, *SAS Data Process Organization*.
503 SAS Data, *Linje 1*, no. 6, 1996.

Middleware

Decades of IT development made the systems portfolio of most corporations, including SAS, a mix of several technological platforms. When a transformation process started from about 1990, IT and business needed tools to overcome the "Babel Tower" of technology. C/s technology paved the way for increased productivity and a systems upgrade to management, user, and customer levels. Open communication was made possible through standardized protocols and multi-protocol routers and reached a climax with the Internet protocol TCP/IP.

SAS' information systems however, as in most corporations, covered single functions only. Increasing efforts to create integrated systems to obtain a radical rise in productivity and quality, internally and towards customers, made companies look for solutions to overcome the problem of information islands. If information management was to move forward it needed easy and quick access to information across various applications. IT industries began to market products to that end, so-called middleware. Nevertheless, it was still an immature technology by the late 1990s. Furthermore, these new products tended to be object-oriented, whereas existing corporations' information systems were historic products of previous technologies. Many IT companies started to focus on solving the problem of information system integration of several platforms from the mid-1990s.

One road to solve the problem of information islands and multi-technology platforms was to combine middleware with a new top level of object technology to create systems messaging.[504] A second road to take was by building so-called data or information warehouses, a method called data mining. The idea was simply to build a huge relational database covering broad segments of a corporation, for example all economy systems or all personnel systems, or even larger parts. With sophisticated tools and information systems, management might access the warehouse for needed information and follow-up. SAS Data started developing such a warehouse from the mid-1990s, but the idea did not catch on with SAS management. The customer database and yield management system of 1992 might be considered examples of the warehouse approach. By the late 1990s, the warehouse and middleware interoperability concept had not yet materialized. In the market however, application server technologies emerged that promised to break down the walls of separated information systems.

---

504 SAS Data, *Linje 1*, no. 8, 1995. See also above, *The IT Industry*.

Information Systems

Corporate

General corporate management planning used information systems only to some degree, mainly for aircraft investments planning.[505] When SAS prepared its large fleet renewal during the 1990s, sophisticated software logic helped to simulate various aircraft types and sizes according to forecasted traffic patterns and corporate goals of optimization.

The three-year airline resource or business plans (ARP), the second level of planning, were being prepared by division management and gathered at corporate level to state the final goals of SAS airline and its divisions. For top management, this would require limited information system support, because most calculations and investigations were carried out at divisional level.

The annual budget formed the third level of planning. OBS handled budget transactions created in divisions and distributed valid budget transactions to the general ledger system. In the early 1990s, OBS was renewed as OBS2 and turned into a c/s system based on DB2.

In 1992, SDD had already produced a concept for strategic management information systems at corporate level, the Business Intelligence Concept (BIC). In 1995, the information systems planning group (ISPG) and SAS Data laid out plans for a future systems information warehouse (SIW). The SIW project intended to develop common databases across applications and functions. Such information warehouses would be supermarkets of common data and common interfaces to make available the enormous amounts of data needed for various management purposes. SAS' yield management system for passenger optimization might be considered a SIW.

By the late 1990s, SIW plans and projects had not surpassed these initial steps of the mid-1990s. Nor were plans seen for external business intelligence systems as a basis of management analysis and follow-up on market developments.

Traffic

Client/Server Systems

The arrival of open airline competition in Europe made SAS management press for tools to follow traffic development closely and for quick and precise

---

505 SDD, *Profil*, no. 1, 1992. SAS Data, *Linje 1*, no. 13, 1994, no. 8, 1995. Interview: *Poul Strand-Holm.*

reactions to competitor initiatives and changing customer travel patterns. The new client/server technology made it easier to develop such software.

Since the mid-1980s, a number of traffic follow-up systems had emerged.[506] By the late 1980s, these follow-up systems made up some kind of spaghetti information: the timetable system TPTS generated SAS traffic, TRAF followed up on a traffic statistics system, IRIS that replaced LRS did route accounting follow-up, Charges II handled charges, and Qualisas followed up on quality of flights. These systems had different goals. To improve follow-up on the individual flight, a system was created that would be the only source for common follow-up information (BFU-Data Collection). When the traffic follow-up systems showed different results, it was now known that it was because they reflected the corporation in different ways, and not because they built on different realities. A new fares system was developed to cover an increasing number of fares and fares changes, too.

In the early 1990s, these planning and follow-up systems were turned into true c/s systems based on IBM's relational database management system, DB2.[507] Business Systems Division (Commercial Division by then) bought a PC-system, Macheup, which enabled planners to move part of the timetable data from the mainframe system to the PC for local information processing. Having finished processing, the result was sent back to the mainframe and distributed to other systems and interested parties. The PC system made timetable changes quicker and easier, and made more detailed traffic analysis possible.

Up to this point destination-pairs, the routes between two cities, were considered. Now, the individual flight might be studied, following statistics for certain days and certain times of the day. Support systems were added for current analysis of booking developments and comparisons with the previous year. In 1998, two more support systems were added, simulating effects of traffic program changes for the whole SAS route network.

The load factor took the bearings of business development and it was, therefore, the factor most intensely studied every day for each flight. The client/server systems allowed fast reactions to changing competitor prices or departures. Route managers and Marketing & Sales people watched these matters closely – Business Systems Division being responsible for formulating an optimum timetable and price policy, and Marketing & Sales (since 1994) for marketing and selling the products, including current changes.

Since the early 1990s, traffic program optimization and current operations to ensure an optimum load factor and profit for every individual flight had

---

506 SDS/SDN, *UPTIME*, no. 3-4, 1989.
507 Interviews: *Stael von Holstein, Stefan Anderson, Anders Eriksson.*

been the driving force of systems development. Furthermore, all other parts of SAS benefited from its reinforced optimizing efforts. Stations wanted to make rotations as short as possible (i.e., the time aircraft spent on the ground) and tried to optimize ground operations for flight arrival and departure. Operations needed to know the physical movements of the plane to optimize crew employment. Technical was interested in adjusting the timetable to optimize maintenance work. SAS took an increasing interest in integration and automation of total corporate information flow to cut costs and raise productivity and flexibility, driven by customer demands and competitor initiatives.

A New Timetable System

During the 1990s, the speed of changes and pressure on the information systems grew. As a consequence, TPTS limitations became more obvious.[508] The hierarchical database of TPTS lacked flexibility in information access and processing, in spite of all the follow-up and client/server systems added to the mainframe system. Urged on by the practical problem of the year 2000, which TPTS was not able to handle, from 1995 the Business Systems Division prepared a new timetable system based on a DB2 relational database and a PC user interface on Windows. The same SDS people who had made the old TPTS of the 1970s developed the new Timetable Database (TDB). Many systems connected to the timetable had to be converted to fit TDB. They included PALCO, RESAID, CARIN/CAREX, CRU80, TT (Tandem), Charges, OPUS, and BFU. In 1996, TDB was implemented and SDS took over timetable administration, which had been done externally by Enator for many years.

Passenger

Marketing & Sales

From the early 1990s, Marketing & Sales functions were reinforced to meet competition.[509] They were upgraded to divisional level in 1994. Marketing & Sales Division expanded even more in 1998 when taking over reservations and distribution activities from the phased-out Information Systems Division.

The most important new SAS products were the loyalty program of Euro-Bonus, which sought to attach frequent travelers more closely to SAS, and the low price product Jackpot.[510] EuroBonus that became a crucial part of the SAS market strategy during the 1990s was based on a new database, Columbus.

---

508 SDS/SDN, *UPTIME*, no. 10, 1994. SAS Data, *Linje 1*, no. 3, 6, 1995, no. 10, 1996.
509 SAS, *Annual Reports*, 1993 and 1997.
510 SDS/SDN, *UPTIME*, no. 11, 1991. Interview: *Per Møller-Jensen*. SAS, *Annual Report*, 1997.

Columbus was a DB2 based database and c/s system with a graphic interface. Information on customers came to Columbus from Diners (credit card), RESAID (booking), PAH (check-in) and IMPALA (interline prorating). The number of EuroBonus members grew to exceed one million in the late 1990s, providing valuable marketing information for individual customers.

Since the mid-1990s, product development and marketing targeted travel flow and service improvement to widen the options of each traveler.[511] At the same time, it tried to attach individual customers (EuroBonus), agents (Partner Agent Program), and companies (SAS Corporate Program) more closely to SAS by way of loyalty programs.

From the early 1990s, the Automated Ticketing and Boarding (ATB) project worked to create a completely automated system for sales information flow, based on such systems as PNR, TICS, PAS, and PALCO.[512] In ATB, the ticket and boarding card merged into one document. It took years to develop ATB, and the system was gradually being implemented from the mid-1990s.

ATB reflected a tremendous IT upgrade of the distribution information chain. From the mid-1990s, this distribution chain was completely automated. It reached from the RESAID booking inventory, traffic program and fares at one end, via travel agencies and sales offices, to global distributors at the other end. Information flow, systems, and functions were continually being improved to make sure that SAS products could easily be found, booked, and sold.

Electronic Ticketing, including TravelPass, added a further dimension to ATB. Passengers could book and check-in easily and quickly by themselves, reducing costs for SAS and improving services for the customer. The c/s ATB was the second sales and marketing strategic system, EuroBonus Columbus being the other one.

Customer-based sales systems were developed, too. From the mid-1990s, direct telephony sales grew considerably. With interactive voice response, computer systems informed people of departure and arrival and enabled passengers to book seats themselves. By the late 1990s, SAS introduced a direct sales technology that offered a much better perspective, namely the Internet. The Internet added new dimensions to long distance sales and self-service for customers, as it did to the airline. By way of the Internet, SAS could deal directly with customers and save agency commissions and sales personnel, while adding value to customers. The turn of the millennium will most likely see a SAS breakthrough in Internet technology.

From the early 1990s, sales offices employed a dialog based PC c/s system

511 SAS Data, *Linje 1*, no. 5, 1997. Interview: *Erik Berggren-Lindberg*.
512 Interviews: *Hannes Lebert, Erik Berggren-Lindberg*.

that was an adjusted version of Qantas' Quick Access.[513] On the screen, the salesperson could work simultaneously with the four most used programs (i.e. reservations, check-in, sales, and hotels), quickly executing telephone bookings. Graphic interfaces and PCs were introduced for front line personnel, too. A c/s Closed Fares system on DB2 was developed for deals with agents. In back office, Marketing & Sales Division introduced client/server systems for financial and employee planning and follow-up, just like the other divisions.

A Sales Force Automation (SFA) system, including a mobile PC, was developed for marketing in the field and to travel agencies.[514] SFA showed how agents sold on various levels, including follow-up on market share and development of various products for various agents. In the late 1990s, TV and Internet commercials were introduced. A new Statistical Passenger Information System (SPI) in Revenue Information, including SIW plans, was added to these initiatives for improved systems in planning, budgeting, follow-up, and revenue analysis.

Reservations

RESAID

When TERESE closed down in 1991, SAS was left with the old Unisys RES.[515] In 1992, the new international distribution system, AMADEUS, took over distribution from SAS RES. The reduced RES, renamed RESAID (Reservation Inventory Documentation), was an enlarged inventory of SAS reservations that included many services made available to travel agencies and sales offices. It also formed the basis of SAS' yield management system, the Origin Destination Movement Management System, ORD.

RESAID in the 1990s made transactions at a speed and volume that transcended pre-1990 levels by miles. Furthermore, RESAID had turned into a very complex system that interfaced with more than 200 other systems.[516]

By the late 1990s, plans were being developed to phase out Unisys and migrate its large systems to some other platform, such as IBM S/390.[517] Once more, the uncertain future of corporate Unisys and SAS' intentions to reduce the number of technology standards called for migration. In case of no phase out, the new Unisys ClearPath technology concept would probably be introduced. Star Alliance cooperation on a common platform or, less likely, a total outsourcing, might be other options for reservations. The choice would depend on a combination of strategic considerations and potentials.

---

513 SDD, *Profil*, no. 4, 1992. SDS/SDN, *UPTIME*, no. 1, 1993.
514 SAS Data, *Linje 1*, no. 5, 1995, no. 4, 1996. Interview: *Erik Berggren-Lindberg*.
515 SDD, *Profil*, no. 43/44, 1991. Interview: *Arne Hansen*.
516 See Figure, *RESAID System Environment*.
517 SAS, *Technical Platform Strategy*.

Resaid System Environment 1991

Source: SAS Data.

Distribution

SMART

Since 1984, SMART had been the leading travel distributor in Scandinavia. In 1992 it was connected to AMADEUS and during the following years to all large distributors of the world.518 Furthermore, the arrival of open international competition made SMART turn into a competitive business of its own. SMART used a graphic interface on its terminals from 1990, followed by a true c/s that was connected to SAS via its Scala economy system. SMART became a 100 % SAS-owned company in 1994, operated by SDS Tandem.

AMADEUS

In the early 1990s, two international European distribution systems started working, namely GALILEO (Swissair, KLM, British Airways, Alitalia), and AMADEUS (Iberia, Lufthansa, Air France, and SAS).[519] In 1991, the Gulf Crisis made SAS give up its joint ownership of AMADEUS for financial reasons. Ownership was no longer that important either, because AMADEUS became an open distribution system and individual business unit.

National distribution systems, including SMART, were connected to AMADEUS and individual airline reservations systems' inventories, including SAS' RESAID, continued to interface with AMADEUS.

At its operations center in Munich, a gigantic database was established, where connected companies entered all their bookings by way of thousands of terminals. All terminals at SAS' sales offices and agents were linked to both AMADEUS and RESAID for bookings. Having made a reservation through AMADEUS on an SAS flight, this part of the so-called »record PNR« returned to RESAID, enabling SAS to control its flights.[520]

Since the advent of AMADEUS, SAS flights and fares appeared on all screens of connected companies. To prevent unfair competition, EU standardized the distribution systems display, based on a neutral presentation. AMADEUS and GALILEO worked according to this standard and as a precondition for access to the European market, American distribution systems and Asian ABACUS followed suit. A cooperation attempt between AMADEUS and American Airlines' SABRE did not succeed, but the two systems communicated and updated each other.

Developments towards open global distribution systems were being pushed forward by international travel agencies that wanted access to all large distribution systems of the world, and by global traffic systems of allied airlines established since the mid-1990s. Through AMADEUS and its connections to other distribution systems, such as GALILEO, American SABRE, APOLLO, WORLD-

---

518 SDS/SDN, *UPTIME*, no. 10, 1990, no. 1, 1992. SAS Data, *Linje 1*, no. 2, 1994.
519 Interviews: *Helle H. Uldal, Göran Pettersson, Björn Boldt-Christmas*.
520 See Figure, *AMADEUS*.

SPAN, and Asian ABACUS, SAS was able to offer globalized access for its products to passenger markets. Since the mid-1990s, all international airlines had been part of a global distribution system, doing business on the same basis of open competition. Controlling a distribution system was no longer the way to create competitiveness. It was the quality of airline products that counted. The objectives of distribution were to make SAS' products visible in all major markets and to ensure that technical and resource limits never prevented SAS from carrying out its market strategy.

These revolutionary changes of distribution and airline business were backed by internal initiatives of the SAS organization.[521] Upgraded distribution activities became a vital part of the Data Distribution Division (1988) and its followers Marketing Automation Division (1990), Support Division (1993), Information Systems (1994), and Marketing & Sales Division (1998).

AMADEUS

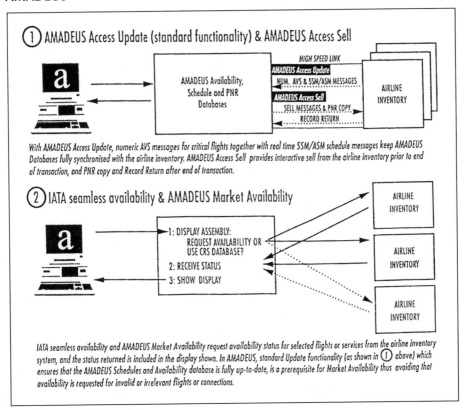

① AMADEUS Access Update (standard functionality) & AMADEUS Access Sell

With AMADEUS Access Update, numeric AVS messages for critical flights together with real time SSM/ASM schedule messages keep AMADEUS Databases fully synchronised with the airline inventory. AMADEUS Access Sell provides interactive sell from the airline inventory prior to end of transaction, and PNR copy and Record Return after end of transaction.

② IATA seamless availability & AMADEUS Market Availability

IATA seamless availability and AMADEUS Market Availability request availability status for selected flights or services from the airline inventory system, and the status returned is included in the display shown. In AMADEUS, standard Update functionality (as shown in ① above) which ensures that the AMADEUS Schedules and Availability database is fully up-to-date, is a prerequisite for Market Availability thus avoiding that availability is requested for invalid or irrelevant flights or connections.

Source: AMADEUS, 1994.

---

521 SAS, *Data Management*, 13/2, 1/6 1988, 16/1 1989, 31/5 1991. SAS, *ARP-88*, -89, -90. SAS, *Annual* Reports, 1994 and 1997.

Revenue Management[522]

ORD/PERMES

During the late 1980s and early 1990s, SAS aimed at building a global travel and traffic system in cooperation with all SAS Group units and several other airlines. Competition increased and SAS had to optimize even more effects of the businessman strategy. As a consequence, a new yield management system was developed to optimize the whole journey. It was called ORD (Origin Destination Movement Management System).[523] ORD covered not only the whole journey but also many more variables of an increasingly complex reality.

The philosophy of the system was developed during the TERESE project, because optimizing had to be coordinated with the routines of the reservations system.[524] ORD specifications were finished before TERESE closed down in 1991. Instead of TERESE, the new ORD yield management system of 1992-1993 was linked to RESAID and AMADEUS. ORD added two new facilities to LEVEL's previous forecasting and optimization services. One was an Early Warning System, a strategic decision support system that enabled management to react swiftly to unexpected changes in sales on forthcoming flights compared with the previous year's figures. Two was the origin and destination system covering the whole journey and not just two city pairs.

ORD was developed in cooperation with the American consulting firm Decision Focus Incorporated (DFI) and SAS Data. While SAS Data took care of computer operations, DFI supplied the expertise of programmers and analysts. DFI had specialized in developing revenue and yield management systems to airlines and as a non-airline firm, it represented a new software trend. ORD ran on a Unix machine that communicated with RESAID through vigorous lines of communication. ORD was a client/server system, having the RESAID mainframe system on one end and a logical system of mathematical and operations analysis on the other.

ORD controlled just 13 % of all SAS departures, while the rest were managed by LEVEL. ORD optimized only those flights with income potential (i.e., flights in great demand). The process went like this. When an employee at a travel agency called up an availability display to see if there were vacant seats on a particular flight, a request was sent to AMADEUS. AMADEUS knew that

---

522 Previously, Yield Management.
523 SDD, *Profil*, no. 3, 1992.
524 Interview: *Helge Rasmussen*.

the flight in question was controlled by the ORD system of SAS. AMADEUS then sent a request to RESAID. Having identified the route, it sent the request on to ORD. ORD handled the matter of whether there was a vacancy or not according to the parameters of the system. The reply was returned to RESAID and then to AMADEUS. This transaction to and fro took place at lightning speed (i.e., within 250 milli seconds).

During the first couple of years after its implementation, ORD was consolidated to include adaptation of new products and personnel training and worked in a satisfactory way. From the mid-1990s, new modules were added to optimize still more fields. This improved version of ORD was called PERMES.

In the early 1990s, Space Control bought a program called Prosam, showing how SAS was displayed by large distribution systems of the world.[525] The EU neutral screen display policy made this controlling system less important.

Revenue Information[526]

Follow-up Systems

Revenue Information's IMPALA IBM mainframe system was not fully implemented until 1992. IMPALA fed and processed SAS and IATA prorated information on interline passenger tickets. The IMPALA IMS database processed more than 2 million tickets every month and presented a general view of income and cost for each flight. Corporate management did not know what SAS earned before Revenue Information had prorated with other airlines. Several SAS functions and groups used revenue information for planning, too, including routes, sales and marketing, but also for operation purposes.

To speed up the frequency of income information, Statistical Passenger Information (SPI) was developed shortly after the final implementation of IMPALA.[527] SPI was a follow-up system with a graphic interface that made information access and presentation easier, but it was not a true c/s system. First, everything was calculated in IMPALA. Then, calculations were transferred to SPI, where sales department and yield management drew on the analytical material. SPI was online connected with several hundred data terminals through out the world deployed for input and output only, excluding local data processing.

---

525 SDD, *Profil*, no. 8, 1993.
526 Previously, Revenue Accounting. Renamed according to international terms.
527 SDD, *Profil*, no. 3, 4, 7, 1992. Interview: *Mogens Meisler*.

Client/Server Systems

Follow-up systems to the mainframe IMPALA for improved analysis and planning was one way to meet open competition. The new client/server technology enabled Revenue Information to go one step further in building a sophisticated superstructure to IMPALA. By way of a DB2 relational database on PCs, client/server systems were developed to increase flexibility and optimization of revenue.

In 1996, client/server plans turned into a project for developing a »Ticket Database«.[528] Instead of SPI on IMS, Revenue Information wanted to produce a flexible system in a graphic environment, based on DB2 and Windows, called the New SPI. IMPALA still formed the basis of client/server systems. IMPALA produced information that was let into the Ticket Database. From the Ticket Database, information was transferred to SPI, getting the same information as always. The Ticket Database and New SPI were developed during 1996-1998.

The purpose of the Ticket Database and New SPI was to create a real-time system. While SPI was loaded once every month, NEW SPI produced a halfway forecast to indicate the direction of development, enabling SAS to react more quickly to movements in the market.

---

528 Interview: *Mogens Meisler.*

IMPALA and Connecting Systems 1994

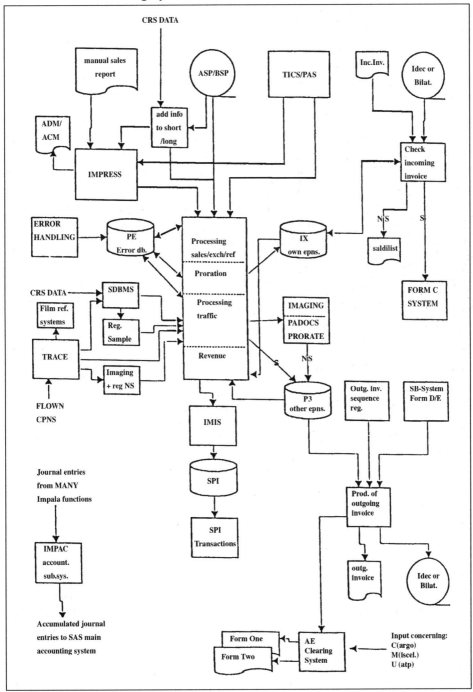

Source: SAS, Revenue Information, 1994.

Cargo

Client/Server Systems

During the 1980s, integrated forwarders and carriers had made deep inroads into SAS Cargo's classical markets of letters and small packets and reduced its Scandinavian market share significantly. Furthermore, in the Scandinavian market the SAS Jetpak door-to-door freight service was turned into an independent company in 1991. Competition continued to increase during the next decade.[529] The early 1990s crisis and radical steps for market adaptation made SAS Cargo a candidate for outsourcing. Reorganization in 1994 stopped such considerations, at least for some years. A process of upgrading started with SAS Cargo and was followed by cooperation with Star Alliance, especially with Lufthansa, the aim being to raise SAS' Scandinavian market share.

Unlike the passenger side, SAS Cargo struggled with the consequences of a globalized business, increasingly driven by large transnational corporations (TNC). Worldwide sophisticated logistics were needed to meet the demands of a new global division of labor, "just-in-time" stock management, and centralized warehousing. The amount of transported goods increased and moved products had to be documented, possibly stored, repacked or quality tested in transit. The whole operation must be handled at the time and prices agreed upon. Furthermore, customers had to be able to control a worldwide flow of components and products, enabling them to react swiftly to market changes. As a consequence, Cargo customers also demanded information from the transport link that might be used directly in their own environment. SAS Cargo and the SAS Data Cargo group would have to upgrade competence and capabilities considerably to live up to these challenges.

In 1991, the Gulf crisis compelled SAS Cargo to close down its plans for a new and comprehensive system of handling, revenue, and management. Then in 1992, SAS granted more than 20 million SEK to develop a number of client/server systems on top of its cargo mainframe handling system, CAREX/CARIN, and its revenue accounting system, CRAS. These systems were called LUCAS.

LUCAS contained a number of applications and as they were implemented, data could be transferred from the mainframe system to be processed locally.[530] Furthermore, the purpose of LUCAS was to draw functions from CAREX/CARIN and CRAS to client/server systems and then, to replace the old files-based mainframe system with a modern database. LUCAS client/server

---

529 SDD, *Profil*, no. 2, 1993. SAS, *Annual Reports*, 1990 to 1997.
530 SDD, *Profil*, no. 8, 1992, no. 2, 1993. SDS/SDN, *UPTIME*, no. 12, 1991. Interviews: *Niels Bloch, Jørgen Herz*.

systems included functions such as TradeVision (i.e., electronic relations with agents), airway bill issuance, paperless transportation, revenue accounting, administration package, and booking/space control.

Whereas the booking and space control system was not developed, some basic handling functions were automated and put on a c/s system with a graphic interface. That included Cargo Monitor, a distributed tool of analysis for cost-performance follow-up, terminal handling, sales follow-up and quality performance that made it possible to see the relationship between the various parts of the application. Cargo Monitor meant to give every station access to the information it »owned«, including lower levels of information. Cargo Monitor had a uniform display presentation.

A new revenue accounting system Cargo Revenue Information System (CRIS) was planned to replace CRAS processing of flown and sold information.[531] Finally, CRIS would be transformed to a modern database intended to include all handling and revenue information. During 1995 to 1996 however, the project foundered for various reasons, including lack of money and great problems in converting the file-based systems of CRAS and CAREX/CARIN to a common database.

Even though LUCAS did not succeed in its overall goals, it managed to introduce a number of handling and revenue accounting client/server systems. Furthermore, it established automatic integration with SAS systems, such as TPTS, PAH, TRAF, ORS, and GML, and by way of Tradevision electronic communications to agents.

During these years, SAS Cargo had no main supplier, being serviced by SDD, SDS, Enator, British Telecom and IDC.[532] Although, SDD operated its systems and together with SDS took part in developing the LUCAS c/s systems, the SDD cargo group never regained the position it had lost in the mid-1980s.

Third Generation System Plans

After long preparations and negotiations, SAS Cargo decided in 1996 to buy a standard Unix system from a firm called Syntegra. It intended to cover handling as well as revenue accounting and the system was to be adjusted to Cargo's own needs.[533] SDD and Unisys offered USAS Cargo, a system that Lufthansa Cargo had just bought. SAS Cargo preferred a non-airline system based on modern distributed technology, however, and wanted to take the great leap forward to a third generation Unix system. In 1998, the large cargo pro-

---

531 Interview: *Kjell Ivarsson.*
532 SDD, *Profil,* no. 8, 1992.
533 SAS Data, *Linje 1,* no. 8, 1996. Interviews: *Niels Bloch, Hans-Henrik Hedegaard.*

ject faulted, because Syntegra was unable to complete it. Moving from two different first generation core systems, CARIN/CAREX Unisys files system and CRAS IBM batch system, to a third generation distributed system turned out to be just as complex as experienced a decade previously.

Once more, SAS Cargo aimed too high when trying to take the great leap forward. As a result, SAS Cargo was left in a vacuum without any new core system. Viable options in this situation were to try again, either with a non-airline system, such as Syntegra, or with an airline cargo system, such as that of Unisys. SAS Cargo might also give up altogether to develop a new system on its own and join with other airlines of the Star Alliance, especially Lufthansa, in a joint project and system, even to the point of a business merger.

Yield Management

On the passenger side, yield management was an important part of the businessman's airline strategy. SAS Cargo never had such sophisticated tools, however. The cargo decline during the 1980s left plenty of room and little need for optimizing. Increased competition did produce some interest in yield management in the late 1980s, however.

The space control department began to practice manual optimizing on intercontinental routes, while on European and Scandinavian routes there were so many flights that there was always room for cargo.[534] Pricing cargo for intercontinental flights required knowledge of production costs, only. From 1993, cargo yield management was a department of its own. Recent plans for a new cargo system also included a subsystem for yield management. As these general plans were never fulfilled, yield management was still left without any computer system. Each flight was optimized on the basis of estimated booking forecasts according to experience, within the framework of capacity, prices, and allotments laid down by budget. Before departure, the cargo load was combined and packed in accordance with rules of balance and weight levels of passengers and luggage.

---

534 Interview: *Kim Christensen.*

Cargo LUCAS Information Flow 1994

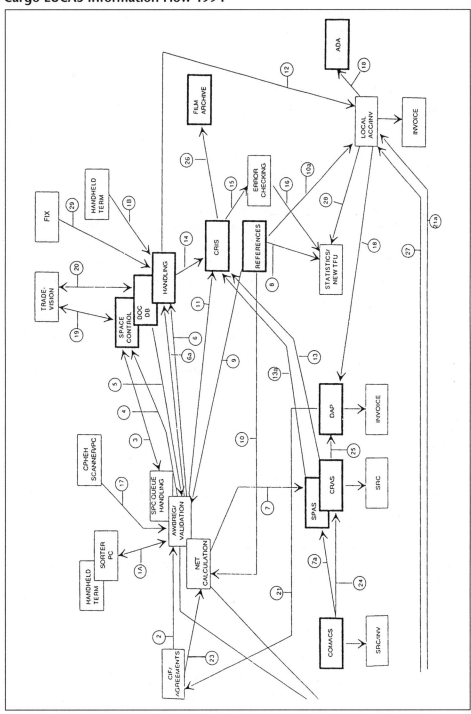

Source: SAS, Cargo.

Station

Client/Server Systems

Finally in 1992, Station implemented its second-generation check-in system, PCI, and load control system, PAH. At the same time, the Gulf War and open competition gave cost reductions first priority. Next, service was upgraded, including later on in 1997, the establishment of a new Traffic Execution Department to combine all resources that affected punctuality and other quality aspects of the daily traffic operations.[535] Automation and client/server solutions were essential parts of this change program.

From the early 1990s, Station Services Division (SSD; previously Traffic Services Division) worked on a big project to automate the passenger sales chain, managed by MAD and later on Information Systems Division.[536] This was the so-called ATB project (Automated Ticketing and Boarding). ATB was part of a grand project to obtain a 30 % productivity rise in station activities. This would require quite different ways of working. In particular, management hoped to reduce working group demarcations and increase flexibility in check-in and boarding areas.

In 1994, ATB tests started at Gothenborg, but it was not until 1997 that automats were generally introduced.[537] Many technical problems were linked to ATB that combined ticket and boarding card into one document on the basis of the PCI check-in systems. Via automat, a booking could be made and partial check-in accomplished. Having entered the card into an automat, passengers would be informed of their seat, gate, and time of flight departure. Arriving at the gate, the passenger ran the card through a gate-reader to gain access to the plane. When a passenger had used the automat, it was registered by the SAS check-in system and matched with luggage information. If the passenger did not board the plane the luggage was removed.

While working on the ATB project, SSD aimed at standardizing Scandinavian airport procedures according to SAS' 1994 reorganization.[538] Front line introduced graphical PC displays that made it much easier to operate systems and move personnel around according to peak demand. With SITA's international CUTE standard all airlines could enter their check-in software in only one terminal in airports throughout the world.

A new delay system, ED Delay, based on c/s technology was developed in

---

535 SAS, *Annual Report*, 1997.
536 SDS/SDN, *UPTIME*, no. 6, 1994. SAS Data, *Linje 1*, no. 2, 1994.
537 SAS Data, *Linje 1*, no. 11, 1996. Interviews: *Hannes Lebert, Poul Strand-Holm.*
538 SDD, *Profil*, no. 7, 1992. SAS Data, *Linje 1*, no. 2, 1994. Interview: *Hannes Lebert.*

the mid-1990s.[539] ED Delay used DB2, OS/2 and other IBM tools, including communication software. Being updated every 15 minutes, the ED Delay informed passengers on delays at CPH, ARL, and FBU. The system replaced manual reporting by station personnel.

Airports and airlines planned to introduce new luggage systems, based on bar coding, to upgrade security control.[540] Just like any other large airline, SAS had its own luggage tracing system, called BAS. In 1994, World Tracer, a worldwide SITA solution, replaced BAS.

Client/server systems were also introduced in work planning.[541] Each of the three Scandinavian capitals had separate station manning systems. In Copenhagen for example, a new SKIFT90 system was being prepared, based on American SABRE StaffPlan and StaffManager management systems, the so-called Production Planning and Resource Disposing System (PORS). StaffPlan handled production planning for 18 months, while StaffManager dealt with disposition on the very same day. It took years to develop, introduce, and integrate these staff manning systems, and they never materialized the way management intended. Unions and employees in the station field blocked radical changes in manning rules, such as going from high peak to low peak manning standards and to introducing flexible manning in check-in and boarding. Furthermore, ATB and distant electronic check-in created other unclarified manning problems in station. Benchmarking and upcoming independent industries, which were to match corporate functions, further reinforced pressure on station management and employees for more radical solutions to these problems. Global Star Alliance was another factor to be considered.

Back office introduced a c/s system to deal with division finance management, too.

By the late 1990s, a number of c/s systems had been built on top of the PCI and PAH mainframe systems, including back office management systems. The IMS hierarchical database was still not replaced by any relational database.

---

539 SDS/SDN, *UPTIME*, no. 19, 1993, no. 7, 1994.
540 SDD, *Profil* no. 5, 1994.
541 SAS Data, *Linje 1*, no. 1, 7, 1995. Interview: *Poul Strand-Holm.*

PAH and Integrated Systems 1994

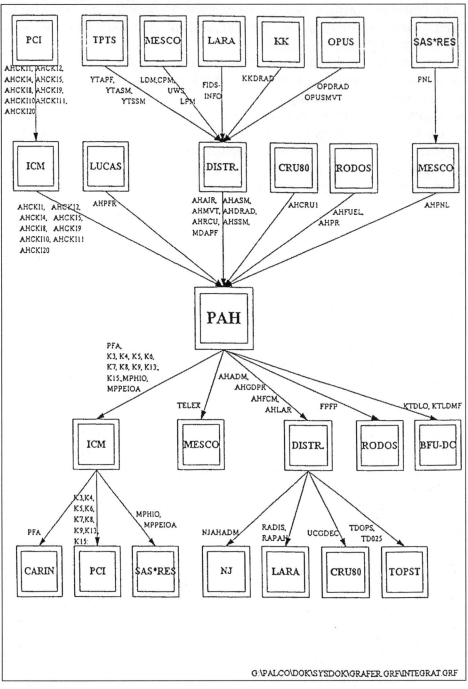

Source: SAS, Station.

Operation

Movement Control

Client/Server System

Shortly after the cut over to OPUS in 1988, the Movement Control Center (MCC) took an interest in a more dynamic graphical interface that was made possible by the PC revolution.[542] PCs with a small DOS program were purchased and by way of automatic updating, a dynamic interface was substituted for the static screen presentation. The new PC interface to OPUS was implemented in 1989-1990.

This PC dialog worked until the mid-1990s when OPUS was turned into a client/server system and the DB2 relational database management system replaced hierarchical IMS in OPUS. Functionalities were drawn out of the mainframe system, typically when obsolete, and replaced by a client/server system in all three Scandinavian capitals. Mainframe and client/server systems continuously communicated and updated each other. This OPUS 2000 project was carried out in 1994 and 1995.

Together with an external software firm, SAS Data Sweden redeveloped OPUS and the OPUS PC section to meet the growing demands of SAS' Movement Control Center's (MCC's) traffic surveillance and disposal system.[543] Traffic disposal could now be performed directly on graphic sling presentations, quickly doing re-disposal by mouse clicks on a PC. Re-disposals were then distributed to all functions and computer systems in SAS that were dependent on these revised aircraft disposition messages. Because SAS MCC was a decentralized function, established in CPH, FBU, and ARN, OPUS2000 was installed on at least three c/s systems, with the IBM mainframe as a super server to keep all MCCs updated and synchronized. Each local MCC had its own LAN, database server, a number of workstations, and communications with central OPUS. A new and forceful network was built to handle increased communications of this c/s system, based on Novell LAN and IBM Token Ring in local networks and a communication manager for communications between network and mainframe. From 1997 to 1998, MCC migrated to the new SAS communications standard, TCP/IP.

Flight Dispatch

In the 1990s, a c/s system was put on top of RODOS (Route Documentation System) that combined huge amounts of information to produce an optimized intercontinental route.[544]

---

542 Interview: *Bent Lund*. Formerly, Operations Control.
543 SDS/SDN, *UPTIME*, no. 8, 1994.
544 SDS/SDN, *UPTIME*, no. 1, 1994. SAS Data, *Linje 1*, no. 4, 1995.

Crew

Client/Server Systems

Crew planning covered the two operation fields Flight Deck and Cabin, through crew bases in the three Scandinavian capitals. Crew bases dealt with administration of check-in and checkout, ticket booking, leave, training, and so on.

Like all other SAS functions, crew planning had to raise its productivity and flexibility when open competition arrived. In 1991, the first OS/2 client/server systems were already developed for crew transport, hotel, and check-in.[545] In 1992, preparations started for a large project, called New Crew Planning (NCP).[546] NCP included various sub-projects for market adaptation, optimizing, legality, organization development, and the future infrastructure of the Operations Division.

NCP was a comprehensive and long-term project. In the short term, the computer part of NCP, called Crew Allocation Information System (CAIS), aimed at developing a client/server system with CRU80. During the following years a number of client/server systems were created. The first system was implemented in 1992 when data from CRU80 was transferred to a Unix server database for local processing. A local system with graphical tools reduced the cycle of crew planning from 24 to 9-12 weeks. Furthermore, the system could do simulation (i.e., it produced alternative proposals, rather than just one master plan and one schedule plan as in the old system).

The client/server system consisted of three modules. The pairing/master plan module was based on a program bought at Volvo Data for automatic pairing construction. Automatic Pairing Construction (APC) included a graphic display, known as Graphic Pairing Construction (GAC), and a legal component called Carmen Rule Construction (CRC). On the basis of the traffic program, the pairing module optimized crew planning automatically, replacing the old manual system.

For the schedule module, a similar combination of an automatic crew assigning system, Automatic Crew Assignment (ACA), and a graphic tool, Graphic Crew Assignment (GCA), was bought. Unlike the master module, ACA/GCA could not optimize, being a direct assignment system. The system replaced much of the manual scheduling, at first produced on large paper schedules, and later entered into the CRU80. The schedule system just automated the function and added extra new facilities.

Graphic tools improved connections between assignment and disposal.

---

545 SDD, *Profil* no. 8, 1991.
546 SDD, *Profil* no. 2, 3, 9, 1992. Interview: *Allan Sørensen*.

Whereas optimizing could be done in master planning or pairing, scheduling and disposal did not have these facilities. As a consequence, current traffic and crew changes kept on creating problems in traffic and planning.

Plans for a New Crew Planning System

Endeavors to reinforce total crew planning resulted in a change of organization in 1994-95, when the three dimensions of pairing, scheduling, and disposal were replaced by a combined master and schedule planning on the one hand and disposal on the other. Disposal was still allocated to Copenhagen, close to movement control, whereas all planning was concentrated in Stockholm. The reorganization was intended to integrate optimizing across the planning dimensions and avoid sub-optimizing. Simultaneously, a new crew planning system was being prepared.

The client/server system was just the first part of a larger project that would substitute a modern relational database system for CRU80. Instead of being dependent on applications, a new system should be based on objects that could be accessed from any system, including a new infrastructure.

Since 1993/94, Crew was preparing an NCP. Analyses were made and requirements described. Further project plans were postponed, however, and by the late 1990s, no decision had yet been made to start developing the new project.

Market developments pressed for new information systems facilities. To adapt to market demands, the traffic program was being changed more and more often and at still shorter notice, leaving no room for a three-month planning cycle. Shorter planning cycles and simulations of alternative solutions were introduced with the client/server system. With the parameter-managed legal part, the user could enter new rules, which would automatically become an integrated part of the system, and not having to wait for SAS Data to reprogram. As mentioned, this system halved planning time. Accordingly, what was needed was adaptation to changes and simulation of alternatives.

From the 1980s, increasing information requirements brought to light CRU80 limitations. If for example, information were needed on crewmembers with gaps in their working schedules who were therefore able to take more work without breaking the rules, the old system would require a long time to deliver a reply. That was why a new DB2 relational database management system should replace the old MVS/IMS system, avoiding the present tendency of sub-optimizing and being able to get quick access to current information.

A number of problems were to be taken care of through the new planning system. One issue was to ensure that a problem was solved on the basis of relevant preconditions. To do that, information on actions had to be stored and the order of priority currently updated, at the same time the system had to wait to solve a problem to the latest possible moment. In the meantime, so many things might have happened, rendering superfluous or having changed the preconditions of the original event. All events should be put into a Unix box with an optimizing module that was able to sort and send information to the person handling the problem.

In the long term, the new crew planning system should be integrated with OPUS for flight disposal. Such integration could, in the case of delays, connect crew with a plane. Decision support systems would produce alternative proposals, including consequence calculations. If for instance Oslo closed for some hours because of fog, no planning tool was available that produced scenarios with calculated consequences for closing for 1 or 2 hours, or more. Often such calculations were done manually, and it took time before plane and crew could be matched. Optimizing to meet increased demands for flexibility was the goal of these endeavors.

Another crew dimensioning problem was caused by the fact that flying peaked at early and late hours of the day, with low loads in between where crew often did not do anything. Traditionally, crew was dimensioned according to peaks, but the growing competition of the 1990s pressed for a better use of resources during the day. Collective agreements stuck to peak manning rules, however. Furthermore, a general airlines policy of moving passengers around to reduce the level of manning was stopped by an EU manning system based on the number of seats in a plane, and not the number of passengers. Thus, organizational barriers accumulated.

Lack of economic consequence calculations in the existing system caused a third problem. Planners at schedule and disposal levels could not see the costs of an alternative plan. The new system intended to include this facility. To do so would require a relational database, because IMS did not produce alternative management reports that provided a different view of a situation.

The increasing speed of rule changes caused a huge backlog in the legality section of CRU80 because all legalities had to be entered whenever there was a change of rules. A future legality infrastructure was looked for that integrated all three planning dimensions in one system. In the existing system for instance, it took half a year before rules were changed according to new collective agreements. In a future legality module, changes would only have to be entered once, automatically updating all other systems.

Plans for NCP were not just hindered by the existence of different technology platforms. SAS crew worked on the basis of a comprehensive set of rules and agreements within three countries. Although the new SAS organization of 1994 aimed at creating Scandinavian units, crew remained an obstacle to intentions of achieving an optimized flow of work and information. American inspired systems, such as individual preferential bidding, collided with Scandinavian ways of collective agreements. Whereas managers could plan for better IT tools, they had no success in changing principles of crew manning and disposal. This inherited conflict might be the reason why a new crew planning system still remained unsettled by the late 1990s.

Technical

Distributed and C/S Systems

Since the mid-1980s, Technical Division (TD) was gradually being reduced. Parts of heavy maintenance were outsourced because new planes required less maintenance, and an increasingly rationalized working process cut costs and personnel. No fundamental change took place in TD's core MOPS mainframe system.[547]

During the first half of the 1990s, TD was pressed even harder by corporate management to reduce costs and upgrade to the economic standards of the market by benchmarking, and a BPR process was initiated to streamline the flow of work and information through TD workshops.[548]

From the mid-1990s and just like the rest of SAS, TD was implementing a process-oriented strategy across all levels and structures of planning and production to improve productivity on the basis of SAS customer demands. During the 1990s, a move towards centralized management and horizontal working processes replaced traditional decentralized and vertical structures.

Since the mid-1990s, TD management had been working on the sensitive problem of softening the collective agreements to improve flexibility and productivity. Although some success was achieved in overcoming old barriers of working group demarcations and principles of peak manning, there was still some way to go by the end of the millennium.

While MOPS remained the IT foundation of TD, new technologies made it possible to add facilities to the mainframe systems from the mid-1980s. The PC paved the way for automation of documentary work (i.e., technical documents and working cards for individual jobs), the so-called Technical Documentation (TEDOC), and Operations Documentation (OPDOC). During the late 1980s and early 1990s other distributed systems spread throughout the workshop bases. As a consequence of local developments, many different technical standards for PCs and local networks were introduced. The PC-systems just worked as terminal systems, improved by a graphical interface.

---

547 SAS, *Information Technology Applications in Aircraft Maintenance & Engineering*, 1991.
548 Interviews: *John Dueholm, Mindor Lundström*.

All subsystems of MOPS – RELS, LIPS, BOWAC, and so on – were given graphic interfaces on PCs, to a certain degree tailored to their respective fields.[549] A »Harmony« system was developed for planning aircraft checks. MOPS user manuals were converted to a DB2 database and maintained by PC Word. Line Maintenance worked with systems on three different machines, IBM, Unisys, and Tandem. By way of a standard tool, Easel, the three systems MOPS (IBM), MATS (Unisys), MECS (Tandem) were connected. A few additional c/s were added to improve planning and optimization. Those included a system to show how many delays were caused by technical problems and night-job planning at the Arlanda workshop, and a system for recording flight traffic irregularities and its consequences for technical maintenance planning.

Since the mid-1990s, management had worked on tidying up the technological mess and focusing on one standard, namely Windows. A process started to replace terminals with intelligent workstations. Fundamentally, information work in the workshops did not change, however, compared with the terminal-structure of the l970s and 1980s. The new PCs with graphic interfaces did lighten input and output jobs, but they functioned as dedicated terminals. Client/server systems were created for planning of the workshop jobs, only. Although client/server systems were deployed in technical maintenance planning, optimized planning was not started until the late 1990s, based on Microsoft Windows and NT. Unfinished plans circulated throughout the 1990s to automate connections with the main suppliers, Boeing and McDonnell Douglas (now merged).

By the late 1990s, MOPS still made up the basis of technical maintenance. Having been prepared for the year 2000, no new system was considered as a substitute for MOPS.[550]

MOVEX

Plans for developing MATS 2 collapsed during the Gulf Crisis in 1991. In 1993, tenders were invited for a new material planning system. The Swedish firm Intensia was contracted to produce the system, under the very noses of SAS Data. SAS Data proposed a system developed by Unisys/Iberia, but TD wanted a non-airline system (i.e., a standard system that had proved itself in different businesses). TD chose a system called MOVEX, based on the IBM AS/400 technology. SAS Data was to operate the system.[551]

MOVEX was implemented in 1996 having been much modified to adapt

---

549 SDS/SDN, *UPTIME*, no. 21, 1991, no. 1, 1993. SAS Data, *Linje 1*, no. 1- 2, 1995.
     Interview: *Mindor Lundström.*
550 Interview: *Mindor Lundström.*
551 SAS Data, *Linje 1*, no. 1, 3, 10, 1996. Interview: *John Dueholm.*

to the demands of SAS. Using the AS/400, terminals were replaced with true PCs. Contrary to its predecessor MATS, MOVEX included an optimizing function and was integrated with MOPS.

Finance[552]

Client/Server Systems

By the early 1990s, the new mainframe accounting system, GLM, had finally replaced its old predecessor. At the same time, increased pressure for financial control to keep down costs and to adapt to an environment of open competition called for upgraded management and IT tools. As a result, a new and stronger staff unit, Corporate Finance and Control (CFC), was formed with the SAS reorganization in 1994.[553]

While GLM was being stabilized on corporate and divisional levels, a new PC consolidating or management system, Hyperion, was being prepared to replace terminal Business Manager. Implemented in 1995, Hyperion was a client/server system built on top of the GLM mainframe system. It used Windows for client interface, and data processing from GLM was much improved and speedier. Furthermore, PCs were connected in LANs, so that more people were able to work with the same data at the same time. Before being sent to corporate Hyperion, data were consolidated at divisional level. Divisions planned to introduce Hyperion, too, being urged to concentrate on one standard, and such systems were gradually being implemented from 1995.

A Third Generation System

In 1997, Corporate Finance & Control (CFC) decided to replace GLM and its many connected systems with a modern corporate-wide standard system based on a relational database. While Human Resources at the same time chose a SAP system, CFC decided upon Oracle Financials' application and database on a Unix server with a Windows interface. The new system was being implemented during 1998-99.[554]

SAS' Purchase Statistics System, PUSS, was converted to an Oracle database and to Unix. At the same time, the old administration system for foreign stations, Commercial Accounting or COMACS, was phased out and replaced by Oracle.[555]

---

552 Previously, Accounting.
553 Interviews: *Ulla Edlund, John Schmidt-Hansen.*
554 Interview: *John Schmidt-Hansen.*
555 SAS Data, *Linje 1,* no. 4 and 10, 1996.

Based on Windows and Unix, SAS Data used a SCALA economy system in three versions. When SAS Data merged in 1997, SCALA was made into one system, too.[556]

Personnel

Client/Server System

From the early 1990s, pressure increased on salary systems. The number and complexity of rules and laws kept on growing, as did SAS personnel connections with authorities, banks, and insurance companies. Second generation SAS information systems of the 1980s extended internal automation of functions and external integration with other systems.

Except for Travel Order, few client/server systems for personnel were introduced for front line and back office before the mid-1990s.[557] Travel Order enabled personnel to do several transactions themselves, such as booking and ticketing leisure travels. The Travel Order system was developed on DB2, first in Sweden, and then in an adopted form in Norway and Denmark.

A Third Generation System

Large programs of rationalization and reorganization since the early 1990s had brought to light the information shortcomings of existing systems. In particular, the intentions of the 1994 SAS reorganization to create a true Scandinavian organization and introduce a personnel policy for upgraded flexibility, time limited employment, and personnel development, made these deficiencies apparent.

In 1994, the first corporate personnel staff was formed, Human Resources. Right away, the new Human Resources management formed a project group to prepare a common Scandinavian information system for salary and administration, plans that were never fulfilled during the existing PERS/PINS system.[558] First, the project group needed to produce a common platform of requirements and search the market for a standard system to be bought, based on one modern relational database and c/s technology.

Human Resources wanted a common database and a uniform information structure that would create a flexible system giving quick access to information and information processing for management purposes. Management information was not easily obtained in existing systems. For instance, it was difficult to know the actual number of personnel in SAS, even within the in-

---

556 SAS Data, *Linje 1*, no. 4, 1994, no. 1, 1995, no. 1, 1997.
557 SDS/SDN, *UPTIME*, no. 21, 1991. SDD, *Profil*, no. 4, 1992. Interview: *Lars Nilsson*.
558 Interviews: *Lars Nilsson, John Schmidt-Hansen*.

dividual area. Total integration of the three regional systems was not intended in the new system, however, because it would be too complex to integrate three different national systems. A platform was to be made for a gradual replacement of the various parts of the old systems, too.

Just like with PERS/PINS 15 years earlier, a process of agreeing on common data objects and functions was started and just like then, national differences caused the project to be drawn out. The main problem was to try to make three different national complexes of laws and rules (i.e., the management part and logic of the system), uniform. Searching the market, the leading packaged software vendor, SAP, was chosen to deliver its HR module.

From the mid-1990s, a project group had been working on pre-studies of phase one (i.e., standardizing all concepts and objects of personnel systems to adapt to SAP). Standardizing was a time-consuming process, probably continuing for years. Phase one included prototyping (i.e., making dialog models of each function). Ernst & Young did this job, with SAS Data as a sub-supplier.

In 1997, it was decided to start phase two, which would remake all PERS systems, including interfaces, and convert them to SAP. While working to standardize objects, HR management decided to start a parallel SAP converting process, both planned to end in the year 2000. Many unforeseen problems may postpone that plan, however, as defining the data basis made slow progress. The new system would have an 80 % uniform core and the rest would be left for national adoptions.

Unlike PERS/PINS, SAP was a true personnel system. It covered all the personnel functions, such as time registration, time scheduling, training administration, and workflow (i.e., any vital aspect of the labor process). SAP integrated all modules in a common database, including a graphic interface.

Still for reasons of organization and history much personnel information on collective agreements, training, and so forth, remained at divisional level. These included station, crew, and maintenance. Only a distant future might see an integration of all these personnel systems.

Other Systems

Besides central systems, several other systems were used for back office,[559] domestic,[560] and subsidiaries,[561] during the 1990s.

---

559 Since the mid-1980s, PC word and calculation packages gradually spread in back office activities. Since the early 1990s, an expanded market has made SAS turn completely to Windows-based office packages, including new products such as e-mail. LAN technology developed, too, benefiting from common printers etc. (SDS/SDN, *UPTIME*, no. 1 and 18, 1993). Since the mid-1990s, a highly automated, integrated and standardized office environment emerged within the new SAS communications infrastructure, based on Microsoft Windows products and in addition, Lotus Notes for document handling and Netscape for Internet browsing (SAS Data, *Linje 1*, no. 1, 2, 3, 8, 1995, no. 10 and 11, 1996). At management level, all divisions and staff units introduced c/s systems for control and follow-up.

560 In addition to central SAS systems, a number of local systems emerged for domestic traffic. The largest SAS market, SAS Sweden, was most sophisticated in that respect. Several Tandem based systems were taken over from Linjeflyg in 1992 and later on converted to c/s systems with modern graphic interfaces, including information on station, timetables, passenger numbers, transfer, traffic, luggage, and personnel (SAS Data, *Linje 1*, no. 4, 1997).

561 SAS subsidiaries, such as SAS Commuter, SAS Trading, and SAS International Hotels had IT departments and systems of their own but used SAS Data for operation and communication (except Commuter). Outsourced units including Diners, Leisure, and Service Partner had their own IT departments and systems, too, until integrated into other large corporations (SDS/SDN, *UPTIME*, no. 8, 1988, no. 8, 1994. SDD, *Profil*, no. 4 and 5, 1992. SAS, *Annual Report*, 1997).

IT Paradigms of C/S and Emerging Web

The second paradigm was that of networked open client/server systems. In this paradigm, computer systems included large numbers of computers sharing resources and cooperatively processing data over standardized networks. Client/server systems gave managers and other users access to information and technology of the corporation.

The client/server paradigm dominated the 1990s, within the framework of an open and globalized economy. SAS wanted to create a profitable business, including every flight and link of the organization. Internal reorganization and global alliances were introduced to make that come true. Whereas traditional rationalization focused on internal cost cutting within a bureaucratic organization, the efforts of the 1990s aimed at breaking down the bureaucracy of SAS and introducing a different kind of organization. With cross-functional process innovation of the organization and its IT and with strategic management supported by a new and open IT infrastructure, management looked for radical increases in productivity and adaptability. That implied a true process of reorganization.

Contrary to previous cost-cutting goals, benchmarking methods were introduced to make sure that all activities of SAS lived up to the best standards in the market. When SAS changed its strategy from the travel chain concept to core business, it resorted to outsourcing of non-strategic parts of the organization, too. At the same time, SAS moved from a highly decentralized organization to an increasingly centralized organization on the strategic level. Consolidation and competence upgrading had top priority and were preferred to outsourcing in order to make SAS a more integrated and competent organization.

Cross-functional systems, such as automatic ticketing and boarding and Flight Follow-Up, were introduced to increase productivity as well as revenue. The many c/s systems for operation, planning, and follow-up had the same goals. In general, the new IT infrastructure was intended to create a foundation for improved integration, automation, optimization, and revenue. Customer relations were increasingly automated and oriented towards direct sales. New automated services were intended to individualize choices of air travel, too. The Columbus database and EuroBonus loyalty program created stronger links to a huge number of frequent passengers. Internally, reorganization and IT developments aimed at giving corporate management an increasing grasp of the organization, including much improved tools for follow-up and market adaptation.

In this way, control of internal and external information processing of the organization moved upwards towards the level of strategic management, improving its capability for competing in a rapidly changing economic environment. The transformation of the organization and its IT was a revolutionary process in its intentions but in practice, mostly a gradual process of innovation, based on learning and often troublesome transformation of deeply rooted structures and mentalities.

From the mid-1990s, electronic links were increasingly built between airlines of the global Star Alliance, covering market relations, such as traffic and frequent flyer programs. Operative systems relations would most likely follow in the near future, and perhaps merger at lower levels.

By the late 1990s, a third paradigm was emerging to replace the second paradigm of networked open client/server systems, namely that of the ubiquitous information systems of the Internet and its Web. Since 1998, all SAS communications were based on the Internet protocol, and SAS determinedly targeted this technology for commercial purposes, as did most corporations of the world. The Web implied increased access to information and knowledge, use of virtual applications and organization, and in particular changed external relations. From the late 1990s, SAS started to build direct customer links via the Internet, probably to be followed by Star Alliance relationships. Still, SAS had a long way to go to be a true knowledge and virtual organization.

CONCLUSIONS

The present study examines the changing relationship between business and IT within the SAS corporation. It is a business history, focusing on the development and importance of IT since the late 1950s. During these four decades, modern business, including IT-industries and the application of information systems, changed and expanded in revolutionary ways. The economic and IT environment on which SAS was dependent is established. Analytical and theoretical gains from history and the social sciences are merged into a historical and theoretical approach to the study of firms and their application of IT.

Airlines follow the trend of economic growth and trade on the one hand, and on the other hand, they work as an enabler of industrial development. Western economies expanded enormously from the 1950s to the early 1970s. These golden years of growth and prosperity were the founding era of modern airlines, including traffic, technology, and organization. The recession of the 1970s and early 1980s compelled airlines to reorganize and prepare for a world of increased competition and global reach. The moderate economic growth of the 1980s saw the start of these trends, with a complete breakthrough in the expanding 1990s in a way that has revolutionized modern business.

As the speed and scope of industrialization increased, so did the application of computer and communications technology. IT, as these combined computer and communications technologies are called, worked to enable economies and corporations to expand continuously. An IT industry emerged to serve and fuel these new demands for information processing.

The 1950s to 1970s

While the 1950s, 1960, and 1970s were the founding decades of airlines and IT they also ended a business era. Since the end of the 19th century, mass-producing, and multi-unit corporations had dominated the industrial world. Mass-production was based on the idea that increases in productivity depended on increasing division of labor according to the potentials of the market. Standardization and specialized mechanization pushed productivity further ahead, reaching its climax with the assembly line of Ford.

The SAS organization and business expanded and worked within this Fordist environment. The main tool for increased mass-production was investments in new aircraft technology. During the three decades of the 1950s, 1960s, and 1970s, SAS invested in two generations of propeller and two generations of jet planes. Soon, computers were needed to make this machine-like organization run in an efficient way.

By the late 1950s, SAS suffered from serious transaction problems, as did all leading airlines. The arrival of jet planes made this looming transaction crisis even deeper. Problems were most clearly felt in the reservation system that made up the lifeline of airlines. Computer reservation systems became the answer to this bottleneck of information and reduced income.

Through three expanded versions, computer reservations and check-in systems were built from the late 1950s to the late 1970s, and combined with SAS' telecommunications system that was also expanded continuously. The reservations system included availability in the first stage, added booking in the next stage, and covered passenger name recording, ticketing, and accounting recording in the final stage. To make and handle computer systems, a separate data processing department called Data Services, was organized during the 1960s. Several hundreds computer professionals were organized in subfunctions of computer operations, programming and systems development, and communications.

Around the core technology of reservations system, computer applications were developed during the 1970s for all major functions of SAS. That included planning and operation of timetable, passenger reservation, check-in, operations control, revenue accounting, cargo, crew, technical maintenance and materiel supply, accounting and salaries. Far from all activities were automated, and IT-supported planning was limited to tactical levels of the timetable, crew, and maintenance. All these first generation systems were file-based, except for maintenance, and they were mainly operative in their focus, according to the predominant technology of the time. Links were built between the systems for the continuous transfer of information, too.

The computer professionals of SAS developed all systems internally. Systems were based on a certain method of development and organized in ad hoc projects. IT vendors delivered only hardware and systems software, including operating systems. Two IT vendors completely dominated the airlines industry from the 1960s, namely IBM and Unisys (originally called Univac). They even marketed standardized systems of reservations and cargo, based on systems developed in one or more airlines. Centrally operated mainframes were the technology of the day.

During the 1970s, Data Services was organized in areas, corresponding to the main functions of SAS. This alignment of computer and user departments did not create much cooperation between the two parties. On the contrary, the computer professionals of Data Services came to monopolize computer knowledge, estranging users from centrally operated and developed computer systems. The technical knowledge needed to handle computers was so demanding that only experts could do it. Often SAS was short of qualified computer people, as were other large organizations of the day. As a result, a very powerful and self-assured culture developed within the group of computer professionals concentrated to the Copenhagen center.

The prime mover of computer applications at SAS was the continuous fight to remain profitable, pressed by rising costs on the one hand and relatively falling prices on the other. SAS also had to expand computer applications and capacity to handle the increasing volume and speed of information transactions, particularly in reservations. Finally, as all other leading airlines introduced and developed computer applications, SAS had to follow suit. Primarily, computer applications were introduced and expanded to replace employees and thereby increase productivity. As a consequence, SAS could expand its activities with almost the same number of employees during the 1960s and 1970s.

The general economic crisis of the 1970s gradually undermined the profitability of SAS, and other leading airlines, as prices of fuel, wages, and duties went sky high. A general crisis by the late 1970s resulted in a deficit for SAS and all other airlines, too. Radical changes had to be made.

The 1980s

The breakthrough of economic recession in the West during the 1970s, while Japanese corporations successfully conquered large portions of Western markets, was the beginning of the end of Fordism. Japan's success was based on a more productive way of organizing business that was developed while transferring American technology to Japan during the 1950s and 1960s. Eventually, Western corporations introduced this new model of business to regain their lost competitiveness.

Fordism was so deeply rooted in western economies and thinking that it took years before a radical restructuring of business had been carried out, however. The main problem was lack of competitiveness. Western corporations fell short of Japanese productivity, and lacked flexibility towards changing market conditions. Finally, government regulations and protectionism hampered international trade. These structural problems were only gradually understood. Immediately, it was obvious to Western management that productivity had to be raised, and the computer was the only tool around that promised such improvement.

As a consequence, computer technology was elevated to being of the utmost strategic importance during the 1980s. Billions of dollars were invested to automate manufacturing, design, and administrative functions still done manually or by less sophisticated IT. At the same time, corporations began to pay more attention to markets, compelled by Japanese success and Western failure. Gradually, the supply-driven economy of mass-producing Fordism was replaced by an increased market orientation. Computer technology was one answer in order to raise productivity. Increased market awareness was another answer, namely to increase revenue. Still to their astonishment, Western corporations found themselves continuously surpassed by Japanese corporations, during the 1980s.

SAS was no exception to this development. SAS chose a solution that was even more radical than other companies, becoming a kind of conceptual leader during the early 1980s. By 1981, SAS was transformed into a market-driven organization focusing on one large group of passengers, namely the frequent-traveling and full-price-paying businessman. The Businessman's Airline strategy meant to increase revenue by transporting a greater share of Scandinavian businessmen by air. As Europe was still a regulated area of air traffic and most Scandinavian businessmen moved within this part of the world, SAS concentrated on European passenger traffic. Intercontinental and cargo traffic that used to dominate was given less attention.

Furthermore, investments in new aircraft technology were no longer of prime importance. SAS wanted to produce service to businessmen, not technology. A satisfied customer was the most valuable asset, not the latest aircraft technology. A decentralized unit of results was the leading SAS management principle, distinguishing between profit-based customer departments and cost-based production departments of the organization. Production departments produced services for customer-oriented departments.

The whole SAS organization was reorganized to serve the needs of the businessman. Market orientation towards this segment included IT and the data department of SAS. SAS was further divisionalized according to functional principles, and the data department was turned into a division called SAS Data. Furthermore, a strategic reorientation of SAS Data and SAS was introduced. SAS Data had to adapt to the new business strategy and in general, consider itself a deliverer of computer services to the divisions of SAS. Management of divisions and business considerations should be the driving force of IT, rather than matters of technology.

The market strategy was successful and SAS became a very profitable business during the 1980s. Making the deep-rooted Fordist bureaucracy market-oriented turned out to be a very difficult task, however. Economic success did not make such change easier and furthermore, divisions were completely estranged from a strategy that made them the driving force of IT development. For two decades, SAS Data had monopolized the IT knowledge at SAS. Small groups of computer people had emerged throughout the departments and divisions of SAS, but generally there was little IT competence in user organizations.

Accordingly, not much changed in practice. During the 1980s, a second generation of computer applications was developed to automate most operative activities and tactical planning, including highly increased levels of technical, social, and economic rules of business. These systems were built around database management systems that also allowed increased management decision support. Applications were still developed in-house and on mainframe computers. SAS was more than ever driven by mainframe applications developed by in-house computer professionals. Increased automation was the viable option for SAS, as it was for all other Western corporations, in order to increase productivity and handle information at growing volumes and speed.

Since the mid-1980s, SAS had upgraded its business and IT strategy to meet the growing competition in the airlines industry. The businessman's airline strategy was extended to include the SAS Group of many affiliated travel companies. The strategy of business-driven IT was determinedly enforced during the late 1980s. SAS invested more than ever in IT, including an improved reservation and distribution system to meet coming open competition. In the development of new IT applications, market conditions were introduced to make SAS Data compete with other service vendors. This boded future radical changes.

Since the late 1970s, thousands of terminals had spread throughout the SAS organization to ensure direct information entering and presentation relating to the large mainframe systems. Furthermore, it brought daily work and operative personnel in contact with distant computer systems. Rapid diffusion of terminals created an emerging appetite for user computing. The spread of PCs from the early 1980s only wetted this appetite for hands-on computing. During the 1980s, PCs spread in their hundreds at SAS and gave users knowledge of the potentials of distributed computing. PCs did not mean much within the world of applications, however, because they lacked capacity and links to the mainframe databases. Only word processing spread to a considerable degree, because it applied for stand-alone software.

What the PCs and other IT developments did was to cherish visions of a reformed future that might bring back economic growth and improved competitiveness to the Western world. Not until the late 1980s, did those visions become part of a new reality. By then, corporate management decided to carry out radical changes in business organization and to enforce the strategy of business-driven IT. This deeply influenced SAS Data, which was turned into three national computer business units and compelled to learn to live on the premises of the market.

The 1990s

By 1990, SAS had learned, as in many other Western corporations, that cost reductions and big computer investments were not enough to be competitive. A new world-economy was emerging, and more radical measures had to be taken to survive in an approaching situation of open competition.

The new world-economy that broke through by the early 1990s built on two pillars. One was a qualitative move towards international production and globalized conditions of business. Corporations began determinedly to reorganize their activities along global lines. Governmental policies transformed to fuel a process of global liberalization, replacing traditional protectionism. As a consequence, competition increased rapidly, and firms had to concentrate on their core competence and business and leave a growing number of secondary activities to the market. While globalization worked to widen industrialization it also caused a deepening of industrialization. As a result, new, reorganized and expanding global industries and firms emerged to cover this growing market of former bureaucratic activities.

Two, the IT industry or industries went through a revolutionary change and expansion. Chip technology escalated and paved the way for computing practically any kind of information. Networking developed to produce an electronic infrastructure, fuelled by the breakthrough of the Internet since the mid-1990s. A rapidly expanding packaged software industry emerged to cover the growing demands of client/server software, including applications and system software. The 9/10 of the computer applications iceberg that used to be developed in-house became visible and commercialized. Demands for reorganized businesses along global and flexible lines created huge markets for business services, including systems integration and outsourcing. Generally, the IT client/server and networking revolution paved the way for globalized business and an IT industry of huge dimensions. By the late 1990s, an even greater revolution may be on its way, as the Internet and a profound process of computerizing of most social activities prepare to meet in an electronic and virtual reality.

To SAS these new emerging realities of business and IT became relevant when the Gulf War of 1990-1991 made visible the need to restructure the Fordist organization of the past. In the first place, SAS had to cut costs drastically to adapt to a situation of halved traffic. Next, so-called client/server systems were introduced, particularly in market-oriented parts of SAS. Client/server systems were packaged software purchased in the market, put on top of the mainframe databases. This software took data from the mainframe systems to be processed on the PC with relational database management systems used for improved planning and management follow-up. As a consequence, time of planning and reactions to market changes were much reduced. Needs for still faster improvement of productivity and adaptation to market changes put an increasing pressure on IT operation and development. In large numbers, client/server systems moved in to make such improvements feasible. They changed the relationship between IT and business and created what might be labeled a client/server IT paradigm of the 1990s.

Client/server systems were part of a general reorganization process. During the first half of the 1990s, market-related activities and systems were being increasingly automated and horizontally integrated. This business process engineering (BPR) approach had yet another and important additional characteristic. Rationalization was market-driven. Unless internal activities created value for customers and/or worked according to the best standards in the competitive field of SAS, they were met with the alternative, either to comply with these demands or to be outsourced for a destiny in the marketplace.

This was a head-on attack on Fordist structures of organization. BPR dominated the activities of the first half of the 1990s. As a consequence of this upgraded organization, SAS reorganized in 1994 to concentrate on its core activities and increasingly, along Scandinavian lines. Management was upgraded, simultaneously. The main goal was to create a flexible organization working at radically increased levels of productivity and adaptability.

The reorganization of 1994 was revolutionary in another sense, too. Finally, management broke with its Scandinavian regional organization. The need to upgrade core competence required a final break with the historic regions. Upgraded strategic management at one end was met with local responsibility for results at the other end. Carrying on this process of transformation during the 1990s, SAS had to overcome the extra problem of having three different national structures of organization and legal systems.

IT was a vital tool of the cross-organizational automation and market-oriented products development. As a consequence, the three national IT business units were once more closely tied to SAS with the 1994 reorganization. Principles of account management were introduced to create a close strategic alignment of IT and airline. By 1997, the three IT units merged into one unit, still a separate subsidiary. Determinedly, IT was made an integrated part of strategic management and systems.

Since the mid-1990s, SAS focused on revenue-gaining activities and process innovation throughout the organization to create horizontal flows of work and information. The process innovation approach was intended to make the radical restructuring of BPR into a permanent and deepening process of change. Externally, SAS became part of the global Star Alliance. As merger was not an option of the time, only alliances allowed for open global competition.

Electronic relations between SAS and customers opened for quite new developments, reaching new dimensions with the arrival of the Internet. The Internet created an electronic infrastructure of open standards. Reservation, ticketing, check-in, and boarding headed for customer automation, including IT facilities in airport and on board. To meet the new demands of open competition and communication, SAS and SAS Data had worked since the early 1990s to turn the proprietary communication system into a system of open standards. This was achieved gradually from the mid-1990s, reaching a peak by the late 1990s when it was moved onto the Internet standard.

By the late 1990s, SAS Data was still closely related to SAS, and SAS was more than ever dependent on its large database systems and communications. SAS worked to integrate and upgrade its IT and business competence, while still being dependent on its large legacy systems. Some systems were being transformed into a new and third generation of systems, while others were renewed by way of client/server systems.

By the turn of the millennium, a knowledge approach to internal and external loads of data might be dimly seen by SAS. To carry out such a perspective was not just a matter of management decision. The reorganization of the early 1990s and a focus on process organization and core competence since the mid-1990s had made it clear that radical changes in the SAS organization would have to be a general and common learning process. Management, employees, IT, embedded knowledge, and cultures had to be upgraded to rising levels of competence and integration.

By the late 1990s, barriers of legacy systems and organization still slowed down this transformation process, however. Increasingly competitive global business and IT, including Star Alliance, put an ever-greater pressure on SAS. Core competence and business focus on one hand and on the other hand, maturing industries for outsourcing activities moved SAS management closer to taking measures of a profound nature in order to remain a competitive business in the long run. Radical restructuring may be just around the corner and pressures on legacy barriers will most likely intensify.

Dansk Resumé

Afhandlingen undersøger udviklingen i samspillet mellem virksomheden Scandinavian Airlines (SAS) og dens brug af informations teknologi (IT) i perioden fra 1950'erne til slutningen af 1990'erne. Hovedvægten ligger på belysningen af den informations teknologiske udvikling.

Fremstillingen bygger på et større materiale i form af arkivalier og andet internt materiale, trykte beretninger og talrige interviews af ledere fra alle SAS's og SAS Data's hovedfunktioner samt en hel del tidligere ledere. Dertil kommer den relevante teoretiske og historiske litteratur.

Redegørelsen for den historiske udvikling af firmaet SAS og dets brug af IT er den første grundlæggende undersøgelse af sin art. Endvidere skildrer afhandlingen denne problemstilling i sammenhæng med de samfundsforhold, som er bestemmende for udviklingen, og som SAS spiller direkte sammen med. Det drejer sig om følgende forhold: 1. Den generelle økonomiske udvikling i verden i perioden, 2. Den globale udvikling af luftfartsindustrien, og 3. Den globale udvikling af IT-industrien og dens anvendelse i forretningslivet.

Til grund for den historiske undersøgelse er den relevante samfundsvidenskabelige og historiske teoridannelse søgt integreret til et samlet perspektiv på den valgte problemstilling. Der er i både teori og analyse lagt vægt på at opnå en helhedsforståelse.

Informations teknologien opfattes på denne baggrund som en teknologi, der er dybt integreret i forretningslivet og dets organisationer. IT er bærer af den information eller viden, som ligger til grund for de økonomiske aktiviteter i virksomheden og i virksomhedens forhold til omverdenen. IT adskiller sig fra alle tidligere ikke-digitale teknologier ved ikke fysisk at afspejle, men ved logisk at repræsentere informationen om den samfundsmæssige virkelighed. Det gør IT til en generel teknologi, der kan anvendes i alle sammenhænge, hvor den samfundsmæssige information er digitaliseret.

Den historiske udvikling præges af to dominerende forretningsmodeller med en overgangsperiode i 1980'erne. Udgangspunktet er den måde arbejdsprocessen er organiseret på. Den første industrielle model, som har sin rod i det andet industrielle gennembrud omkring 1900, præger de første årtier efter anden verdenskrig. Disse Fordistisk lignende organisationer dominerer forretningslivet i kraft af masseproduktion og en høj grad af specialisering inden for en hierarkisk organisation. I 1970'erne og 1980'erne udfordres denne vestlige forretningsmodel af en mere fleksibel japansk udgave, der lægger vægt på evnen til tilpasning over for forandringer i omverdenen og en netværks lignende organisering i forhold til leverandører og kunder. Fra omkring 1990 tager Vestens forretningsliv denne organisationsform til sig og forbedrer den til en højproduktiv, markedsorienteret, global og fleksibel netorganisering omkring virksomhedernes kerne kompetence. 1980'erne udgør her en overgangstid.

Når Vestens store virksomheder, anført af de amerikanske, i 1990'erne i den grad generobrer dominansen på verdensmarkedet, så hænger det især sammen med, at den nye organisationsform kædes sammen med en revolutionerende udvikling af IT. Computere og telekommunikation finder sammen i en ny elektronisk infrastruktur, som omspænder hele verden. Den nye elektroniske infrastruktur og den samtidige omvæltning af computerteknologien giver helt nye muligheder for forretningslivet. I løbet af få år sker der en omfattende globalisering, hvor det økonomiske samspil over grænserne ikke længerne primært præges af varehandel mellem producent og kunder, men af en international organisering af produktionen. Derved bindes verden sammen på en måde, som tvinger alle firmaer til at anlægge globale strategier, ofte indgå globale alliancer eller direkte fusionere til større enheder.

Firmaet SAS og dets anvendelse af IT følger hovedtrækkene i den generelle udvikling. Det gælder også alle andre førende luftfartselskaber. SAS ekspanderer voldsomt fra 1950'erne til 1970'erne, indtil det rammes af den generelle økonomiske krise. Det er i denne periode det klassiske luftfartselskab udformes. SAS søger at bevare sin konkurrenceevne ved anskaffelse af stadig mere teknologisk avancerede fly med stigende kapacitet, dvs. øget masseproduktion. Luftfarten foregår og udvikler sig inden for en statslig reguleret lufttrafik, som reelt giver de nationale selskaber monopol på at beflyve deres egne regioner. SAS er organiseret som et traditionel masseproducerende bureaukrati, men adskiller sig fra de fleste større firmaer og luftfart selskaber ved også at have en geografisk opdeling på de tre nordiske lande.

For at håndtere den stigende trafik indføres IT til at varetage informationsbehandlingen inden for alle hovedfunktioner. Denne første generelle IT struktur er opbygget omkring centrale computersystemer, som brugerne ikke har nogen egentlig indflydelse på. Reservations systemet udgør omdrejningspunktet.

Fra begyndelsen af 1980'erne omlægges SAS til en markedsorienteret virksomhed, der fokuserer på én hovedkundegruppe: den hyppigt rejsende og fuldt betalende forretningsmand. Den nye strategi bliver en stor succes. Strategien bygger også på en reorientering af trafikken mod passagerer i Skandinavien og især mellem Skandinavien og Europa. Derved flyttes tyngdepunktet væk fra de interkontinentale ruter og fragt transporten, som hidtil havde spillet en dominerende rolle. Igennem 1980'erne søger SAS ledelsen, mestendels forgæves, at gøre hele det traditionelle bureaukrati markedsorienteret.

I løbet af 1980'erne udbygges IT-systemerne til at automatisere stort set alle operative og taktiske funktioner, bundet sammen i omfattende spaghettiagtige net. Disse systemer er baseret på en mere avanceret teknologi end tidligere i form af databaser og øget kommunikation, men teknologien lægger sig tæt op ad tidligere systemer og det traditionelle bureaukrati. IT cementerer således den traditionelle organisation. Samtidig er den forøgede automatisering imidlertid forudsætningen for det følgende årtis revolutionerende udvikling. 1980'erne udgør således både afslutningen på den første traditionelle periode inden for organisation og IT og grundlaget for de efterfølgende store forandringer.

Fra begyndelsen af 1990'erne slår den åbne og globale konkurrence igennem i luftfarten. Årtiet begynder med en økonomisk krise efter Golfkrigen. Krisen og den forestående liberalisering af luftfarten tvinger SAS, og andre luftfart selskaber, til at gennemføre en radikal ændring af organisationen. Det traditionelle bureaukrati bliver sat under heftige angreb ved at blive målt efter den til enhver tid bedste markeds standard med risiko for, at det enkelte interne forretningsområde kan blive solgt, hvis det ikke kan måle sig med konkurrerende firmaer på markedet. Det bliver stadig tydeligere, at SAS ikke blot udgør ét firma, men i virkeligheden består af en række selvstændige interne "firmaer", der varetager hver sin del af den samlede værdikæde. Muligheden for at omdanne disse områder til selvstændige selskaber vokser. SAS Data udskilles således som tre selvstændige datterselskaber, omend tæt knyttet til moderselskabet.

Stærkt faldende priser og accelererende konkurrence gør det nødvendigt med en langt mere produktiv og fleksibel organisation, der hurtigt kan omstille sig efter de hastigt skiftende markedsforhold. En sådan proces- og markedsorienteret organisation begynder at udkrystallisere sig i SAS i løber af anden halvdel af 1990'erne.

Fra midten af 1990'erne erkender SAS ledelsen nødvendigheden af at knytte SAS Data og SAS tættere sammen for at kunne gennemføre et spring fremad i kompetence udviklingen. Videns-, service- og teknologikravene til firmaet forstærkes markant. Den skandinaviske organisationsform med regionale enheder må herunder lade livet. Samtidig indgår SAS i en global fly alliance for at kunne tilbyde skandinaver et globalt trafiknet og for at matche organisationen til en stadig mere skærpet global konkurrence. Omstillingsprocessen sker imidlertid gradvist, fordi de bureaukratiske organisationsformer stikker dybt i SAS og bunder i tilsvarende samfundsstrukturer.

Parallelt med denne organisatoriske og forretningsmæssige udvikling gennemgår IT-området en lige så revolutionerende forvandling. Hidtil var SAS' bærende IT-systemer blevet udviklet internt af SAS Data. Nu går man imidlertid over til at købe applikationer på et nyt og ekspanderende software marked. Det er de såkaldte client/server systemer. De lægges oven på de eksisterende store systemer, hvorved tyngdepunktet i anvendelse og udvikling flytter over på brugersiden. Forretningsmæssige hensyn bliver nu helt afgørende for IT-udviklingen. Det stiller nye og radikale krav til SAS Data om at blive forretningsorienteret og konkurrencedygtig.

Tempoet i udviklingen af nye systemer og systemændringer forøges markant. Adgangen til information og informationsbehandlingen på tværs af eksisterende systemer forstærkes ligeledes betydeligt. Et mere helheds- og videnspræget syn på IT og IT-systemer breder sig. En ny og åben IT-infrastruktur opbygges, som letter samspillet med omverdenen, herunder alliancepartnere. Denne åbne struktur antager endnu mere radikal karakter som følge af Internettets samtidige gennembrud. Dermed opnås en fælles teknologisk standard og informationskanal, som giver mulighed for elektroniske baserede relationer både internt i virksomheden og eksternt i forhold til andre virksomheder og til kunder i et hidtil uset omfang. Fra slutningen af 1990'erne åbner der sig herved nye perspektiver, ikke mindst for direkte kundekontakt.

1990'ernes forretningsliv og IT præges således af radikale forandringer. En fleksibel og markedsorienteret organisation tager over, som realiseres gennem den nye client/server teknologi og den åbne elektroniske kommunikations teknologi. Ved slutningen af 1990'erne peger den voldsomme ekspansion af Internet og elektronisk handel på, at client/server 'paradigmet' snart vil blive afløst af et såkaldt Web-'paradigme'. De store systemer med rod i de foregående årtier danner imidlertid stadig grundlag for SAS' basale informationsarbejde. De lader sig ikke uden videre udskifte, også fordi den relevante teknologi på markedet først modnes efterhånden. Udskiftningen vanskeliggøres også af, at systemerne arbejder døgnet rundt på højtryk for at holde firmaet i luften, også i bogstaveligste forstand. En endnu større barriere skal søges i årtiers rodfæstede organisationsforhold.

SOURCES AND REFERENCES

SAS Sources

Archives

SAS

Betänkande avgivet av skandinavisk kommitté för Reorganisation af SAS (report on SAS reorganization), 1961.
K 1971.
P 1973.
V 1981-1986.
ARP 1987-1993.

SAS, Data Management

– Systems plans, 1962-1994.
– Divisions plans, 1981-1993.
– Correspondance, 1962-1994.
– Data Organization plans and reports, 1963-1993.
– SDG minutes of meetings, 1981-1982.

Corporate Strategies and Plans

– Availability System, 1961.
– Description of SASCO, 1963.
– Information Systems, 1970.
– SASCO. SAS Computer System, 1974.
– Data Services, 1978.
– Data Services, 1980.
– SASMO. SAS Data Models, 1980.
– ADB-Strategisk Plan for SAS Data (IT strategic plan for SAS Data), 1981.
– Information Processing Strategy, 1984.
– Airlines Greybook, 1985.
– Business and Data Model, 1988.
– Information Systems Policies, 1989.
– Handbook of IT Policies and Standards within SAS Airline, 1990.
– Savings through Standards, 1991, 1992, 1993, 1994.
– SDG Forbedringsaktiviteter 1998-2001. Handlingsplaner (action plans), 1998.
– SDG Technical Platform Strategy, 1998.

Systems Descriptions

– The MATS system, 1969.
– MOPS Masterplan Handbook, 1972.
– MOPS Development Manual, 1974.
– MOPS System Handbok (system handbook), 1977.
– MOPS COST System Overview, 1978.
– MOPS: ROCO, RELS, MOCO, MRS, BOWAC, LIPS Systems Handbooks, 1975-1986.

– MOPS Information Handbook, 1980-1987.
– Information Technology Applications in Aircraft Maintenance & Engineering, 1991.
– ACS System Handbok (system handbook), 1973-1977.
– ACS System Handbok (system handbook), 1983.
– GLM Systemforvalter Handbok (System management handbook), 1993.
– PERS/RINS Rutinhandbok (system handbook), 1982–83.
– PERS System, CPH, 1988
– Cargo Manual, 1993.
– PA-Systemets Använderhandbok (the PA-System User Handbook), 1993.

SAS Data

SDD, Vi er her, 1989 (we are here).
SDD, Hvidbog om SAS Data Danmark A/S. Tekster vedrørende etablering af SAS Data
  Danmark A/S (White book on the making of SAS Data Denmark, Ltd.), 1989.
SDD, Forandring af en dataafdeling. Fra intern afdeling til aktieselskab. Status over 2 års
  forandringsproces i SAS Data Danmark (Changing an IT department to a joint stock
  company. Drawing up the balance sheet after two years of change), 1990.
SDD, Projektlederguide (project management guide), 1990.
SDD, Fremad mod 1995 (forward towards 1995) (1991).
SDD, Guide (organization handbook), 1992.
SDD, Business Plan 1994–1996, 1993.
SD, Organization Papers, 1997.

Organs and Reports

House Organ and Handbooks

SAS Nytt, 1951-1963.
Inside SAS, 1964-1998.
SAS, Telefonkatalog, 1993-1997 (Telephone Catalogue).
SAS, Travel Book, 1994-1998.

House Organs/SAS Data

Data Services News, 1970-1979.
Data Services Bulletin, 1980-1981.
Data News, 1981-1985.
Data Ventilen, 1986-1987.
UPTIME, 1988-1994 (Sweden/Norway)
SDS/SDN, Nätvärlden, 1991.
Profil, 1989-1994 (Denmark).
Linje 1, 1994-1998.

Annual Reports

SAS, Annual Reports, 1946-1997.
SAS, Environmental Reports, 1995-1997.
SAS, Yearbooks, 1967-1980.

Interviews

SAS

Information Strategies & Processes

Björn Boldt-Christmas
(Vicepresident of DDD/ISD, 1987-1998. Left SAS) (Int., 1995).

Lars Swärd
(Secretary of Information Systems Strategies, 1988-1998. Left SAS) (Int., 1995).

Business System Division

Carl-Axel Stael von Holstein
(Head of Business Control, in the 1980s and 1990s) (Int., 1995).

Stefan Andersson
(Head of Statistical Systems, Business Control, in the 1980s and 1990s) (Int., 1995).

Helge Rasmussen
(IT Manager, Revenue Management, in the 1990s) (Int., 1995).

Mogens Meisler
(Vicepresident SDD, 1988-1990. Director, Revenue Information, since 1990) (Int., 1995).

Robert Skoog
(Manager, Cargo, since the 1970s) (Int., 1995).

Niels Bloch
(Manager Cargo Procedures & Systemsupport, since the 1970s) (Int., 1995).

Kjell Ivarsson
(Manager, Cargo Revenue Accounting, since the 1980s) (Int., 1995).

Kim Christensen
(Manager, Cargo Yield Management & Space Control, since the 1980s) (Int., 1995).

Marketing & Sales Division

Eric Berggren-Lindberg
(Head of Business Control, in the 1990s) (Int., 1995).

Per Møller-Jensen
(Head of Marketing, in the 1990s) (Int., 1995).

Göran Pettersson
(Director, Distribution Services, since the late 1980s) (Int., 1995).

Station Services Division

Hannes Lebert
Vicepresident, Station & Sales Support, in the 1990s) (Int., 1995).

Technical Division

Mindor Lundström
Manager, Information Systems, since the 1970s) (Int., 1995).

Erik Normann
  (Director Business Control, 1994-1996. Left SAS) (Int., 1995).
John Dueholm
  (Vicepresident, in 1994. Left SAS) (Int., 1995).

Operation Division

Allan Sørensen
  (Manager, Crew Allocation, since the 1980s) (Int., 1995).
Bent Lund
  (Manager IT Systems, Movement Control, since the 1970s) (Int., 1997).
Jan Pedro Sördelund
  (Manager IS/IT Standards, in the 1990s) (Int., 1995).

Corporate Finance & Control

Agneta Peyron-Malmquist
  (Manager, Corporate Accounting/Financial Systems, in the 1990s) (Int., 1995).
Per-Erik Jegbert
  (Corporate Accounting/Financial Systems, since the 1960s) (Int., 1995).
Ulla Edlund
  (Vicepresident, Corporate Accounting, since 1994) (Int., 1995).

Human Resources

Lars Nilsson
  (Manager, Systems Development Human Resources, since the 1970s) (Int., 1995).

SAS Data

General

Torsten Bergner
  (Manager Technical Operations, in the 1950s and 1960s. In the 1970s and the 1980s, technological advisor to the SAS President. Retired) (Interview, 1995).
Arne Hansen
  (Head of SDD, 1963-1988. Retired) (Int., 1995).
Curt Ekström
  (Vicepresident of SAS Data, 1981-1986. CEO of AMADEUS, 1986-1991. In the 90s, President of BA, Speedwing) (Int., 1995).
Mogens Meisler
  (Vicepresident of SDD, 1988-1990. Since 1990, head of Revenue Information) (Int., 1995).
John Dueholm
  (Vicepresident of SDD, 1990-1993. Head of Technical, CPH, 1993-1994. Vicepresident Technical Division, 1994. Left SAS) (Int., 1995).
Tage E. Christiansen
  (Vicepresident of SDD, 1993-1996. Left SAS) (Int., 1995).
Knut Hallen
  (Head of SDN, in the 1980s and 1990s) (Int., 1997).

Gjermund Gullberg
  (Business Controller SDN, in the 1980s and 1990s) (Int., 1997).
Björn Lilja
  (Head of SDS, 1990-1998. Left SAS) (Int., 1995).
Hans-Henrik Hedegaard
  (Vicepresident of SAS Data, since 1996) (Int., 1998).

Functions

Anders Eriksson
  (SDS, Manager of Traffic & Technical Systems, in the 1980s and 1990s) (Int., 1995).
Helle H. Uldal
  (SDD, Key Account Manager, Space Control Services/Distribution, since 1994) (Int., 1995).
Henrik Røge
  (SDD, Key Account Manager, Cargo, 1994-1997) (Int., 1995).
Jørgen Hertz
  (SDD, Systems developer/consultant, Cargo, in the 1980s and 1990) (Int., 1995).
Mogens B. Friis
  (SDD, Systems developer/consultant, Crew, during the 1980s and early 1990s. Key Account Manager, Technical/Operation, 1994-1997) (Int., 1995).
Poul Strand-Holm
  (SDD, Systems developer/consultant, Stations, during the 1980s and early 1990s. Key Account Manager, Stations & Sales, since 1994) (Int., 1997).
John Schmidt-Hansen
  (SDD, Systems developer/consultant, Personnel, in the 1980s and early 1990s. Key Account Manager, SDD, since 1994) (Int., 1997).
Dan Sjøland
  (SDD, Unisys systems operation, since the 1970s. Manager Unisys System Software, 1994-1998) (Int., 1997).
Bjarne Karpanschof
  (SDD, IBM systems operation, since the 1970s. Manager IBM System Software, since 1994) (Int., 1997).
Mogens Kischovsky
  (SDD, Systems developer, in the 1980s. Head of Systems Development, CPH, in the late 1980s and early 1990s) (Left SAS) (Int., 1995).
Henning Andersen
  (SDD, Manager Communications, from the 1960s to the mid 1980s) (Retired) (Int., 1997).
Ole Skyt Johansson
  (SDD, General Manager, Communications, since the mid 1980s) (Int., 1997).
Johnny Daugaard
  (SD, Director of Administration & Business Control, Production Management, since 1997) (Int., 1997).

References

Allen, Th. J. and Scott Morton, M. S. (Ed.) (1994), *Information Technology and the Corporation of the 1990s. Research Studies* (Oxford: Oxford University Press).

Andersen Consulting (1997-1998), *Annual Reports 1996-1997* (WWW).

Applegate, L., McFarlan, W., and McKenney, J. L. (1992), *Corporate Information Systems Management*, 3rd Ed. (Chicago: Irwin).

Applegate, L., McFarlan, W., and McKenney, J. L. (1996), *Corporate Information Systems Management*, 4th Ed. (Chicago: Irwin).

Applegate, L. M. (1994), "Managing in an Information Age: The Organization for the 90s", In Baskerville, *Transforming Organizations with Information Technology*, pp. 15-94.

Andersen, P. B., Holmqvist, B. & Jensen, J. J. (Ed.) (1993), *The Computer as Medium* (New York: Cambridge University Press).

Baskerville, R. et al (Ed.) (1994), *Transforming Organizations with Information Technology: Proceedings of the IFIP WG8.2 Conference on Information Technology and the New Emergent Forms of Organizations, Ann Arbor, Michigan, USA, 11-13 August 1994* (Amsterdam: North Holland)

Beniger, J. R. (1986), *The Control Revolution. Technological and Economic Origins of the Information Society* (Camdbrige, Mass.: Harvard University Press).

Bertelsen, T., et al (Red.) (1991), *EDB-LEX: Det store informatik-leksikon* (IT dictionary) (Copenhagen: Gad).

Berthelsen, S. (Red.) (1985), *Et liv i luften* (a life in the air) (Copenhagen: Bogan).

Bijker, W. E., and Law, J. (Eds.) (1992), *Shaping Technology, Building Society* (Cambridge, Mass.: The MIT Press).

Bjørn-Andersen, N., and Turner, J. A. (1994), "Creating the Twenty-First Century Organization: The Metamorphosis of Oticon", in Baskerville, *Transforming Organizations with Information Technology*, pp. 379-394.

Borum, F. et al (1992), *Social Dynamics of the IT Field. The Case of Denmark* (Berlin: De Gruyter).

Bradley, S. P., Hausman, J. A., Nolan, R. L. (1993), *Globalization, Technology, and Competition. The Fusion of Computers and Telecommunications in the 1990s* (Boston, Mass.: Harvard Business School Press).

Brancker, J. W. S. (1977), *IATA and What It Does* (Leiden: Sitjhoff).

British Airways (1998), *Annual Report 1997* (WWW).

Buraas, A. (1972), *Fly over fly: Historien om SAS* (a history of SAS) (Oslo: Gyldendal).

Buraas, A. (1973), *The Making of SAS* (Oslo: Gyldendal).

Buraas, A. (1979), *The SAS Saga: A History of Scandinavian Airlines System* (Oslo: Gyldendal).

Carlzon, J. (1985), *Riv pyramiderne ned! En bog om chefen, lederen og det nye menneske* (tear down the pyramids) (Copenhagen, Gyldendal).

Cash, J. I., McFarlan, F. W., and McKenney, J. L. (1988), *Corporate Information Systems Management: the Issues Facing Corporate Executives*, 2nd Ed. (Homewood, Ill.: Irwin).

Ceruzzi, P. E. (1989*), Beyond the Limits: Flight Enters the Computer Age* (Cambridge, Mass.: MIT Press).

Chandler, A. D., Jr. (1962), *Strategy and Structure: Chapters in the History of the Industrial Enterprise* (Cambridge, Mass.: The M. I. T. Press).

Chandler, A. D., Jr. (1977), *The Visible Hand. The Managerial Revolution in American Business* (Cambridge, Mass.: The Belknap Press of Harvard University Press).

Chandler, A. D., Jr. (1990), *Scale and Scope. The Dynamics of Industrial Capitalism* (Cambridge, Mass.: The Belknap Press of Harvard University Press).

Chandler, A. D. (1992), "Organizational Capabilities and the Economic History of Industrial Enterprise", in *Journal of Economic Perspectives*, vol 6, no. 3, pp. 79-100.

Chandler, A. D., Hagström, P., Sölvell, Ö. (Ed.) (1998), *The Dynamic Firm. The Role of Technology, Strategy, Organization, and Regions* (Oxford: Oxford University Press).

Christensen, J. (1993), "Historical Trends in Computer and Information Technology", in Andersen, P. B., B. Holmqvist, B., & Jensen, J. J. (Ed.), *The Computer as Medium*, pp. 422-451.

Coleman, K. G. et al (Eds.) (1996), *Reengineering MIS. Aligning Information Technology and Business Operations* (Harrisburg, USA: Idea Group Publishing).

Copeland, D. and McKenney, J. (1988), "Airline Reservations: Lesson from History", *MIS Quarterly*, vol. 12, no. 3, pp. 353-372.

Cortada, J. W. (1996), *Information Technology as Business History: Issues in the History and Management of Computers* (Westport, Conn.: Greenwood Press).

Cortada, J. W, (1996), *A Bibliographic Guide to the History of Computer Applications, 1950-1990* (Westport, Conn.: Greenwood Press).

Cortada, J. W. (1990), *A Bibliographic Guide to the History of Computing, Computers and the Information Processing Industry* (New York: Greenwood Press).

Cortada, J. W. (1996), *Second Bibliographic Guide to the History of Computing, Computers, and the Information Processing Industry* (Westport, Conn. London: Greenwood Press).

Davenport, Th. D. (1993), *Process Innovation. Reengineering Work through Information Technology Technology* (Boston, Mass.: Harvard Business School Press).

Davis, G. B. (1974), *Management Information Systems: Conceptual Foundations, Structure, and Development* (New York: McGraw-Hill)

Davis, G. B., Olson, M. H. (1985), *Management Information Systems: Conceptual Foundations, Structure, and Development*, 2nd Ed. (New York: McGraw-Hill).

Deans, P. C., Karwan, K. R (1994), *Global Information Systems and Technology. Focus on the Organization and its Functional Areas* (Harrisburg, USA: Idea Group Publishing).

Dienel, H.-L., and Lynth, P. (Ed.) (1998), *Flying the Flag. European Commercial Air Transport since 1945* (London: MacMillan Press).

Dosi, G. et al (Eds.) (1988), *Technical Change and Economic Theory* (London: Pinter Publishers).

Dosi, G. et al (Eds.) (1992), *Technology and Enterprise in a Historical Perspective* (Oxford: Oxford University Press).

Dosi, G. and Malerba, F. (Eds.) (1996), *Organization and Strategy in the Evolution of the Enterprise* (London: MacMillan Press).

Dosi, G., Teece, D. J., Syntry, J. (Eds.) (1998), *Technology, Organization, and Competitiveness: Perspectives on Corporate Change* (Oxford University Press, Oxford).

Dunning, J. H. (1993), *The Globalization of Business: The Challenge of the 1990s* (London: Routledge).

Dunning, J. H: (Ed.) (1993-1994), *Transnational Corporations*, vol. 1-20 (London: Routledge).

Dunning, J. H. (Ed.) (1997), *Governments, Globalization, and the International Business* (Oxford: Oxford University Press).

Earl, M. J. (1989), *Management Strategies for Information Technology* (London: Prentice-Hall).

Earl, M. J. (1996), *Information Management. The Organizational Dimension* (Oxford: Oxford University Press).

Early, G. (1992), "Airline Reservation Systems", in *Macmillan Encyclopedia of Computers* (New York: Macmillan), pp. 33-40.

Ekström, C. (1985), "SAS' strategi för dataverksamheten" (SAS' IT strategi) (1985), in *Nordisk DATANytt*, 1, pp. 10-15.

EU (1997), *The Single Market Review. Impact on Services. AIR TRANSPORT.*

EU (1998), *Transport Research. Fourth Framework Programme. Air Transport VII-69.*

Forester, T. (1993), *Silicon Samurai: How Japan Conquered the World's IT Industry* (Oxford: Blackwell).

Freeman, C. (1982), *The Economics of Industrial Innovation,* 2nd Ed. (London: Pinter).

Freeman, C. and Soete, I. G. L. (Eds.) (1987), *Technical Change and Full Employment* (Oxford: Basil Blackwell).

Friedman, A. L. (1989), *Computer Systems Development: History, Organization, and Implementation* (Chichester: John Wiley).

Galliers, R. D., Baets, W. R. J. (Ed.) (1998), *Information Technology and Organizational Transformation: Information for the 21st Century Organization* (Chichester:Wiley).

Galliers, R. D., Leidner, D. E., Baker, B. S: H. (Ed.) (1994), *Strategic Information Management. Challenges and Strategies in Managing Information Systems* (Oxford: Butterworth-Heinemann).

Hagrup, K. (1975), *Luftfarten og fremtiden* (aviation and the future) (Copenhagen: Chr. Erichsen).

Hammer, M. (1996), *Beyond Reengineering. Work and Our Lives* (London: HarperCollins Business).

Hammer, M. and Champy, J. (1993), *Reengineering the Corporation. A Manifesto for Business Revolution* (London: Nicholas Brealey).

Harris, B. (1993), *BABS, BEACON, and BOADICEA. A History of Computing at British Airways and its Predecessor Airlines* (Hounslow, UK: Speedwing Press).

Harvard Business Review, 1960-1998.

Hopper, M. D. (1990), "Rattling SABRE – New Ways to Compete on Information", in *Harvard Business Review*, May-June, pp. 118-125.

Hughes, T. P. (1983), *Networks of Power. Electrification in Western Society*, (Baltimore: The John Hopkins University Press).

IATA (1971-1998), *World Air Transport Statistics, 1970-1997.*
IBM (1997-98), *Annual Reports*, 1996-1997.
IDC (1993), *The European Application Solutions Marketplace, 1991-1997.*
IDC (1996), *Consulting and Management Services* (Bulletin).
IDC (1996), *1996 Worldwide Software Review and Forecast.*
IDC (1997), *ERP Consulting and Integration Services in Western Europe.*
IDC (1997), *European Outsourcing Markets and Trends, 1995-2001.*
IDC (1997), *1997 European Network Management and Monitoring Services.*
IDC (1997), *European Network Product Support Services Markets and Trends*, 1995–2001.
IDC (1997), *1997 Global IT Survey.*
IDC (1997), *Riding the Wave. An Analysis of Outsourcing Market Leaders in Western Europe.*
IDC (1997), *SAP's Component-Enabled Business Framework* (Bulletin).
IDC (1997), *Vendor Performance in European IT Markets 1996.*
IDC (1998), *Cross-Industry Applications: 1997 World Market and Trends.*
IDC (1998), *1998 Global IT Survey.*
IDC (1998), *Programmer Development Tools Synopsis: 1998 Worldwide Markets and Trends.*
IDC (1998), *The Third Paradigm.*
IDC (1998), *Vertical-Industry Applications: 1998 Worldwide Markets and Trends.*
Igbaria, M., Tan, M. (Eds.) (1998), *The Virtual Workplace* (Hersey, USA: Idea Group Publishing).
IRMA Conference Proceedings: Challenges for Information Management in a World Economy (1993). Managing Social and Economic Change with IT (1994). Managing Information and Communications in a Changing Global Environment (1995). IT Management and Organizational Innovations (1996). Managing IT Resources and Applications in the World Economy (1997). Effective Utilization and Management of Emerging Information Technologies (1998).

Jönscher, C. (1994), "An Economic Study of the Information Technology Revolution", in Allen, Th. J. & Scott Morton, M. S. (Ed.), *Information Technology and the Corporation of the 1990s*, pp. 5-42.

Kaplinsky, R. (1984), *Automation. The Technology and Society* (London: Longman).

Langlois, R. N., Foss, N. J. (1997), *Capabilities and Governance: the Rebirth of Production in the Theory of Economic Organization* (Copenhagen: Danish Research Unit for Industrial Dynamics)
Lebow, I. (1995), *Information Highways and Byways. From the Telegraph to the 21st Century* (New York: IEEE Press).

Maddison, A. (1991), *Dynamic Forces in Capitalist Developmen: A Long-Run Comparative View* (Oxford: Oxford University Press).
Maddison, A. (1995), *Monitoring the World Economy 1820-1992* (Paris: OECD).
Marx, K. (1962-1966/1867-1894), *Das Kapital*, I-III (Berlin: Dietz Verlag).

McFarlan. M. W. (1984), "Information technology changes the way you compete", in *Harvard Business Review*, May-June, pp. 98-103.

McKenney, J. (1995), *Waves of Change. Business Evolution through Information Technology* (Harvard Business School Press, Boston, Mass.).

McNurlin, B. C., and Sprague, R. H., Jr. (1989), *Information Systems Management in Practice*, 2nd Ed. (Englewood Cliffs, New Jersey: Prentice-Hall).

Microsoft (1997-1998), *Annual Reports 1996-1997* (WWW).

Mintzberg, H. (1979), *The Structuring of Organizations: A Synthesis of the Research* (Englewood Cliffs, New Jersey: Prentice-Hall).

Mintzberg, H. (1983), *Structure in Fives. Designing Effective Organizations* (Englewood Cliffs, New Jersey: Prentice-Hall).

Mintzberg, H., Quinn, J. B. (1988), *The Strategy Process: Concepts, Contexts, Cases* (Englewood Cliffs, New Jersey: Prentice-Hall).

Montgomery, A. A. (Ed.) (1995), *Resource-Based and Evolutionary Theories of the Firm: towards a Synthesis* (Boston, Mass.: Kluwer Academic Publishers).

Morrison, S. A., and Winston, C. (1995), *The Evolution of the Airline Industry* (Washington, D. C.: The Brookings Institute).

Nelson, R. E. and Winter, S. G. (1982), *An Evolutionary Theory of Economic Change* (Cambridge, Mass.: The Belknap Press of Harvard University Press)

Nolan, R. L. (1979), "Managing the Crisis in Data Processing", in *Harvard Business Review*, March–April, pp. 115-126.

Nolan, R. L. and Croson, D. C. (1995), *Creative Destruction. A Six-Stage Process for Transforming the Organization* (Boston, Mass.: Harvard Business School Press).

OECD (1988), *New Technologies in the 1990s* (Paris: OECD).

OECD (1991), *Convergence between Communications Technologies* (Paris: OECD).

OECD (1992), *Technology and Economy* (Paris: OECD).

OECD (1993), *International Air Transport* (Paris: OECD).

OECD (1996), *Globalization of Industries* (Paris: OECD).

OECD (1997), *Communications Outlook* (Paris: OECD).

OECD (1997), *The Future of International Air Transport Policy* (Paris: OECD).

OECD (1997), *Information Technology Outlook* (Paris: OECD).

OECD (1997-1998), *Economic Outlook 1997-1998*.

OECD (1998), *The Economic and Social Impacts of Electronic Commerce* (Paris: OECD).

Pedersen, M. K (1996), *A Theory of Informations* (Roskilde, Denmark: Samfundslitteratur & Roskilde Universitetsforlag).

Piore, M. J. and Sabel, Ch. F. (1984), *The Second Industrial Divide. Possibilities for Prosperity* (New York: Basic Books).

Porter, M. E. (1980), *Competitive Strategy: Techniques for Analyzing Industries and Competitors* (New York: Free Press).

Porter. M. E. (1985), *Competitive Advantage. Creating and Sustaining Superior Performance* (New York: Free Press).

Porter, M. E. and Miller, V. E. (1985), "How Information Gives You Competitive Advantage", *Harvard Business Review*, July-Aug., pp. 149-160.

Porter, M. E. (1990), *The Competitive Advantage of Nations* (London: Macmillan).

Rosenberg, N. (1982), *Inside the Blackbox: Technology and Economics* (Cambridge: Cambridge University Press).

Rosenberg, N. (1993), *Exploring the Blackbox. Technology, Economics, and History* (Cambridge: Cambridge University Press).

The SABRE Group (1998), *Annual Report 1997* (WWW).

SAP (1997-1998), *Annual Reports 1996-1997* (WWW).

Svenska Transportarbetarförbundet (1983), *Datautveckling inom Civilflyget. Delrapport om personalens uppfatning om datasystemens effekter* (employees' experienced labor effects of computer development within civil aviation) (Stockholm).

SAS (1996), *The First Fifty Years* (Stockholm: SAS).

SAS (1961), "International Inquiry Answering Service", in *Data Processing*, July-September, pp. 3-14.

Schumpeter, J. A. (1961/1934), *The Theory of Economic Development: An Inquiry into Profits, Capital, Credit, Interest, and the Business Cycle* (Cambridge, Mass.: Harvard University Press).

Schumpeter, J. A. (1939), *Business Cycles: A Theoretical, Historical and Statistical Analysis of the Capitalist Process*, I-II (New York).

Selling, R. (1992), *Legend and Legacy. The Story of Boeing and its People* (Seattle: Boeing).

Sprague, R. H., Jr., and McNurlin, B. C. (1992), *Information Systems Management in Practice*, 3rd Ed. (Englewood Cliffs, New Jersey: Prentice-Hall).

Sprague, R. H., Jr., and McNurlin, B. C. (1996), *Information Systems Management in Practice*, 4th Ed. (Englewood Cliffs, New Jersey: Prentice-Hall).

Sterling, C. H. (1996), *Commercial Air Transport Books: An Annotated Bibliography of Airlines, Airliners, and the Air Transport Industry* (McLean, Virginia: Paladwr Press).

Synnott, W. R. (1987), *The Information Weapon: Winning Customers and Markets with Technology* (New York: Wiley).

Targowski, A. S. (1996), *Global Information Infrastructure. The Birth, Vision, and, Architecture* (Harrisburg, USA: Idea Group Publishing).

Thomsen, R. (Ed.) (1975-1976), *Hovedlinier i Nordens Historie*, vol. 3-4 (an outline of Nordic history) (Copenhagen: Gyldendal).

UN, *Statistical Yearbook 1950-1995* (Washington, D. C.: UN).

UN (1990-1998), *World Investment Report 1990-1998* (Washington, D. C.: UN).

U. S. Department of Commerce (1998), *The Emerging Digital Economy* (Washington, D. C.: U. S. Department of Commerce).

Willcocks, L., Feeny, D., Islei, G. (1997), *Managing IT as a Strategic Resource* (London: McGraw-Hill).

Williamson, O. E. (1975), *Markets and hierarchies: Analysis and Anti-Trust Implications. A Study in the Economics of Internal Organization* (New York: Free Press).

Williamson, O. E. (1985), *The Economic Institutions of Capitalism: Firms, Market, Relational Contracting* (New York: Free Press).

Williamson, O. E. (1996), *The Mechanisms of Governance* (New York: Oxford University Press).

Williamson, O. E., and Winter, G. (Ed.) (1991), *The Nature of the Firm: Origins, Evolution, and Development* (New York: Oxford University Press)

Wiseman, C. (1988), *Strategic Information Systems* (Homewood, Ill.: Irwin).

Wit, D. de (1994), *The Shaping of Automation. A Historical Analysis of the Interaction between Technology and Organization, 1950-1985* (Hilversum, the Netherlands: Verloren).

Womack, J. P, Jones, D. T., Roos, D. (1990), *The Machine that Changed the World* (New York: Rawson Associates).

World Bank (1994-1998), *Annual Reports 1993-1997.*

WWW (1998), Boeing homepage.

WWW (1998), SAS homepage.

WWW (1998), SAS Cargo homepage.

WWW (1998), SAS Data homepage.

WWW (1998), British Airways homepage.

WWW (1998), Speedwing homepage.

WWW (1998), American Airlines homepage.

WWW (1998), The SABRE Group homepage.

WWW (1998), Lufthansa homepage.

Zoboff, S. (1988), *In the Age of the Smart Machine.*

INDEX